The Editor

J. M. Opal is Associate Professor of History at McGill University. He is the author of *Beyond the Farm: National Ambitions in Rural New England*. His new book, *Avenging the People: Andrew Jackson, the Southern Borderlands, and the Ordeal of American Democracy*, centers on vengeance and on the man who built both his public and his private life around its pursuit.

A NORTON CRITICAL EDITION

Thomas Paine
COMMON SENSE
AND OTHER WRITINGS

AUTHORITATIVE TEXTS

CONTEXTS

INTERPRETATIONS

Edited by

J. M. OPAL
McGill University

W · W · NORTON & COMPANY · *New York* · *London*

W. W. Norton & Company has been independent since its founding in 1923, when William Warder Norton and Mary D. Herter Norton first published lectures delivered at the People's Institute, the adult education division of New York City's Cooper Union. The firm soon expanded its program beyond the Institute, publishing books by celebrated academics from America and abroad. By mid-century, the two major pillars of Norton's publishing program—trade books and college texts—were firmly established. In the 1950s, the Norton family transferred control of the company to its employees, and today—with a staff of four hundred and a comparable number of trade, college, and professional titles published each year—W. W. Norton & Company stands as the largest and oldest publishing house owned wholly by its employees.

This title is printed on permanent paper containing 30 percent post-consumer waste recycled fiber.

The text of this book is composed in Fairfield Medium with the display set in Bernhard Modern.
Book design by Antonina Krass.
Composition by Westchester
Manufacturing by Courier
Production manager: Sean Mintus

Library of Congress Cataloging-in-Publication Data

Paine, Thomas, 1737–1809.
    Common sense and other writings : authoritative texts, contexts, interpretations / Thomas Paine ; edited by J. M. Opal.—1st ed.
        p. cm.—(A Norton critical edition)
    Includes bibliographical references and index.
    ISBN 978-0-393-97870-4 (pbk.)
1. Political science—Early works to 1800.   I. Opal, J. M.   II. Title.
    JC177.A5 2011
    320.51—dc23

                                                                    2011046436

W. W. Norton & Company, Inc., 500 Fifth Avenue, New York, NY 10110-0017
wwnorton.com

W. W. Norton & Company Ltd., Castle House, 75/76 Wells Street
London W1T 3QT

1   2   3   4   5   6   7   8   9   0

Contents

Introduction

Thomas Paine and the Revolutionary Enlightenment, 1770s–1790s

In 1805, the seventy-year-old John Adams, former revolutionary and ex-president of the United States, knew whom to blame for the sorry state of the world. Having lost much of his optimism but none of his honesty through the years, Adams found ample reason to despair. The present day, he opined, was an "Age of Frivolity," a time of "Folly, Vice, Frenzy, [and] Barbarity." The American Revolution had been a good thing, Adams allowed. But it had degenerated into social and moral confusion, as evidenced by his defeat at the hands of Thomas Jefferson four years earlier. Meanwhile, the upheavals in Europe and the Caribbean had brought war, atrocity, and Napoleon. And all the calamities seemed to trace to one man, one name: "I know not whether any man in the world has had more influence on its inhabitants or affairs for the last thirty years than Tom Paine." Once beloved for his 1776 pamphlet, *Common Sense*, Paine now epitomized what Adams most reviled. A "mongrel between pig and puppy, begotten by a wild boar on a bitch wolf," Paine had loosed a "career of mischief" across the globe. "Call it then the Age of Paine," Adams wrote with a sigh.[1]

Priding themselves on balance and objectivity, historians try to avoid this sort of personal attack. Yet they have long been guilty of favoring certain nations, usually their own, while documenting and explaining the past. In the United States especially, the dominant historical narrative sees the American Revolution as exclusively *American*, as if its origins, ideas, and legacies belonged to only the thirteen British colonies of North America. Indeed, Americans often dissociate their revolution from all others, carving out a special historical space for the founding of their country. In this way, the tumultuous final decades of the eighteenth century are stripped down and simplified, forced into a comforting tale of national destiny. In this way, too, Thomas Paine is remembered primarily as the

1. Adams to Benjamin Waterhouse, October 29, 1805, quoted in Craig Nelson, *Thomas Paine: Enlightenment, Revolution, and the Birth of Modern Nations* (New York, 2007), 9.

man whose pamphlet helped begin the American Revolution in 1776, as if he simply faded away thereafter. From this nation-centered perspective, John Adams's rant about an "Age of Paine" becomes all the more puzzling. Why would Adams, himself a revolutionary leader, lament an age of revolution? What "mischief" and "frenzy" was he talking about? What was so dangerous about the author of *Common Sense*?

To understand why Paine inspired such passions, we need to jettison our national blinders and approach great events like the American, French, and Haitian revolutions as global phenomena. For such upheavals were caused by ideas and forces that came from many different places and peoples, compelling changes in the lives and cultures of many different nations and empires. As a leading voice of what we might call the Revolutionary Enlightenment, Thomas Paine understood the global nature of the human drama. In fact, he embraced it. "My attachment is to all the world and not to any particular part," he reported in 1778. Paine read and wrote about slaves in western Africa, peasants in South Asia, and farmers in Pennsylvania. He took an active role in the destruction of monarchy in France and North America and did his best to depose the ruling class of his native Britain. He saw the Haitian Revolution, that nightmare of the wealthy and powerful across the Atlantic world, as "the natural consequence of Slavery" and called for worldwide rebellion against oppression and exploitation. As a group of Ohio radicals later proclaimed, he was a "Great Champion of Human Rights, whose very soul could not be confined to a single state or country." During the last quarter of the eighteenth century, Paine's devout commitment to global emancipation and human dignity—along with his sharp wit and reckless pen—took him from obscurity to celebrity to infamy.[2]

I. Enlightenment or Revolution?

As soon as he began to publish his thoughts in the 1770s, when he was already in his late thirties, Thomas Paine conveyed a deep dislike of the British government. He was repelled not only by its central institutions of king, church, and Parliament but also by the everyday authority of its judges, sheriffs, aristocrats, and military officers. He was outraged by their arrogance, their privilege, their careless wielding of power. "If I have any where expressed myself

2. Thomas Paine, "The American Crisis, #VII," November 11, 1778, in Moncure Daniel Conway, ed., *The Writings of Thomas Paine* (Routledge, 1996), I:278–79; Conway, *The Life of Thomas Paine* (New York, 1908), I:323; "Address of the President," in *The Paine Festival: Celebration of the 119th Anniversary of the Birth of Thomas Paine, at Cincinnati, January 19, 1856* (Cincinnati, 1856).

overwarmly," he would later announce, "'tis from a fixt immovable hatred I have, and ever had, to cruel men and cruel measures." There is no doubt that Paine did, at times, express himself "overwarmly," and that he did, at bottom, hate all forms of cruelty. But where did his intense feelings come from? What made Paine such a fierce critic of his own government and even his own countrymen? With few written records of his early life, we are left to tease out the origins of his political and moral instincts, to make educated guesses about the roots of his ideology.[3]

The son of Joseph and Francis Cocke Pain (no "e"), Thomas was born in the small village of Thetford, England, eighty miles from London, in 1737. His father was a member of the Society of Friends, or Quakers, who were known across the English-speaking world as dour oddballs who addressed each other as "thee" and "thou" and refused to doff their hats to their social betters. None but God deserved worship, the Friends insisted, and everyone—including women, vagrants, and black slaves—carried a tiny piece of God's grace inside them. From these curious beliefs came the Quakers' equally strange customs of allowing women to speak during meetings and of denouncing slavery. In Paine's day, being a Quaker did not bring the cruel persecution that Europe's Jews and Gypsies endured, but it did mean general suspicion and official exclusion from the halls of power. (Friends could not sit in Parliament until 1828, nor attend Oxford and Cambridge until 1871.) As a boy, Thomas went to Quaker meetings even though he was baptized and confirmed in the Church of England, after the manner of his mother's more respectable family.[4]

Even with a prominent lawyer as his maternal grandfather, young Thomas surely knew that his household sat low on England's steep and intricate social pyramid. The kingdom's elite, about 5 percent of the total population, was composed of a venerable landed gentry along with a newer business and merchant class. These two elements of the ruling class increasingly intermarried, much as the government itself and the capitalist institutions centered at the Bank of England increasingly worked in tandem to foster a cohesive and dynamic system of power. For all the might and promise of the British Empire, however, perhaps one Englishman in two lived in severe poverty. The English poor (and their counterparts in Scotland and Ireland) scratched out a living from small wages and piecework, moving from their villages to London and then back again. The rural

3. Paine, "The American Crisis, No. 2" January 13, 1777, in Philip S. Foner, ed., *The Life and Major Writings of Thomas Paine* (Secaucus, N.J., 1948), 72.
4. Nelson, *Thomas Paine*, 12–50; Roy Porter, *English Society in the Eighteenth Century* (1982; rev. ed., New York 1991), 98–142, 182–86; Eric Foner, *Tom Paine and Revolutionary America* (New York, 1976), 1–18.

population rented farms, worked in artisan shops, and "bound out" their children as servants and apprentices. Joseph Pain was a master corset maker and small farmer, so the family probably had enough food and firewood to make ends meet. But young Thomas, like most English children, had little formal education. Instead of pursuing a career of his own choice, he would have to follow his father's trade to escape destitution.[5]

After working as an apprentice in the family trade, Thomas essentially ran away by sailing with a privateer—a government-sanctioned pirate—in 1757. Here he discovered one key to Britain's power: its huge fleet of merchant vessels and naval ships. He also encountered the coarse and brutal world of the Atlantic economy. During times of war, common throughout the eighteenth century, the Royal Navy could not man all of its vessels. So, it hired large men with clubs to press people into service, literally dragging passersby onto ships that departed for years on end. Abandoned wives and children could only wonder where their husbands and fathers had gone. (Despite protests, Parliament repeatedly affirmed the legality of pressing.) Back on the docks of cities like London, Bristol, and Liverpool, ships arrived with cargoes of lumber and tobacco from North America and spices and calicoes from southern Asia. Others departed for the west coast of Africa, where they took on loads of enslaved people for sale on Caribbean and American plantations. When they returned, these ships filled the docks with the stench of the suffering and dying humans trapped inside during the long journey across the Atlantic. Few Englishmen besides the Quakers cared, because slavery seemed crudely predictable within this prehumanitarian world.[6]

By modern standards, this was indeed a cruel place. Childbirth was perilous for both mothers and babies, and medical care barely surpassed the grim standards of medieval times. The backways and shanties of its metropolis made up what one historian calls "a vertiginous maw of human depravity," where people amused themselves through cockfights, dogfights, and bare-knuckled boxing. Everywhere, the institutions of the state tried to police a social order in which common folk were supposed to defer to the ruling class. Courts announced the death penalty for dozens of crimes, most of them involving property; crowds gathered to watch petty thieves choke and kick on the noose. Titled aristocrats held exclusive rights to hunt in the king's forests, while poor families did without meat

---

5. Porter, *English Society in the Eighteenth Century*, 48–97. On the cultural assumption of following a trade, see J. M. Opal, *Beyond the Farm: National Ambitions in Rural New England* (Philadelphia, 2008).

6. Daniel J. Ennis, "Naval Impressement in Tobias Smollet's *Roderick Random*," *Albion* 32 (summer 2000), 234–35; Adam Hochschild, *Bury the Chains: Prophets and Rebels in the Fight to Free an Empire's Slaves* (Boston, 2005), 222–24.

and firewood. Only about one in six English men, and no women, enjoyed the right to vote. Thomas Paine never approached the required sum of property, and even if he had, Thetford was a "rotten borough," represented not by local voters but by an insulated, uncaring elite. Perhaps the most common reminder of the standing order came in the form of the debtors' jail, where those who could not deliver the sums they promised in private transactions were confined by public authorities.[7]

As he returned from his brief adventure at sea, Paine ran into these hard realities of English life. He struggled during the 1750s to make do as a corset maker, a teacher, a tobacconist, and an excise officer. We might imagine him casting about, wondering at the origins of the hardships and miseries all around. In 1760, his first wife, Mary, who was herself an orphan, died while delivering their first child (the baby also died). He rarely mentioned his early years or private life in any of his writings, partly because of eighteenth-century conventions for public men and partly because there was little he wanted to recall. Indeed, Tom Paine had a dark, lonely streak that would later manifest in bitter attacks on his homeland and a fondness for the numbing power of drink.[8]

Especially after he made his way to London in 1766, however, Paine discovered another side of Britain, one that centered on the word *enlightened*. Like the Renaissance three centuries earlier, the eighteenth-century Enlightenment revolutionized the way people thought and thus how they behaved. Based on the work of Isaac Newton and other scientists of the seventeenth century, who had discovered natural laws behind everyday phenomena, enlightened ideas took hold in urban settings across Europe during the mid-1700s. At the heart of the movement was the belief that human society, no less than the natural world, could be understood and then improved through conscious effort rather than divine intervention. By applying their reason to solve their problems, instead of submitting to the will of fate or God, people could render themselves more decent, healthy, and happy. According to the first *Encyclopédie*, published (and also banned) in France during the 1760s, man was "a feeling, reflecting, thinking being, who freely walks the earth" and "lives in society." He was not damned or depraved, but capable of moral and intellectual progress.[9]

7. Nelson, *Thomas Paine*, 22; Douglas Hay, "Property, Authority and the Criminal Law," in Hay et al., eds. *Albion's Fatal Tree: Crime and Society in Eighteenth-Century England* (New York, 1975), 17–64.
8. Nelson, *Thomas Paine*, 38. Paine's many detractors routinely accused him of chronic drunkenness, and by his own admission he occasionally drank heavily. But, as Nelson notes, "there is no serious evidence of chronic alcoholism" (p. 258).
9. Nelly S. Hoyt and Thomas Cassirer, trans. *Encyclopédie: Selections: Diderot, D'Alembert, and a Society of Men of Letters* (Indianapolis, 1956), 243.

In relative terms, Britain offered fertile soil for enlightened ideas. Its dense population and maritime economy brought large numbers of people, Paine included, into urbane milieus where fresh ideas circulated. In coffeehouses and merchants' taverns, a cosmopolitan culture of reading and debating enabled everyday people to air their thoughts on affairs of state. Although aristocratic to the core, the British government did not tyrannize its subjects as did the crowned heads of France, Spain, the German states, or Russia. More to the point, it could *not* do so, because the day-to-day governance of the realm had long splintered into local clusters of power and influence. Different parts of the ruling class grudgingly shared this power, opening room for dissent within the wider society. Especially since the civil wars of the 1640s and so-called Glorious Revolution of 1689, a set of personal liberties—the "rights of Englishmen"—had taken root in both law and custom, prohibiting agents of the state from entering homes without a warrant or convicting persons without a trial. The freedom of the press was more uncertain, but the sheer mass of newspapers and pamphlets in London and other cities made effective censorship difficult. Britons of all ranks boasted of their liberty, defining themselves against such presumably enslaved peoples as the French or Turks.[1]

Thomas Paine did not passively absorb Enlightenment values or take for granted the political rights of British subjects. He sought them out, attending scientific lectures in London in 1757 and joining a debating club in the town of Lewes, where he ran a tobacco shop with his landlord, in 1768. By the early 1770s, he was rubbing shoulders with some of the leading lights of the day: the historian Edward Gibbon, the playwright Oliver Goldsmith, and the author Samuel Johnson. These men prided themselves on their freedom from prejudice and superstition, their ability to take an "enlarged" and "impartial" view of the world. They called this trait "liberality" and used it to denounce those who clung to ancient fears and inherited oppressions. By the 1770s, the words *liberal* and *enlightened* had become almost interchangeable. A liberal person was not only rational but also sympathetic, willing to show compassion to strangers and foreigners no less than to friends or family. These ideas would lead some philosophers to call for "the extinction of all national prejudice and enmity," the end of every "wretched partiality" in favor of a "UNIVERSAL BENEVOLENCE" toward the entire world. In the preface to his *Complete History of England*, which Paine read and cited, the novelist-historian Tobias Smollet pronounced himself "free

1. Linda Colley, *Britons: Forging the Nation, 1707–1837* (New Haven, Conn., 1992); John Brewer, *The Pleasures of the Imagination: English Culture in the Eighteenth Century* (London, 1997).

from all national jealousy and prejudice," liberated from "that illiberal partiality which has disgraced the works of many English historians." The premise behind such declarations—that the past was full of darkness and bigotry, from which humankind was just emerging—became a cornerstone of Paine's thinking.[2]

But Enlightenment did not necessarily mean or encourage revolution. That was true only of those societies, like France, where the *ancien régime* was both inflexible and vulnerable. Throughout Europe and its plantations, in fact, ruling elites were often the first to claim enlightened status. They used top-down reforms in education, law, and science to refine and enhance their authority; others sought greater efficiencies in the production of cash crops such as sugar, which meant wringing more blood and sweat from their slaves. Especially in Britain, with its growing professional class and strong civil society, liberal and enlightened measures gradually took hold in the moderation of penal codes, the removal of traditional market regulations, and, decades later, the campaign against the Atlantic slave trade. If he had been born to a wealthier family or had found a suitable patron, Thomas Paine might well have joined a long line of reformers whose efforts made Britain one of the most stable kingdoms in Europe. Yet Paine was the child of Quakers and artisans, and he carried the fury of Britain's underclass along with the optimism of its educated elite. He enjoyed the conversation of philosophers and scientists but identified with the struggles of sailors and vagrants. Much more than other liberals, he was willing to accept revolutionary means to achieve enlightened ends.[3]

Even for Thomas Paine, however, the ingrained habit and forms of deference died hard. In a 1767 letter to his superiors in the Excise office, he used the words *humble* and *humbly* four times in one paragraph. Five years later, he asked for better pay and treatment for his coworkers in his first pamphlet, *The Case of the Officers of Excise*. He spent much of the winter of 1772–73 trying in vain to find a member of Parliament who might read and respond to his work. Meanwhile, he neglected his shop back in Lewes, leaving it to the care of his second wife, Elizabeth, whom he had married in 1771. During the spring and summer of 1774, disaster struck Paine again and again. He sold his possessions, defaulted his debts, and signed a separation agreement with his wife, which was made easier by the fact that the marriage had never been consummated. (This was nobody's business but his own, Paine would say.) So at

2. J. M. Opal, "The Labors of Liberality: Christian Benevolence and National Prejudice in the American Founding," *Journal of American History* 94 (March 2008), 1087; Tobias Smollet, *A Complete History of England* (London, 1757), I:1.
3. Isaac Kramnick, *Republicanism and Bourgeois Radicalism: Political Ideology in Late Eighteenth-Century England and America* (Ithaca, N.Y., 1990), 133–60.

the age of thirty-seven, he was a broke, divorced unknown: liberal, enlightened, and unemployed.[4]

Late in 1774, the tenth year of a growing dispute between Britain and its North American colonies, Paine met the most famous American, Benjamin Franklin. This inventor-philosopher-politician wrote a brief letter on Paine's behalf, describing the rootless Englishman as "an ingenious worthy young man." Armed, at last, with a patron, Paine boarded a ship bound for Philadelphia. He would later explain this decision by noting that he had once read a "pleasing natural history" of Virginia, and had always wanted to see the other side of the Atlantic. But desperation must have been a factor too. Most Europeans knew America as a wild, backward place. A famed naturalist from France even posited that all life forms degenerated in the New World, which explained its dull humans and small animals. (An indignant Thomas Jefferson later tried to use a moose skeleton to refute these charges.) Then again, the North American colonies also held a special place in the imagination of Europe's liberals and nonconformists. "[America] may become the last asylum of British liberty," Tobias Smollet prophesized in 1757. Some day, Great Britain would be "enslaved by domestic despotism or foreign domination," worn down by the weight of wars, taxes, and the past itself. When that happened, "those colonies sent off by our forefathers may receive and entertain their sons as hapless exiles and ruined refugees." An exile from failure and a refugee from despair, Thomas Paine arrived in Philadelphia just before New Years' Day, 1775.[5]

II. The Evil Empire

Two years before he set sail for North America, a scandal hit Britain that deeply moved Paine, alerting him as no book ever could to imperial cruelty. Since the early 1600s, an English business firm known as the East India Company had used armed force and clever dealing to build a trading empire through much of South Asia. Around 1750, the company began to claim dominion over large swaths of the East Indies, driving British foreign policy and raising fears of corruption in high places. From 1766 to 1769, Robert Clive and other company leaders set off a speculative boom in London over East India stock, all the while enriching themselves with bribes, diamonds, and land cessions from the region of Bengal, in what is now eastern India and Bangladesh. When the stock crashed, London buzzed with rumors about the "eastern plunderers" and "nabobs" (a

---

4   Nelson, *Thomas Paine*, 39, 43–45.
5. Franklin quoted in Nelson, *Thomas Paine*, 49; Paine quoted in Nelson, *Thomas Paine*, 48; Smollet, *Complete History of England*, IV:661.

corruption of *nawab,* or Muslim ruler in India) of the company; when a terrible famine struck Bengal in 1770, many blamed the company's disruption of regional trade and rice production. In 1772, Lord Clive—his title a reward for his military exploits in India— appeared before a select committee of Parliament, whose findings were reprinted in the *London Chronicle* and other papers. Tom Paine read the report.[6]

It was a horror story. Gathering records and testimony reaching back to the 1750s, the select committee found that company agents had systematically profited at the expense of both the Indian people and the British taxpayers. They had also set India's many compet- ing rulers against one another, stoking civil wars while building their own army of native recruits, called *sepoys.* The British military, in service to the company, had not acted according to their nation's enlightened self-image. In 1764, for example, Major Hector Munro had faced a mutiny among his *sepoys.* By his own admission, given without a trace of regret, he had summoned twenty-four mutineers in front of all the troops, then ordered them to be tied to cannons and "blown away." This obscene display of British firepower burned into Paine's memory, as did other atrocities reported in the newspa- pers. Among these was the "punishment of the Breeches," in which an Indian was dressed in tight pants and tied to a pole, then forced to eat. Over a period of days, he died from exposure to his own excre- ment. "We have outdone the Spaniards in Peru!" wrote one reader in London. "We have murdered, deposed, plundered, usurped—nay, what think you of the famine in Bengal, in which three millions per- ished [?]".[7]

Parliament did not think too much about it. In May 1773, just as Tom Paine was giving up on his petition for the excise officers, its members essentially exonerated Clive, even praising him for his "great and meritorious service" to Britain. (Still, Clive's honor had been tarnished, and he never recovered.) Especially because the government then bailed out the company by granting it a new monopoly over tea sales in the American colonies, we can imagine Paine's sense of indignation. Parliament could not be bothered to listen to a humble petition from its dutiful servants, yet it lavished the rich and well connected with favors? Paine's own labors counted for nothing, while Lord Clive's plunder won him fame and fortune?

6. J. M. Opal, "*Common Sense* and Imperial Atrocity: How Tom Paine Saw South Asia in North America," *Common-place* 8 (July 2009), www.common-place.org/vol-09/no-4/ form/opal.shtml.
7. *The Minutes of the Select Committee Appointed by the House of Commons* (London, 1772), 55; *The London Evening-Post,* March 31–April 2, 1772; Horace Walpole to Hor- ace Mann, March 5, 1772 in W. S. Lewis, ed., *The Yale Edition of Horace Mann's Cor- respondence* (New Haven, Conn., 1939), XXIII:387.

And no one—*no one*—would be punished for killing all those innocent Asians?[8]

Once he arrived in Philadelphia, added the "e" to his last name,
and recovered from a severe illness, Paine's pent-up anger found
free rein. No longer at the center of the empire, in the literal shad-
ows of Parliament, Paine was free to reinvent himself. Franklin's
letter helped him land a job as editor of *The Pennsylvania Magazine:
Or, American Monthly Museum*, launched in early 1775 as Philadelphia's eighth newspaper. He and two other men wrote most of the
articles, using pen names like Humanus and Atlanticus. Gathering
articles and reports from all over the city and colonies, Paine
learned about the imports and merchant fleet of Philadelphia, the
ethnic diversity and Quaker origins of Pennsylvania, and the growing rift between colonial authorities and Parliament. He must have
been especially curious about the Boston Tea Party of December
1773, during which angry colonists refused the East India Company's monopoly-insured product.[9]

Paine wrote some two dozen articles during 1775, ranging in topic
from a dream sequence in which he met Alexander the Great
(reincarnated as a bug) to an instructional piece on building a
frame house "so as to represent brick." Two essays, in particular, capture his maturing ideology of revolutionary Enlightenment—of overthrowing the past to make room for a future built on reason and
sympathy, logic and justice. In "Reflections on the Life and Death of
Lord Clive," written soon after word arrived that Clive had killed
himself, Paine told his American readers of the recent calamities in
Bengal. Clive's lust for power and dominion had left a trail of woe for
the people of India, whom Paine symbolized as a "wailing widow"
and a "crying orphan." Wherever Clive and the East India Company
had ventured, "murder and rapine" had followed, with "famine and
wretchedness" not far behind. But these evil deeds had haunted
Clive, Paine wrote, and judgment, though deferred, would not be
denied: "A conqueror more fatal than himself beset him, and revenged
the injuries done to India." In *African Slavery in America*, separately
printed because the owner of the *Pennsylvania Magazine* did not want
his name attached to it, Paine also attacked the "savage practice" of
slavery as a daring violation of divine law. That law boiled down to
the Golden Rule, universally applied in the liberal spirit: "Christians
are taught to *account all men their neighbors; and love their neighbours as themselves; and do to all men as they would be done by.*"[1]

8. Opal, "*Common Sense* and Imperial Atrocity."
9. Nelson, *Thomas Paine*, 52, 60–61; Frank Smith, "New Light on Thomas Paine's First
   Year in America, 1775," *American Literature* 1 (January 1930), 347–71.
1. Thomas Paine, "Reflections on the Life and Death of Lord Clive," in Conway, ed.,
   Writings of Thomas Paine, I:30, 33; Paine, "African Slavery in America," in ibid., I:4, 6.

On the afternoon of April 24, 1775, five days after Paine's anonymous assault on slavery was printed, express riders brought news
of bloodshed between British regulars and local militia in Massachusetts. We might imagine Paine digesting this news over brandy
or coffee at the Indian Queen tavern, one of his favorite haunts. The
reports that arrived at the magazine's office spoke of thirty to forty
militiamen, "innocently amusing themselves" on the town green,
facing down a thousand British redcoats, who then opened fired
"without the least provocation." One dispatch said that some of the
Americans had taken refuge in the town church, whereupon the
redcoats "pointed their guns in and killed three." Another reported
that the British had searched for rebel leaders at their homes, "and
not finding them there, killed the woman of the house and all the
children, and set fire to the house." They then marched on, "firing
and killing hogs, geese, cattle, and everything that came in their
way, and burning houses." Blending fact and exaggeration, these
reports speak to the advanced network of communication—and
propaganda—that rebel leaders in North America had fashioned
over the past few years.[2]

They had a great deal of convincing to do. Perhaps one-quarter
to one-third of the 2.5 million colonists were Loyalists or Tories,
staunch supporters of a British government they considered the most
liberal and enlightened on earth. Many other Americans had no problem condemning certain "corruptions" in Parliament while still praising the king and the British Constitution. Loyalism prevailed among
the Quakers of Pennsylvania, through much of Long Island and New
York City, and in parts of the southern backcountry. Even the rebellious Whigs or Patriots who dreamed of a republic—a government
and society run by and for the people—spoke with respect, even
reverence, for British law and civilization. They often protested Parliament's heavy-handed actions on the basis of their *membership* in
the British Empire, not their independence from it. As free-born
subjects of Britain, they argued, they did not deserve the degraded
treatment or secondary status of Ireland (colonized by the English
since the 1500s) or Poland (partitioned by its neighbors in 1772).
They could not bear any comparisons to darker-skinned and "savage"
peoples. As John Adams snarled in 1765, "We won't be their negroes."[3]

Even in the summer and fall of 1775, after fighting had started
in New England, most colonials hesitated on the brink and declared
their fealty to King George III. It was Paine, the recent émigré from

---

2. "To all Friends of America Liberty," *The Pennsylvania Gazette: Or, American Monthly
   Museum* (Philadelphia), April 1775.
3. Adams, writing as "Humphrey Ploughjogger" in the *Boston Gazette*, quoted in T. H.
   Breen, *The Marketplace of Revolution: How Consumer Politics Shaped American Independence* (New York, 2004), 202.

Britain, who was most critical of British society and culture, most willing to denounce the empire itself rather than its corruptions. In an October 1775 essay, "A Serious Thought," he all but shouted at his readers to wake up to their peril. "When I reflect on the horrid cruelties exercised by the British in the East-Indies," he announced, "[and] read of the wretched natives being blown away, for no other crime than because, sickened with the miserable scene, they refused to fight," he was sure "that the Almighty, in compassion to mankind, will curtail the power of Britain." Their empire was guilty of "a thousand instances of barbarity," he insisted, chief among them the ongoing crime of the African slave trade. Asia and Africa had already suffered from British "barbarity"—and North America would be next. (Paine could not have known that on the very day he published these words, a British warship shelled a coastal town in Maine for refusing to surrender its cannon.) To convince his adopted countrymen of their prospects and perils, Paine then set to work on the pamphlet that transformed his life.[4]

The "Introduction" of *Common Sense*, which was first printed on January 10, 1776, reframed the Anglo-American controversy in terms of Enlightenment thought and feeling. They also used images of imperial atrocities past, present, and future, surely drawn from Paine's reading of British history and of recent events in the East Indies. "The laying a Country desolate with Fire and Sword, declaring War against the natural rights of all Mankind, and extirpating the Defenders thereof from the Face of Earth, is the Concern of every Man to whom Nature hath given the Power of feeling." The abuses you have suffered are no mere anomaly, no simple corruption, Paine told his readers. They were the means the empire would use to reduce you to subservience, so that it could plunder the country and feed its appetite for tax money and natural resources. "Fire and Sword" had come to America, and much worse was on the way. In this essay and others, Paine was instrumental in spreading news (and rumors) of British plans to incite slave revolts and Indian massacres.[5]

As of December 1775, when Paine wrote his famous pamphlet, had the British really brought the violence seen in the East Indies to the thirteen colonies? To what extent were they guilty of the desolating, extirpating war Paine evoked? Besides the initial fighting in and around Boston and the offer made by Virginia's royal governor in November to free those slaves and servants who fought for His Majesty, good evidence for Paine's charges include the October 18 bom-

---

4. Paine, "A Serious Thought," in Conway, *Writings of Thomas Paine*, I:65–66.
5. Peter Silver, *Our Savage Neighbors: How Indian War Transformed Early America* (New York, 2008), 230, 234, 241–42.

bardment of what is now Falmouth, Maine. Well over a hundred homes were destroyed; and most of the town was consumed by fire. Still, the British captain had given enough advance warning for the inhabitants to depart, so no one died in the attack. One might even argue that it was the Americans who were the aggressors at this early phase of the war; during the fall and early winter, a rebel force had invaded Québec. Yet Paine saw events in terms of a clear and grim pattern in English and British history. Beginning with the Norman Conquest, running through the cruel repression of the Irish and Scottish, and proceeding to the "prodigious" crimes in Bengal, British forces serving brutish kings had destroyed those in their way. Indeed, the most radical component of *Common Sense* was not the call for independence but the reason given for that goal: the British Empire was savage and cruel, uncivilized and insatiable.[6]

Having seized his readers' attention with this shocking claim, Paine explored the roots of political society more generally. "Society is produced by our wants, and government by our wickedness," he argued. "The former promotes our happiness *positively* by uniting our affections, the latter *negatively* by restraining our vices." Society derived from the human instinct to associate with other humans, which also gave rise to that jewel of enlightened morality, universal benevolence. Government was the price people paid for their vices. This distinction enabled Paine to present government as an artificial thing, at best a necessary evil and at worst a monstrous absurdity. If we prevent ourselves from being "dazzled with show," Paine reflected, we find that most governments, whether among the ancient Jews or the contemporary Europeans, were nothing but frauds or punishments. He urged Americans to trust the more "natural" forms of authority, such as those derived from the family and religion, and to dispel the unnatural grip of imperial rule.[7]

Determined to uproot the beliefs, claims, and assumptions that supported monarchy, he used extensive excerpts and close readings of the Old Testament to argue that God had never intended a king for Israel. Instead, monarchy had come to the Jews as a punishment. And what of the British government? Where did its present head, King George III, derive his authority? His target in sight, Paine began a ruthless exposé of the royal family. It seems, he wrote, that William the Conqueror, illegitimate son of a French nobleman,

6. Robert Middlekauff, *The Glorious Cause: The American Revolution, 1773–1789* (New York, 1982), 250–311; James S. Leamon, "Falmouth, the American Revolution, and the Price of Moderation," in Joseph Conforti, ed., *Creating Portland: History and Place in Northern New England* (Lebanon, N.H., 2005), 44–71.
7. Robert Ferguson, "The Commonalities of *Common Sense*," *William and Mary Quarterly* 57 (July 2000), 465–504.

had invaded England in 1066 and introduced a feudal system headed by a king. *That* was the bedrock of the British throne. While making and repeating this point, Paine clearly enjoyed himself. "A French bastard landing with an armed banditti, and establishing himself king of England against the consent of the natives, is in plain terms a very paltry rascally original.—It certainly hath no divinity in it." Throw off the "dark covering of antiquity," he dared in the name of Enlightenment, and you find nothing but a long line of untalented degenerates at the helm of state, bumbling their people into foolish wars. Building on the (literally) illegitimate origins of the British monarchy, Paine used the family metaphor to charge George III with murder most foul. "Even brutes do not devour their young, nor savages make war upon their families."

Before reviewing the rest of *Common Sense*, it is important to pause and refute two common misconceptions about the pamphlet and its author: first, that it is a simple attack on all public authority and, second, that he only used biblical text to appeal to a pious audience. Paine was neither an anarchist nor a libertarian. He wanted to remake law and authority so as to secure human rights. Society, for him, was not the sum total of people acting selfishly but the medium through which they behaved virtuously—that is, with an eye to their duties as well as their rights, their equality as well as their liberty. To understand those rights and duties, Paine drew from his Quaker origins, repeatedly using Christian parables and sayings as well as direct quotes from Scripture. (He also echoed English prejudices against Catholicism and Islam.) Again and again, he used the Golden Rule, which he sometimes called "the law of reciprocity," to support his arguments. True to Enlightenment liberality, he extended that law beyond the literal sense of *neighbor,* demanding goodwill and fairness to all humanity. Such principles were the true and just foundations of authority, for they derived from Nature or God, not treachery or force.

In contrast to the dry, learned pamphlets of eighteenth-century erudition, *Common Sense* had the edgy satire and furious wit of British dissenters like Jonathan Swift, who had famously proposed that the English eat the small children of Ireland. Paine's first major essay has a brash beauty to it, an uncompromising flair that translated well into one-liners and tavern talk. It was meant to startle and upset, to draw laughs, and to be read aloud. Paine combined sweeping maxims about humanity ("Time makes more converts than reason") with irreverent jabs at the high and mighty (nature shows her dislike of hereditary rule by giving us "an *ass for a lion*"). By openly appealing to the "passions and feelings of mankind," the pamphlet also swept away a traditional theory of politics whereby a dispassionate elite oversaw public affairs, protecting the masses from their own emotions. As the historian Nicole Eustace has observed, *Common Sense* made an important contribution to political and moral philosophy by insisting that *everyone*, not just the learned and well born, could or should feel for strangers. Paine argued for a new kind of equality: the equality of sympathy.[8]

Having exposed the roots of monarchy and the behavior of the British state, Paine finished his pamphlet with a ringing endorsement of American independence. He explained that the British fleet was not as mighty as it seemed, that the "United Colonies" of North America could be defended with relative ease, and that the rest of the world would welcome the new nation. "The sun never shined on a cause of greater worth" than American independence, Paine mused. Rather than cringe under the wing of a brutal empire and ruffian king, Americans could form a country that will be "the glory of the earth." Of what value were the musty, ignored "rights of Englishmen" when Americans could inspire all mankind? "Freedom hath been hunted round the globe," Paine warned, but now it found a new home: "O! receive the fugitive, and prepare in time an asylum for mankind."

III. The Limits of Humanity

Selling for two shillings, or about $15 today, *Common Sense* swept through the colonies in a matter of weeks. Within months, copies circulated in London, Edinburgh, Berlin, and Warsaw. The total number sold in North America during the early months of 1776 is a point of controversy, but there is no doubt that tens of thousands of Americans—perhaps well over a hundred thousand—bought copies or read sections of the pamphlet. The circulation of Paine's work dwarfed that of all other revolutionary pamphlets and may have reached one in five American adults. Paine's best-seller did not *cause* Americans to embrace independence; it focused and intensified their grievances, pushing the terms of the Anglo-American crisis beyond the point of reconciliation. "[Y]ou have declared the sentiments of millions," one reader told Paine. "Your production may justly be compared to a land-flood that sweeps all before it." During the spring and early summer of 1776, at least ninety documents demanding American independence—drafted by towns, grand juries, and legislatures—appeared in the thirteen colonies/states, and in June the Virginia radical and slaveholder Thomas Jefferson drafted a national statement for the Continental Congress. (Jefferson's first draft included a furious indictment of British involvement in the slave trade; Congress deleted it before presenting the final draft on

8. Nicole Eustace, *Passion Is the Gale: Emotion, Power, and the Coming of the American Revolution* (Chapel Hill, N. C., 2008), 439–79.

July 4, 1776.) Unknown a year before, Thomas Paine had become a household name throughout the Western world.[9]

The war started very badly for the American rebels. In August, a huge armada of British troops, supplemented by hired soldiers from Hesse-Kassel and other German states, landed on Long Island and routed George Washington's Continental Army. Paine marched with the Continental troops (who called him, simply, "Common Sense") as they retreated into northern New Jersey and Pennsylvania. In pursuit, the British commanders generally treated Washington as a legitimate foe rather than the leader of a "banditti," even though international law—the "law of nations"—recommended no quarter to rebels or traitors. They meant to isolate the radicals and restore the obedience of the colonials, securing this corner of the empire for strategic and economic advantage over the French and other rivals. But British and Hessian soldiers also plundered and terrified civilians and, in many confirmed cases, raped women. Thomas Paine was there to tell the world all about it.[1]

The "eyes of all Europe" were upon the American colonies, Paine wrote in the spring of 1776. What Paine wanted them to see was "the havoc and destruction of unnatural war . . . the burning and depopulating of towns and cities." He wanted them to know the naked cruelty of imperial violence. When a writer who called himself Cato scolded that such seditious words would bring foreign troops to America's shores, Paine retorted: "Were they coming, Cato . . . it would be impossible for them to exceed, or even to equal the cruelties practiced by the British army in the East-Indies." Writing as The Forrester, the pen name of an eighteenth-century Whig and the surname of an eleventh-century rebel against William the Conqueror, Paine condemned the British as a vile horde. As usual, the scandals from the East Indies clinched his point. "The tying men to the mouths of cannon and '*blowing them away,*'" he noted, "was never acted by any but an English General, or approved by any but a British Court." In December 1776, he wrote a series of essays called *The American Crisis*, the first of which famously declared that these were the times that tried men's souls.[2]

9. Nelson, *Thomas Paine*, 92; Pauline Maier, *American Scripture: Making the Declaration of Independence* (New York, 1997), 48–49. For estimates of between 120,000 and 150,000 copies sold, see Ferguson, "The Commonalities of *Common Sense*," 466 and 466n; for more conservative figures, consult Trish Loughram, "Disseminating *Common Sense*: Thomas Paine and the Problem of the Early National Bestseller," *American Literature* 78 (March 2006), 1–28.

1. David Hackett Fischer, *Washington's Crossing* (New York, 2004), 176–80; Mary Beth Norton, *Liberty's Daughters: The Revolutionary Experience of American Women, 1750–1800* (Boston, 1980), 202–4.

2. Paine, "The Forrester's Letters, No. 2" March 28, 1776, and "The Forrester's Letters, No. 3," April 22, 1776, in Conway, ed., *Writings of Thomas Paine*, I:72, 77.

They also tried Paine's principles. *"Our plan is peace for ever,"* he had appealed to the Quakers in an appendix to *Common Sense.* "We fight neither for revenge nor conquest; neither from pride nor passion; we are not insulting the world with our fleets and armies, not ravaging the globe for plunder." Because he believed in the dignity and equality of humankind, Paine abhorred military force and violence. Firepower was the tool of the oppressor, the source of unjust and unnatural inequalities. But how could the plain and unoffending peoples of the earth, be they slaves from Africa, *sepoys* in Bengal, or farmers at Lexington, resist the bloody imperialists? What could Americans do but fight the empire? "Whoever considers the unprincipled enemy we have to cope with," Paine warned three months after Lexington and Concord, "will not hesitate to declare that nothing but arms or miracles can reduce them to reason and moderation." Here again, we see how Paine's love of liberty was bound up with an ethical code that set down rules and restrictions—*thou shalt nots*—for people and nations alike. As he liked to say, he *knew* the English, and they had to be "reduced" or brought under the laws of morality: "They have lost sight of the limits of humanity."[3]

This tension between peace and violence, rights and duties, human passion and moral law ran through the entire American war effort. Desperate to win the support and respect of European rulers, statesmen like Washington and Jefferson stressed that the United States was a nation of laws that obeyed the law of nations. An important way to do so was to avoid—or at least condemn—revenge, the signature vice of "savage" or "barbaric" peoples. Vengeance was not only unenlightened but anti-Christian, and Paine noted that the New Testament explicitly disallowed revenge. But British atrocities (or rumors thereof) enraged the rebels. When stories of British arsonists reached the Continental Congress in 1781, one delegate suggested employing people to "reduce to ashes the towns of Great Britain." Paine made similar threats. "You ought to know, gentlemen," he wrote in an open letter to British commissioners, "that England and Scotland are far more exposed to incendiary desolation than America." We speak English and know your customs, he warned darkly. One of us could slip into London and set fire to the Bank of England.[4]

Even as he threatened the British with revolutionary violence and "incendiary mischief," though, Paine worked to build America's

3. Paine, "Epistle to Quakers," in Conway, ed., *Writings of Thomas Paine*, I:122 (this was added to the February 14 edition of *Common Sense* along with an appendix replying to Loyalist writers); Paine, "Thoughts on Defensive War," *Pennsylvania Gazette*, July 1775.
4. The motion in the Continental Congress was made on September 20, 1781, by John Mathews and seconded by James Varnum. See *Journals of the Continental Congress, 1774–1789*, memory.loc.gov/ammem/amlaw/lwjc.html (accessed September 23, 2011).

reputation as a good global citizen and trading partner. Like most Enlightenment figures, he tightly associated peace and commerce. A free exchange of each nation's surpluses, he assumed, would not only benefit every nation in material terms but also promote an "enlarged" and "liberal" mentality. "Our plan is commerce," Paine advised; the United States wanted to "shake hands with all the world." He served on the Committee for Foreign Affairs during 1777 and 1778, during which the new nation signed the Treaty of Amity and Commerce with France. Rejecting the imperial policy by which the major powers monopolized trade with their colonies, this agreement was based on reciprocity, the equal standing of both countries "in the eyes of the world." In a later agreement with Prussia, the United States also embraced a new diplomatic theory that gave neutral countries the right to trade with warring nations. The treaty also called for novel restrictions on the violence of war. In the event of conflict, all women and children, farmers, artisans, fishermen, scholars, and any person "whose occupations are for the common benefit of mankind" were not to be harmed or harassed. Prisoners were to be treated just as the opposing army provided for its own troops.[5]

With the end of major fighting in North America in 1781 and the formal declaration of peace in 1783, Paine exulted that a new age had dawned. The empire had been beaten, the Enlightenment vindicated. In place of the "system of war," in which domestic tyranny gave rise to foreign aggression and vice versa, a new global society of reciprocal trade and equal rights was at hand. As common people gained more control over public affairs, nations would no longer "insult" and make war on each other, because common people did not want to conquer and dominate. That was the evil of kings and despots, of William the Conqueror and Lord Clive. Instead, government would (and *should*, in Paine's view) promote the happiness and progress of the society it represented. The law of nations would change, too, so that it more clearly favored the peaceful and more brightly reflected "that spirit of universal justice which ought to preside equally over all mankind."[6]

Across the Atlantic world, in fact, the 1780s brought out liberal plans for global peace and commerce, for the elimination of "tyrant custom" and the advance of human happiness. These plans combined Enlightened and Christian values, harnessing the power of reason to the cause of justice. In Britain, France, and the United

---

5. Treaty of Amity and Commerce with France, February 6, 1778; Treaty of Amity and Commerce between His Majesty the King of Prussia and the United States of America, September 10, 1785, at www.avalon.law.yale.edu/18th_century/fr1788-1.asp and www.avalon.law.yale.edu/18th_century/prus1788.asp, respectively (accessed December 17, 2010).

6. Paine, "Public Good," December 30, 1780 in Conway, ed., *Writings of Thomas Paine*, II:35.

States, ministers and statesmen as well as activists denounced the Atlantic slave trade. Four survivors of that trade published their own accounts in London; of these, the most popular was that of Olaudah Equiano, which described the iron muzzles and thumb screws used to torture slaves, while the most furious was that of Quobna Ottobah Cugoano, which warned of "the long suspended vengeance" awaiting slaveholders. Whig statesmen in Britain, including Paine's future nemesis, Edmund Burke, charged the East India Company with abusing the people of India and shaming the standards of civility. The philosophers Immanuel Kant and Jeremy Bentham drew up new theories of human morality and historical progress, suggesting plans for a "universal and permanent peace" on earth. As for Thomas Paine, he designed an iron bridge that could be taken down and transported as needed—a fitting invention for a global enthusiast for trade—and traveled back to Europe, reporting in 1787 that some "very extraordinary change" was happening in France.[7]

Two years later, on July 14, 1789, a Paris crowd attacked the Bastille prison, symbol of absolute monarchy and the *ancien régime*. The values and ideas of this early period of the French Revolution were similar to those of its American counterpart: natural rights, the sovereignty of the people, representative government, and civil society. Yet the sheer pace and scope of the changes involved in deposing monarchy were far more dramatic in France, where thousands of peasants still traveled to Versailles palace each year to see King Louis XVI, trusting that his royal touch would cure them of scrofula. The reforms demanded by liberal aristocrats in France soon gave way to something much more daring and dangerous. Over the span of only three years, as food shortages and bloody riots shook its social order, France passed from an absolute to a constitutional monarchy and then to a radical republic. In the name of the people and the nation, a revolutionary convention abolished all vestiges of feudalism and many of Catholicism, even introducing a new calendar that marked time, not from the birth of Christ, but from the birth of the republic. Time, no less than society, was to begin anew.[8]

Many European and American liberals and radicals praised and welcomed these sweeping changes. Thomas Jefferson, for one, was living in Paris when the Bastille fell, and for years he was certain that he had witnessed "the first chapter of the history of European liberty." In August 1792, the French Republic announced nineteen foreigners to be honorary *citoyens*; Paine was one of them, and although he spoke no French he took a seat in the new National

7. Paine, "Prospects on the Rubicon," August 20, 1787, in Conway, ed., *Writings of Thomas Paine*, II:206.
8. Simon Schama, *Citizens: A Chronicle of the French Revolution* (New York, 1989).

Assembly that fall. "[T]he cause of France," he declared to its delegates, "is the cause of all mankind." Yet conservative voices on both
sides of the Atlantic recoiled from the tremendous passions and
raw violence emanating from Paris. From the outset, John Adams
saw mischief where Jefferson saw promise, and over the next several years the so-called Federalists made opposition to the French
Revolution a major theme of American politics. In Britain, Edmund
Burke's *Reflections on the Revolution in France* (1790) faulted the
French radicals for rejecting the good sense of the past. Enlightenment universalism had gone too far, he argued. It was erasing the
loyalties, the traditions, and even the "prejudices" that made liberty
safe, orderly, and enduring.[9]

Paine's reply to Burke came in the form of another best-seller, a
two-part, book-length classic of progressive and radical ideas called
The Rights of Man (1791–92). Part I of Paine's new book defended
the French Revolution along with the key premise of the Revolutionary Enlightenment: that the earth belonged to the living, who
could alter or abolish their inheritance to suit their needs and rights.
That power, in turn, did not derive from any particular document,
national privilege, or sectarian religion. It belonged to all of humanity, whose rights were nothing less than sacred. In effect, Paine
lifted humanity into direct interface with the divine, imbuing each
person with a dignity that no other person could rightly deny. "The
duty of man," he proclaimed, "is plain and simple, and consists but
of two points. His Duty to God, which every man must feel; and
with respect to his neighbour, to do as he would be done by." Convinced that liberated citizens would never forget those duties while
claiming their rights, Paine rejected all earthly authority but that
of the duly represented people of each political community: "the
nation."

Part II of *Rights of Man* moved well beyond the call for liberation. "Why is it," he dared to ask, "that scarcely any are executed but
the poor?" Why did so many live in poverty and desperation, while a
few indulged their every wish? Exploring the roots of poverty and
social misery, Paine suggested a national pension system, universal
education, and other means of "rendering governments more conducive to the general happiness of mankind." Rather than a defense of
customary liberties or an attack on corrupt government, this was a
manifesto for a new social and political order. Let the old order fall
to ashes, Paine exalted. Let the British stop their plunders in India,
the Spanish release their colonies in South America, and the "hor-

---

9. Thomas Jefferson to Diodati, August 3, 1789, in Julian P. Boyd, ed., *The Papers of
Thomas Jefferson* (Princeton, N.J., 1958), XV:326; Paine, "Address to People of France,"
September 25, 1792, in Conway, ed., *Writings of Thomas Paine*, III:97.

rid practice of war" disappear forever. A new world was waiting, in which people would live in peace and government would serve society, not vice versa. "In stating these matters," he avowed, "I speak an open and disinterested language, dictated by no passion but that of humanity . . . my country is the world, and my religion is to do good." In her *Vindication of the Rights of Women* (1792) the British writer Mary Wollstonecraft subtly faulted Paine for neglecting half of the human species. But this first statement of modern feminism shared the crucial premise, not only of Paine's work, but also of radical politics most generally: that today's power arrangements came from yesterday's thinking, and should be changed to make a better tomorrow. Together, the works of Paine and Wollstonecraft in the early 1790s signal the high-water mark of the Revolutionary Enlightenment.[1]

Then, within years, it collapsed into violence and fear. In August 1791, the deadly vengeance that Cugoano had prophesized came true on the Caribbean island of Saint Domingue, where the brutalized African slaves rose up against the wealthy French masters. They slaughtered the whites and torched the hated plantation homes and sugar refineries. Terrified French refugees fled to the United States, where slaveholders wondered if this worst nightmare would soon come to their homes. In Europe, a coalition of monarchies planned to reinstate Louis XVI, thereby crushing the revolutionary spirit before it spread. The British government continued its crackdown, aided by "king and church" rioters who burned Paine in effigy and broke up radical meetings. In December 1792, Paine was convicted in absentia for seditious libel. The next year, French revolutionaries began to sing "*La Marseillaise*," whose chorus line warned the invaders with a new kind of nationalism: "Let's march, let's march, that the impure blood should water the furrows of our fields." In Paris, Paine kept his faith in the revolution, recommending (through an interpreter) that France support an uprising in Ireland.[2]

During the winter of 1792–93, the National Convention tried and convicted Louis XVI—now Louis Capet, just another *citoyen*—of high treason. Paine supported the trial but objected to the penalty: death by guillotine. "My language has always been that of liberty *and* humanity," he explained. Public executions violated his creed, because they arose from "a spirit of revenge rather than a spirit of justice." The final vote in the convention was close (361 to 334),

1. Christine Stansell, *The Feminist Promise: 1792 to the Present* (New York, 2010), 17–26. Paine never attacked patriarchal laws and customs in a systematic way, and he often referred to the "natural" distinctions of male and female. But he was not blind to the global oppression of women, as evidenced by his August 1775 essay, "An Occasional Letter on the Female Sex."
2. Hochschild, *Bury the Chains*, 241–79.

and some deputies probably voted for death out of fear for their own necks. On January 21, 1793, Louis Capet managed some brave final words before being decapitated in front of a huge crowd. Some say the crowd chanted, *"Vive la nation!"*; others insist that the people of Paris watched in grim silence, afraid to look at one another. Over the next year and a half, some forty thousand people (mostly commoners) perished in "the Terror." Convinced, with good reason, that Europe's aristocracy would never allow the Republic to endure, the French government declared war on virtually all of Europe, Britain included. They welcomed revolutionaries everywhere to rise up against existing institutions. Conservatives were appalled. This was no "common political war with an old recognized member of the commonwealth of Christian Europe," Burke warned, but a desperate struggle for civilization itself. Seventeen years after he condemned the British for forgetting the limits of humanity, Thomas Paine found himself committed to a pariah nation that made total war on its enemies.[3]

IV. For God and Country

Alexis de Tocqueville once noted that the French Revolution originally behaved much like a missionary religion, in that it sought converts the world over. In fact, it required sweeping changes of its neighbors. "Of all the surprises that [it] launched on a startled world," he reflected, "this surely was the most astounding." This expansionary imperative was in some ways a reflection of the Revolutionary Enlightenment's stress on universal rights and shared humanity. Yet by the late 1790s, the radical republic no longer tried to erase national boundaries in the name of humanity, but to conquer Europe in the name of France. Helped along by the pen of Thomas Paine, the American Revolution—a colonial insurrection more than a social upheaval—had also addressed itself to the "cause of all mankind." But by the time an artillery officer named Napoleon Bonaparte seized control of France in 1799, the United States had also withdrawn into a much more exclusive and conservative form of nationalism. No one's influence or reputation suffered more in this new climate than that of Tom Paine.[4]

By the end of 1793, Paine observed, "the just and humane principles" of the French Revolution "had been departed from." In addition to the mass beheadings of the Terror, many thousands of

3. Edmund Burke, "Letters on a Regicide Peace . . . Letter IV, to the Earl Fitzwilliam," *The Works of the Right Honourable Edmund Burke* (London, 1812), IX:10; Schama, *Citizens*, 634–35; Jack Fruchtman Jr., *Thomas Paine: Apostle of Freedom* (New York, 1994), 295, 481.
4. Alexis de Tocqueville, *The Old Regime and the French Revolution*, trans. Stuart Gilbert (New York, 1955), 11.

peasants in the Vendée region, who refused to give up their religion in the name of the republic, were massacred as traitors. Not coincidentally, Paine began to drink heavily. He still supported the French Republic, which along with the United States seemed to be the only obstacles to British world domination. Indeed, his deeper loyalty to global republican revolution remained even as the revolutionaries turned on him. When the radical Jacobins seized power in late 1793, they began to suspect rather than welcome foreigners. The enemies of the Revolution were everywhere, and they had to be eliminated. On December 28, agents of the Committee of General Surety and Surveillance arrested Paine and the only other foreign-born convention deputy, who was later guillotined. When an American official tried to obtain Paine's release, the authorities noted that he had been born in Britain before accepting French citizenship, which, to their minds, disqualified him from American protection. The cosmopolitan ideal of the Enlightenment had imploded. Once a citizen of the world, Paine was now a man without a country.[5]

Imprisoned in Paris's Luxembourg Palace, Paine nursed his private demons. What, he mused, had Britain ever done but plunder and destroy and conspire? Why, he wondered, did the president of the United States, to whom he had dedicated Part I of *Rights of Man*, not arrange for his release? Issued in late 1794, he published a full version of *The Age of Reason*, his third and final best-seller, the following year. It remains his most elusive and tortured work. Judged by its cover, the book appears to renounce the "passions and feelings of mankind" in favor of cold, pitiless rationality. Quoted out of context, it seems to advocate atheism (the belief in no God or religion), when in truth it calls for deism (the belief in God but no religion). Paine's goal was to destroy the authority of the sacred texts to promote love and awe of Creation itself. To do so, he excoriated what he saw as the discrepancies and lies of the Old Testament, in particular. The bloody actions of the ancient Jews, done in the name of Jehovah, were "as shocking to humanity" as anything done by the fanatics of Paris or "the English government in the East Indies." Ever since, Pharisees and hypocrites had used religious dogma to keep the masses from their sacred rights. Here he reiterated his lifelong opposition to violence and domination. Yet in his zeal to uncover the human corruptions of divine precepts, Paine also mocked some of the moral traditions that he had long embraced. His sweeping denunciation of the Abrahamic canon alienated countless thousands and unborn generations.[6]

5. Paine, *The Age of Reason*, in Conway, ed., *Writings of Thomas Paine*, IV:85. This quote appears in the preface to the second part of the book.
6. Paine, *The Age of Reason*, in Conway, ed., *Writings of Thomas Paine*, IV:90.

Given Great Britain's situation in the late 1790s, one can understand why many Englishmen came to hate Tom Paine. The conservative writer Hannah More, among many, counseled Britain's poor
to appreciate their liberty, venerate their king, and cast away airy
dreams of universal rights and human equality. Meanwhile, Irish
rebels rose up against the English occupation while Napoleon's
armies swept across Europe and reached to Egypt. Many feared that
French soldiers would soon reenact the Conquest of 1066. Thomas
Paine not only supported that idea but actively *planned* such an
attack in 1797, offering his ideas to the Directory, the somewhat less
radical French government that had taken charge two years earlier.
That year, he also published *Agrarian Justice*, the contents of which
stirred the deepest fear of Britain's upper and middle classes—the
deliberate reordering of society in pursuit of an egalitarian ideal of
justice. In the midst of Britain's greatest crisis, Paine became public
enemy number two, behind Napoleon. A vicious "biography," commissioned by the British government, reported that Paine was a liar,
a drunkard, a wife beater, and a physically ugly man who could not
consummate his second marriage due to either "natural imbecility"
or "philosophical indifference." The turn against Paine in the United
States, on the other hand, requires more explanation. For what happened there speaks not only to the fate of the Revolutionary Enlightenment but also to the competing models of nationalism that have
shaped Western civilization ever since.[7]

To Paine's mind, a nation was a defined territory in which the
inhabitants shared certain laws, beliefs, and public institutions. Its
government was bound not only to secure the rights and safety of
the people but also to improve their lives through liberal trade, fair
taxes, and basic protections for the aged, the sick, and the poor.
This enthusiasm for robust national policy—"the public affairs of a
Nation," in his words—reflects Paine's exposure to French radicalism and its emphasis on the "nation" as an indivisible body of political and social equals. But these ideas ran counter to popular
Anglo-American fears of centralized government; during the debates
over a new U.S. Constitution in the late 1780s, Paine was actually
closer in spirit to the elite Federalists than he was to their more
populist, local-minded opponents. By the 1790s, his belief that public authority ought to promote the people's happiness also ran
squarely into a new conservative ideology, led by Alexander Hamilton, which called on government to secure liberty against equality—
that is, to contain the democratization of society by protecting the

---

7. Francis Oldys, *The Life of Thomas Paine* (Boston, 1796), 12; Alfred Owen Aldridge,
"Thomas Paine's Plan for a Descent on England," *William and Mary Quarterly* 14 (January 1957), 74–84. First printed in London, *Life of Paine* was commissioned by the British government and written by Scottish lawyer George Chalmers.

investments of the wealthy and enabling them to direct and profit from economic change. Paine's democratic nationalism thus had little traction in the sprawling American republic. Moreover, many Americans now stressed God's particular favor over their nation. Rather than "universal benevolence" on the model of the New Testament, they spoke of a new chosen people, a new Israel that had to guard against the "cargoes of infidelity" arriving from France.[8]

Especially after he denounced George Washington in a bitter, rambling letter from 1796, Paine became a poster boy for everything Americans loved to hate. He became an alcoholic atheist who stood with infidel France, with which the United States fought an undeclared war at sea during 1797 and 1798. (Much to his credit, President John Adams managed to avoid an all-out conflict.) *Common Sense* was long forgotten, while *The Age of Reason* was denounced from every pulpit. In 1798, a prominent minister from Charlestown, Massachusetts warned of a worldwide conspiracy to overthrow Christianity, led by a mysterious cabal known as the Bavarian Illuminati. Years later, another pastor from New England wondered if a yellow fever outbreak in New Hampshire and a deadly earthquake in South America were both punishments from God, meted out because the people living in those places had read Thomas Paine.[9]

The aging radical shrugged off such attacks. They confirmed his disdain for superstition and bigotry and fed his self-image as righteous dissident from unjust power, fearless advocate of hidden truth. But how was he to answer a pamphlet published in New York during 1797, which defended Washington's policy of noninterference with the wars of the French Revolution? How could he reply to its rebuke of the "hellish principles of retaliation," or brush aside its condemnation of French aggression? "America has ever pursued a system of peace," the author explained. "She wishes to be at peace with the world, and to do justice to all." The vindictive fury of the French Revolution had exposed Paine to the gentler side of his own principles.[1]

---

8. Opal, "Labors of Liberality," 1106; Evan Radcliffe, "Revolutionary Writing, Moral Philosophy, and Universal Benevolence in the Eighteenth Century," *Journal of the History of Ideas* 54 (April 1993), 221–40. For various views of post-Revolution conservatism in the United States, see Terry Bouton, *Taming Democracy: The People, "The Founders," and the Troubled Ending of the American Revolution* (New York, 2007), 171–265; Carole Smith-Rosenberg, *This Violent Empire: The Birth of an American National Identity* (Chapel Hill, N.C., 2009).

9. Jonathan Plummer, *The Dreadful Earthquake and the Fatal Spotted Fever* (Newburyport, Mass.?, 1812?). The mysterious provenance of this text and its extravagant language suggests it might have been a satire of anti-Paine attacks, but even if so, it suggests how intense those attacks were. For Paine's unwise and unhinged attack on Washington, see Joseph J. Ellis, *Founding Brothers: The Revolutionary Generation* (New York, 2001), 126.

1. *A Letter to Thomas Paine, In Answer to His Scurrilous Epistle Addressed to our Late Worthy President* (New York, 1797), 9, 18.

Even as his reputation collapsed, Paine kept a special confidence in the United States. He had always ignored the bitter divisions within American society and politics and rarely dwelled on Americans' treatment of slaves and native peoples. The economic prosperity of the new nation during the 1790s, powered by the ongoing war in Europe and the resulting demand for American exports, vindicated his faith in the American experiment. When his old friend Thomas Jefferson defeated John Adams and the Federalists in 1800, completing a peaceful transfer of power back to what Jefferson called "the Spirit of 1776," Paine decided on a final voyage across the Atlantic. Back in 1774, he had traveled in safe, if seasick anonymity to North America. Now, in 1802, he was a celebrity and a fugitive. Fearing capture by the Royal Navy, which was fanned out through the Atlantic sea lanes, Paine waited for a lull in the fighting to board a ship heading west.[2]

The nation Paine returned to was full of individuals who were too busy pursuing their own happiness—not that of society or humanity—to bother with this icon of tumultuous days gone by. To be sure, Americans loved (and loved to talk about) liberty and equality, and more and more of them were taking an active role in public affairs and political decisions. But the democracy they were creating was more practical and individualistic than the brave new world Paine had once evoked. It left much more room for rights and far less space for duties than he and other democratic radicals hoped for. Above all, it was committed to territorial expansion and economic growth at the expense of native peoples and slaves, not to mention poorer farmers and tradesmen who had more modest aspirations for themselves and their country. Now in power, Jefferson tired of Paine's relentless hostility to the status quo. Semiretired, Paine lived in and around New York City, writing letters and declarations that no one read. When he dined in public, it was said, people stared at him as if he were an orangutan.[3]

In early 1809 he grew ill, refusing on his deathbed to renounce deism. He died on June 8 and was buried on a farm the next day; only a tiny crowd gathered to pay any respects. Ten years later, William Cobbett, an English journalist who had once reviled Paine but then converted to radicalism, tried to exhume the body and bring it back to England. There Cobbett planned a great monument to the great revolutionary. The British authorities were not amused, and the British public was not interested. Cobbett tried, and failed, to exhibit Paine's remains for a fee. "Poor Tom Paine!"

2. Merrill D. Peterson, *Thomas Jefferson and the New Nation: A Biography* (New York, 1970), 681–82.
3. Peterson, Ibid., 711–13.

exclaimed a nursery rhyme. "Where he has gone or how he fares; Nobody knows and nobody cares."[4]

His ideas discredited, Paine's reputation bottomed out in the English-speaking world during the early nineteenth century. In the United States, the 1820s was a decade of both nationalist swagger and evangelical piety. Amid the glow of military victory over Britain in 1815 and the fervor of a mass revival known as the Second Great Awakening, no one associated with the memory of a citizen of the world who had called Christianity a fraud. In Britain, too, Paine's assaults on imperialism seemed peevish and outdated as the empire triumphed over Napoleon and then expanded into South Asia, Africa, the Caribbean, and China. The East India Company, for its part, prospered as the world's largest drug dealer, bringing opium to China at the point of many guns. Then again, a growing workers' movement saw Paine as an early spokesman for those of small means and modest ambitions. After 1830, workingmen's parties and associations pushing for democratic reforms in the United States also rediscovered Paine as the common man's philosopher.

Against a nineteenth-century backdrop of industrialization and imperial rivalry, Paine's image waxed and waned. Nationalist radicals in British India, often educated in Christian schools, used secreted copies of *The Age of Reason* and *Rights of Man* to attack imperial rule. Theodore Roosevelt, a progressive imperialist and devout nationalist, deemed Paine a "filthy little atheist" in 1898. The argument continued into the twentieth and twenty-first centuries. Cold warriors tied him to communism, while a wide range of Americans tried to seize the author of *Common Sense* for their own understandings of the United States at the 1976 bicentennial. Conservative icon and then president Ronald Reagan cited Paine's opposition to government interference in trade and commerce while a new group of right-wing hawks known as neoconservatives later used Paine's description of America as "the cause of all mankind" to support sweeping plans for American hegemony. The Paine Anti-Defamation League issued a sharp rebuttal, promising to guard Paine's legacy against those who used his words without due regard to basic context or common sense. Undeterred, Glenn Beck published *Glenn Beck's Common Sense* in 2009.[5]

What do all of these postmortem adoptions mean? With what groups or causes should we associate the great radical? Freethinkers

---

4. Nelson, *Thomas Paine*, 8, 1–9; Paul Collins, *The Trouble with Tom: The Strange Aftermath and Times of Thomas Paine* (New York, 2005).
5. Theodore Roosevelt, *Gouverneur Morris* (1898; New York, 1972), 289; Harvey J. Kaye, "The Lost Founder," *The American Prospect*, July 2005; "The Paine Anti-Defamation League," at www.thomaspainefriends.org/anti-defamation.htm (accessed January 28, 2011); Glenn Beck, *Glenn Beck's Common Sense* (New York, 2009).

and deists can certainly claim Paine as their own, although no more than Quakers can. Workers' radicals rightly see him as one of their early champions, although he was no Marxist—property, he always said, was a natural and essential right, as long as it derived from labor instead of speculation or plunder. As for the notion that Paine would support the antiregulatory demands of business interests or the military adventures of latter-day imperialists, all that can be said is that he intuitively favored the weak over the strong, the poor over the rich, the marginalized over the mighty. His avowed and fundamental purpose was to challenge privilege and prejudice, to defy tyranny and cruelty. If you either possess or desire a great deal of money and power, Paine is not your man.

More to the point, though, Paine belongs to none of the groups or ideologies that have claimed him since his death, because he was a product above all of a *period*—a phase in Western and Atlantic history that encompasses the American and early French revolutions. Only in that window of time could someone advocate so easily for new freedoms from unjust government *and* new ways to promote and establish public happiness. Only at that moment of intellectual and cultural creativity could someone so seamlessly empathize with colonized Asians, enslaved Africans, and rebellious Americans. And only by recovering what the revolutionary Enlightenment was and was not, by steeping ourselves in the world Paine knew and helped shape, can we begin to learn from that moment rather than to hoard it for ourselves.

V. How to Use This Norton Critical Edition

This book is divided into three parts: a selection of Paine's own writings from the 1770s to 1790s, a sample of original documents from those turbulent decades, and a section of interpretive essays by historians looking back on Paine's legacy and those of the American and French revolutions. These documents, in turn, focus on three major themes, each of which roughly correlates with the 1770s, the 1780s, and the 1790s: rebellion against imperial rule and monarchy, global citizenship and the spread of Enlightenment hopes and ideas, and reaction against such thinking amid the violence and chaos of the French Revolution.

In addition to the complete text of *Common Sense*, we have included selections of Paine's writings that touch on the themes and events discussed in the introduction. His work spans an enormous range of topics, from the abuses of the East India Company in South Asia to the prospects for American trade with Europe and Africa. Did he rely on a similar set of ethical and political ideas throughout his career? Do we find significant changes in his thinking and arguments, or basic continuity? Was he conscious of the tensions we now see in his thinking between liberty and equality, or did he assume that they were natural allies in the larger fight against monarchy, aristocracy, slavery, poverty, bigotry, and oppression?

The primary documents, as well, are as varied and wide-ranging as Paine himself, so it might be helpful to consider how he would have approached or understood each one. In what way does each author agree or disagree with Paine's premises? How would Paine have reacted to each source in his various roles as British subject, American revolutionary, and, later, French delegate? While imagining Paine reading these sources, try to keep track of where he was when each was written, so as to trace the movement of revolutionary and Enlightenment ideas back and forth across the Atlantic. The temporal context is vital, too. Certain ideas and phrases "sounded" different before and after the ratification of the American Constitution or the creation of the French Republic, because they relied on different memories of what had already happened and on varying assumptions as to what was possible.

The last section offers four different interpretations of Paine and his work. The first two consider the early phases of his career, focusing on *Common Sense* and the independence movement in North America. Robert A. Ferguson shows how Paine was able to appeal to many different Americans by asking for a moral reorientation on the part of the reader. Nathan Perl-Rosenthal uncovers a religious argument against monarchy that contributed to the success (and to the writing) of that pamphlet. The other authors discuss Paine on the other side of the Atlantic as both revolution and reaction spread during the 1780s and 1790s. For both Gary Kates and Gregory Claeys, Paine revised the simple call for liberation that had characterized his early work to confront the far more vexing problems of class exploitation and social inequality. His efforts to this effect—and the powerful rebuttals they provoked—speak to the bitterly divided traditions of democracy and nationalism that came out of the late eighteenth century.

J. M. OPAL

The Texts of
COMMON SENSE
AND OTHER WRITINGS

Common Sense

Addressed to the Inhabitants of America . . . [What follows is the third edition of Common Sense, *published on Feb. 14, 1776. In that edition, Paine also included an appendix directed at Quakers, which is not included here.]*

Perhaps the sentiments contained in the following pages, are not yet sufficiently fashionable to procure them general favour; a long habit of not thinking a thing *wrong*, gives it a superficial appearance of being *right*, and raises at first a formidable outcry in defense of custom. But the tumult soon subsides. Time makes more converts than reason.

As a long and violent abuse of power, is generally the means of calling the right of it in question (and in Matters too which might never have been thought of, had not the Sufferers been aggravated into the inquiry) and as the King of England hath undertaken in his *own Right*, to support the Parliament in what he calls *Theirs*, and as the good people of this country are grievously oppressed by the combination, they have an undoubted privilege to inquire into the pretensions of both, and equally to reject the usurpation of either.

In the following sheets, the author hath studiously avoided every thing which is personal among ourselves. Compliments as well as censure to individuals make no part thereof. The wise, and the worthy, need not the triumph of a pamphlet; and those whose sentiments are injudicious, or unfriendly, will cease of themselves unless too much pains are bestowed upon their conversion.

The cause of America is in a great measure the cause of all mankind. Many circumstances hath, and will arise, which are not local, but universal, and through which the principles of all Lovers of Mankind are affected, and in the Event of which, their Affections are interested. The laying a Country desolate with Fire and Sword, declaring War against the natural rights of all Mankind, and extirpating the Defenders thereof from the Face of the Earth, is the Concern of every man to whom Nature hath given the Power of feeling; of which Class, regardless of Party Censure, is

THE AUTHOR.

3

P. S. The Publication of this new Edition hath been delayed, with a View of taking notice (had it been necessary) of any Attempt to refute the Doctrine of Independence: As no Answer hath yet appeared, it is now presumed that none will, the Time needful for getting such a Performance ready for the Public being considerably past.

Who the Author of this Production is, is wholly unnecessary to the Public, as the Object for Attention is the *doctrine itself*, not the *man*. Yet it may not be unnecessary to say, that he is unconnected with any party, and under no sort of influence public or private, but the influence of reason and principle.

Philadelphia, February 14, 1776

On the Origin and Design of Government in General, with Concise Remarks on the English Constitution

Some writers have so confounded society with government, as to leave little or no distinction between them; whereas they are not only different, but have different origins. Society is produced by our wants, and government by our wickedness; the former promotes our happiness *positively* by uniting our affections, the latter *negatively* by restraining our vices. The one encourages intercourse, the other creates distinctions. The first is a patron, the last a punisher.

Society in every state is a blessing, but Government, even in its best state, is but a necessary evil; in its worst state an intolerable one: for when we suffer, or are exposed to the same miseries *by a government*, which we might expect in a country *without government*, our calamity is heightened by reflecting that we furnish the means by which we suffer. Government, like dress, is the badge of lost innocence; the palaces of kings are built upon the ruins of the bowers of paradise. For were the impulses of conscience clear, uniform and irresistibly obeyed, man would need no other lawgiver; but that not being the case, he finds it necessary to surrender up a part of his property to furnish means for the protection of the rest; and this he is induced to do by the same prudence which in every other case advises him, out of two evils to choose the least. *Wherefore*, security being the true design and end of government, it unanswerably follows that whatever *form* thereof appears most likely to ensure it to us, with the least expense and greatest benefit, is preferable to all others.[1]

1. Paine relies here on the theory of a "social contract" by which individuals gave up the natural right of self-defense in return for security and safety from the law and the state. The classic formulations of this theory appeared a decade before Paine became politi-

In order to gain a clear and just idea of the design and end of government, let us suppose a small number of persons settled in some sequestered part of the earth, unconnected with the rest; they will then represent the first peopling of any country, or of the world. In this state of natural liberty, society will be their first thought. A thousand motives will excite them thereto; the strength of one man is so unequal to his wants, and his mind so unfitted for perpetual solitude, that he is soon obliged to seek assistance and relief of another, who in his turn requires the same. Four or five united would be able to raise a tolerable dwelling in the midst of a wilderness, but one man might labour out the common period of life without accomplishing any thing; when he had felled his timber he could not remove it, nor erect it after it was removed; hunger in the mean time would urge him to quit his work, and every different want would call him a different way. Disease, nay even misfortune, would be death; for, though neither might be mortal, yet either would disable him from living, and reduce him to a state in which he might rather be said to perish than to die.

Thus necessity, like a gravitating power, would soon form our newly arrived emigrants into society, the reciprocal blessings of which would supersede, and render the obligations of law and government unnecessary while they remained perfectly just to each other; but as nothing but Heaven is impregnable to vice, it will unavoidably happen that in proportion as they surmount the first difficulties of emigration, which bound them together in a common cause, they will begin to relax in their duty and attachment to each other; and this remissness will point out the necessity of establishing some form of government to supply the defect of moral virtue.

Some convenient tree will afford them a State House, under the branches of which the whole Colony may assemble to deliberate on public matters. It is more than probable that their first laws will have the title only of regulations and be enforced by no other penalty than public disesteem. In this first parliament every man by natural right will have a seat.

But as the Colony increases, the public concerns will increase likewise, and the distance at which the members may be separated, will render it too inconvenient for all of them to meet on every occasion as at first, when their number was small, their habitations near, and the public concerns few and trifling. This will point out the convenience of their consenting to leave the legislative part to be managed by a select number chosen from the whole body, who are supposed to have the same concerns at stake which those have who

cally active: Jean-Jacques Rousseau, *The Social Contract, Or Principles of Political Right* (1762), and Henry Home, Lord Kames, *Historical Law-Tracts* (1761).

appointed them, and who will act in the same manner as the whole body would act were they present. If the colony continue encreasing, it will become necessary to augment the number of representatives, and that the interest of every part of the colony may be attended to, it will be found best to divide the whole into convenient parts, each part sending its proper number: and that the *elected* might never form to themselves an interest separate from the *electors*, prudence will point out the propriety of having elections often: because as the *elected* might by that means return and mix again with the general body of the *electors* in a few months, their fidelity to the public will be secured by the prudent reflection of not making a rod for themselves. And as this frequent interchange will establish a common interest with every part of the community, they will mutually and naturally support each other, and on this (not on the unmeaning name of king) depends the *strength of government, and the happiness of the governed*.

Here then is the origin and rise of government; namely, a mode rendered necessary by the inability of moral virtue to govern the world; here too is the design and end of government, viz. freedom and security. And however our eyes may be dazzled with show, or our ears deceived by sound; however prejudice may warp our wills, or interest darken our understanding, the simple voice of nature and reason will say, 'tis right.

I draw my idea of the form of government from a principle in nature which no art can overturn, viz. that the more simple any thing is, the less liable it is to be disordered, and the easier repaired when disordered; and with this maxim in view I offer a few remarks on the so much boasted constitution of England.[2] That it was noble for the dark and slavish times in which it was erected, is granted. When the world was overrun with tyranny the least remove therefrom was a glorious rescue. But that it is imperfect, subject to convulsions, and incapable of producing what it seems to promise is easily demonstrated.

Absolute governments, (tho' the disgrace of human nature) have this advantage with them, they are simple; if the people suffer, they know the head from which their suffering springs; know likewise the remedy; and are not bewildered by a variety of causes and cures. But the constitution of England is so exceedingly complex, that the nation may suffer for years together without being able to discover in which part the fault lies; some will say in one and some in another, and every political physician will advise a different medicine.

2. The British Constitution referred to the entire corpus of laws and political structures—the constituted authority—of the British realm, not to a single document or charter. Many of the "rights of Englishmen," though, could be found in the 1689 Declaration of Rights, which followed the so-called Glorious Revolution.

I know it is difficult to get over local or long standing prejudices, yet if we will suffer ourselves to examine the component parts of the English constitution, we shall find them to be the base remains of two ancient tyrannies, compounded with some new Republican materials.

First. — The remains of monarchical tyranny in the person of the king.

Secondly. — The remains of aristocratical tyranny in the persons of the peers.

Thirdly. — The new Republican materials, in the persons of the commons, on whose virtue depends the freedom of England.

The two first, by being hereditary, are independent of the people; wherefore in a *constitutional sense* they contribute nothing towards the freedom of the State.

To say that the constitution of England is an *union* of three powers, reciprocally *checking* each other, is farcical; either the words have no meaning, or they are flat contradictions.

First. — That the king it not to be trusted without being looked after; or in other words, that a thirst for absolute power is the natural disease of monarchy.

Secondly. — That the commons, by being appointed for that purpose, are either wiser or more worthy of confidence than the crown.

But as the same constitution which gives the commons a power to check the King by withholding the supplies, gives afterwards the king a power to check the commons, by empowering him to reject their other bills; it again supposes that the King is wiser than those whom it has already supposed to be wiser than him. A mere absurdity!

There is something exceedingly ridiculous in the composition of monarchy; it first excludes a man from the means of information, yet empowers him to act in cases where the highest judgment is required. The state of a king shuts him from the world, yet the business of a king requires him to know it thoroughly; wherefore the different parts, by unnaturally opposing and destroying each other, prove the whole character to be absurd and useless.

Some writers have explained the English constitution thus: the king, say they, is one, the people another; the Peers are a house in behalf of the king, the commons in behalf of the people; but this hath all the distinctions of a house divided[3] against itself; and though

---

3. From the New Testament, Matthew 12:25, in which Jesus responds to the Pharisees, who had accused him of using satanic powers to drive away demons. The King James translation is: "And Jesus knew their thoughts, and said unto them, Every kingdom divided against itself is brought to desolation, and every city or house divided against itself shall not stand." Abraham Lincoln would use this metaphor in a famous 1858 speech decrying the spread of slavery.

the expressions be pleasantly arranged, yet when examined they appear idle and ambiguous; and it will always happen, that the nicest construction that words are capable of, when applied to the description of something which either cannot exist, or is too incomprehensible to be within the compass of description, will be words of sound only, and though they may amuse the ear, they cannot inform the mind: for this explanation includes a previous question, viz. *How came the king by a power which the people are afraid to trust, and always obliged to check?* Such a power could not be the gift of a wise people, neither can any power, *which needs checking,* be from God; yet the provision which the constitution makes supposes such a power to exist.

But the provision is unequal to the task; the means either cannot or will not accomplish the end, and the whole affair is a *felo de se:*[4] for as the greater weight will always carry up the less, and as all the wheels of a machine are put in motion by one, it only remains to know which power in the constitution has the most weight, for that will govern: and tho' the others, or a part of them, may clog, or, as the phrase is, check the rapidity of its motion, yet so long as they cannot stop it, their endeavours will be ineffectual, the first moving power will at last have its way, and what it wants in speed is supplied by time.

That the crown is this overbearing part in the English constitution needs not be mentioned, and that it derives its whole consequence merely from being the giver of places and pensions is self-evident; wherefore, though we have been wise enough to shut and lock a door against absolute monarchy, we at the same time have been foolish enough to put the crown in possession of the key.

The prejudice of Englishmen, in favour of their own government, by king, lords and Commons, arises as much or more from national pride than reason. Individuals are undoubtedly safer in England than in some other countries: but the *will* of the king is as much the *law* of the land in Britain as in France, with this difference, that instead of proceeding directly from his mouth, it is handed to the people under the formidable shape of an act of parliament. For the fate of Charles the First[5] hath only made kings more subtle—not more just.

Wherefore, laying aside all national pride and prejudice in favour of modes and forms, the plain truth is that *it is wholly owing to the constitution of the people, and not to the constitution of the government* that the crown is not as oppressive in England as in Turkey.

4. Referring to suicide or self-murder (Latin). Paine suggests that the British constitution undermines itself—and the liberties of the British people—by building on a series of contradictions.
5. A Stuart king (1600–1649) who ran afoul of the powerful aristocrats in Parliament after he took the throne in 1625. The English Civil War broke out in 1642, pitting Royalists against Puritan forces led by Oliver Cromwell. The Puritans prevailed, and Charles was executed by order of Parliament. The monarchy was restored, under Charles's son, in 1660.

An inquiry into the *constitutional errors* in the English form of government, is at this time highly necessary; for as we are never in a proper condition of doing justice to others, while we continue under the influence of some leading partiality, so neither are we capable of doing it to ourselves while we remain fettered by any obstinate prejudice. And as a man who is attached to a prostitute is unfitted to choose or judge of a wife, so any prepossession in favour of a rotten constitution of government will disable us from discerning a good one.

Of Monarchy and Hereditary Succession

Mankind being originally equals in the order of creation, the equality could only be destroyed by some subsequent circumstance: the distinctions of rich and poor may in a great measure be accounted for, and that without having recourse to the harsh ill-sounding names of oppression and avarice. Oppression is often the *consequence*, but seldom or never the *means* of riches; and tho' avarice will preserve a man from being necessitously poor, it generally makes him too timorous to be wealthy.

But there is another and great distinction for which no truly natural or religious reason can be assigned, and that is the distinction of men into KINGS and SUBJECTS. Male and female are the distinctions of nature, good and bad the distinctions of Heaven; but how a race of men came into the world so exalted above the rest, and distinguished like some new species, is worth inquiring into, and whether they are the means of happiness or of misery to mankind.

In the early ages of the world, according to the scripture chronology there were no kings; the consequence of which was, there were no wars; it is the pride of kings which throws mankind into confusion. Holland, without a king hath enjoyed more peace for this last century than any of the monarchical governments in Europe. Antiquity favours the same remark; for the quiet and rural lives of the first patriarchs have a happy something in them, which vanishes when we come to the history of Jewish royalty.[6]

Government by kings was first introduced into the world by the Heathens, from whom the children of Israel copied the custom. It was the most prosperous invention the Devil ever set on foot for the promotion of idolatry. The heathens paid divine honours to their deceased kings, and the christian world hath improved on the plan by doing the same to their living ones. How impious is the title of

---

6. Here Paine begins his extended inquiry into the Hebrew Scriptures or Old Testament, drawing from Judges 6–8 and 1 Samuel 5–8 and 12. His reading of these passages is thorough and credible, but also convenient; in particular, he omits the story of Saul, who seems to receive God's command to rule as king over Israel.

sacred majesty applied to a worm, who in the midst of his splendor is crumbling into dust!

As the exalting one man so greatly above the rest cannot be justified on the equal rights of nature, so neither can it be defended on the authority of scripture; for the will of the Almighty as declared by Gideon, and the prophet Samuel, expressly disapproves of government by kings. All anti-monarchical parts of scripture have been very smoothly glossed over in monarchical governments, but they undoubtedly merit the attention of countries which have their governments yet to form. *"Render unto Cesar the things which are Cesar's"* is the scripture doctrine of courts, yet it is no support of monarchical government, for the Jews at that time were without a king, and in a state of vassalage to the Romans.

Near three thousand years passed away, from the Mosaic account of the creation, till the Jews under a national delusion requested a king. Till then their form of government (except in extraordinary cases where the Almighty interposed) was a kind of republic, administered by a judge and the elders of the tribes. Kings they had none, and it was held sinful to acknowledge any being under that title but the Lord of Hosts. And when a man seriously reflects on the idolatrous homage which is paid to the persons of Kings, he need not wonder that the Almighty, ever jealous of his honour, should disapprove a form of government which so impiously invades the prerogative of Heaven.

Monarchy is ranked in scripture as one of the sins of the Jews, for which a curse in reserve is denounced against them. The history of that transaction is worth attending to. The children of Israel being oppressed by the Midianites, Gideon marched against them with a small army, and victory thro' the divine interposition decided in his favour. The Jews, elate with success, and attributing it to the generalship of Gideon, proposed making him a king, saying, *Rule thou over us, thou and thy son, and thy son's son.* Here was temptation in its fullest extent; not a kingdom only, but an hereditary one; but Gideon in the piety of his soul replied, *I will not rule over you, neither shall my son rule over you.* THE LORD SHALL RULE OVER YOU. Words need not be more explicit: Gideon doth not *decline* the honour, but denieth their right to give it; neither doth he compliment them with invented declarations of his thanks, but in the positive style of a prophet charges them with disaffection to their proper Sovereign, the King of Heaven.

About one hundred and thirty years after this, they fell again into the same error. The hankering which the Jews had for the idolatrous customs of the Heathens, is something exceedingly unaccountable; but so it was, that laying hold of the misconduct of Samuel's two sons, who were intrusted with some secular concerns, they came in an abrupt and clamorous manner to Samuel, saying, *Behold thou art old, and they sons walk not in thy ways, now make us a king to judge us like all the other nations.* And here we cannot observe but that their motives were bad, viz. that they might be *like* unto other nations, i. e. the Heathens, whereas their true glory lay in being as much *unlike* them as possible. *But the thing displeased Samuel when they said, give us a King to judge us; and Samuel prayed unto the Lord, and the Lord said unto Samuel, hearken unto the voice of the people in all that they say unto thee, for they have not rejected thee, but they have rejected me,* THAT I SHOULD NOT REIGN OVER THEM. *According to all the works which they have done since the day that I brought them up out of Egypt even unto this day, wherewith they have forsaken me, and served other Gods: so do they also unto thee. Now therefore hearken unto their voice, howbeit, protest solemnly unto them and show them the manner of the king that shall reign over them,* i.e. not of any particular king, but the general manner of the kings of the earth whom Israel was so eagerly copying after. And notwithstanding the great distance of time and difference of manners, the character is still in fashion. *And Samuel told all the words of the Lord unto the people, that asked of him a king. And he said, This shall be the manner of the King that shall reign over you. He will take your sons and appoint them for himself for his chariots and to be his horsemen, and some shall run before his chariots* (this description agrees with the present mode of impressing men) *and he will appoint him captains over thousands and captains over fifties, will set them to clear his ground and to reap his harvest, and to make his instruments of war, and instruments of his chariots, And he will take your daughters to be confectionaries, and to be cooks, and to be bakers* (this describes the expense and luxury as well as the oppression of Kings) *and he will take your fields and your vineyards, and your olive yards, even the best of them, and give them to his servants. And he will take the tenth of your seed, and of your vineyards, and give them to his officers and to his servants* (by which we see that bribery, corruption, and favouritism, are the standing vices of Kings) *and he will take the tenth of your men servants, and your maid servants, and your goodliest young men, and your asses, and put them to his work: and he will take the tenth of your sheep, and ye shall be his servants, and ye shall cry out in that day because of your king which ye shell have chosen,* AND THE LORD WILL NOT HEAR YOU IN THAT DAY. This accounts for the continuation of Monarchy; neither do the characters of the few good kings which have lived since, either sanctify the title, or blot out the sinfulness of the origin; the high encomium of David takes no notice of him *officially as a king,* but only as a *man* after God's own heart. *Nevertheless the people refused to obey the voice of Samuel, and they said, Nay, but we will have a king over us, that we may be like all the nations, and that our king may judge us, and go out before us and fight our battles.* Samuel continued to reason with them but to no purpose; he set before them their ingratitude, but all would not avail; and seeing them fully bent on their folly, he cried out, *I will call unto the Lord, and he shall send thunder and rain* (which was then a punishment, being in the time of wheat harvest) *that ye may perceive and see that your wickedness is great which ye have done in the sight of the Lord,* IN ASKING YOU A KING. *So Samuel called unto the Lord, and the Lord sent thunder and rain that day, and all the people greatly feared the Lord and Samuel. And all the people said unto Samuel, Pray for thy servants unto the Lord thy God that we die not, for* WE HAVE ADDED UNTO OUR SINS THIS EVIL, TO ASK A KING. These portions of scripture are direct and positive. They admit of no equivocal construction. That the Almighty hath here entered his protest against monarchical government is true, or the scripture is false. And a man hath good reason to believe that there is as much of kingcraft as priestcraft in withholding the scripture from the public in Popish countries. For monarchy in every instance is the Popery of government.

To the evil of monarchy we have added that of hereditary succession; and as the first is a degradation and lessening of ourselves, so the second, claimed as a matter of right, is an insult and imposition on posterity. For all men being originally equals, no *one* by *birth* could have a right to set up his own family in perpetual preference to all others for ever, and though himself might deserve *some* decent degree of honours of his contemporaries, yet his descendants might be far too unworthy to inherit them. One of the strongest natural proofs of the folly of hereditary right in Kings, is that nature disapproves it, otherwise she would not so frequently turn it into ridicule, by giving mankind an *ass for a lion.*[7]

Secondly, as no man at first could possess any other public honors than were bestowed upon him, so the givers of those honors could have no power to give away the right of posterity, and though they might say "We choose you for *our* head," they could not without manifest injustice to their children say "that your children and your children's children shall reign over *ours* forever." Because such an unwise, unjust, unnatural compact might (perhaps) in the next succession put them under the government of a rogue or a fool. Most wise men in their private sentiments have ever treated hereditary right with contempt; yet it is one of those evils which when once established is not easily removed: many submit from fear, others from superstition, and the more powerful part shares with the king the plunder of the rest.

---

7. Paine refers to Aesop's fable "The Ass in Lion's Skin," in which an ass dresses in the skin of a lion and tries to frighten other animals and his master.

This is supposing the present race of kings in the world to have had an honorable origin: whereas it is more than probable, that, could we take off the dark covering of antiquity and trace them to their first rise, we should find the first of them nothing better than the principal ruffian of some restless gang, whose savage manners of pre-eminence in subtilty obtained him the title of chief among plunderers; and who by increasing in power and extending his depredations, overawed the quiet and defenseless to purchase their safety by frequent contributions. Yet his electors could have no idea of giving hereditary right to his descendants, because such a perpetual exclusion of themselves was incompatible with the free and restrained principles they professed to live by. Wherefore, hereditary succession in the early ages of monarchy could not take place as a matter of claim, but as something casual or complemental; but as few or no records were extant in those days, the traditionary history stuffed with fables, it was very easy, after the lapse of a few generations, to trump up some superstitious tale conveniently timed, Mahomet-like,[8] to cram hereditary right down the throats of the vulgar. Perhaps the disorders which threatened, or seemed to threaten, on the decease of a leader and the choice of a new one (for elections among ruffians could not be very orderly) induced many at first to favour hereditary pretensions; by which means it happened, as it hath happened since, that what at first was submitted to as a convenience was afterwards claimed as a right.

England since the conquest hath known some few good monarchs, but groaned beneath a much larger number of bad ones, yet no man in his senses can say that their claim under William the Conqueror is a very honourable one. A French bastard landing with an armed Banditti and establishing himself king of England against the consent of the natives, is in plain terms a very paltry rascally original—It certainly hath no divinity in it. However it is needless to spend much time in exposing the folly of hereditary right, if there are any so weak as to believe it, let them promiscuously worship the ass and lion, and welcome. I shall neither copy their humility, nor disturb their devotion.

Yet I should be glad to ask how they suppose kings came at first? The question admits but of three answers, viz. either by lot, by election, or by usurpation. If the first king was taken by lot, it establishes a precedent for the next, which excludes hereditary succession. Saul was by lot, yet the succession was not hereditary, neither does

---

8. This derisive reference to Mohammed (ca. 570–632), founder and prophet of Islam, reflects prejudices that date back to the Crusades. However, eighteenth-century Britons conveyed just as much hostility, and possibly more, to Catholicism. (Paine echoed this hostility in remarks about "Papist" religion and Jesuit missionaries, which Protestants associated with oppression, superstition, and foppish ceremony).

it appear from that transaction that there was any intention it ever should. If the first king of any country was by election, that likewise establishes a precedent for the next; for to say, that the *right* of all future generations is taken away, by the act of the first electors, in their choice not only of a king but of a family of kings for ever, hath no parallel in or out of scripture but the doctrine of original sin, which supposes the free will of all men lost in Adam; and from such comparison, and it will admit of no other, hereditary succession can derive no glory. for as in Adam all sinned, and as in the first electors all men obeyed; as in the one all mankind were subjected to Satan, and in the other to sovereignty; as our innocence was lost in the first, and our authority in the last; and as both disable us from re-assuming some former state and privilege, it unanswerably follows that original sin and hereditary succession are parallels. Dishonour-able rank! inglorious connection! Yet the most subtle sophist can-not produce a juster simile.

As to usurpation, no man will be so hardy as to defend it; and that William the Conqueror was an usurper is a fact not to be con-tradicted. The plain truth is, that the antiquity of English monar-chy will not bear looking into.

But it is not so much the absurdity as the evil of hereditary suc-cession which concerns mankind. Did it ensure a race of good and wise men it would have the seal of divine authority, but as it opens a door to the *foolish*, the *wicked*, and the *improper*, it hath in it the nature of oppression. Men who look upon themselves born to reign, and others to obey, soon grow insolent. Selected from the rest of mankind, their minds are early poisoned by importance; and the world they act in differs so materially from the world at large, that they have but little opportunity of knowing its true interests, and when they succeed in the government are frequently the most igno-rant and unfit of any throughout the dominions.

Another evil which attends hereditary succession is, that the throne is subject to be possessed by a minor at any age; all which time the regency acting under the cover of a king have every opportunity and inducement to betray their trust. The same national misfortune happens when a king worn out with age and infirmity enters the last stage of human weakness. In both these cases the public becomes a prey to every miscreant who can tamper successfully with the follies either of age or infancy.

The most plausible plea which hath ever been offered in favor of hereditary succession is, that it preserves a nation from civil wars; and were this true, it would be weighty; whereas it is the most bare-faced falsity ever imposed upon mankind. The whole history of England disowns the fact. Thirty kings and two minors have reigned in that distracted kingdom since the conquest, in which time there has been (including the Revolution) no less than eight civil wars and nineteen rebellions. Wherefore instead of making for peace, it makes against it, and destroys the very foundation it seems to stand upon.

The contest for monarchy and succession, between the houses of York and Lancaster, laid England in a scene of blood for many years. Twelve pitched battles besides skirmishes and sieges were fought between Henry and Edward. Twice was Henry prisoner to Edward, who in his turn was prisoner to Henry. And so uncertain is the fate of war and the temper of a nation, when nothing but personal matters are the ground of a quarrel, that Henry was taken in triumph from a prison to a palace, and Edward obliged to fly from a palace to a foreign land; yet, as sudden transitions of temper are seldom lasting, Henry in his turn was driven from the throne, and Edward re-called to succeed him. The parliament always following the strongest side.

This contest began in the reign of Henry the Sixth, and was not entirely extinguished till Henry the Seventh, in whom the families were united. Including a period of 67 years, viz. from 1422 to 1489.

In short, monarchy and succession have laid (not this or that kingdom only) but the world in blood and ashes. 'Tis a form of government which the word of God bears testimony against, and blood will attend it.

If we enquire into the business of a king, we shall find that in some countries they may have none; and after sauntering away their lives without pleasure to themselves or advantage to the nation, withdraw from the scene, and leave their successors to tread the same idle round. In absolute monarchies the whole weight of business civil and military lies on the King; the children of Israel in their request for a king urged this plea, "that he may judge us, and go out before us and fight our battles." But in countries where he is neither a judge nor a general, as in England, a man would be puzzled to know what *is* his business.

The nearer any government approaches to a republic, the less business there is for a king. It is somewhat difficult to find a proper name for the government of England. Sir William Meredith[9] calls it a republic; but in its present state it is unworthy of the name, because the corrupt influence of the Crown, by having all the places in its disposal, hath so effectually swallowed up the power, and eaten out the virtue of the house of commons (the republican part in the Constitution) that the government of England is nearly as monarchical as that of France or Spain. Men fall out with names without understanding them. For 'tis the republican and not the

---

9. Meredith (1724–1790) was a member of Parliament for the city of Liverpool who began and ended his career as a Tory but sometimes supported Whig and even radical causes. In a 1773 article in *The Gentleman's Magazine*, he referred to the present British constitution "as a republic, under the administration of a king."

monarchical part of the constitution of England which Englishmen glory in, viz. the liberty of choosing an House of Commons from out of their own body—and it is easy to see that when republican virtues fail, slavery ensues. Why is the Constitution of England sickly, but because monarchy hath poisoned the republic; the crown hath engrossed the commons.

In England a king hath little more to do than to make war and give away places; which, in plain terms, is to empoverish the nation and set it together by the ears. A pretty business indeed for a man to be allowed eight hundred thousand sterling a year[1] for, and worshipped into the bargain! Of more worth is one honest man to society, and in the sight of God, than all the crowned ruffians that ever lived.

Thoughts on the Present State of American Affairs

In the following pages I offer nothing more than simple facts, plain arguments, and common sense: and have no other preliminaries to settle with the reader, than that he will divest himself of prejudice and prepossession, and suffer his reason and his feelings to determine for themselves; that he will put *on*, or rather that he will not put *off*, the true character of a man, and generously enlarge his views beyond the present day.

Volumes have been written on the subject of the struggle between England and America. Men of all ranks have embarked in the controversy, from different motives, and with various designs; but all have been ineffectual, and the period of debate is closed. Arms as the last resource decide the contest; the appeal was the choice of the king, and the continent has accepted the challenge.

It hath been reported of the late Mr. Pelham[2] (who tho' an able minister was not without his faults) that on his being attacked in the House of Commons on the score that his measures were only of a temporary kind, replied, "*they will last my time.*" Should a thought so fatal and unmanly possess the Colonies in the present contest, the name of ancestors will be remembered by future generations with detestation.

The sun never shined on a cause of greater worth. 'Tis not the affair of a City, a County, a province, or a kingdom; but of a continent—of at least one-eighth part of the habitable globe. 'Tis not the concern of a day, a year, or an age; posterity are virtually

---

1. This figure is accurate. The Civil List Act of 1760 restructured payments rendered to the Crown, and the king received an annual amount of £800,000 until 1777, when the sum increased to £900,000.
2. Paine is probably referring to Thomas Pelham, Duke of Newcastle, who served as prime minister and also as first lord of the treasury during much of the Seven Years' War.

involved in the contest, and will be more or less affected even to the end of time, by the proceedings now. Now is the seed-time of Continental union, faith and honour. The least fracture now will be like a name engraved with the point of a pin on the tender rind of a young oak; the wound will enlarge with the tree, and posterity read in it full grown characters.

By referring the matter from argument to arms, a new era for politics is struck; a new method of thinking hath arisen. All plans, proposals, &c. prior to the nineteenth of April, *i.e.* to the commencement of hostilities, are like the almanacks of the last year; which tho' proper then, are superseded and useless now. Whatever was advanced by the advocates on either side of the question then, terminated in one and the same point, viz. a union with Great Britain; the only difference between the parties was the method of effecting it; the one proposing force, the other friendship; but it hath so far happened that the first hath failed, and the second hath withdrawn her influence.

As much hath been said of the advantages of reconciliation, which, like an agreeable dream, hath passed away and left us as we were, it is but right that we should examine the contrary side of the argument, and enquire into some of the many material injuries which these colonies sustain, and always will sustain, by being connected with and dependent on Great Britain. To examine that connection and dependence, on the principles of nature and common sense, to see what we have to trust to, if separated, and what we are to expect, if dependent.

I have heard it asserted by some, that as America has flourished under her former connection with Great Britain, the same connection is necessary towards her future happiness, and will always have the same effect. Nothing can be more fallacious than this kind of argument. We may as well assert that because a child has thrived upon milk, that it is never to have meat, or that the first twenty years of our lives is to become a precedent for the next twenty. But even this is admitting more than is true; for I answer roundly that America would have flourished as much, and probably much more, had no European power taken any notice of her. The commerce by which she hath enriched herself are the necessaries of life, and will always have a market while eating is the custom of Europe.

But she has protected us, say some. That she hath engrossed us is true, and defended the continent at our expense as well as her own, is admitted; and she would have defended Turkey from the same motive, viz.—for the sake of trade and dominion.

Alas! we have been long led away by ancient prejudices and made large sacrifices to superstition. We have boasted the protection of Great Britain, without considering, that her motive was *interest* not *attachment*; and that she did not protect us from *our enemies* on *our account*; but from *her enemies* on *her own account*, from those who had no quarrel with us on any *other account*, and who will always be our enemies on the *same account*. Let Britain waive her pretensions to the Continent, or the Continent throw off the dependence, and we should be at peace with France and Spain, were they at war with Britain. The miseries of Hanover's last war ought to warn us against connections.[3]

It hath lately been asserted in parliament, that the Colonies have no relation to each other but through the Parent Country, i.e. that Pennsylvania and the Jerseys and so on for the rest, are sister Colonies by the way of England; this is certainly a very roundabout way of proving relationship, but it is the nearest and only true way of proving enmity (or enemyship, if I may so call it.) France and Spain never were, nor perhaps ever will be, our enemies as *Americans*, but as our being the *subjects of Great Britain*.

But Britain is the parent country, say some. Then the more shame upon her conduct. Even brutes do not devour their young, nor savages make war upon their families. Wherefore, the assertion, if true, turns to her reproach; but it happens not to be true, or only partly so, and the phrase *parent* or *mother country* hath been jesuitically adopted by the king and his parasites, with a low papistical design of gaining an unfair bias on the credulous weakness of our minds. Europe, and not England, is the parent country of America. This new World hath been the asylum for the persecuted lovers of civil and religious liberty from *every part* of Europe. Hither have they fled, not from the tender embraces of the mother, but from the cruelty of the monster; and it is so far true of England, that the same tyranny which drove the first emigrants from home, pursues their descendants still.

In this extensive quarter of the globe, we forget the narrow limits of three hundred and sixty miles (the extent of England) and carry our friendship on a larger scale; we claim brotherhood with every European christian, and triumph in the generosity of the sentiment.

It is pleasant to observe by what regular gradations we surmount the force of local prejudices, as we enlarge our acquaintance with the world. A man born in any town in England divided into parishes, will naturally associate most with his fellow parishioners (because their interests in many cases will be common) and distinguish him by the name of *neighbor*; if he meet him but a few miles

---

3. This is dubious. The British American colonists certainly fought with the French, the Spanish, and their Indian allies because of European conflicts, but they also encroached on the lands of these powers and of Indian tribes in New England, the Southeast, and the trans-Appalachian west. These invasive settlements triggered much of the violence of the colonial period.

from home, he drops the narrow idea of a street, and salutes him by the name of *townsman*; if he travel out of the county and meet him in any other, he forgets the minor divisions of street and town, and calls him *countrymen*, i.e. *countryman*; but if in their foreign excursions they should associate in France, or any other part of *Europe*, their local remembrance would be enlarged into that of *Englishman*. And by a just parity of reasoning, all Europeans meeting in America, or any other quarter of the globe, are *countrymen*; for England, Holland, Germany, or Sweden, when compared with the whole, stand in the same places on the larger scale, which the divisions of street, town, and county do on the smaller ones; Distinctions too limited for continental minds. Not one third of the inhabitants, even of this province [Pennsylvania], are of English descent.[4] Wherefore I reprobate the phrase of parent or mother country applied to England only, as being false, selfish, narrow and ungenerous.

But, admitting that we were all of English descent, what does it amount to? Nothing. Britain, being now an open enemy, extinguishes every other name and title: and to say that reconciliation is our duty, is truly farcical. The first king of England, of the present line (William the Conqueror) was a Frenchman, and half the peers of England are descendants from the same country; wherefore, by the same method of reasoning, England ought to be governed by France.

Much hath been said of the united strength of Britain and the Colonies, that in conjunction they might bid defiance to the world. But this is mere presumption; the fate of war is uncertain, neither do the expressions mean anything; for this continent would never suffer itself to be drained of inhabitants, to support the British arms in either Asia, Africa, or Europe.

Besides, what have we to do with setting the world at defiance? Our plan is commerce, and that, well attended to, will secure us the peace and friendship of all Europe; because it is the interest of all Europe to have America a *free port*. Her trade will always be a protection, and her barrenness of gold and silver secure her from invaders.

---

4. As a rough estimate, this figure is accurate, but only for Pennsylvania. Settled by English Quakers during the late 1600s, Pennsylvania took in tens of thousands of German, Scotch, and Scotch-Irish immigrants during the middle third of the eighteenth century. The five years right before the outbreak of the Revolution saw a huge influx of Scotch-Irish into the Cumberland Valley of Pennsylvania, and by 1790, the first census found that only 25.8 percent of the state's residents were of English origin. New York and Delaware were also highly diverse, with large numbers of Germans, Dutch, and Scottish and smaller communities of Swedes, Swiss, Norwegians, and Jews. Yet the white populations of New England and the southern colonies were predominantly English, albeit with a Scottish and German presence, and in the colonies as a whole the English made up perhaps two thirds of the white total, not one-third. Africans and African Americans made up large percentages of the total population throughout the South (and in New York City and Philadelphia), with large black majorities in some coastal areas of South Carolina.

I challenge the warmest advocate for reconciliation to show a single advantage that this continent can reap by being connected with Great Britain. I repeat the challenge; not a single advantage is derived. Our corn will fetch its price in any market in Europe, and our imported goods must be paid for buy them where we will.

But the injuries and disadvantages which we sustain by that connection, are without number; and our duty to mankind at large, as well as to ourselves, instruct us to renounce the alliance: because, any submission to, or dependence on, Great Britain, tends directly to involve this continent in European wars and quarrels; and sets us at variance with nations who would otherwise seek our friendship, and against whom we have neither anger nor complaints. As Europe is our market for trade, we ought to form no partial connection with any part of it. It is the true interest of America to steer clear of European contentions, which she never can do, while, by her dependence on Britain, she is made the makeweight in the scale of British politics.

Europe is too thickly planted with Kingdoms to be long at peace, and whenever a war breaks out between England and any foreign power, the trade of America goes to ruin, *because of her connection with Britain*. The next war may not turn out like the last, and should it not, the advocates for reconciliation now will be wishing for separation then, because neutrality in that case would be a safer convoy than a man of war. Every thing that is right or reasonable pleads for separation. The blood of the slain, the weeping voice of nature cries, 'TIS TIME TO PART. Even the distance at which the Almighty hath placed England and America is a strong and natural proof that the authority of the one over the other, was never the design of heaven. The time likewise at which the Continent was discovered, adds weight to the argument, and the manner in which it was peopled, encreases the force of it. The reformation was preceded by the discovery of America: As if the Almighty graciously meant to open a sanctuary to the persecuted in future years, when home should afford neither friendship nor safety.

The authority of Great Britain over this continent, is a form of government, which sooner or later must have an end: And a serious mind can draw no true pleasure by looking forward, under the painful and positive conviction that what he calls "the present constitution" is merely temporary. As parents, we can have no joy, knowing that *this government* is not sufficiently lasting to ensure any thing which we may bequeath to posterity: And by a plain method of argument, as we are running the next generation into debt, we ought to do the work of it, otherwise we use them meanly and pitifully. In order to discover the line of our duty rightly, we should take our children in our hand, and fix our station a few years farther into life; that eminence will present a prospect, which a few present fears and prejudices conceal from our sight.

Though I would carefully avoid giving unnecessary offence, yet I am inclined to believe, that all those who espouse the doctrine of reconciliation, may be included within the following descriptions. Interested men, who are not to be trusted, weak men who *cannot* see, prejudiced men who *will not* see, and a certain set of moderate men who think better of the European world than it deserves; and this last class, by an ill-judged deliberation, will be the cause of more calamities to this continent than all the other three.

It is the good fortune of many to live distant from the scene of present sorrow; the evil is not sufficiently brought to *their* doors to make *them* feel the precariousness with which all American property is possessed. But let our imaginations transport us a few moments to Boston; that seat of wretchedness will teach us wisdom, and instruct us for ever to renounce a power in whom we can have no trust. The inhabitants of that unfortunate city who but a few months ago were in ease and affluence, have now no other alternative than to stay and starve, or turn out to beg. Endangered by the fire of their friends if they continue within the city and plundered by the soldiery if they leave it, in their present situation they are prisoners without the hope of redemption, and in a general attack for their relief they would be exposed to the fury of both armies.[5]

Men of passive tempers look somewhat lightly over the offences of Great Britain, and, still hoping for the best, are apt to call out, "*Come, come, we shall be friends again for all this.*" But examine the passions and feelings of mankind. Bring the doctrine of reconciliation to the touchstone of nature, and then tell me whether you can hereafter love, honour, and faithfully serve the power that hath carried fire and sword into your land? If you cannot do all these, then are you only deceiving yourselves, and by your delay bringing ruin upon posterity. Your future connection with Britain, whom you can neither love nor honour, will be forced and unnatural, and being formed only on the plan of present convenience, will in a little time fall into a relapse more wretched than the first. But if you say, you can still pass the violations over, then I ask, hath your house been burnt? Hath your property been destroyed before your face? Are your wife and children destitute of a bed to lie on, or bread to live on? Have you lost a parent or a child by their hands, and yourself the ruined and wretched survivor? If you have not, then are you

---

5. Following the fighting of April 19, 1775, British regulars retreated into Boston, where colonial militia trapped them. After the battle of Bunker Hill on June 17, militia and the Continental Army besieged the city until the British evacuated in March 1776. During that time, the local population suffered from shortages and from a terrifying outbreak of smallpox, which swept across North America during the war years.

not a judge of those who have. But if you have, and can still shake hands with the murderers, then are you unworthy the name of husband, father, friend or lover, and whatever may be your rank or title in life, you have the heart of a coward, and the spirit of a sycophant.

This is not inflaming or exaggerating matters, but trying them by those feelings and affections which nature justifies, and without which, we should be incapable of discharging the social duties of life, or enjoying the felicities of it. I mean not to exhibit horror for the purpose of provoking revenge, but to awaken us from fatal and unmanly slumbers, that we may pursue determinately some fixed object. 'Tis not in the power of Britain or of Europe to conquer America, if she do not conquer herself by *delay* and *timidity*. The present winter is worth an age if rightly employed, but if lost or neglected, the whole continent will partake of the misfortune; and there is no punishment which that man will not deserve, be he who, or what, or where he will, that may be the means of sacrificing a season so precious and useful.

'Tis repugnant to reason, to the universal order of things to all examples from former ages, to suppose, that this continent can longer remain subject to any external power. The most sanguine in Britain doth not think so. The utmost stretch of human wisdom cannot, at this time, compass a plan short of separation, which can promise the continent even a year's security. Reconciliation is *now* a fallacious dream. Nature hath deserted the connection, and art cannot supply her place. For, as Milton wisely expresses, "never can true reconcilement grow where wounds of deadly hate have pierced so deep."[6]

Every quiet method for peace hath been ineffectual. Our prayers have been rejected with disdain; and hath tended to convince us, that nothing flatters vanity, or confirms obstinacy in Kings more than repeated petitioning—and nothing hath contributed more than that very measure to make the Kings of Europe absolute: Witness Denmark and Sweden.[7] Wherefore, since nothing but blows will do, for God's sake, let us come to a final separation, and not leave the next generation to be cutting throats, under the violated unmeaning names of parent and child.

6. John Milton (1608–1674) was a devout Puritan and antimonarchist. This quotation is from Book 4 of *Paradise Lost*, first published in 1667.
7. The Scandinavian kingdoms had long warred with one another while dividing power between monarchs, aristocratic landlords, and deputies and, to some extent, common subjects. In 1720, for example, a new constitution in Sweden provided for popular elections to the *riksdag*, or parliament, and later reforms gave substantial freedom of the press. But in 1772, the same year that Russia, Prussia, and Austria partitioned Poland and the British Parliament held hearings about atrocities in South Asia, Gustavus III centralized power after months of wrangling and petitioning by the deputies. Paine's reference to Denmark is less obvious, but may refer to Frederick III's seizure of power after a long war with Sweden in the 1650s.

To say, they will never attempt it again is idle and visionary, we thought so at the repeal of the stamp act, yet a year or two undeceived us; as well may we suppose that nations, which have been once defeated, will never renew the quarrel.

As to government matters, 'tis not in the power of Britain to do this continent justice: The business of it will soon be too weighty, and intricate, to be managed with any tolerable degree of convenience, by a power, so distant from us, and so very ignorant of us; for if they cannot conquer us, they cannot govern us. To be always running three or four thousand miles with a tale or a petition, waiting four or five months for an answer, which when obtained requires five or six more to explain it in, will in a few years be looked upon as folly and childishness—There was a time when it was proper, and there is a proper time for it to cease.

Small islands not capable of protecting themselves, are the proper objects for kingdoms to take under their care; but there is something very absurd, in supposing a continent to be perpetually governed by an island. In no instance hath nature made the satellite larger than its primary planet, and as England and America, with respect to each other, reverses the common order of nature, it is evident they belong to different systems: England to Europe, America to itself.

I am not induced by motives of pride, party, or resentment to espouse the doctrine of separation and independence; I am clearly, positively, and conscientiously persuaded that it is the true interest of this continent to be so; that every thing short of *that* is mere patchwork, that it can afford no lasting felicity,—that it is leaving the sword to our children, and shrinking back at a time, when, a little more, a little farther, would have rendered this continent the glory of the earth.

As Britain hath not manifested the least inclination towards a compromise, we may be assured that no terms can be obtained worthy the acceptance of the continent, or any ways equal to the expense of blood and treasure we have been already put to.

The object, contended for, ought always to bear some just proportion to the expense. The removal of North,[8] or the whole detestable junto, is a matter unworthy the millions we have expended. A temporary stoppage of trade, was an inconvenience, which would have sufficiently balanced the repeal of all the acts complained of, had such repeals been obtained; but if the whole continent must take up arms, if every man must be a soldier, 'tis scarcely worth our while to fight against a contemptible ministry only. Dearly, dearly,

8. Lord Frederick North (1713–1792) served as prime minister from 1770 to 1782. Sympathetic to colonial protests and hesitant to coerce obedience, he nonetheless oversaw the British war effort against the Americans, as King George III and the more hawkish majority of Parliament demanded.

do we pay for the repeal of the acts, if that is all we fight for; for in a just estimation 'tis as great a folly to pay a Bunker-hill price for law, as for land. As I have always considered the independency of this continent, as an event, which sooner or later must arrive, so from the late rapid progress of the continent to maturity, the event could not be far off. Wherefore, on the breaking out of hostilities, it was not worth the while to have disputed a matter, which time would have finally redressed, unless we meant to be in earnest; otherwise, it is like wasting an estate on a suit at law, to regulate the trespasses of a tenant, whose lease is just expiring. No man was a warmer wisher for reconciliation than myself, before the fatal nineteenth of April 1775,[9] but the moment the event of that day was made known, I rejected the hardened, sullen tempered Pharaoh of England for ever; and disdain the wretch, that with the pretended title of FATHER OF HIS PEOPLE, can unfeelingly hear of their slaughter, and composedly sleep with their blood upon his soul.

But admitting that matters were now made up, what would be the event? I answer, the ruin of the continent. And that for several reasons.

First. The powers of governing still remaining in the hands of the king, he will have a negative over the whole legislation of this continent. And as he hath shewn himself such an inveterate enemy to liberty, and discovered such a thirst for arbitrary power; is he, or is he not, a proper man to say to these colonies, *"You shall make no laws but what I please."* And is there any inhabitant in America so ignorant, as not to know, that according to what is called the *present constitution,* that this continent can make no laws but what the king gives it leave to; and is there any man so unwise, as not to see, that (considering what has happened) he will suffer no Law to be made here, but such as suit *his* purpose? We may be as effectually enslaved by the want of laws in America, as by submitting to laws made for us in England. After matters are made up (as it is called) can there be any doubt, but the whole power of the crown will be exerted, to keep this continent as low and humble as possible? Instead of going forward we shall go backward, or be perpetually quarrelling or ridiculously petitioning.—We are already greater than the king wishes us to be, and will he not hereafter endeavour to make us less? To bring the matter to one point. Is the power who is jealous of our prosperity, a proper power to govern us? Whoever says *No* to this question is an *independent,* for independency means no more, than, whether we shall make our own laws, or, whether the king, the greatest enemy this continent hath, or can have, shall tell us, *"there shall be no laws but such as I like."*

9. Massacre at Lexington [Paine's note].

But the king you will say has a negative in England; the people there can make no laws without his consent. In point of right and good order, it is something very ridiculous, that a youth of twenty-one (which hath often happened) shall say to several millions of people, older and wiser than himself, I forbid this or that act of yours to be law. But in this place I decline this sort of reply, tho' I will never cease to expose the absurdity of it, and only answer, that England being the king's residence, and America not so, make quite another case. The king's negative *here* is ten times more dangerous and fatal than it can be in England, for *there* he will scarcely refuse his consent to a bill for putting England into as strong a state of defence as possible, and in America he would never suffer such a bill to be passed.

America is only a secondary object in the system of British politics, England consults the good of *this* country, no farther than it answers her *own* purpose. Wherefore, her own interest leads her to suppress the growth of ours in every case which doth not promote her advantage, or in the least interferes with it. A pretty state we should soon be in under such a second-hand government, considering what has happened! Men do not change from enemies to friends by the alteration of a name: And in order to shew that reconciliation *now* is a dangerous doctrine, I affirm, *that it would be policy in the king at this time, to repeal the acts for the sake of reinstating himself in the government of the provinces;* in order, that HE MAY ACCOMPLISH BY CRAFT AND SUBTILITY, IN THE LONG RUN, WHAT HE CANNOT DO BY FORCE AND VIOLENCE IN THE SHORT ONE. Reconciliation and ruin are nearly related.

Secondly. That as even the best terms, which we can expect to obtain, can amount to no more than a temporary expedient, or a kind of government by guardianship, which can last no longer than till the colonies come of age, so the general face and state of things, in the interim, will be unsettled and unpromising. Emigrants of property will not choose to come to a country whose form of government hangs but by a thread, and who is every day tottering on the brink of commotion and disturbance; and numbers of the present inhabitants would lay hold of the interval, to dispose of their effects, and quit the continent.

But the most powerful of all arguments, is, that nothing but independence, *i. e.* a continental form of government, can keep the peace of the continent and preserve it inviolate from civil wars. I dread the event of a reconciliation with Britain now, as it is more than probable, that it will followed by a revolt somewhere or other, the consequences of which may be far more fatal than all the malice of Britain.

Thousands are already ruined by British barbarity; (thousands more will probably suffer the same fate.) Those men have other feelings than us who have nothing suffered. All they *now* possess is liberty, what they before enjoyed is sacrificed to its service, and having nothing more to lose, they disdain submission. Besides, the general temper of the colonies, towards a British government, will be like that of a youth, who is nearly out of his time; they will care very little about her: And a government which cannot preserve the peace, is no government at all, and in that case we pay our money for nothing; and pray what is it that Britain can do, whose power will be wholly on paper, should a civil tumult break out the very day after reconciliation? I have heard some men say, many of whom I believe spoke without thinking, that they dreaded an independence, fearing that it would produce civil wars. It is but seldom that our first thoughts are truly correct, and that is the case here; for there are ten times more to dread from a patched up connection than from independence. I make the sufferers case my own, and I protest, that were I driven from house and home, my property destroyed, and my circumstances ruined, that as a man, sensible of injuries, I could never relish the doctrine of reconciliation, or consider myself bound thereby.

The colonies have manifested such a spirit of good order and obedience to continental government, as is sufficient to make every reasonable person easy and happy on that head. No man can assign the least pretence for his fears, on any other grounds, that such as are truly childish and ridiculous, viz. that one colony will be striving for superiority over another.

Where there are no distinctions there can be no superiority, perfect equality affords no temptation. The republics of Europe are all (and we may say always) in peace. Holland and Switzerland are without wars, foreign or domestic: Monarchical governments, it is true, are never long at rest; the crown itself is a temptation to enterprising ruffians at *home*; and that degree of pride and insolence ever attendant on regal authority, swells into a rupture with foreign powers, in instances, where a republican government, by being formed on more natural principles, would negotiate the mistake.

If there is any true cause of fear respecting independence, it is because no plan is yet laid down. Men do not see their way out—Wherefore, as an opening into that business, I offer the following hints; at the same time modestly affirming, that I have no other opinion of them myself, than that they may be the means of giving rise to something better. Could the straggling thoughts of individuals be collected, they would frequently form materials for wise and able men to improve into useful matter.

Let the assemblies be annual, with a President only. The representation more equal.[1] Their business wholly domestic, and subject to the authority of a Continental Congress.

Let each colony be divided into six, eight, or ten, convenient districts, each district to send a proper number of delegates to Congress, so that each colony send at least thirty. The whole number in Congress will be least 390. Each Congress to sit and to choose a president by the following method. When the delegates are met, let a colony be taken from the whole thirteen colonies by lot, after which, let the whole Congress choose (by ballot) a president from out of the delegates of that province. In the next Congress, let a colony be taken by lot from twelve only, omitting that colony from which the president was taken in the former Congress, and so proceeding on till the whole thirteen shall have had their proper rotation. And in order that nothing may pass into a law but what is satisfactorily just, not less than three fifths of the Congress to be called a majority.—He that will promote discord, under a government so equally formed as this, would have joined Lucifer in his revolt.

But as there is a peculiar delicacy, from whom, or in what manner, this business must first arise, and as it seems most agreeable and consistent that it should come from some intermediate body between the governed and the governors, that is, between the Congress and the people, let a CONTINENTAL CONFERENCE be held, in the following manner, and for the following purpose.

A committee of twenty-six members of Congress, viz. two for each colony. Two members for each House of Assembly, or Provincial Convention; and five representatives of the people at large, to be chosen in the capital city or town of each province, for, and in behalf of the whole province, by as many qualified voters as shall think proper to attend from all parts of the province for that purpose; or, if more convenient, the representatives may be chosen in two or three of the most populous parts thereof. In this conference, thus assembled, will be united, the two grand principles of business, *knowledge* and *power*. The members of Congress, Assemblies, or Conventions, by having had experience in national concerns, will be able and useful

---

1. The nature of representation was one of the central debates of eighteenth-century politics. How many people or places could a single person responsibly represent? Should each "interest" or class or locality in the society have their own delegates in a congress or parliament or should the representative try to consider the larger needs of the nation as well as the particular demands of his constituents? Interestingly, Paine seems to have argued for both theories; he favored large assemblies to give each part of the population its due, yet also wanted the representatives to consider the good of the nation and of humanity in making decisions. Later in this essay, he cites James Burgh's *Political Disquistions* (1774), which argued on behalf of the unrepresented Americans against the Crown.

counsellors, and the whole, being impowered by the people will have a truly legal authority.

The conferring members being met, let their business be to frame a CONTINENT[A]L CHARTER, or Charter of the United Colonies; (answering to what is called the Magna Charta of England) fixing the number and manner of choosing members of Congress, members of Assembly, with their date of sitting, and drawing the line of business and jurisdiction between them: Always remembering, that our strength is continental, not provincial. Securing freedom and property to all men, and above all things, the free exercise of religion, according to the dictates of conscience; with such other matter as is necessary for a charter to contain. Immediately after which, the said Conference to dissolve, and the bodies which shall be chosen comfortable to the said charter, to be the legislators and governors of this continent for the time being: Whose peace and happiness, may God preserve. Amen.

Should any body of men be hereafter delegated for this or some similar purpose, I offer them the following extracts from that wise observer on governments, *Dragonetti*.[2] "The science" says he "of the politician consists in fixing the true point of happiness and freedom. Those men would deserve the gratitude of ages, who should discover a mode of government that contained the greatest sum of individual happiness, with the least national expense."

But where says some is the King of America? I'll tell you friend, he reigns above, and doth not make havoc of mankind like the Royal Brute of Britain. Yet that we may not appear to be defective even in earthly honors, let a day be solemnly set apart for proclaiming the charter; let it be brought forth placed on the divine law, the Word of God; let a crown be placed thereon, by which the world may know, that so far as we approve as monarchy, that in America THE LAW IS KING. For as in absolute governments the King is law, so in free countries the law *ought* to be King; and there ought to be no other. But lest any ill use should afterwards arise, let the crown at the conclusion of the ceremony be demolished, and scattered among the people whose right it is.

A government of our own is our natural right: And when a man seriously reflects on the precariousness of human affairs, he will become convinced, that it is infinitely wiser and safer, to form a constitution of our own in a cool deliberate manner, while we have it in our power, than to trust such an interesting event to time and

---

2. "Dragonetti on virtue and rewards" [Paine's note]. Giacinto Dragonetti, *A Treatise on Rewards and Virtues* (1769), originally published in Italian in 1765. Dragonetti was no radical—he later became president of the Royal Court of Sicily—but like most Enlightenment figures he sought liberal reforms in government, so that authority aligned with reason instead of fear.

chance. If we omit it now, some Massanello[3] may hereafter arise, who laying hold of popular disquietudes, may collect together the desperate and discontented, and by assuming to themselves the powers of government, may sweep away the liberties of the continent like a deluge. Should the government of America return again into the hands of Britain, the tottering situation of things, will be a temptation for some desperate adventurer to try his fortune; and in such a case, what relief can Britain give? Ere she could hear the news, the fatal business might be done; and ourselves suffering like the wretched Britons under the oppression of the Conqueror. Ye that oppose independence now, ye know not what ye do: ye are opening a door to eternal tyranny, by keeping vacant the seat of government. There are thousands, and tens of thousands, who would think it glorious to expel from the continent, that barbarous and hellish power, which hath stirred up the Indians and Negroes to destroy us, the cruelty hath a double guilt, it is dealing brutally by us, and treacherously by them.[4]

To talk of friendship with those in whom our reason forbids us to have faith, and our affections wounded through a thousand pores instruct us to detest, is madness and folly. Every day wears out the little remains of kindred between us and them, and can there be any reason to hope, that as the relationship expires, the affection will increase, or that we shall agree better, when we have ten times more and greater concerns to quarrel over than ever?

Ye that tell us of harmony and reconciliation, can ye restore to us the time that is past? Can ye give to prostitution its former innocence? Neither can ye reconcile Britain and America. The last cord now is broken, the people of England are presenting addresses against us. There are injuries which nature cannot forgive; she would cease to be nature if she did. As well can the lover forgive the ravisher of his mistress, as the continent forgive the murders of Britain. The Almighty hath implanted in us these unextinguishable feelings for good and wise purposes. They are the guardians of his image in our hearts. They distinguish us from the herd of common animals. The social compact would dissolve, and justice be extirpated from

---

3. Reference to Tommasso Aniello (1620–1647), a fisherman of Naples who led a popular revolt against Spanish rule, only to be killed after ten days in power. His memory lived on to inspire unrest among the maritime workers of the Atlantic world—and fear among its ruling elites.
4. Along with another biblical reference (Luke 23:34, in which Christ forgives those about to crucify him) this passage alludes to the November 1775 proclamation by John Murray, Earl of Dunmore and last royal governor of Virginia, offering freedom to those slaves and servants who fled their rebel masters and served in His Majesty's military. Tens of thousands of slaves would indeed escape to British lines during the war; for them, the British army was one of liberation, or at least opportunity. Beset by white American settlers, most Indian nations also supported the British or remained neutral during the war.

the earth, or have only a casual existence were we callous to the touches of affection. The robber, and the murderer, would often escape unpunished, did not the injuries which our tempers sustain, provoke us into justice.

O ye that love mankind! Ye that dare oppose, not only the tyranny, but the tyrant, stand forth! Every spot of the old world is overrun with oppression. Freedom hath been hunted round the globe. Asia and Africa have long expelled her.—Europe regards her like a stranger, and England hath given her warning to depart. O! receive the fugitive, and prepare in time an asylum for mankind.

Of the Present Ability of America; with Some Miscellaneous Reflections

I have never met with a man, either in England or America, who hath not confessed his opinion, that a separation between the countries would take place one time or other: And there is no instance in which we have shown less judgment, than in endeavoring to describe, what we call, the ripeness or fitness of the continent for independence.

As all men allow the measure, and vary only in their opinion of the time, let us, in order to remove mistakes, take a general survey of things, and endeavor if possible to find out the *very* time. But I need not go far, the inquiry ceases at once, for the *time hath found us*. The general concurrence, the glorious union of all things, proves the fact.

'Tis not in numbers but in unity that our great strength lies; yet our present numbers are sufficient to repel the force of all the world. The continent hath at this time the largest body of armed and disciplined men of any power under Heaven: and is just arrived at that pitch of strength, in which no single colony is able to support itself, and the whole, when united, is able to do any thing. Our land force is already sufficient, and as to naval affairs, we cannot be insensible that Britain would never suffer an American man of war to be built, while the Continent remained in her hands. Wherefore, we should be no forwarder an hundred years hence in that branch than we are now; but the truth is, we should be less so, because the timber of the Country is every day diminishing, and that which will remain at last, will be far off or difficult to procure.

Were the continent crowded with inhabitants, her sufferings under the present circumstances would be intolerable. The more seaport-towns we had, the more should we have both to defend and to lose. Our present numbers are so happily proportioned to our wants, that no man need be idle. The diminution of trade affords an army, and the necessities of an army create a new trade.

Debts we have none: and whatever we may contract on this account will serve as a glorious memento of our virtue. Can we but leave posterity with a settled form of government, an independent constitution of its own, the purchase at any price will be cheap. But to expend millions for the sake of getting a few vile acts repealed, and routing the present ministry only, is unworthy the charge, and is using posterity with the utmost cruelty; because it is leaving them the great work to do, and a debt upon their backs from which they derive no advantage. Such a thought is unworthy a man of honour, and is the true characteristic of a narrow heart and a peddling politician.

The debt we may contract doth not deserve our regard if the work be but accomplished. No nation ought to be without a debt. A national debt is a national bond; and when it bears no interest, is in no case a grievance. Britain is oppressed with a debt of upwards of one hundred and forty millions sterling, for which she pays upwards of four millions interest. And as a compensation for her debt, she has a large navy; America is without a debt, and without a navy; yet for the twentieth part of the English national debt, could have a navy as large again. The navy of England is not worth at this time more than three millions and a half sterling.

The first and second editions of this pamphlet were published without the following calculations, which are now given as a proof that the above estimation of the navy is a just one. See *Entic's naval history, intro.* page 56.[5]

The charge of building a ship of each rate, and furnishing her with masts, yards, sails, and rigging, together with a proportion of eight months boatswain's and carpenter's sea-stores, as calculated by Mr. Burchett, Secretary to the navy.

For a ship of 100 guns,	....	35,553 £
90 "	....	29,886
80 "	....	23,638
70 "	....	17,785
60 "	....	14,197
50 "	....	10,606
40 "	....	7,558
30 "	....	5,846
20 "	....	3,710

5. John Entick, *A New Naval History* (1757). Entick also published children's spellers, dictionaries, and a history of the war between France and Britain that raged across the globe from 1754 to 1763.

And hence it is easy to sum up the value, or cost, rather, of the whole British navy, which, in the year 1757, when it was at its greatest glory, consisted of the following ships and guns:

Ships	Guns	Cost of One	Cost of All
6	100	55,553 £	213,318 £
12	90	29,886	358,632
12	80	23,638	283,656
43	70	17,785	764,755
35	60	14,197	496,895
40	50	10,605	424,240
45	40	7,558	340,110
58	20	3,710	215,180

85 sloops, bombs, and fireships, one with another at	2,000	170,000
Cost,		3,266,786 £
Remains for guns,		233,214
Total,		3,500,000 £

No country on the globe is so happily situated, or so internally capable of raising a fleet as America. Tar, timber, iron, and cordage are her natural produce. We need go abroad for nothing. Whereas the Dutch, who make large profits by hiring out their ships of war to the Spaniards and Portuguese, are obliged to import most of the materials they use. We ought to view the building a fleet as an article of commerce, it being the natural manufactory of this country. 'Tis the best money we can lay out. A navy when finished is worth more than it cost. And is that nice point in national policy, in which commerce and protection are united. Let us build; if we want them not, we can sell; and by that means replace our paper currency with ready gold and silver.

In point of manning a fleet, people in general run into great errors; it is not necessary that one-fourth part should be sailors. The terrible privateer, Captain Death, stood the hottest engagement of any ship last war, yet had not twenty sailors on board, though her complement of men was upwards of two hundred. A few able and social sailors will soon instruct a sufficient number of active landsmen in the common work of a ship. Wherefore we never can be more capable of beginning on maritime matters than now, while our timber is standing, our fisheries blocked up, and our sailors and shipwrights out of employ. Men of war, of seventy and eighty guns, were built forty years ago in New England, and why not the same now? Ship building is America's greatest pride, and in which she will, in time, excel the whole world. The great empires of the east are mainly inland, and consequently excluded from the possibility of rivalling her. Africa is in a state of barbarism; and no power in Europe hath either such an extent of coast, or such an internal supply of materials. Where nature hath given the one, she hath withheld the other; to America only hath she been liberal to both. The vast empire of Russia is almost shut out from the sea; wherefore her boundless forests, her tar, iron and cordage are only articles of commerce.

In point of safety, ought we to be without a fleet? We are not the little people now which we were sixty years ago; at that time we might have trusted our property in the streets, or fields rather, and slept securely without locks or bolts to our doors and windows. The case is now altered, and our methods of defence ought to improve with our increase of property. A common pirate, twelve months ago, might have come up the Delaware, and laid the city of Philadelphia under contribution for what sum he pleased; and the same might have happened to other places. Nay, any daring fellow, in a brig of fourteen or sixteen guns, might have robbed the whole Continent, and carried off half a million of money. These are circumstances which demand our attention, and point out the necessity of naval protection.

Some perhaps will say, that after we have made it up with Britain, she will protect us. Can they be so unwise as to mean that she will keep a navy in our harbors for that purpose? Common sense will tell us that the power which hath endeavoured to subdue us, is of all others the most improper to defend us. Conquest may be effected under the pretence of friendship; and ourselves, after a long and brave resistance, be at last cheated into slavery. And if her ships are not to be admitted into our harbours, I would ask, how is she going to protect us? A navy three or four thousand miles off can be of little use, and on sudden emergencies, none at all. Wherefore if we must hereafter protect ourselves, why not do it for ourselves? Why do it for another?

The English list of ships of war is long and formidable, but not a tenth part of them are at any time fit for service, numbers of them are not in being; yet their names are pompously continued in the list; if only a plank be left of the ship; and not a fifth part of such as are fit for service can be spared on any one station at one time. The East and West Indies, Mediterranean, Africa, and other parts, over which Britain extends her claim, make large demands upon her navy. From a mixture of prejudice and inattention we have contracted a false notion respecting the navy of England, and have talked as if we should have the whole of it to encounter at once, and for that reason supposed that we must have one as large; which not being instantly practicable, has been made use of by a set of disguised Tories to discourage our beginning thereon. Nothing can be further from truth than this; for if America had only a twentieth part of the naval force of Britain, she would be by far an over-match for her; because, as we neither have, nor claim any foreign dominion, our whole force would be employed on our own coast, where we should, in the long run, have two to one the advantage of those who had three or four thousand miles to sail over before they could attack us, and the same distance to return in order to refit and recruit. And although Britain, by her fleet, hath a check over our trade to Europe, we have as large a one over her trade to the West Indies, which, by laying in the neighborhood of the Continent, lies entirely at its mercy.[6]

Some method might be fallen on to keep up a naval force in time of peace, if we should judge it necessary to support a constant navy. If premiums were to be given to merchants to build and employ in their service ships mounted with twenty, thirty, forty, or fifty guns (the premiums to be in proportion to the loss of bulk to the merchant) fifty or sixty of those ships, with a few guardships on constant duty, would keep up a sufficient navy, and that without burdening ourselves with the evil so loudly complained of in England, of suffering their fleet in time of peace to lie rotting in the docks. To unite the sinews of commerce and defence is sound policy; for when our strength and our riches play into each other's hand, we need fear no external enemy.

In almost every article of defence we abound. Hemp flourishes even to rankness so that we need not want cordage. Our iron is superior to that of other countries. Our small arms equal to any in the world. Cannon we can cast at pleasure. Saltpetre and gunpowder we are every day producing. Our knowledge is hourly improving. Resolution is our inherent character, and courage hath never yet forsaken us. Wherefore, what is it that we want? Why is it that we hesitate? From Britain we can expect nothing but ruin. If she is once admitted to the government of America again, this Continent will not be worth living in. Jealousies will be always arising; insurrections will be constantly happening; and who will go forth to quell them? Who will venture his life to reduce his own countrymen to a foreign obedience? The difference between Pennsylvania and Connecticut, respecting some unlocated lands, shows the insignificance of a British government, and fully proves that nothing but Continental authority can regulate Continental matters.

Another reason why the present time is preferable to all others is, that the fewer our numbers are, the more land there is yet unoccupied, which, instead of being lavished by the king on his worthless dependents, may be hereafter applied, not only to the discharge of

---

6. In 1775, the value of British tax revenues from the island of Jamaica—like Saint Domingue, a sugar colony built on an especially horrifying form of slavery—nearly equaled the revenues it collected from all thirteen mainland colonies combined.

the present debt, but to the constant support of government. No nation under Heaven hath such an advantage as this.

The infant state of the Colonies, as it is called, so far from being against, is an argument in favour of independence. We are sufficiently numerous, and were we more so we might be less united. 'Tis a matter worthy of observation that the more a country is peopled, the smaller their armies are. In military numbers, the ancients far exceeded the moderns; and the reason is evident, for trade being the consequence of population, men became too much absorbed thereby to attend to anything else. Commerce diminishes the spirit, both of patriotism and military defence. And history sufficiently informs us that the bravest achievements were always accomplished in the non-age of a nation. With the increase of commerce, England hath lost its spirit. The city of London, notwithstanding its numbers, submits to continued insults with the patience of a coward. The more men have to lose, the less willing are they to venture. The rich are in general slaves to fear, and submit to courtly power with the trembling duplicity of a spaniel.

Youth is the seed-time of good habits, as well in nations as in individuals. It might be difficult, if not impossible, to form the Continent into one government half a century hence. The vast variety of interests, occasioned by an increase of trade and population, would create confusion. Colony would be against colony. Each being able would scorn each other's assistance; and while the proud and foolish gloried in their little distinctions the wise would lament that the union had not been formed before. Wherefore the present time is the true time for establishing it. The intimacy which is contracted in infancy, and the friendship which is formed in misfortune, are of all others the most lasting and unalterable. Our present union is marked with both these characters; we are young, and we have been distressed; but our concord hath withstood our troubles, and fixes a memorable era for posterity to glory in.

The present time, likewise, is that peculiar time which never happens to a nation but once, *viz.* the time of forming itself into a government. Most nations have let slip the opportunity, and by that means have been compelled to receive laws from their conquerors, instead of making laws for themselves. First, they had a king, and then a form of government; whereas the articles or charter of government should be formed first, and men delegated to execute them afterwards; but from the errors of other nations let us learn wisdom, and lay hold of the present opportunity—*To begin government at the right end.*

When William the Conqueror subdued England, he gave them law at the point of the sword; and, until we consent that the seat of government in America be legally and authoritatively occupied, we shall be in danger of having it filled by some fortunate ruffian, who may treat us in the same manner, and then, where will be our freedom? where our property?

As to religion, I hold it to be the indispensable duty of government to protect all conscientious professors thereof, and I know of no other business which government hath to do therewith. Let a man throw aside that narrowness of soul, that selfishness of principle, which the niggards of all professions are so unwilling to part with, and he will be at once delivered of his fears on that head. Suspicion is the companion of mean souls, and the bane of all good society. For myself, I fully and conscientiously believe that it is the will of the Almighty that there should be a diversity of religious opinions among us. It affords a larger field for our christian kindness. Were we all of one way of thinking, our religious dispositions would want matter for probation; and on this liberal principle, I look on the various denominations among us to be like children of the same family, differing only, in what is called their Christian names.[7]

In [earlier] pages I threw out a few thoughts on the propriety of a Continental Charter, (for I only presume to offer hints, not plans) and in this place I take the liberty of re-mentioning the subject, by observing that a charter is to be understood as a bond of solemn obligation, which the whole enters into, to support the right of every separate part, whether of religion, professional freedom, or property. A firm bargain and a right reckoning make long friends.

In a former page I have likewise mentioned the necessity of a large and equal representation; and there is no political matter which more deserves our attention. A small number of electors, or a small number of representatives, are equally dangerous. But if the number of the representatives be not only small, but unequal, the danger is increased. As an instance of this, I mention the following: when the petition of the associators was before the House of Assembly of Pennsylvania, twenty-eight members only were present; all the Bucks county members, being eight, voted against it, and had seven of the Chester members done the same, this whole province had been governed by two counties only, and this danger it is always exposed to. The unwarrantable stretch likewise, which that house made in their last sitting, to gain an undue authority over the delegates of that province, ought to warn the people at large how they trust power out of their own hands. A set of instructions for their delegates were put together, which in point of sense and business would have dishonoured a school-boy, and after being approved by a *few*, a *very few*, without doors, were carried into the house, and there

---

7. In *Rights of Man*, Paine would develop this argument for religious diversity, likening each religion to a gift that grateful children offered to a common parent.

passed *in behalf of the whole colony*; whereas, did the whole colony know with what ill will that house had entered on some necessary public measures, they would not hesitate a moment to think them unworthy of such a trust.

Immediate necessity makes many things convenient, which if continued would grow into oppressions. Expedience and right are different things. When the calamities of America required a consultation, there was no method so ready, or at that time so proper, as to appoint persons from the several houses of assembly for that purpose; and the wisdom with which they have proceeded hath preserved this Continent from ruin. But as it is more than probable that we shall never be without a CONGRESS, every well wisher to good order must own that the mode for choosing members of that body deserves consideration. And I put it as a question to those who make a study of mankind, whether *representation* and *election* is not too great a power for one and the same body of men to possess? When we are planning for posterity, we ought to remember that virtue is not hereditary.

It is from our enemies that we often gain excellent maxims, and are frequently surprised into reason by their mistakes. Mr. Cornwall (one of the Lords of the Treasury) treated the petition of the New York Assembly with contempt, because *that* house, he said, consisted but of twenty-six members, which trifling number, he argued, could not with decency be put for the whole. We thank him for his involuntary honesty.[8]

To CONCLUDE, however strange it may appear to some, or however unwilling they may be to think so, matters not, but many strong and striking reasons may be given to show that nothing can settle our affairs so expeditiously as an open and determined declaration for independence. Some of which are,

First. — It is the custom of nations, when any two are at war, for some other powers, not engaged in the quarrel, to step in as mediators, and bring about the preliminaries of a peace: but while America calls herself the subject of Great Britain, no power, however well disposed she may be, can offer her mediation. Wherefore, in our present state we may quarrel on for ever.[9]

Secondly. — It is unreasonable to suppose, that France or Spain will give us any kind of assistance, if we mean only to make use of that assistance for the purpose of repairing the breach, and

---

8. Those who would fully understand of what great consequence a large and equal representation is to a state, should read Burgh's political Disquisitions [Paine's note].

9. Paine refers to a code of international conduct often called *Le Droit des Gens* or Law of Nations, as devised by European theorists such as Emerich Vattel and Samuel Pufendorf. This code granted far more protection and respect to the soldiers of foreign nations than it did to rebels and insurgents.

strengthening the connection between Britain and America; because, those powers would be sufferers by the consequences.

Thirdly. — While we profess ourselves the subjects of Britain, we must, in the eyes of foreign nations, be considered as rebels. The precedent is somewhat dangerous to *their peace*, for men to be in arms under the name of subjects; we, on the spot, can solve the paradox: but to unite resistance and subjection, requires an idea much too refined for common understanding.

Fourthly. — Were a manifesto to be published, and despatched to foreign courts, setting forth the miseries we have endured, and the peaceful methods which we have ineffectually used for redress; declaring at the same time that not being able longer to live happily or safely under the cruel disposition of the British court, we had been driven to the necessity of breaking off all connections with her; at the same time, assuring all such Courts of our peaceable disposition towards them, and of our desire of entering into trade with them: Such a memorial would produce more good effects to this Continent than if a ship were freighted with petitions to Britain.

Under our present denomination of British subjects, we can neither be received nor heard abroad: the custom of all courts is against us, and will be so, until by an independence we take rank with other nations.

These proceedings may at first seem strange and difficult, but like all other steps which we have already passed over, will in a little time become familiar and agreeable; and until an independence is declared, the Continent will feel itself like a man who continues putting off some unpleasant business from day to day, yet knows it must be done, hates to set about it, wishes it over, and is continually haunted with the thoughts of its necessity.

The American Crisis #6
October 20, 1778

To the Earl of Carlisle, General Clinton, and William Eden, Esq., British Commissioners at New York.[1] There is a dignity in the warm passions of a Whig, which is never to be found in the cold malice of a Tory. In the one nature is only heated—in the other she is poisoned. The instant the former has it in his power to punish, he feels a disposition to forgive; but the canine venom of the latter knows no relief but revenge.[2] This general distinction will, I believe, apply in all cases, and suits as well the meridian of England as America.

As I presume your last proclamation will undergo the strictures of other pens, I shall confine my remarks to only a few parts thereof. All that you have said might have been comprised in half the compass. It is tedious and unmeaning, and only a repetition of your former follies, with here and there an offensive aggravation. Your cargo of pardons will have no market. It is unfashionable to look at them— even speculation is at an end. They have become a perfect drug, and no way calculated for the climate.

In the course of your proclamation you say, "The policy as well as the benevolence of Great Britain have thus far checked the extremes of war, when they tended to distress a people still considered as their fellow subjects, and to desolate a country shortly to become again a source of mutual advantage." What you mean by "the benevolence of Great Britain" is to me inconceivable. To put a plain question; do you consider yourselves men or devils? For until this point is settled, no determinate sense can be put upon the expression. You have already equalled and in many cases excelled, the savages of either

---

1. This letter is a reply to an offer sent by British commissioners to the Continental Congress in June 1778. Responding to news of the two treaties, signed in February 1778, between the United States and Louis XVI's France, the British proposed a restoration of the empire in which the Americans would have representation in Parliament, while submitting to its authority. Before the Franco-American treaties, many Britons continued to think of Americans as fellow subjects and to criticize the decision to compel them to obedience; afterward, support for the war seems to have increased for a time in Britain.
2. In the late eighteenth century, revenge was widely considered "savage" and criminal, a direct violation of the most basic agreement of civil society. What makes this essay so compelling is the tension it reveals between an American self-image of civility and lawfulness and a powerful desire for retaliation.

Indies; and if you have yet a cruelty in store you must have imported it, unmixed with every human material, from the original ware-house of hell.

To the interposition of Providence, and her blessings on our endeavors, and not to British benevolence are we indebted for the short chain that limits your ravages. Remember you do not, at this time, command a foot of land on the continent of America. Staten Island, York Island, a small part of Long Island, and Rhode Island, circumscribe your power; and even those you hold at the expense of the West Indies. To avoid a defeat, or prevent a desertion of your troops, you have taken up your quarters in holes and corners of inac-cessible security; and in order to conceal what every one can per-ceive, you now endeavor to impose your weakness upon us for an act of mercy. If you think to succeed by such shadowy devices, you are but infants in the political world; you have the A, B, C, of stratagem yet to learn, and are wholly ignorant of the people you have to con-tend with.[3] Like men in a state of intoxication, you forget that the rest of the world have eyes, and that the same stupidity which con-ceals you from yourselves exposes you to their satire and contempt.

The paragraph which I have quoted, stands as an introduction to the following: "But when that country[4] professes the unnatural design, not only of estranging herself from us, but of mortgaging herself and her resources to our enemies, the whole contest is changed: and the question is how far Great Britain may, by every means in her power, destroy or render useless, a connection con-trived for her ruin, and the aggrandizement of France. Under such circumstances, the laws of self-preservation must direct the conduct of Britain, and, if the British colonies are to become an accession to France, will direct her to render that accession of as little avail as possible to her enemy."

I consider you in this declaration, like madmen biting in the hour of death. It contains likewise a fraudulent meanness; for, in order to justify a barbarous conclusion, you have advanced a false position. The treaty we have formed with France is open, noble, and gener-ous. It is true policy, founded on sound philosophy, and neither a surrender or mortgage, as you would scandalously insinuate. I have seen every article, and speak from positive knowledge. In France, we have found an affectionate friend and faithful ally; in Britain, we have found nothing but tyranny, cruelty, and infidelity.

---

3. Having failed to subdue New England in 1775–76 and having lost an army of seven thousand men as prisoners after the battle of Saratoga, New York, in October 1777, the British military was in the midst of a major change in strategy against the American rebels. During 1779 and 1780, British forces would turn to the South, eventually con-quering much of South Carolina and Virginia.
4. America. [Paine's note]

But the happiness is, that the mischief you threaten, is not in your power to execute; and if it were, the punishment would return upon you in a ten-fold degree. The humanity of America has hitherto restrained her from acts of retaliation, and the affection she retains for many individuals in England, who have fed, clothed and comforted her prisoners, has, to the present day, warded off her resentment, and operated as a screen to the whole. But even these considerations must cease, when national objects interfere and oppose them. Repeated aggravations will provoke a retort, and policy justify the measure. We mean now to take you seriously up upon your own ground and principle, and as you do, so shall you be done by.

You ought to know, gentlemen, that England and Scotland, are far more exposed to incendiary desolation than America, in her present state, can possibly be. We occupy a country, with but few towns, and whose riches consist in land and annual produce. The two last can suffer but little, and that only within a very limited compass. In Britain it is otherwise. Her wealth lies chiefly in cities and large towns, the depositories of manufactures and fleets of merchantmen. There is not a nobleman's country seat but may be laid in ashes by a single person. Your own may probably contribute to the proof: in short, there is no evil which cannot be returned when you come to incendiary mischief. The ships in the Thames, may certainly be as easily set on fire, as the temporary bridge was a few years ago; yet of that affair no discovery was ever made; and the loss you would sustain by such an event, executed at a proper season, is infinitely greater than any you can inflict. The East India House and the Bank, neither are nor can be secure from this sort of destruction, and, as Dr. Price[5] justly observes, a fire at the latter would bankrupt the nation. It has never been the custom of France and England when at war, to make those havocs on each other, because the ease with which they could retaliate rendered it as impolitic as if each had destroyed his own.

But think not, gentlemen, that our distance secures you, or our invention fails us. We can much easier accomplish such a point than any nation in Europe. We talk the same language, dress in the same habit, and appear with the same manners as yourselves. We can pass from one part of England to another unsuspected; many of us are as well acquainted with the country as you are, and should you impolitically provoke us, you will most assuredly lament the effects of it. Mischiefs of this kind require no army to execute them. The means are obvious, and the opportunities unguardable. I hold up a

5. Richard Price, a liberal clergyman and political radical, had opposed war with the rebellious Americans in a 1776 pamphlet, *Observations on the Nature of Civil Liberty*. In it he noted that coin—much of it kept at the Bank of England—was the basis of England's paper credit and that its destruction would cripple the economy.

warning to our senses, if you have any left, and "to the unhappy people likewise, whose affairs are committed to you." I call not with the rancor of an enemy, but the earnestness of a friend, on the deluded people of England, lest, between your blunders and theirs, they sink beneath the evils contrived for us.

"He who lives in a glass house," says a Spanish proverb, "should never begin throwing stones." This, gentlemen, is exactly your case, and you must be the most ignorant of mankind, or suppose us so, not to see on which side the balance of accounts will fall. There are many other modes of retaliation, which, for several reasons, I choose not to mention. But be assured of this, that the instant you put your threat into execution, a counter-blow will follow it. If you openly profess yourselves savages, it is high time we should treat you as such, and if nothing but distress can recover you to reason, to punish will become an office of charity.

While your fleet lay last winter in the Delaware, I offered my service to the Pennsylvania Navy Board then at Trenton, as one who would make a party with them, or any four or five gentlemen, on an expedition down the river to set fire to it, and though it was not then accepted, nor the thing personally attempted, it is more than probable that your own folly will provoke a much more ruinous act. Say not when mischief is done, that you had not warning, and remember that we do not begin it, but mean to repay it. Thus much for your savage and impolitic threat.

In another part of your proclamation you say, "But if the honors of a military life are become the object of the Americans, let them seek those honors under the banners of their rightful sovereign, and in fighting the battles of the united British Empire, against our late mutual and natural enemies." Surely! the union of absurdity with madness was never marked in more distinguishable lines than these. Your rightful sovereign, as you call him, may do well enough for you, who dare not inquire into the humble capacities of the man; but we, who estimate persons and things by their real worth, cannot suffer our judgments to be so imposed upon; and unless it is your wish to see him exposed, it ought to be your endeavor to keep him out of sight. The less you have to say about him the better. We have done with him, and that ought to be answer enough. You have been often told so. Strange! that the answer must be so often repeated. You go a-begging with your king as with a brat, or with some unsaleable commodity you were tired of; and though every body tells you no, no, still you keep hawking him about. But there is one that will have him in a little time, and as we have no inclination to disappoint you of a customer, we bid nothing for him.

The impertinent folly of the paragraph that I have just quoted, deserves no other notice than to be laughed at and thrown by, but the principle on which it is founded is detestable. We are invited to submit to a man who has attempted by every cruelty to destroy us, and to join him in making war against France, who is already at war against him for our support.

Can Bedlam, in concert with Lucifer, form a more mad and devilish request? Were it possible a people could sink into such apostacy they would deserve to be swept from the earth like the inhabitants of Sodom and Gomorrah.[6] The proposition is an universal affront to the rank which man holds in the creation, and an indignity to him who placed him there. It supposes him made up without a spark of honor, and under no obligation to God or man.

What sort of men or Christians must you suppose the Americans to be, who, after seeing their most humble petitions insultingly rejected; the most grievous laws passed to distress them in every quarter; an undeclared war let loose upon them, and Indians and negroes invited to the slaughter;[7] who, after seeing their kinsmen murdered, their fellow citizens starved to death in prisons, and their houses and property destroyed and burned; who, after the most serious appeals to heaven, the most solemn abjuration by oath of all government connected with you, and the most heart-felt pledges and protestations of faith to each other; and who, after soliciting the friendship, and entering into alliances with other nations, should at last break through all these obligations, civil and divine, by complying with your horrid and infernal proposal. Ought we ever after to be considered as a part of the human race? Or ought we not rather to be blotted from the society of mankind, and become a spectacle of misery to the world? But there is something in corruption, which, like a jaundiced eye, transfers the color of itself to the object it looks upon, and sees every thing stained and impure; for unless you were capable of such conduct yourselves, you would never have supposed such a character in us. The offer fixes your infamy. It exhibits you as a nation without faith; with whom oaths and treaties are considered as trifles, and the breaking them as the breaking of a bubble. Regard to decency, or to rank, might have taught you better; or pride inspired you, though virtue could not. There is not left a step in the degradation of character to which you can now descend; you have put your foot on the ground floor, and the key of the dungeon is turned upon you.

---

6. In Genesis 19, God destroys the cities of Sodom and Gomorrah for their faithlessness and sinfulness.
7. In addition to a reminder of Lord Dunmore's offer of freedom to Virginia's slaves and servants (see n. 4, p. 29), Paine refers here to British support for several Indian nations that attacked American settlements during the war. In a 1782 public letter addressed to British commander Sir Guy Carleton, he argued that the British, who pretended to humanity and civility, were even worse than the Indians, who at least made no secret of being ruled by "the horridness of revenge."

That the invitation may want nothing of being a complete monster, you have thought proper to finish it with an assertion which has no foundation, either in fact or philosophy; and as Mr. Ferguson,[8] your secretary, is a man of letters, and has made civil society his study, and published a treatise on that subject, I address this part to him.

In the close of the paragraph which I last quoted, France is styled the "natural enemy" of England, and by way of lugging us into some strange idea, she is styled "the late mutual and natural enemy" of both countries. I deny that she ever was the natural enemy of either; and that there does not exist in nature such a principle. The expression is an unmeaning barbarism, and wholly unphilosophical, when applied to beings of the same species, let their station in the creation be what it may. We have a perfect idea of a natural enemy when we think of the devil, because the enmity is perpetual, unalterable and unabateable. It admits, neither of peace, truce, or treaty; consequently the warfare is eternal, and therefore it is natural. But man with man cannot arrange in the same opposition. Their quarrels are accidental and equivocally created. They become friends or enemies as the change of temper, or the cast of interest inclines them. The Creator of man did not constitute them the natural enemy of each other. He has not made any one order of beings so. Even wolves may quarrel, still they herd together. If any two nations are so, then must all nations be so, otherwise it is not nature but custom, and the offence frequently originates with the accuser. England is as truly the natural enemy of France, as France is of England, and perhaps more so. Separated from the rest of Europe, she has contracted an unsocial habit of manners, and imagines in others the jealousy she creates in herself. Never long satisfied with peace, she supposes the discontent universal, and buoyed up with her own importance, conceives herself the only object pointed at.[9] The expression has been often used, and always with a fraudulent design; for when the idea of a natural enemy is conceived, it prevents all other inquiries, and the real cause of the quarrel is hidden in the universality of the conceit. Men start at the notion of a natural enemy, and ask no other question. The cry obtains credit like the alarm of a mad dog, and is one of those kind of tricks, which, by operating on the common passions, secures their interest through their folly.

8. Adam Ferguson (1724–1816) was professor of moral philosophy in the University of Edinburgh and author of *An Essay on the History of Civil Society* (1767) and *Institutes of Moral Philosophy* (1769).
9. In this indictment of his native country, Paine revisits the Corinthians' view of the ancient Athenians. As recounted by Thucydides, the Athenians were "incapable of either living a quiet life themselves or of allowing anyone else to do so."

But we, sir, are not to be thus imposed upon. We live in a large world, and have extended our ideas beyond the limits and prejudices of an island. We hold out the right hand of friendship to all the universe, and we conceive that there is a sociality in the manners of France, which is much better disposed to peace and negotiation than that of England, and until the latter becomes more civilized, she cannot expect to live long at peace with any power. Her common language is vulgar and offensive, and children suck in with their milk the rudiments of insult—"The arm of Britain! The mighty arm of Britain! Britain that shakes the earth to its center and its poles! The scourge of France! The terror of the world! That governs with a nod, and pours down vengeance like a God." This language neither makes a nation great or little; but it shows a savageness of manners, and has a tendency to keep national animosity alive. The entertainments of the stage are calculated to the same end, and almost every public exhibition is tinctured with insult. Yet England is always in dread of France,—terrified at the apprehension of an invasion, suspicious of being outwitted in a treaty, and privately cringing though she is publicly offending. Let her, therefore, reform her manners and do justice, and she will find the idea of a natural enemy to be only a phantom of her own imagination.

Little did I think, at this period of the war, to see a proclamation which could promise you no one useful purpose whatever, and tend only to expose you. One would think that you were just awakened from a four years' dream, and knew nothing of what had passed in the interval. Is this a time to be offering pardons, or renewing the long forgotten subjects of charters and taxation? Is it worth your while, after every force has failed you, to retreat under the shelter of argument and persuasion? Or can you think that we, with nearly half your army prisoners, and in alliance with France, are to be begged or threatened into submission by a piece of paper? But as commissioners at a hundred pounds sterling a week each, you conceive yourselves bound to do something, and the genius of ill-fortune told you, that you must write.

For my own part, I have not put pen to paper these several months. Convinced of our superiority by the issue of every campaign, I was inclined to hope, that that which all the rest of the world now see, would become visible to you, and therefore felt unwilling to ruffle your temper by fretting you with repetitions and discoveries. There have been intervals of hesitation in your conduct, from which it seemed a pity to disturb you, and a charity to leave you to yourselves. You have often stopped, as if you intended to think, but your thoughts have ever been too early or too late.

There was a time when Britain disdained to answer, or even hear a petition from America. That time is past and she in her turn is petitioning our acceptance. We now stand on higher ground, and offer her peace; and the time will come when she, perhaps in vain, will ask it from us. The latter case is as probable as the former ever was. She cannot refuse to acknowledge our independence with greater obstinacy than she before refused to repeal her laws; and if America alone could bring her to the one, united with France she will reduce her to the other. There is something in obstinacy which differs from every other passion; whenever it fails it never recovers, but either breaks like iron, or crumbles sulkily away like a fractured arch. Most other passions have their periods of fatigue and rest; their suffering and their cure; but obstinacy has no resource, and the first wound is mortal. You have already begun to give it up, and you will, from the natural construction of the vice, find yourselves both obliged and inclined to do so.

If you look back you see nothing but loss and disgrace. If you look forward the same scene continues, and the close is an impenetrable gloom. You may plan and execute little mischiefs, but are they worth the expense they cost you, or will such partial evils have any effect on the general cause? Your expedition to Egg Harbor, will be felt at a distance like an attack upon a hen-roost, and expose you in Europe, with a sort of childish frenzy. Is it worth while to keep an army to protect you in writing proclamations, or to get once a year into winter quarters? Possessing yourselves of towns is not conquest, but convenience, and in which you will one day or other be trepanned. Your retreat from Philadelphia, was only a timely escape, and your next expedition may be less fortunate.[1]

It would puzzle all the politicians in the universe to conceive what you stay for, or why you should have stayed so long. You are prosecuting a war in which you confess you have neither object nor hope, and that conquest, could it be effected, would not repay the charges: in the mean while the rest of your affairs are running to ruin, and a European war kindling against you. In such a situation, there is neither doubt nor difficulty; the first rudiments of reason will determine the choice, for if peace can be procured with more advantages than even a conquest can be obtained, he must be an idiot indeed that hesitates.[2]

1. British forces under Sir William Howe had captured Philadelphia in 1777, but to no discernible military advantage. Unlike European powers, the American union was too decentralized to suffer much from the capture of its nominal capital. Realizing as much, Sir Henry Clinton, who succeeded Howe, evacuated the city in June 1778.
2. Paine was surely aware that the war against the American colonies had many influential critics in Britain, including Edmund Burke and Adam Smith. The war was especially unpopular in the region east of London, where many Separatists (Congregationalists, the descendants of Puritans) had personal and religious ties to New England. Public and parliamentary support for the war would collapse after news of the defeat at Yorktown, Virginia, in 1781, leading a new ministry under Lord Shelburne to make peace.

But you are probably buoyed up by a set of wretched mortals, who, having deceived themselves, are cringing, with the duplicity of a spaniel, for a little temporary bread. Those men will tell you just what you please. It is their interest to amuse, in order to lengthen out their protection. They study to keep you amongst them for that very purpose; and in proportion as you disregard their advice, and grow callous to their complaints, they will stretch into improbability, and season their flattery the higher. Characters like these are to be found in every country, and every country will despise them.

—COMMON SENSE.

From Rights of Man, Part First
February 1791

Among the incivilities by which nations or individuals provoke and irritate each other, Mr. Burke's pamphlet on the French Revolution is an extraordinary instance. Neither the People of France, nor the National Assembly, were troubling themselves about the affairs of England, or the English Parliament; and that Mr. Burke should commence an unprovoked attack upon them, both in Parliament and in public, is a conduct that cannot be pardoned on the score of manners, nor justified on that of policy.

There is scarcely an epithet of abuse to be found in the English language, with which Mr. Burke has not loaded the French Nation and the National Assembly. Everything which rancour, prejudice, ignorance or knowledge could suggest, is poured forth in the copious fury of near four hundred pages. In the strain and on the plan Mr. Burke was writing, he might have written on to as many thousands. When the tongue or the pen is let loose in a frenzy of passion, it is the man, and not the subject, that becomes exhausted.

Hitherto Mr. Burke has been mistaken and disappointed in the opinions he had formed of the affairs of France; but such is the ingenuity of his hope, or the malignancy of his despair, that it furnishes him with new pretences to go on. There was a time when it was impossible to make Mr. Burke believe there would be any Revolution in France. His opinion then was, that the French had neither spirit to undertake it nor fortitude to support it; and now that there is one, he seeks an escape by condemning it.

Not sufficiently content with abusing the National Assembly, a great part of his work is taken up with abusing Dr. Price[1] (one of the best-hearted men that lives) and the two societies in England known by the name of the Revolution Society and the Society for Constitutional Information.

---

1. Richard Price was among the first Unitarians, a group of liberal Christians who combined Enlightenment skepticism about religious dogma with a humanitarian emphasis on good works, forgiveness, and love.

Dr. Price had preached a sermon on the 4th of November, 1789,[2] being the anniversary of what is called in England the Revolution, which took place 1688. Mr. Burke, speaking of this sermon, says: "The political Divine proceeds dogmatically to assert, that by the principles of the Revolution, the people of England have acquired three fundamental rights:

1. To choose our own governors.
2. To cashier them for misconduct.
3. To frame a government for ourselves."

Dr. Price does not say that the right to do these things exists in this or in that person, or in this or in that description of persons, but that it exists in the whole; that it is a right resident in the nation. Mr. Burke, on the contrary, denies that such a right exists in the nation, either in whole or in part, or that it exists anywhere; and, what is still more strange and marvellous, he says: "that the people of England utterly disclaim such a right, and that they will resist the practical assertion of it with their lives and fortunes." That men should take up arms and spend their lives and fortunes, not to maintain their rights, but to maintain they have not rights, is an entirely new species of discovery, and suited to the paradoxical genius of Mr. Burke.

The method which Mr. Burke takes to prove that the people of England have no such rights, and that such rights do not now exist in the nation, either in whole or in part, or anywhere at all, is of the same marvellous and monstrous kind with what he has already said; for his arguments are that the persons, or the generation of persons, in whom they did exist, are dead, and with them the right is dead also. To prove this, he quotes a declaration made by Parliament about a hundred years ago, to William and Mary, in these words: "The Lords Spiritual and Temporal, and Commons, do, in the name of the people aforesaid" (meaning the people of England then living) "most humbly and faithfully submit themselves, their heirs and posterities, for EVER." He quotes a clause of another Act of Parliament made in the same reign, the terms of which he says, "bind us" (meaning the people of their day), "our heirs and our posterity, to them, their heirs and posterity, to the end of time."

Mr. Burke conceives his point sufficiently established by producing those clauses, which he enforces by saying that they exclude the right of the nation for ever. And not yet content with making such

---

2. Price delivered *A Discourse on the Love of our Country* to a group of English reformers and radicals. In addition to applauding the French Revolution and warning "slavish governments and slavish hierarchies" everywhere, Price condemned the "wretched partiality" that nations had for themselves, calling instead for a "universal benevolence" toward all people.

declarations, repeated over and over again, he farther says, "that if the people of England possessed such a right before the Revolution" (which he acknowledges to have been the case, not only in England, but throughout Europe, at an early period), "yet that the English Nation did, at the time of the Revolution, most solemnly renounce and abdicate it, for themselves, and for all their posterity, for ever."

As Mr. Burke occasionally applies the poison drawn from his horrid principles, not only to the English nation, but to the French Revolution and the National Assembly, and charges that august, illuminated and illuminating body of men with the epithet of usurpers, I shall, sans ceremonie, place another system of principles in opposition to his.

The English Parliament of 1688 did a certain thing, which, for themselves and their constituents, they had a right to do, and which it appeared right should be done. But, in addition to this right, which they possessed by delegation, they set up another right by assumption, that of binding and controlling posterity to the end of time. The case, therefore, divides itself into two parts; the right which they possessed by delegation, and the right which they set up by assumption. The first is admitted; but with respect to the second, I reply—

There never did, there never will, and there never can, exist a Parliament, or any description of men, or any generation of men, in any country, possessed of the right or the power of binding and controlling posterity to the "end of time," or of commanding for ever how the world shall be governed, or who shall govern it; and therefore all such clauses, acts or declarations by which the makers of them attempt to do what they have neither the right nor the power to do, nor the power to execute, are in themselves null and void. Every age and generation must be as free to act for itself in all cases as the age and generations which preceded it.[3] The vanity and presumption of governing beyond the grave is the most ridiculous and insolent of all tyrannies. Man has no property in man; neither has any generation a property in the generations which are to follow. The Parliament or the people of 1688, or of any other period, had no more right to dispose of the people of the present day, or to bind or to control them in any shape whatever, than the parliament or the people of the present day have to dispose of, bind or control those who are to live a

3. The idea that generations no less than individuals had civil and natural rights circulated among a small circle of Anglo-American radicals as well as French *philosophes* during the late 1780s. Besides Paine, these included Dr. Richard Gem of Britain, Thomas Jefferson's physician during the Virginian's sojourn in Europe. In a letter from Paris written eight weeks after the fall of the Bastille, Jefferson passed on his doctor's ideas to James Madison. "I set out on this ground, which I suppose to be self-evident," Jefferson wrote, "that the *earth belongs in usufruct to the living*; that the dead have neither powers nor rights over it." Jefferson also corresponded with Paine during the heady summer and fall of 1789, and later complimented both parts of *Rights of Man*.

hundred or a thousand years hence. Every generation is, and must be, competent to all the purposes which its occasions require. It is the living, and not the dead, that are to be accommodated. When man ceases to be, his power and his wants cease with him; and having no longer any participation in the concerns of this world, he has no longer any authority in directing who shall be its governors, or how its government shall be organised, or how administered.

I am not contending for nor against any form of government, nor for nor against any party, here or elsewhere. That which a whole nation chooses to do it has a right to do. Mr. Burke says, No. Where, then, does the right exist? I am contending for the rights of the living, and against their being willed away and controlled and contracted for by the manuscript assumed authority of the dead, and Mr. Burke is contending for the authority of the dead over the rights and freedom of the living. There was a time when kings disposed of their crowns by will upon their death-beds, and consigned the people, like beasts of the field, to whatever successor they appointed. This is now so exploded as scarcely to be remembered, and so monstrous as hardly to be believed. But the Parliamentary clauses upon which Mr. Burke builds his political church are of the same nature.

The laws of every country must be analogous to some common principle. In England no parent or master, nor all the authority of Parliament, omnipotent as it has called itself, can bind or control the personal freedom even of an individual beyond the age of twenty-one years. On what ground of right, then, could the Parliament of 1688, or any other Parliament, bind all posterity for ever?

Those who have quitted the world, and those who have not yet arrived at it, are as remote from each other as the utmost stretch of mortal imagination can conceive. What possible obligation, then, can exist between them—what rule or principle can be laid down that of two nonentities, the one out of existence and the other not in, and who never can meet in this world, the one should control the other to the end of time?

In England it is said that money cannot be taken out of the pockets of the people without their consent. But who authorised, or who could authorise, the Parliament of 1688 to control and take away the freedom of posterity (who were not in existence to give or to withhold their consent) and limit and confine their right of acting in certain cases for ever?

A greater absurdity cannot present itself to the understanding of man than what Mr. Burke offers to his readers. He tells them, and he tells the world to come, that a certain body of men who existed a hundred years ago made a law, and that there does not exist in the nation, nor ever will, nor ever can, a power to alter it. Under how many subtilties or absurdities has the divine right to govern been imposed on the credulity of mankind? Mr. Burke has discovered a new one, and he has shortened his journey to Rome by appealing to the power of this infallible Parliament of former days, and he produces what it has done as of divine authority, for that power must certainly be more than human which no human power to the end of time can alter.

But Mr. Burke has done some service—not to his cause, but to his country—by bringing those clauses into public view. They serve to demonstrate how necessary it is at all times to watch against the attempted encroachment of power, and to prevent its running to excess. It is somewhat extraordinary that the offence for which James II. was expelled, that of setting up power by assumption, should be re-acted, under another shape and form, by the Parliament that expelled him. It shows that the Rights of Man were but imperfectly understood at the Revolution, for certain it is that the right which that Parliament set up by assumption (for by the delegation it had not, and could not have it, because none could give it) over the persons and freedom of posterity for ever was of the same tyrannical unfounded kind which James attempted to set up over the Parliament and the nation, and for which he was expelled. The only difference is (for in principle they differ not) that the one was an usurper over living, and the other over the unborn; and as the one has no better authority to stand upon than the other, both of them must be equally null and void, and of no effect.

From what, or from whence, does Mr. Burke prove the right of any human power to bind posterity for ever? He has produced his clauses, but he must produce also his proofs that such a right existed, and show how it existed. If it ever existed it must now exist, for whatever appertains to the nature of man cannot be annihilated by man. It is the nature of man to die, and he will continue to die as long as he continues to be born. But Mr. Burke has set up a sort of political Adam, in whom all posterity are bound for ever. He must, therefore, prove that his Adam possessed such a power, or such a right.

The weaker any cord is, the less will it bear to be stretched, and the worse is the policy to stretch it, unless it is intended to break it. Had anyone proposed the overthrow of Mr. Burke's positions, he would have proceeded as Mr. Burke has done. He would have magnified the authorities, on purpose to have called the right of them into question; and the instant the question of right was started, the authorities must have been given up.

It requires but a very small glance of thought to perceive that although laws made in one generation often continue in force through succeeding generations, yet they continue to derive their force from the consent of the living. A law not repealed continues in force, not because it cannot be repealed, but because it is not repealed; and the non-repealing passes for consent.

But Mr. Burke's clauses have not even this qualification in their favour. They become null, by attempting to become immortal. The nature of them precludes consent. They destroy the right which they might have, by grounding it on a right which they cannot have. Immortal power is not a human right, and therefore cannot be a right of Parliament. The Parliament of 1688 might as well have passed an act to have authorised themselves to live for ever, as to make their authority live for ever. All, therefore, that can be said of those clauses is that they are a formality of words, of as much import as if those who used them had addressed a congratulation to themselves, and in the oriental style of antiquity had said: O Parliament, live for ever!

The circumstances of the world are continually changing, and the opinions of men change also; and as government is for the living, and not for the dead, it is the living only that has any right in it. That which may be thought right and found convenient in one age may be thought wrong and found inconvenient in another. In such cases, who is to decide, the living or the dead?

As almost one hundred pages of Mr. Burke's book are employed upon these clauses, it will consequently follow that if the clauses themselves, so far as they set up an assumed usurped dominion over posterity for ever, are unauthoritative, and in their nature null and void; that all his voluminous inferences, and declamation drawn therefrom, or founded thereon, are null and void also; and on this ground I rest the matter.

We now come more particularly to the affairs of France. Mr. Burke's book has the appearance of being written as instruction to the French nation; but if I may permit myself the use of an extravagant metaphor, suited to the extravagance of the case, it is darkness attempting to illuminate light.

* * *

"We have seen," says Mr. Burke, "the French rebel against a mild and lawful monarch, with more fury, outrage, and insult, than any people has been known to rise against the most illegal usurper, or the most sanguinary tyrant." This is one among a thousand other instances, in which Mr. Burke shows that he is ignorant of the springs and principles of the French Revolution.

It was not against Louis XVI. but against the despotic principles of the Government, that the nation revolted. These principles had not their origin in him, but in the original establishment, many centuries back: and they were become too deeply rooted to be removed, and the Augean stables of parasites and plunderers too abominably filthy to be cleansed by anything short of a complete and universal Revolution. When it becomes necessary to do anything, the whole heart and soul should go into the measure, or not attempt it. That crisis was then arrived, and there remained no choice but to act with determined vigor, or not to act at all. The king was known to be the friend of the nation, and this circumstance was favorable to the enterprise. Perhaps no man bred up in the style of an absolute king, ever possessed a heart so little disposed to the exercise of that species of power as the present King of France.[4] But the principles of the Government itself still remained the same. The Monarch and the Monarchy were distinct and separate things; and it was against the established despotism of the latter, and not against the person or principles of the former, that the revolt commenced, and the Revolution has been carried.

Mr. Burke does not attend to the distinction between men and principles, and, therefore, he does not see that a revolt may take place against the despotism of the latter, while there lies no charge of despotism against the former.

The natural moderation of Louis XVI. contributed nothing to alter the hereditary despotism of the monarchy. All the tyrannies of former reigns, acted under that hereditary despotism, were still liable to be revived in the hands of a successor. It was not the respite of a reign that would satisfy France, enlightened as she was then become. A casual discontinuance of the practice of despotism, is not a discontinuance of its principles: the former depends on the virtue of the individual who is in immediate possession of the power; the latter, on the virtue and fortitude of the nation. In the case of Charles I. and James II. of England, the revolt was against the personal despotism of the men; whereas in France, it was against the hereditary despotism of the established Government. But men who can consign over the rights of posterity for ever on the authority of a mouldy parchment, like Mr. Burke, are not qualified to judge of this Revolution. It takes in a field too vast for their views to explore, and proceeds with a mightiness of reason they cannot keep pace with.

But there are many points of view in which this Revolution may be considered. When despotism has established itself for ages in a country, as in France, it is not in the person of the king only that it resides. It has the appearance of being so in show, and in nominal authority; but it is not so in practice and in fact. It has its standard everywhere. Every office and department has its despotism, founded

---

4. Louis XVI had in fact pursued a number of reforms in the face of his kingdom's mounting social and political problems. For example, he criticized the regressive taxation of the poor and forbade the use of torture on witnesses. In 1788, upon summoning the three "Estates" of France into a general assembly, he invited the common people to submit *cahiers*, or reports, of their many problems.

upon custom and usage. Every place has its Bastille, and every Bastille its despot. The original hereditary despotism resident in the person of the king, divides and sub-divides itself into a thousand shapes and forms, till at last the whole of it is acted by deputation. This was the case in France; and against this species of despotism, proceeding on through an endless labyrinth of office till the source of it is scarcely perceptible, there is no mode of redress. It strengthens itself by assuming the appearance of duty, and tyrannies under the pretence of obeying.

When a man reflects on the condition which France was in from the nature of her government, he will see other causes for revolt than those which immediately connect themselves with the person or character of Louis XVI. There were, if I may so express it, a thousand despotisms to be reformed in France, which had grown up under the hereditary despotism of the monarchy, and became so rooted as to be in a great measure independent of it. Between the Monarchy, the Parliament, and the Church there was a rivalship of despotism; besides the feudal despotism operating locally, and the ministerial despotism operating everywhere. But Mr. Burke, by considering the king as the only possible object of a revolt, speaks as if France was a village, in which everything that passed must be known to its commanding officer, and no oppression could be acted but what he could immediately control. Mr. Burke might have been in the Bastille his whole life, as well under Louis XVI. as Louis XIV., and neither the one nor the other have known that such a man as Burke existed. The despotic principles of the government were the same in both reigns, though the dispositions of the men were as remote as tyranny and benevolence.

What Mr. Burke considers as a reproach to the French Revolution (that of bringing it forward under a reign more mild than the preceding ones) is one of its highest honors. The Revolutions that have taken place in other European countries, have been excited by personal hatred. The rage was against the man, and he became the victim. But, in the instance of France we see a Revolution generated in the rational contemplation of the Rights of Man, and distinguishing from the beginning between persons and principles.

But Mr. Burke appears to have no idea of principles when he is contemplating Governments. "Ten years ago," says he, "I could have felicitated France on her having a Government, without inquiring what the nature of that Government was, or how it was administered." Is this the language of a rational man? Is it the language of a heart feeling as it ought to feel for the rights and happiness of the human race? On this ground, Mr. Burke must compliment all the Governments in the world, while the victims who suffer under them, whether sold into slavery, or tortured out of existence, are wholly forgotten. It is power, and not principles, that Mr. Burke venerates; and under this abominable depravity he is disqualified to judge between them. Thus much for his opinion as to the occasions of the French Revolution. I now proceed to other considerations.

I know a place in America called Point-no-Point, because as you proceed along the shore, gay and flowery as Mr. Burke's language, it continually recedes and presents itself at a distance before you; but when you have got as far as you can go, there is no point at all. Just thus it is with Mr. Burke's three hundred and sixty-six pages. It is therefore difficult to reply to him. But as the points he wishes to establish may be inferred from what he abuses, it is in his paradoxes that we must look for his arguments.

As to the tragic paintings by which Mr. Burke has outraged his own imagination, and seeks to work upon that of his readers, they are very well calculated for theatrical representation, where facts are manufactured for the sake of show, and accommodated to produce, through the weakness of sympathy, a weeping effect. But Mr. Burke should recollect that he is writing history, and not plays, and that his readers will expect truth, and not the spouting rant of high-toned exclamation.

When we see a man dramatically lamenting in a publication intended to be believed that "The age of chivalry is gone! that The glory of Europe is extinguished for ever! that The unbought grace of life (if anyone knows what it is), the cheap defence of nations, the nurse of manly sentiment and heroic enterprise is gone!" and all this because the Quixot age of chivalry nonsense is gone, what opinion can we form of his judgment, or what regard can we pay to his facts? In the rhapsody of his imagination he has discovered a world of wind mills, and his sorrows are that there are no Quixots to attack them. But if the age of aristocracy, like that of chivalry, should fall (and they had originally some connection) Mr. Burke, the trumpeter of the Order, may continue his parody to the end, and finish with exclaiming: "Othello's occupation's gone!"

Notwithstanding Mr. Burke's horrid paintings, when the French Revolution is compared with the Revolutions of other countries, the astonishment will be that it is marked with so few sacrifices; but this astonishment will cease when we reflect that principles, and not persons, were the meditated objects of destruction. The mind of the nation was acted upon by a higher stimulus than what the consideration of persons could inspire, and sought a higher conquest than could be produced by the downfall of an enemy. Among the few who fell there do not appear to be any that were intentionally singled out. They all of them had their fate in the circumstances of the moment, and were not pursued with that long, cold-blooded unabated revenge which pursued the unfortunate Scotch in the affair of 1745.[5]

Through the whole of Mr. Burke's book I do not observe that the Bastille is mentioned more than once, and that with a kind of implication as if he were sorry it was pulled down, and wished it were built up again. "We have rebuilt Newgate," says he, "and tenanted the mansion; and we have prisons almost as strong as the Bastille for those who dare to libel the queens of France." As to what a madman like the person called Lord George Gordon[6] might say, and to whom Newgate is rather a bedlam than a prison, it is unworthy a rational consideration. It was a madman that libelled, and that is sufficient apology; and it afforded an opportunity for confining him, which was the thing that was wished for. But certain it is that Mr. Burke, who does not call himself a madman (whatever other people may do), has libelled in the most unprovoked manner, and in the grossest style of the most vulgar abuse, the whole representative authority of France, and yet Mr. Burke takes his seat in the British House of Commons! From his violence and his grief, his silence on some points and his excess on others, it is difficult not to believe that Mr. Burke is sorry, extremely sorry, that arbitrary power, the power of the Pope and the Bastille, are pulled down.

Not one glance of compassion, not one commiserating reflection that I can find throughout his book, has he bestowed on those who lingered out the most wretched of lives, a life without hope in the most miserable of prisons. It is painful to behold a man employing his talents to corrupt himself. Nature has been kinder to Mr. Burke than he is to her. He is not affected by the reality of distress touching his heart, but by the showy resemblance of it striking his imagination. He pities the plumage, but forgets the dying bird. Accustomed to kiss the aristocratical hand that hath purloined him from himself, he degenerates into a composition of art, and the genuine soul of nature forsakes him. His hero or his heroine must be a tragedy-

5. In 1745, the heir of the deposed Stuart kings landed in Scotland and sought to overthrow the British government. These rebels, called Jacobites, had considerable support in the Scottish Highlands, but they were routed in the Battle of Culloden in April 1746. The victorious commander, the Duke of Cumberland, proceeded to punish the Highlands. Harrowing accounts of these reprisals appeared in histories written by Tobias Smollet, which Paine read and cited. Smollet described the English as "lay[ing] waste the country with fire and sword," a phrase Paine repeatedly used while denouncing British militarism.

6. Gordon (1751–1793) sat in Parliament during the War of the American Revolution and then played a key role in the violent anti-Catholic riots of 1780. Protesting the Roman Catholic relief act of 1778, which granted some civil protections to the despised papists, Gordon and other leaders of the so-called Protestant Associations held a huge rally on June 2, 1780, to present a petition to Parliament. After a week of violence against Catholic churches, peoples, and properties, some ten thousand soldiers managed to restore order. In the end, sixty-two rioters were sentenced to death, and twenty-five were eventually hanged.

victim expiring in show, and not the real prisoner of misery, sliding into death in the silence of a dungeon.

As Mr. Burke has passed over the whole transaction of the Bastille (and his silence is nothing in his favour), and has entertained his readers with reflections on supposed facts distorted into real falsehoods, I will give, since he has not, some account of the circumstances which preceded that transaction. They will serve to show that less mischief could scarcely have accompanied such an event when considered with the treacherous and hostile aggravations of the enemies of the Revolution.

The mind can hardly picture to itself a more tremendous scene than what the city of Paris exhibited at the time of taking the Bastille,[7] and for two days before and after, nor perceive the possibility of its quieting so soon. At a distance this transaction has appeared only as an act of heroism standing on itself, and the close political connection it had with the Revolution is lost in the brilliancy of the achievement. But we are to consider it as the strength of the parties brought man to man, and contending for the issue. The Bastille was to be either the prize or the prison of the assailants. The downfall of it included the idea of the downfall of despotism, and this compounded image was become as figuratively united as Bunyan's Doubting Castle and Giant Despair.[8]

The National Assembly, before and at the time of taking the Bastille, was sitting at Versailles, twelve miles distant from Paris. About a week before the rising of the Partisans, and their taking the Bastille, it was discovered that a plot was forming, at the head of which was the Count D'Artois, the king's youngest brother, for demolishing the National Assembly, seizing its members, and thereby crushing, by a coup de main, all hopes and prospects of forming a free government. For the sake of humanity, as well as freedom, it is well this plan did not succeed. Examples are not wanting to show how dreadfully vindictive and cruel are all old governments, when they are successful against what they call a revolt.

This plan must have been some time in contemplation; because, in order to carry it into execution, it was necessary to collect a large military force round Paris, and cut off the communication between that city and the National Assembly at Versailles. The troops destined for this service were chiefly the foreign troops in the pay of

7. Dating back to 1370, the Bastille had held political prisoners, often at the express and secret orders of the French kings. But Louis XVI issued few such orders, and only seven prisoners—guarded by over a hundred soldiers—remained there in 1789. Louis had even initiated plans for the prison's demolition five years earlier.
8. A reference to John Bunyan's *Pilgrims' Progress* (1678), which was a staple of devotional literature among Protestant dissenters in North America and Europe. Two travelers, Christian and Hopeful, are imprisoned for a time in Doubting Castle, when they suddenly realize that they hold the key to their liberation within their own hearts.

France, and who, for this particular purpose, were drawn from the distant provinces where they were then stationed. When they were collected to the amount of between twenty-five and thirty thousand, it was judged time to put the plan into execution. The ministry who were then in office, and who were friendly to the Revolution, were instantly dismissed and a new ministry formed of those who had concerted the project, among whom was Count de Broglio, and to his share was given the command of those troops. The character of this man as described to me in a letter which I communicated to Mr. Burke before he began to write his book, and from an authority which Mr. Burke well knows was good, was that of "a high-flying aristocrat, cool, and capable of every mischief."

While these matters were agitating, the National Assembly stood in the most perilous and critical situation that a body of men can be supposed to act in. They were the devoted victims, and they knew it. They had the hearts and wishes of their country on their side, but military authority they had none. The guards of Broglio surrounded the hall where the Assembly sat, ready, at the word of command, to seize their persons, as had been done the year before to the Parliament of Paris. Had the National Assembly deserted their trust, or had they exhibited signs of weakness or fear, their enemies had been encouraged and their country depressed. When the situation they stood in, the cause they were engaged in, and the crisis then ready to burst, which should determine their personal and political fate and that of their country, and probably of Europe, are taken into one view, none but a heart callous with prejudice or corrupted by dependence can avoid interesting itself in their success.

The Archbishop of Vienne was at this time President of the National Assembly—a person too old to undergo the scene that a few days or a few hours might bring forth. A man of more activity and bolder fortitude was necessary, and the National Assembly chose (under the form of a Vice-President, for the Presidency still resided in the Archbishop) M. de la Fayette; and this is the only instance of a Vice-President being chosen. It was at the moment that this storm was pending (July 11th) that a declaration of rights was brought forward by M. de la Fayette, and is the same which is alluded to earlier. It was hastily drawn up, and makes only a part of the more extensive declaration of rights agreed upon and adopted afterwards by the National Assembly. The particular reason for bringing it forward at this moment (M. de la Fayette has since informed me) was that, if the National Assembly should fall in the threatened destruction that then surrounded it, some trace of its principles might have the chance of surviving the wreck.

Everything now was drawing to a crisis. The event was freedom or slavery. On one side, an army of nearly thirty thousand men; on the other, an unarmed body of citizens—for the citizens of Paris, on whom the National Assembly must then immediately depend, were as unarmed and as undisciplined as the citizens of London are now. The French guards had given strong symptoms of their being attached to the national cause; but their numbers were small, not a tenth part of the force that Broglio commanded, and their officers were in the interest of Broglio.

Matters being now ripe for execution, the new ministry made their appearance in office. The reader will carry in his mind that the Bastille was taken the 14th July; the point of time I am now speaking of is the 12th. Immediately on the news of the change of ministry reaching Paris, in the afternoon, all the playhouses and places of entertainment, shops and houses, were shut up. The change of ministry was considered as the prelude of hostilities, and the opinion was rightly founded.

The foreign troops began to advance towards the city. The Prince de Lambesc, who commanded a body of German cavalry, approached by the Place of Louis XV., which connects itself with some of the streets. In his march, he insulted and struck an old man with a sword. The French are remarkable for their respect to old age; and the insolence with which it appeared to be done, uniting with the general fermentation they were in, produced a powerful effect, and a cry of "To arms! to arms!" spread itself in a moment over the city.

Arms they had none, nor scarcely anyone who knew the use of them; but desperate resolution, when every hope is at stake, supplies, for a while, the want of arms. Near where the Prince de Lambesc was drawn up, were large piles of stones collected for building the new bridge, and with these the people attacked the cavalry. A party of French guards upon hearing the firing, rushed from their quarters and joined the people; and night coming on, the cavalry retreated.

The streets of Paris, being narrow, are favourable for defence, and the loftiness of the houses, consisting of many stories, from which great annoyance might be given, secured them against nocturnal enterprises; and the night was spent in providing themselves with every sort of weapon they could make or procure: guns, swords, blacksmiths' hammers, carpenters' axes, iron crows, pikes, halberts, pitchforks, spits, clubs, etc., etc. The incredible numbers in which they assembled the next morning, and the still more incredible resolution they exhibited, embarrassed and astonished their enemies. Little did the new ministry expect such a salute. Accustomed to slavery themselves, they had no idea that liberty was capable of such inspiration, or that a body of unarmed citizens would dare to face the military force of thirty thousand men. Every moment of this day was employed in collecting arms, concerting plans, and arranging themselves into the best order which such an instantaneous movement could afford. Broglio continued lying round the city, but made no further advances this day, and the succeeding night passed with as much tranquility as such a scene could possibly produce.

But defence only was not the object of the citizens. They had a cause at stake, on which depended their freedom or their slavery. They every moment expected an attack, or to hear of one made on the National Assembly; and in such a situation, the most prompt measures are sometimes the best. The object that now presented itself was the Bastille; and the eclat of carrying such a fortress in the face of such an army, could not fail to strike terror into the new ministry, who had scarcely yet had time to meet. By some intercepted correspondence this morning, it was discovered that the Mayor of Paris, M. Defflesselles, who appeared to be in the interest of the citizens, was betraying them; and from this discovery, there remained no doubt that Broglio would reinforce the Bastille the ensuing evening. It was therefore necessary to attack it that day; but before this could be done, it was first necessary to procure a better supply of arms than they were then possessed of.

There was, adjoining to the city a large magazine of arms deposited at the Hospital of the Invalids, which the citizens summoned to surrender; and as the place was neither defensible, nor attempted much defence, they soon succeeded. Thus supplied, they marched to attack the Bastille; a vast mixed multitude of all ages, and of all degrees, armed with all sorts of weapons. Imagination would fail in describing to itself the appearance of such a procession, and of the anxiety of the events which a few hours or a few minutes might produce. What plans the ministry were forming, were as unknown to the people within the city, as what the citizens were doing was unknown to the ministry; and what movements Broglio might make for the support or relief of the place, were to the citizens equally as unknown. All was mystery and hazard.

That the Bastille was attacked with an enthusiasm of heroism, such only as the highest animation of liberty could inspire, and carried in the space of a few hours, is an event which the world is fully possessed of. I am not undertaking the detail of the attack, but bringing into view the conspiracy against the nation which provoked it, and which fell with the Bastille. The prison to which the new ministry were dooming the National Assembly, in addition to its being the high altar and castle of despotism, became the proper object to begin with. This enterprise broke up the new ministry, who began now to fly from the ruin they had prepared for others. The troops of Broglio dispersed, and himself fled also.

Mr. Burke has spoken a great deal about plots, but he has never once spoken of this plot against the National Assembly, and the liberties of the nation; and that he might not, he has passed over all the circumstances that might throw it in his way. The exiles who have fled from France, whose case he so much interests himself in, and from whom he has had his lesson, fled in consequence of the miscarriage of this plot.[9] No plot was formed against them; they were plotting against others; and those who fell, met, not unjustly, the punishment they were preparing to execute. But will Mr. Burke say that if this plot, contrived with the subtilty of an ambuscade, had succeeded, the successful party would have restrained their wrath so soon? Let the history of all governments answer the question.

Whom has the National Assembly brought to the scaffold? None. They were themselves the devoted victims of this plot, and they have not retaliated; why, then, are they charged with revenge they have not acted?[1] In the tremendous breaking forth of a whole people, in which all degrees, tempers and characters are confounded, delivering themselves, by a miracle of exertion, from the destruction meditated against them, is it to be expected that nothing will happen? When men are sore with the sense of oppressions, and menaced with the prospects of new ones, is the calmness of philosophy or the palsy of insensibility to be looked for? Mr. Burke exclaims against outrage; yet the greatest is that which himself has committed. His book is a volume of outrage, not apologised for by the impulse of a moment, but cherished through a space of ten months; yet Mr. Burke had no provocation—no life, no interest, at stake.

* * *

I have now to follow Mr. Burke through a pathless wilderness of rhapsodies, and a sort of descant upon governments, in which he asserts whatever he pleases, on the presumption of its being believed, without offering either evidence or reasons for so doing.

Before anything can be reasoned upon to a conclusion, certain facts, principles, or data, to reason from, must be established, admitted, or denied. Mr. Burke with his usual outrage, abused the Declaration of the Rights of Man, published by the National Assembly of France, as the basis on which the constitution of France is built. This he calls "paltry and blurred sheets of paper about the rights of man." Does Mr. Burke mean to deny that man has any rights? If he

9. Nobles, aristocrats, and clergymen began fleeing France in the summer of 1789, after the collapse of royal authority in Paris and the spread of violence and a "Great Fear" in the countryside. Many of these early émigrés found refuge in Britain. After 1792, larger waves of refugees, including bourgeois and peasants, fled to countries all over Europe, some joining royalist forces in hopes of crushing the revolution. In total, perhaps 130,000 fled.

1. The revolutionaries of Paris would lose such claims to mercy after September 2, 1792, when a mob assailed a group of priests on their way to prison. Agitated by news of Prussian troops invading France and by rumors of counterrevolutionary plots in the capital, crowds rampaged for five days, killing and sometimes mutilating priests, aristocrats, and even the forty-three teenage inhabitants of an insane asylum at Bicêtre.

does, then he must mean that there are no such things as rights anywhere, and that he has none himself; for who is there in the world but man? But if Mr. Burke means to admit that man has rights, the question then will be: What are those rights, and how man came by them originally?

The error of those who reason by precedents drawn from antiquity, respecting the rights of man, is that they do not go far enough into antiquity. They do not go the whole way. They stop in some of the intermediate stages of an hundred or a thousand years, and produce what was then done, as a rule for the present day. This is no authority at all. If we travel still farther into antiquity, we shall find a direct contrary opinion and practice prevailing; and if antiquity is to be authority, a thousand such authorities may be produced, successively contradicting each other; but if we proceed on, we shall at last come out right; we shall come to the time when man came from the hand of his Maker. What was he then? Man. Man was his high and only title, and a higher cannot be given him. But of titles I shall speak hereafter.

We are now got at the origin of man, and at the origin of his rights. As to the manner in which the world has been governed from that day to this, it is no farther any concern of ours than to make a proper use of the errors or the improvements which the history of it presents. Those who lived an hundred or a thousand years ago, were then moderns, as we are now. They had their ancients, and those ancients had others, and we also shall be ancients in our turn. If the mere name of antiquity is to govern in the affairs of life, the people who are to live an hundred or a thousand years hence, may as well take us for a precedent, as we make a precedent of those who lived an hundred or a thousand years ago. The fact is, that portions of antiquity, by proving everything, establish nothing. It is authority against authority all the way, till we come to the divine origin of the rights of man at the creation. Here our enquiries find a resting-place, and our reason finds a home. If a dispute about the rights of man had arisen at the distance of an hundred years from the creation, it is to this source of authority they must have referred, and it is to this same source of authority that we must now refer.

Though I mean not to touch upon any sectarian principle of religion, yet it may be worth observing, that the genealogy of Christ is traced to Adam. Why then not trace the rights of man to the creation of man? I will answer the question. Because there have been upstart governments, thrusting themselves between, and presumptuously working to un-make man.

If any generation of men ever possessed the right of dictating the mode by which the world should be governed for ever, it was the first generation that existed; and if that generation did it not, no succeeding generation can show any authority for doing it, nor can set any up. The illuminating and divine principle of the equal rights of man (for it has its origin from the Maker of man) relates, not only to the living individuals, but to generations of men succeeding each other. Every generation is equal in rights to generations which preceded it, by the same rule that every individual is born equal in rights with his contemporary.

Every history of the creation, and every traditionary account, whether from the lettered or unlettered world, however they may vary in their opinion or belief of certain particulars, all agree in establishing one point, the unity of man; by which I mean that men are all of one degree, and consequently that all men are born equal, and with equal natural right, in the same manner as if posterity had been continued by creation instead of generation, the latter being the only mode by which the former is carried forward; and consequently every child born into the world must be considered as deriving its existence from God.[2] The world is as new to him as it was to the first man that existed, and his natural right in it is of the same kind.

The Mosaic account of the creation, whether taken as divine authority or merely historical, is full to this point, the unity or equality of man. The expression admits of no controversy. "And God said, Let us make man in our own image. In the image of God created he him; male and female created he them." The distinction of sexes is pointed out, but no other distinction is even implied. If this be not divine authority, it is at least historical authority, and shows that the equality of man, so far from being a modern doctrine, is the oldest upon record.

It is also to be observed that all the religions known in the world are founded, so far as they relate to man, on the unity of man, as being all of one degree. Whether in heaven or in hell, or in whatever state man may be supposed to exist hereafter, the good and the bad are the only distinctions. Nay, even the laws of governments are obliged to slide into this principle, by making degrees to consist in crimes and not in persons.

It is one of the greatest of all truths, and of the highest advantage to cultivate. By considering man in this light, and by instructing him to consider himself in this light, it places him in a close connection with all his duties, whether to his Creator or to the creation, of which he is a part; and it is only when he forgets his origin, or, to use a more fashionable phrase, his birth and family, that he becomes dissolute. It is not among the least of the evils of the present existing

---

2. Along with most theologians of the time, eighteenth-century Enlightenment thinkers believed that all humans had a common ancestry and origin. Thus they often argued that racial differences stemmed from environmental factors.

governments in all parts of Europe that man, considered as man, is thrown back to a vast distance from his Maker, and the artificial chasm filled up with a succession of barriers, or sort of turnpike gates, through which he has to pass. I will quote Mr. Burke's catalogue of barriers that he has set up between man and his Maker. Putting himself in the character of a herald, he says: "We fear God—we look with awe to kings—with affection to Parliaments with duty to magistrates—with reverence to priests, and with respect to nobility." Mr. Burke has forgotten to put in "chivalry." He has also forgotten to put in Peter.

The duty of man is not a wilderness of turnpike gates, through which he is to pass by tickets from one to the other. It is plain and simple, and consists but of two points. His duty to God, which every man must feel; and with respect to his neighbor, to do as he would be done by.[3] If those to whom power is delegated do well, they will be respected: if not, they will be despised; and with regard to those to whom no power is delegated, but who assume it, the rational world can know nothing of them.

Hitherto we have spoken only (and that but in part) of the natural rights of man. We have now to consider the civil rights of man, and to show how the one originates from the other. Man did not enter into society to become worse than he was before, nor to have fewer rights than he had before, but to have those rights better secured. His natural rights are the foundation of all his civil rights. But in order to pursue this distinction with more precision, it will be necessary to mark the different qualities of natural and civil rights.

A few words will explain this. Natural rights are those which appertain to man in right of his existence. Of this kind are all the intellectual rights, or rights of the mind, and also all those rights of acting as an individual for his own comfort and happiness, which are not injurious to the natural rights of others. Civil rights are those which appertain to man in right of his being a member of society. Every civil right has for its foundation some natural right pre-existing in the individual, but to the enjoyment of which his individual power is not, in all cases, sufficiently competent. Of this kind are all those which relate to security and protection.

From this short review it will be easy to distinguish between that class of natural rights which man retains after entering into society and those which he throws into the common stock as a member of society.

---

3. In addition to the derisive aside on turnpikes, the much-resented toll roads of the eighteenth century, this passage is important for the glimpse it offers of Paine's moral theory. His two-part definition of the "duty of man" most obviously recalls Christ's articulation of the greatest commandments (Matthew 22:37–40): to love God with all one's heart, soul, and mind and to love one's neighbor as oneself.

The natural rights which he retains are all those in which the Power to execute is as perfect in the individual as the right itself. Among this class, as is before mentioned, are all the intellectual rights, or rights of the mind; consequently religion is one of those rights. The natural rights which are not retained, are all those in which, though the right is perfect in the individual, the power to execute them is defective. They answer not his purpose. A man, by natural right, has a right to judge in his own cause; and so far as the right of the mind is concerned, he never surrenders it. But what availeth it him to judge, if he has not power to redress? He therefore deposits this right in the common stock of society, and takes the arm of society, of which he is a part, in preference and in addition to his own. Society grants him nothing. Every man is a proprietor in society, and draws on the capital as a matter of right.

From these premises two or three certain conclusions will follow:

First, That every civil right grows out of a natural right; or, in other words, is a natural right exchanged.

Secondly, That civil power properly considered as such is made up of the aggregate of that class of the natural rights of man, which becomes defective in the individual in point of power, and answers not his purpose, but when collected to a focus becomes competent to the Purpose of every one.

Thirdly, That the power produced from the aggregate of natural rights, imperfect in power in the individual, cannot be applied to invade the natural rights which are retained in the individual, and in which the power to execute is as perfect as the right itself.

We have now, in a few words, traced man from a natural individual to a member of society, and shown, or endeavoured to show, the quality of the natural rights retained, and of those which are exchanged for civil rights. Let us now apply these principles to governments.

In casting our eyes over the world, it is extremely easy to distinguish the governments which have arisen out of society, or out of the social compact, from those which have not; but to place this in a clearer light than what a single glance may afford, it will be proper to take a review of the several sources from which governments have arisen and on which they have been founded.

They may be all comprehended under three heads.

First, Superstition.

Secondly, Power.

Thirdly, The common interest of society and the common rights of man.

The first was a government of priestcraft, the second of conquerors, and the third of reason.

When a set of artful men pretended, through the medium of oracles, to hold intercourse with the Deity, as familiarly as they now march up the back-stairs in European courts, the world was completely under the government of superstition. The oracles were consulted, and whatever they were made to say became the law; and this sort of government lasted as long as this sort of superstition lasted.

After these a race of conquerors arose, whose government, like that of William the Conqueror, was founded in power, and the sword assumed the name of a sceptre. Governments thus established last as long as the power to support them lasts; but that they might avail themselves of every engine in their favor, they united fraud to force, and set up an idol which they called Divine Right, and which, in imitation of the Pope, who affects to be spiritual and temporal, and in contradiction to the Founder of the Christian religion, twisted itself afterwards into an idol of another shape, called Church and State. The key of St. Peter and the key of the Treasury became quartered on one another, and the wondering cheated multitude worshipped the invention.

When I contemplate the natural dignity of man, when I feel (for Nature has not been kind enough to me to blunt my feelings) for the honour and happiness of its character, I become irritated at the attempt to govern mankind by force and fraud, as if they were all knaves and fools, and can scarcely avoid disgust at those who are thus imposed upon.

We have now to review the governments which arise out of society, in contradistinction to those which arose out of superstition and conquest.

It has been thought a considerable advance towards establishing the principles of Freedom to say that Government is a compact between those who govern and those who are governed; but this cannot be true, because it is putting the effect before the cause; for as man must have existed before governments existed, there necessarily was a time when governments did not exist, and consequently there could originally exist no governors to form such a compact with.

The fact therefore must be that the individuals themselves, each in his own personal and sovereign right, entered into a compact with each other to produce a government: and this is the only mode in which governments have a right to arise, and the only principle on which they have a right to exist.

To possess ourselves of a clear idea of what government is, or ought to be, we must trace it to its origin. In doing this we shall easily discover that governments must have arisen either out of the people or over the people. Mr. Burke has made no distinction. He investigates nothing to its source, and therefore he confounds everything; but he has signified his intention of undertaking, at some future opportunity, a comparison between the constitution of England and France. As he thus renders it a subject of controversy by throwing the gauntlet, I take him upon his own ground. It is in high challenges that high truths have the right of appearing; and I accept it with the more readiness because it affords me, at the same time, an opportunity of pursuing the subject with respect to governments arising out of society.

But it will be first necessary to define what is meant by a Constitution. It is not sufficient that we adopt the word; we must fix also a standard signification to it.

A constitution is not a thing in name only, but in fact. It has not an ideal, but a real existence; and wherever it cannot be produced in a visible form, there is none. A constitution is a thing antecedent to a government, and a government is only the creature of a constitution. The constitution of a country is not the act of its government, but of the people constituting its government. It is the body of elements, to which you can refer, and quote article by article; and which contains the principles on which the government shall be established, the manner in which it shall be organised, the powers it shall have, the mode of elections, the duration of Parliaments, or by what other name such bodies may be called; the powers which the executive part of the government shall have; and in fine, everything that relates to the complete organisation of a civil government, and the principles on which it shall act, and by which it shall be bound. A constitution, therefore, is to a government what the laws made afterwards by that government are to a court of judicature. The court of judicature does not make the laws, neither can it alter them; it only acts in conformity to the laws made: and the government is in like manner governed by the constitution.

Can, then, Mr. Burke produce the English Constitution? If he cannot, we may fairly conclude that though it has been so much talked about, no such thing as a constitution exists, or ever did exist, and consequently that the people have yet a constitution to form.

Mr. Burke will not, I presume, deny the position I have already advanced—namely, that governments arise either out of the people or over the people. The English Government is one of those which arose out of a conquest, and not out of society, and consequently it arose over the people; and though it has been much modified from the opportunity of circumstances since the time of William the Conqueror, the country has never yet regenerated itself, and is therefore without a constitution.

I readily perceive the reason why Mr. Burke declined going into the comparison between the English and French constitutions, because he could not but perceive, when he sat down to the task, that no such a thing as a constitution existed on his side the question. His book is certainly bulky enough to have contained all he could say on this subject, and it would have been the best manner in which people could have judged of their separate merits. Why then has he declined the only thing that was worth while to write upon? It was the strongest ground he could take, if the advantages were on his side, but the weakest if they were not; and his declining to take it is either a sign that he could not possess it or could not maintain it.

Mr. Burke said, in a speech last winter in Parliament, "that when the National Assembly first met in three Orders (the Tiers Etat, the Clergy, and the Noblesse), France had then a good constitution." This shows, among numerous other instances, that Mr. Burke does not understand what a constitution is. The persons so met were not a constitution, but a convention, to make a constitution.

The present National Assembly of France is, strictly speaking, the personal social compact. The members of it are the delegates of the nation in its original character; future assemblies will be the delegates of the nation in its organised character. The authority of the present Assembly is different from what the authority of future Assemblies will be. The authority of the present one is to form a constitution; the authority of future assemblies will be to legislate according to the principles and forms prescribed in that constitution; and if experience should hereafter show that alterations, amendments, or additions are necessary, the constitution will point out the mode by which such things shall be done, and not leave it to the discretionary power of the future government.

A government on the principles on which constitutional governments arising out of society are established, cannot have the right of altering itself. If it had, it would be arbitrary. It might make itself what it pleased; and wherever such a right is set up, it shows there is no constitution. The act by which the English Parliament empowered itself to sit seven years, shows there is no constitution in England. It might, by the same self-authority, have sat any great number of years, or for life. The bill which the present Mr. Pitt brought into Parliament some years ago, to reform Parliament, was on the same erroneous principle.[4] The right of reform is in the nation in its original character, and the constitutional method would

---

4. In 1783 and again in 1785, William Pitt the Younger introduced a series of reforms aimed, in his words, to improve "a beautiful frame of government." The proposed changes would have shortened each sitting of Parliament and enhanced the representation of growing cities—that is, they would have modestly democratized and modernized the governance of the realm without making any fundamental changes to social, political, and economic order. His proposals were defeated, and substantial changes to the electorate and to Parliament waited until 1828.

be by a general convention elected for the purpose. There is, more-over, a paradox in the idea of vitiated bodies reforming themselves.

From these preliminaries I proceed to draw some comparisons. I have already spoken of the declaration of rights; and as I mean to be as concise as possible, I shall proceed to other parts of the French Constitution.

The constitution of France says that every man who pays a tax of sixty sous per annum (2s. 6d. English) is an elector. What article will Mr. Burke place against this? Can anything be more limited, and at the same time more capricious, than the qualification of elec-tors is in England? Limited—because not one man in an hundred (I speak much within compass) is admitted to vote. Capricious—because the lowest character that can be supposed to exist, and who has not so much as the visible means of an honest livelihood, is an elector in some places: while in other places, the man who pays very large taxes, and has a known fair character, and the farmer who rents to the amount of three or four hundred pounds a year, with a prop-erty on that farm to three or four times that amount, is not admitted to be an elector. Everything is out of nature, as Mr. Burke says on another occasion, in this strange chaos, and all sorts of follies are blended with all sorts of crimes. William the Conqueror and his descendants parcelled out the country in this manner, and bribed some parts of it by what they call charters to hold the other parts of it the better subjected to their will. This is the reason why so many of those charters abound in Cornwall; the people were averse to the Government established at the Conquest, and the towns were garri-soned and bribed to enslave the country. All the old charters are the badges of this conquest, and it is from this source that the capri-ciousness of election arises.

The French Constitution says that the number of representatives for any place shall be in a ratio to the number of taxable inhabitants or electors. What article will Mr. Burke place against this? The county of York, which contains nearly a million of souls, sends two county members; and so does the county of Rutland, which contains not an hundredth part of that number. The old town of Sarum,[5] which contains not three houses, sends two members; and the town of Manchester, which contains upward of sixty thousand souls, is not admitted to send any. Is there any principle in these things? It is admitted that all this is altered, but there is much to be done yet, before we have a fair representation of the people. Is there anything

5. Old Sarum was the most notorious of the so-called rotten boroughs of eighteenth-century England. Defenders of the British government, including Edmund Burke, would argue that all the king's subjects were virtually represented in Parliament and that to demand instead local and direct representation would be to encourage a "narrow" and "partial" politics, rather than one built on a broader appreciation of public good.

by which you can trace the marks of freedom, or discover those of wisdom? No wonder then Mr. Burke has declined the comparison, and endeavored to lead his readers from the point by a wild, unsystematical display of paradoxical rhapsodies.

The French Constitution says that the National Assembly shall be elected every two years. What article will Mr. Burke place against this? Why, that the nation has no right at all in the case; that the government is perfectly arbitrary with respect to this point; and he can quote for his authority the precedent of a former Parliament.

The French Constitution says there shall be no game laws, that the farmer on whose lands wild game shall be found (for it is by the produce of his lands they are fed) shall have a right to what he can take; that there shall be no monopolies of any kind—that all trades shall be free and every man free to follow any occupation by which he can procure an honest livelihood, and in any place, town, or city throughout the nation. What will Mr. Burke say to this? In England, game is made the property of those at whose expense it is not fed; and with respect to monopolies, the country is cut up into monopolies. Every chartered town is an aristocratical monopoly in itself, and the qualification of electors proceeds out of those chartered monopolies. Is this freedom? Is this what Mr. Burke means by a constitution?

In these chartered monopolies, a man coming from another part of the country is hunted from them as if he were a foreign enemy. An Englishman is not free of his own country; every one of those places presents a barrier in his way, and tells him he is not a freeman—that he has no rights. Within these monopolies are other monopolies. In a city, such for instance as Bath, which contains between twenty and thirty thousand inhabitants, the right of electing representatives to Parliament is monopolised by about thirty-one persons. And within these monopolies are still others. A man even of the same town, whose parents were not in circumstances to give him an occupation, is debarred, in many cases, from the natural right of acquiring one, be his genius or industry what it may.[6]

Are these things examples to hold out to a country regenerating itself from slavery, like France? Certainly they are not, and certain am I, that when the people of England come to reflect upon them they will, like France, annihilate those badges of ancient oppression, those traces of a conquered nation. Had Mr. Burke possessed talents similar to the author of "On the Wealth of Nations," he would have

6. In decrying the various restrictions on residence and travel that covered the British countryside, Paine echoes Adam Smith's critique in *The Wealth of Nations*. To inhibit the movement of laborers from town to town, Smith argued, was an "evident violation of natural liberty and justice." This may explain Paine's reference to Smith two paragraphs later.

comprehended all the parts which enter into, and, by assemblage, form a constitution. He would have reasoned from minutiae to magnitude. It is not from his prejudices only, but from the disorderly cast of his genius, that he is unfitted for the subject he writes upon. Even his genius is without a constitution. It is a genius at random, and not a genius constituted. But he must say something. He has therefore mounted in the air like a balloon, to draw the eyes of the multitude from the ground they stand upon.

Much is to be learned from the French Constitution. Conquest and tyranny transplanted themselves with William the Conqueror from Normandy into England, and the country is yet disfigured with the marks. May, then, the example of all France contribute to regenerate the freedom which a province of it destroyed!

* * *

The French Constitution says, There shall be no titles; and, of consequence, all that class of equivocal generation which in some countries is called "aristocracy" and in others "nobility," is done away, and the peer is exalted into the MAN.

Titles are but nicknames, and every nickname is a title. The thing is perfectly harmless in itself, but it marks a sort of foppery in the human character, which degrades it. It reduces man into the diminutive of man in things which are great, and the counterfeit of women in things which are little. It talks about its fine blue ribbon like a girl, and shows its new garter like a child. A certain writer, of some antiquity, says: "When I was a child, I thought as a child; but when I became a man, I put away childish things."[7]

It is, properly, from the elevated mind of France that the folly of titles has fallen. It has outgrown the baby clothes of Count and Duke, and breeched itself in manhood. France has not levelled, it has exalted. It has put down the dwarf, to set up the man. The punyism of a senseless word like Duke, Count or Earl has ceased to please. Even those who possessed them have disowned the gibberish, and as they outgrew the rickets, have despised the rattle. The genuine mind of man, thirsting for its native home, society, contemns the gewgaws that separate him from it. Titles are like circles drawn by the magician's wand, to contract the sphere of man's felicity. He lives immured within the Bastille of a word, and surveys at a distance the envied life of man.

Is it, then, any wonder that titles should fall in France? Is it not a greater wonder that they should be kept up anywhere? What are they? What is their worth, and "what is their amount?" When we think or speak of a Judge or a General, we associate with it the ideas

7. 1 Corinthians 13:11.

of office and character; we think of gravity in one and bravery in the other; but when we use the word merely as a title, no ideas associate with it. Through all the vocabulary of Adam there is not such an animal as a Duke or a Count; neither can we connect any certain ideas with the words. Whether they mean strength or weakness, wisdom or folly, a child or a man, or the rider or the horse, is all equivocal. What respect then can be paid to that which describes nothing, and which means nothing? Imagination has given figure and character to centaurs, satyrs, and down to all the fairy tribe; but titles baffle even the powers of fancy, and are a chimerical nondescript.

But this is not all. If a whole country is disposed to hold them in contempt, all their value is gone, and none will own them. It is common opinion only that makes them anything, or nothing, or worse than nothing. There is no occasion to take titles away, for they take themselves away when society concurs to ridicule them. This species of imaginary consequence has visibly declined in every part of Europe, and it hastens to its exit as the world of reason continues to rise. There was a time when the lowest class of what are called nobility was more thought of than the highest is now, and when a man in armour riding throughout Christendom in quest of adventures was more stared at than a modern Duke. The world has seen this folly fall, and it has fallen by being laughed at, and the farce of titles will follow its fate. The patriots of France have discovered in good time that rank and dignity in society must take a new ground. The old one has fallen through. It must now take the substantial ground of character, instead of the chimerical ground of titles; and they have brought their titles to the altar, and made of them a burnt-offering to Reason.

If no mischief had annexed itself to the folly of titles they would not have been worth a serious and formal destruction, such as the National Assembly have decreed them; and this makes it necessary to enquire farther into the nature and character of aristocracy.

That, then, which is called aristocracy in some countries and nobility in others arose out of the governments founded upon conquest. It was originally a military order for the purpose of supporting military government (for such were all governments founded in conquest); and to keep up a succession of this order for the purpose for which it was established, all the younger branches of those families were disinherited and the law of primogenitureship set up.

The nature and character of aristocracy shows itself to us in this law. It is the law against every other law of nature, and Nature herself calls for its destruction. Establish family justice, and aristocracy falls. By the aristocratical law of primogenitureship, in a family of six children five are exposed. Aristocracy has never more than one child. The rest are begotten to be devoured. They are thrown to the cannibal for prey, and the natural parent prepares the unnatural repast.

As everything which is out of nature in man affects, more or less, the interest of society, so does this. All the children which the aristocracy disowns (which are all except the eldest) are, in general, cast like orphans on a parish, to be provided for by the public, but at a greater charge. Unnecessary offices and places in governments and courts are created at the expense of the public to maintain them.

With what kind of parental reflections can the father or mother contemplate their younger offspring? By nature they are children, and by marriage they are heirs; but by aristocracy they are bastards and orphans. They are the flesh and blood of their parents in the one line, and nothing akin to them in the other. To restore, therefore, parents to their children, and children to their parents—relations to each other, and man to society—and to exterminate the monster aristocracy, root and branch—the French Constitution has destroyed the law of PRIMOGENITURESHIP.[8] Here then lies the monster; and Mr. Burke, if he pleases, may write its epitaph.

Hitherto we have considered aristocracy chiefly in one point of view. We have now to consider it in another. But whether we view it before or behind, or sideways, or any way else, domestically or publicly, it is still a monster.

In France aristocracy had one feature less in its countenance than what it has in some other countries. It did not compose a body of hereditary legislators. It was not "a corporation of aristocracy," for such I have heard M. de la Fayette describe an English House of Peers. Let us then examine the grounds upon which the French Constitution has resolved against having such a House in France.

Because, in the first place, as is already mentioned, aristocracy is kept up by family tyranny and injustice.

Secondly. Because there is an unnatural unfitness in an aristocracy to be legislators for a nation. Their ideas of distributive justice are corrupted at the very source. They begin life by trampling on all their younger brothers and sisters, and relations of every kind, and are taught and educated so to do. With what ideas of justice or honour can that man enter a house of legislation, who absorbs in his own person the inheritance of a whole family of children or doles out to them some pitiful portion with the insolence of a gift?

8. In the new United States, ten of the thirteen original states revised their inheritance laws along the lines Paine suggests, abolishing primogeniture and double portions to firstborn sons in favor of equal partition to children. However, these reforms applied to only those who died intestate—that is, without making a will. Any father who wanted to favor or punish certain children retained the power to do so by spelling out his wishes in a will. By contrast, French radicals briefly forced changes in the nation's civil code that compelled equal inheritance and liberalized divorce laws. The Napoleonic Code rescinded such experiments in 1804.

Thirdly. Because the idea of hereditary legislators is as inconsistent as that of hereditary judges, or hereditary juries; and as absurd as an hereditary mathematician, or an hereditary wise man; and as ridiculous as an hereditary poet laureate.

Fourthly. Because a body of men, holding themselves accountable to nobody, ought not to be trusted by anybody.

Fifthly. Because it is continuing the uncivilised principle of governments founded in conquest, and the base idea of man having property in man, and governing him by personal right.

Sixthly. Because aristocracy has a tendency to deteriorate the human species. By the universal economy of nature it is known, and by the instance of the Jews it is proved, that the human species has a tendency to degenerate, in any small number of persons, when separated from the general stock of society, and inter-marrying constantly with each other. It defeats even its pretended end, and becomes in time the opposite of what is noble in man. Mr. Burke talks of nobility; let him show what it is. The greatest characters the world have known have arisen on the democratic floor. Aristocracy has not been able to keep a proportionate pace with democracy. The artificial NOBLE shrinks into a dwarf before the NOBLE of Nature; and in the few instances of those (for there are some in all countries) in whom nature, as by a miracle, has survived in aristocracy, THOSE MEN DESPISE IT.—But it is time to proceed to a new subject.

※　※　※

All religions are in their nature kind and benign, and united with principles of morality. They could not have made proselytes at first by professing anything that was vicious, cruel, persecuting, or immoral. Like everything else, they had their beginning; and they proceeded by persuasion, exhortation, and example. How then is it that they lose their native mildness, and become morose and intolerant?

It proceeds from the connection which Mr. Burke recommends. By engendering the church with the state, a sort of mule-animal, capable only of destroying, and not of breeding up, is produced, called the Church established by Law. It is a stranger, even from its birth, to any parent mother, on whom it is begotten, and whom in time it kicks out and destroys.

The inquisition in Spain does not proceed from the religion originally professed, but from this mule-animal, engendered between the church and the state. The burnings in Smithfield proceeded from the same heterogeneous production; and it was the regeneration of this strange animal in England afterwards, that renewed rancour and irreligion among the inhabitants, and that drove the people called Quakers and Dissenters to America. Persecution is not an original feature in any religion; but it is alway the strongly-marked feature of all law-religions, or religions established by law. Take away the law-establishment, and every religion re-assumes its original benignity. In America, a catholic priest is a good citizen, a good character, and a good neighbour; an episcopalian minister is of the same description: and this proceeds independently of the men, from there being no law-establishment in America.

If also we view this matter in a temporal sense, we shall see the ill effects it has had on the prosperity of nations. The union of church and state has impoverished Spain. The revoking the edict of Nantes[9] drove the silk manufacture from that country into England; and church and state are now driving the cotton manufacture from England to America and France. Let then Mr. Burke continue to preach his antipolitical doctrine of Church and State. It will do some good. The National Assembly will not follow his advice, but will benefit by his folly. It was by observing the ill effects of it in England, that America has been warned against it; and it is by experiencing them in France, that the National Assembly have abolished it, and, like America, have established UNIVERSAL RIGHT OF CONSCIENCE, AND UNIVERSAL RIGHT OF CITIZENSHIP.

* * *

Conclusion

Reason and Ignorance, the opposites of each other, influence the great bulk of mankind. If either of these can be rendered sufficiently extensive in a country, the machinery of Government goes easily on. Reason obeys itself; and Ignorance submits to whatever is dictated to it.

The two modes of the Government which prevail in the world, are—

First, Government by election and representation.

Secondly, Government by hereditary succession.

The former is generally known by the name of republic; the latter by that of monarchy and aristocracy.

Those two distinct and opposite forms erect themselves on the two distinct and opposite bases of Reason and Ignorance.—As the exercise of Government requires talents and abilities, and as talents and abilities cannot have hereditary descent, it is evident that

9. In 1685, by King Louis XIV. The edict (1598) had granted toleration to the *religion prétendue réformée*: Protestant Christianity. This prompted a large movement of French Protestants, known as Huguenots, to North America, notably to the Carolinas. Paine likens this to the movement of English Puritans—among the least tolerant sectarians in Christendom—to North America earlier in the seventeenth century.

hereditary succession requires a belief from man to which his reason cannot subscribe, and which can only be established upon his ignorance; and the more ignorant any country is, the better it is fitted for this species of Government.

On the contrary, Government, in a well-constituted republic, requires no belief from man beyond what his reason can give. He sees the rationale of the whole system, its origin and its operation; and as it is best supported when best understood, the human faculties act with boldness, and acquire, under this form of government, a gigantic manliness.

As, therefore, each of those forms acts on a different base, the one moving freely by the aid of reason, the other by ignorance; we have next to consider, what it is that gives motion to that species of Government which is called mixed Government, or, as it is sometimes ludicrously styled, a Government of this, that and t' other.

The moving power in this species of Government is, of necessity, Corruption. However imperfect election and representation may be in mixed Governments, they still give exercise to a greater portion of reason than is convenient to the hereditary Part; and therefore it becomes necessary to buy the reason up. A mixed Government is an imperfect everything, cementing and soldering the discordant parts together by corruption, to act as a whole. Mr. Burke appears highly disgusted that France, since she had resolved on a revolution, did not adopt what he calls "A British Constitution"; and the regretful manner in which he expresses himself on this occasion implies a suspicion that the British Constitution needed something to keep its defects in countenance.

In mixed Governments there is no responsibility: the parts cover each other till responsibility is lost; and the corruption which moves the machine, contrives at the same time its own escape. When it is laid down as a maxim, that a King can do no wrong, it places him in a state of similar security with that of idiots and persons insane, and responsibility is out of the question with respect to himself. It then descends upon the Minister, who shelters himself under a majority in Parliament, which, by places, pensions, and corruption, he can always command; and that majority justifies itself by the same authority with which it protects the Minister. In this rotatory motion, responsibility is thrown off from the parts, and from the whole.

When there is a Part in a Government which can do no wrong, it implies that it does nothing; and is only the machine of another power, by whose advice and direction it acts. What is supposed to be the King in the mixed Governments, is the Cabinet; and as the Cabinet is always a part of the Parliament, and the members justifying in one character what they advise and act in another, a mixed Government becomes a continual enigma; entailing upon a country by the quantity of corruption necessary to solder the parts, the expense of supporting all the forms of government at once, and finally resolving itself into a Government by Committee; in which the advisers, the actors, the approvers, the justifiers, the persons responsible, and the persons not responsible, are the same persons.

By this pantomimical contrivance, and change of scene and character, the parts help each other out in matters which neither of them singly would assume to act. When money is to be obtained, the mass of variety apparently dissolves, and a profusion of parliamentary praises passes between the parts. Each admires with astonishment, the wisdom, the liberality, the disinterestedness of the other: and all of them breathe a pitying sigh at the burthens of the Nation.

But in a well-constituted republic, nothing of this soldering, praising, and pitying, can take place; the representation being equal throughout the country, and complete in itself, however it may be arranged into legislative and executive, they have all one and the same natural source. The parts are not foreigners to each other, like democracy, aristocracy, and monarchy. As there are no discordant distinctions, there is nothing to corrupt by compromise, nor confound by contrivance. Public measures appeal of themselves to the understanding of the Nation, and, resting on their own merits, disown any flattering applications to vanity. The continual whine of lamenting the burden of taxes, however successfully it may be practised in mixed Governments, is inconsistent with the sense and spirit of a republic. If taxes are necessary, they are of course advantageous; but if they require an apology, the apology itself implies an impeachment. Why, then, is man thus imposed upon, or why does he impose upon himself?

When men are spoken of as kings and subjects, or when Government is mentioned under the distinct and combined heads of monarchy, aristocracy, and democracy, what is it that reasoning man is to understand by the terms? If there really existed in the world two or more distinct and separate elements of human power, we should then see the several origins to which those terms would descriptively apply; but as there is but one species of man, there can be but one element of human power; and that element is man himself. Monarchy, aristocracy, and democracy, are but creatures of imagination; and a thousand such may be contrived as well as three.

From the Revolutions of America and France, and the symptoms that have appeared in other countries, it is evident that the opinion of the world is changing with respect to systems of Government, and that revolutions are not within the compass of political calculations.

The progress of time and circumstances, which men assign to the accomplishment of great changes, is too mechanical to measure the force of the mind, and the rapidity of reflection, by which revolutions are generated: All the old governments have received a shock from those that already appear, and which were once more improbable, and are a greater subject of wonder, than a general revolution in Europe would be now.

When we survey the wretched condition of man, under the monarchical and hereditary systems of Government, dragged from his home by one power, or driven by another, and impoverished by taxes more than by enemies, it becomes evident that those systems are bad, and that a general revolution in the principle and construction of Governments is necessary.

What is government more than the management of the affairs of a Nation? It is not, and from its nature cannot be, the property of any particular man or family, but of the whole community, at whose expense it is supported; and though by force and contrivance it has been usurped into an inheritance, the usurpation cannot alter the right of things. Sovereignty, as a matter of right, appertains to the Nation only, and not to any individual; and a Nation has at all times an inherent indefeasible right to abolish any form of Government it finds inconvenient, and to establish such as accords with its interest, disposition and happiness. The romantic and barbarous distinction of men into Kings and subjects, though it may suit the condition of courtiers, cannot that of citizens; and is exploded by the principle upon which Governments are now founded. Every citizen is a member of the Sovereignty, and, as such, can acknowledge no personal subjection; and his obedience can be only to the laws.

When men think of what Government is, they must necessarily suppose it to possess a knowledge of all the objects and matters upon which its authority is to be exercised. In this view of Government, the republican system, as established by America and France, operates to embrace the whole of a Nation; and the knowledge necessary to the interest of all the parts, is to be found in the center, which the parts by representation form: But the old Governments are on a construction that excludes knowledge as well as happiness; government by Monks, who knew nothing of the world beyond the walls of a Convent, is as consistent as government by Kings.

What were formerly called Revolutions, were little more than a change of persons, or an alteration of local circumstances. They rose and fell like things of course, and had nothing in their existence or their fate that could influence beyond the spot that produced them. But what we now see in the world, from the Revolutions of America and France, are a renovation of the natural order of things, a system of principles as universal as truth and the existence of man, and combining moral with political happiness and national prosperity.

> "I. Men are born, and always continue, free and equal in respect of their rights. Civil distinctions, therefore, can be founded only on public utility.
>
> "II. The end of all political associations is the preservation of the natural and imprescriptible rights of man; and these rights are liberty, property, security, and resistance of oppression.
>
> "III. The nation is essentially the source of all sovereignty; nor can any INDIVIDUAL, or ANY BODY OF MEN, be entitled to any authority which is not expressly derived from it."

In these principles, there is nothing to throw a Nation into confusion by inflaming ambition. They are calculated to call forth wisdom and abilities, and to exercise them for the public good, and not for the emolument or aggrandisement of particular descriptions of men or families. Monarchical sovereignty, the enemy of mankind, and the source of misery, is abolished; and the sovereignty itself is restored to its natural and original place, the Nation. Were this the case throughout Europe, the cause of wars would be taken away.

It is attributed to Henry the Fourth of France, a man of enlarged and benevolent heart, that he proposed, about the year 1610, a plan for abolishing war in Europe. The plan consisted in constituting an European Congress, or as the French authors style it, a Pacific Republic; by appointing delegates from the several Nations who were to act as a Court of arbitration in any disputes that might arise between nation and nation.

Had such a plan been adopted at the time it was proposed, the taxes of England and France, as two of the parties, would have been at least ten millions sterling annually to each Nation less than they were at the commencement of the French Revolution.

To conceive a cause why such a plan has not been adopted (and that instead of a Congress for the purpose of preventing war, it has been called only to terminate a war, after a fruitless expense of several years) it will be necessary to consider the interest of Governments as a distinct interest to that of Nations.

Whatever is the cause of taxes to a Nation, becomes also the means of revenue to Government. Every war terminates with an addition of taxes, and consequently with an addition of revenue; and in any event of war, in the manner they are now commenced and concluded, the power and interest of Governments are increased. War, therefore, from its productiveness, as it easily furnishes the pretence of necessity for taxes and appointments to places and offices, becomes a principal part of the system of old Governments; and to establish any mode to abolish war, however advantageous it might be to Nations, would be to take from such Government the most lucrative of its branches. The frivolous matters upon which war is made, show the disposition and avidity of Governments to uphold the system of war, and betray the motives upon which they act.

Why are not Republics plunged into war, but because the nature of their Government does not admit of an interest distinct from that of the Nation? Even Holland, though an ill-constructed Republic, and with a commerce extending over the world, existed nearly a century without war: and the instant the form of Government was changed in France, the republican principles of peace and domestic prosperity and economy arose with the new Government; and the same consequences would follow the cause in other Nations.

As war is the system of Government on the old construction, the animosity which Nations reciprocally entertain, is nothing more than what the policy of their Governments excites to keep up the spirit of the system. Each Government accuses the other of perfidy, intrigue, and ambition, as a means of heating the imagination of their respective Nations, and incensing them to hostilities. Man is not the enemy of man, but through the medium of a false system of Government. Instead, therefore, of exclaiming against the ambition of Kings, the exclamation should be directed against the principle of such Governments; and instead of seeking to reform the individual, the wisdom of a Nation should apply itself to reform the system.

Whether the forms and maxims of Governments which are still in practice, were adapted to the condition of the world at the period they were established, is not in this case the question. The older they are, the less correspondence can they have with the present state of things. Time, and change of circumstances and opinions, have the same progressive effect in rendering modes of Government obsolete as they have upon customs and manners.—Agriculture, commerce, manufactures, and the tranquil arts, by which the prosperity of Nations is best promoted, require a different system of Government, and a different species of knowledge to direct its operations, than what might have been required in the former condition of the world.

As it is not difficult to perceive, from the enlightened state of mankind, that hereditary Governments are verging to their decline, and that Revolutions on the broad basis of national sovereignty and Government by representation, are making their way in Europe, it would be an act of wisdom to anticipate their approach, and produce Revolutions by reason and accommodation, rather than commit them to the issue of convulsions.

From what we now see, nothing of reform in the political world ought to be held improbable. It is an age of Revolutions, in which everything may be looked for. The intrigue of Courts, by which the system of war is kept up, may provoke a confederation of Nations to abolish it: and an European Congress to patronise the progress of free Government, and promote the civilisation of Nations with each other, is an event nearer in probability, than once were the revolutions and alliance of France and America.

Reasons for Preserving the Life of Louis Capet

[*As Delivered to the National Convention*] *January 15, 1793*

Citizen President,

My hatred and abhorrence of monarchy are sufficiently known: they originate in principles of reason and conviction, nor, except with life, can they ever be extirpated; but my compassion for the unfortunate, whether friend or enemy, is equally lively and sincere.

I voted that Louis should be tried, because it was necessary to afford proofs to the world of the perfidy, corruption, and abomination of the monarchical system. The infinity of evidence that has been produced exposes them in the most glaring and hideous colours; thence it results that monarchy, whatever form it may assume, arbitrary or otherwise, becomes necessarily a centre round which are united every species of corruption, and the kingly trade is no less destructive of all morality in the human breast, than the trade of an executioner is destructive of its sensibility. I remember, during my residence in another country, that I was exceedingly struck with a sentence of M. Autheine, at the Jacobins [Club], which corresponds exactly with my own idea,—"Make me a king to-day," said he, "and I shall be a robber to-morrow."

Nevertheless, I am inclined to believe that if Louis Capet had been born in obscure condition, had he lived within the circle of an amiable and respectable neighbourhood, at liberty to practice the duties of domestic life, had he been thus situated, I cannot believe that he would have shewn himself destitute of social virtues: we are, in a moment of fermentation like this, naturally little indulgent to his vices, or rather to those of his government; we regard them with additional horror and indignation; not that they are more heinous than those of his predecessors, but because our eyes are now open, and the veil of delusion at length withdrawn; yet the lamentable, degraded state to which he is actually reduced, is surely far less imputable to him than to the Constituent Assembly, which, of its own authority, without consent or advice of the people, restored him to the throne.

I was in Paris at the time of the flight, or abdication of Louis XVI., and when he was taken and brought back.[1] The proposal of restoring him to supreme power struck me with amazement; and although at that time I was not a French citizen, yet as a citizen of the world I employed all the efforts that depended on me to prevent it.

A small society, composed only of five persons,[2] two of whom are now members of the Convention, took at that time the name of the Republican Club (Société Républicaine). This society opposed the restoration of Louis, not so much on account of his personal offences, as in order to overthrow the monarchy, and to erect on its ruins the republican system and an equal representation.

With this design, I traced out in the English language certain propositions, which were translated with some trifling alterations, and signed by Achille Duchâtelet, now Lieutenant-General in the army of the French republic, and at that time one of the five members which composed our little party: the law requiring the signature of a citizen at the bottom of each printed paper.[3]

The paper was indignantly torn by Malouet; and brought forth in this very room as an article of accusation against the person who had signed it, the author and their adherents; but such is the revolution of events, that this paper is now received and brought forth for a very opposite purpose—to remind the nation of the errors of that unfortunate day, that fatal error of not having then banished Louis XVI. from its bosom, and to plead this day in favour of his exile, preferable to his death.

The paper in question, was conceived in the following terms:

[*Paine refers here to a proclamation he wrote in 1791 to denounce Louis XVI's attempted escape from France and to call for an end to the French monarchy.*]

Having thus explained the principles and the exertions of the republicans at that fatal period, when Louis was reinstated in full possession of the executive power which by his flight had been suspended, I return to the subject, and to the deplorable situation in which the man is now actually involved.

What was neglected at the time of which I have been speaking, has been since brought about by the force of necessity. The wilful, treacherous defects in the former constitution have been brought

---

1. On October 5, 1789, a large Parisian crowd led by women marched ten miles to Versailles, where Louis XVI and his family were protected by hired Flemish soldiers. The following day, after the crowd had forced itself inside the palace gates and killed three guards, the king and queen returned with the populace and the new National Guard to Paris. There, the king accepted the Declaration of the Rights of Man.
2. In addition to Paine, this society consisted of Condorcet and Achille Duchâtelet, and perhaps also Nicolas de Bonneville and Lanthenas.
3. For the first reprinting of this speech and the one that followed four days later, see Moncure Daniel Conway, *The Writings of Thomas Paine* (New York, 1908), III:119–27.

to light; the continual alarm of treason and conspiracy aroused the nation, and produced eventually a second revolution. The people have beat down royalty, never, never to rise again; they have brought Louis Capet to the bar, and demonstrated in the face of the whole world, the intrigues, the cabals, the falsehood, corruption, and rooted depravity, the inevitable effects of monarchical government. There remains then only one question to be considered, what is to be done with this man?

For myself I seriously confess, that when I reflect on the unaccountable folly that restored the executive power to his hands, all covered as he was with perjuries and treason, I am far more ready to condemn the Constituent Assembly than the unfortunate prisoner Louis Capet.

But abstracted from every other consideration, there is one circumstance in his life which ought to cover or at least to palliate a great number of his transgressions, and this very circumstance affords to the French nation a blessed occasion of extricating itself from the yoke of kings, without defiling itself in the impurities of their blood.

It is to France alone, I know, that the United States of America owe that support which enabled them to shake off the unjust and tyrannical yoke of Britain. The ardour and zeal which she displayed to provide both men and money, were the natural consequence of a thirst for liberty. But as the nation at that time, restrained by the shackles of her own government, could only act by the means of a monarchical organ, this organ—whatever in other respects the object might be—certainly performed a good, a great action.

Let then those United States be the safeguard and asylum of Louis Capet. There, hereafter, far removed from the miseries and crimes of royalty, he may learn, from the constant aspect of public prosperity, that the true system of government consists not in kings, but in fair, equal, and honourable representation.

In relating this circumstance, and in submitting this proposition, I consider myself as a citizen of both countries. I submit it as a citizen of America, who feels the debt of gratitude which he owes to every Frenchman. I submit it also as a man, who, although the enemy of kings, cannot forget that they are subject to human frailties. I support my proposition as a citizen of the French republic, because it appears to me the best, the most politic measure that can be adopted.

As far as my experience in public life extends, I have ever observed, that the great mass of the people are invariably just, both in their intentions and in their objects; but the true method of accomplishing an effect does not always shew itself in the first instance. For example: the English nation had groaned under the despotism of the Stuarts. Hence Charles I. lost his life; yet Charles II. was restored to all the plenitude of power, which his father had lost. Forty years had not expired when the same family strove to reestablish their ancient oppression; so the nation then banished from its territories the whole race. The remedy was effectual. The Stuart family sank into obscurity, confounded itself with the multitude, and is at length extinct.

The French nation has carried her measures of government to a greater length. France is not satisfied with exposing the guilt of the monarch. She has penetrated into the vices and horrors of the monarchy. She has shown them clear as daylight, and forever crushed that system; and he, whoever he may be, that should ever dare to reclaim those rights would be regarded not as a pretender, but punished as a traitor.

Two brothers of Louis Capet have banished themselves from the country;[4] but they are obliged to comply with the spirit and etiquette of the courts where they reside. They can advance no pretensions on their own account, so long as Louis Capet shall live.

Monarchy, in France, was a system pregnant with crime and murders, cancelling all natural ties, even those by which brothers are united. We know how often they have assassinated each other to pave a way to power. As those hopes which the emigrants had reposed in Louis XVI are fled, the last that remains rests upon his death, and their situation inclines them to desire this catastrophe, that they may once again rally around a more active chief, and try one further effort under the fortune of the ci-devant Monsieur and d'Artois. That such an enterprize would precipitate them into a new abyss of calamity and disgrace, it is not difficult to foresee; yet it might be attended with mutual loss, and it is our duty as legislators not to spill a drop of blood when our purpose may be effectually accomplished without it.

It has already been proposed to abolish the punishment of death,[5] and it is with infinite satisfaction that I recollect the humane and excellent oration pronounced by Robespierre on that subject in the Constituent Assembly. This cause must find its advocates in every corner where enlightened politicians and lovers of humanity exist, and it ought above all to find them in this assembly.

Monarchical governments have trained the human race, and inured it to the sanguinary arts and refinements of punishment; and it is exactly the same punishment which has so long shocked the sight and tormented the patience of the people, that now, in their

---

4. Louis's younger brother, the hated compte d'Artois, led the first group of émigrés out of France shortly after the fall of the Bastille in July 1789.

5. Paine's opposition to capital punishment was shared only by Enlightenment radicals and certain religious groups, most notably the Quakers. Such ideas found expression in the new state of Pennsylvania, which banned the death penalty for all but homicide.

turn, they practice in revenge upon their oppressors. But it becomes us to be strictly on our guard against the abomination and perversity of monarchical examples: as France has been the first of European nations to abolish royalty, let her also be the first to abolish the punishment of death, and to find out a milder and more effectual substitute.

In the particular case now under consideration, I submit the following propositions: 1st, That the National Convention shall pronounce sentence of banishment on Louis and his family. 2d, That Louis Capet shall be detained in prison till the end of the war, and at that epoch the sentence of banishment to be executed.

Shall Louis XVI Have Respite?

[Speech in the Convention], January 19, 1793

[READ IN FRENCH BY DEPUTY BANCAL]

Very sincerely do I regret the Convention's vote of yesterday for death.

MARAT [*interrupting*]   I submit that Thomas Paine is incompetent to vote on this question; being a Quaker his religious principles are opposed to capital punishment. [*Much confusion, quieted by cries for "freedom of speech," on which Bancal proceeds with Paine's speech.*]

I have the advantage of some experience; it is near twenty years that I have been engaged in the cause of liberty, having contributed something to it in the revolution of the United States of America. My language has always been that of liberty *and* humanity, and I know that nothing so exalts a nation as the union of these two principles, l under all circumstances. I know that the public mind of France, and particularly that of Paris, has been heated and irritated by the dangers to which they have been exposed; but could we carry our thoughts into the future, when the dangers are ended and the irritations forgotten, what to-day seems an act of justice may then appear an act of vengeance. [*Murmurs.*] My anxiety for the cause of France has become for the moment concern for her honor. If, on my return to America, I should employ myself on a history of the French Revolution, I had rather record a thousand errors on the side of mercy, than be obliged to tell one act of severe justice. I voted against an appeal to the people, because it appeared to me that the Convention was needlessly wearied on that point; but I so voted in the hope that this Assembly would pronounce against death, and for the same punishment that the nation would have voted, at least in my opinion, that is for reclusion during the war, and banishment thereafter. That is the punishment most efficacious, because it includes the whole family at once, and none other can so operate. I am still against the appeal to the primary assemblies, because there is a better method. This Convention has been elected to form a Constitution, which will be submitted to the primary assemblies. After its acceptance a necessary consequence will be an election and another assembly. We cannot suppose that the present Convention will last more than five or six months. The choice of new deputies will express the national opinion, on the propriety or impropriety of your sentence, with as much efficacy as if those primary assemblies had been consulted on it. As the duration of our functions here cannot be long, it is a part of our duty to consider the interests of those who shall replace us. If by any act of ours the number of the nation's enemies shall be needlessly increased, and that of its friends diminished,—at a time when the finances may be more strained than to-day,—we should not be justifiable for having thus unnecessarily heaped obstacles in the path of our successors. Let us therefore not be precipitate in our decisions.

France has but one ally—the United States of America. That is the only nation that can furnish France with naval provisions, for the kingdoms of northern Europe are, or soon will be, at war with her. It unfortunately happens that the person now under discussion is considered by the Americans as having been the friend of their revolution. His execution will be an affliction to them, and it is in your power not to wound the feelings of your ally. Could I speak the French language I would descend to your bar, and in their name become your petitioner to respite the execution of the sentence on Louis.

THURIOT   This is not the language of Thomas Paine.

MARAT   I denounce the interpreter. I maintain that it is not Thomas Paine's opinion. It is an untrue translation.[1]

GARRAN   I have read the original, and the translation is correct.

> *[Prolonged uproar.* PAINE, *still standing in the tribune beside his interpreter, Deputy Bancal, declared the sentiments to be his.]*

Your Executive Committee will nominate an ambassador to Philadelphia; my sincere wish is that he may announce to America that the National Convention of France, out of pure friendship to America, has consented to respite Louis. That people, by my vote, ask you to delay the execution.

Ah, citizens, give not the tyrant of England the triumph of seeing the man perish on the scaffold who had aided my much-loved America to break his chains!

---

1. According to Conway, who in turn relied on early histories of the French Revolution, Paine's speech was having a major effect on the delegates, and Marat interrupted in order to stop any possible swing in opinion.

MARAT [*"launching himself into the middle of the hall"*] Paine voted against the punishment of death because he is a Quaker.

PAINE   I voted against it from both moral motives and motives of public policy.

Agrarian Justice

[*Written 1795–96, First Published in French and English in 1797*]

Author's Inscription

To the Legislature and the Executive Directory of the French Republic.

The plan contained in this work is not adapted for any particular country alone: the principle on which it is based is general. But as the rights of man are a new study in this world, and one needing protection from priestly imposture, and the insolence of oppression too long established, I have thought it right to place this little work under your safeguard. When we reflect on the long and dense night in which France and all Europe have remained plunged by their governments and their priests, we must feel less surprise than grief at the bewilderment caused by the first burst of light that dispels the darkness. The eye accustomed to darkness can hardly bear at first the broad daylight. It is by usage the eye learns to see, and it is the same in passing from any situation to its opposite.

As we have not at one instant renounced all our errors, we cannot at one stroke acquire knowledge of all our rights. France has had the honour of adding to the word *Liberty* that of *Equality*; and this word signifies essentially a principal that admits of no gradation in the things to which it applies. But equality is often misunderstood, often misapplied, and often violated.

Liberty and Property are words expressing all those of our possessions which are not of an intellectual nature. There are two kinds of property. Firstly, natural property, or that which comes to us from the Creator of the universe,—such as the earth, air, water. Secondly, artificial or acquired property,—the invention of men. In the latter equality is impossible; for to distribute it equally it would be necessary that all should have contributed in the same proportion, which can never be the case; and this being the case, every individual would hold on to his own property, as his right share. Equality of natural property is the subject of this little essay. Every individual in the world is born therein with legitimate claims on a certain kind of property, or its equivalent.

The right of voting for persons charged with the execution of the laws that govern society is inherent in the word Liberty, and constitutes the equality of personal rights. But even if that right (of voting) were inherent in property, which I deny, the right of suffrage would still belong to all equally, because, as I have said, all individuals have legitimate birthrights in a certain species of property.

I have always considered the present Constitution of the French Republic the *best organized system* the human mind has yet produced. But I hope my former colleagues will not be offended if I warn them of an error which has slipped into its principle. Equality of the right of suffrage is not maintained. This right is in it connected with a condition on which it ought not to depend; that is, with a proportion of a certain tax called "direct." The dignity of suffrage is thus lowered; and, in placing it in the scale with an inferior thing, the enthusiasm that right is capable of inspiring is diminished. It is impossible to find any equivalent counterpoise for the right of suffrage, because it is alone worthy to be its own basis, and cannot thrive as a graft, or an appendage.

Since the Constitution was established we have seen two conspiracies stranded,—that of Babeuf,[1] and that of some obscure personages who decorate themselves with the despicable name of "royalists." The defect in principle of the Constitution was the origin of Babeuf's conspiracy. He availed himself of the resentment caused by this flaw, and instead of seeking a remedy by legitimate and constitutional means, or proposing some measure useful to society, the conspirators did their best to renew disorder and confusion, and constituted themselves personally into a Directory, which is formally destructive of election and representation. They were, in fine, extravagant enough to suppose that society, occupied with its domestic affairs, would blindly yield to them a directorship usurped by violence.

The conspiracy of Babeuf was followed in a few months by that of the royalists, who foolishly flattered themselves with the notion of doing great things by feeble or foul means. They counted on all

---

1. François-Émile Babeuf (1760–1797) emerged as a radical revolutionary in Paris during the Terror of 1793–94. When the more conservative Directory assumed control of France in 1795, Babeuf was among its most strident critics. During 1796 he called for the seizure of all public and private lands in the name of the people, insisting that the purpose of the Revolution was "to destroy inequality." Executed in 1797, he represents the extreme, protocommunist margin of French politics during the 1790s. Paine was far too committed to individual liberty to tolerate such ideas. At the same time, he also feared the growing power of monarchists and conservatives. Napoleon Bonaparte settled the matter when he took control of France in November 1799.

the discontented, from whatever cause, and tried to rouse, in their turn, the class of people who had been following the others. But these new chiefs acted as if they thought society had nothing more at heart than to maintain courtiers, pensioners, and all their train, under the contemptible title of royalty. My little essay will disabuse them, by showing that society is aiming at a very different end,— maintaining itself.

We all know or should know, that the time during which a revolution is proceeding is not the time when its resulting advantages can be enjoyed. But had Babeuf and his accomplices taken into consideration the condition of France under this constitution, and compared it with what it was under the tragical revolutionary government, and during the execrable reign of Terror, the rapidity of the alteration must have appeared to them very striking and astonishing. Famine has been replaced by abundance, and by the well-founded hope of a near and increasing prosperity.

As for the defect in the Constitution, I am fully convinced that it will be rectified constitutionally, and that this step is indispensable; for so long as it continues it will inspire the hopes and furnish the means of conspirators; and for the rest, it is regrettable that a Constitution so wisely organized should err so much in its principle. This fault exposes it to other dangers which will make themselves felt. Intriguing candidates will go about among those who have not the means to pay the direct tax and pay it for them, on condition of receiving their votes. Let us maintain inviolably equality in the sacred right of suffrage: public security can never have a basis more solid.

Salut et Fraternité.
Your former colleague,
THOMAS PAINE.

Author's English Preface

The following little Piece was written in the winter of 1795 and 96; and, as I had not determined whether to publish it during the present war, or to wait till the commencement of a peace, it has lain by me, without alteration or addition, from the time it was written.

What has determined me to publish it now is, a sermon preached by Watson, *Bishop of Llandaff*. Some of my Readers will recollect, that this Bishop wrote a Book entitled *An Apology for the Bible*, in answer to my *Second Part of the Age of Reason*. I procured a copy of his Book, and he may depend upon hearing from me on that subject.

At the end of the Bishop's Book is a List of the Works he has written. Among which is the sermon alluded to; it is entitled: "The Wisdom and Goodness of God, in having made both Rich and Poor; with an Appendix, containing Reflections on the Present State of England and France."

The error contained in this sermon determined me to publish my AGRARIAN JUSTICE. It is wrong to say God made *rich* and *poor*; he made only *male* and *female*; and he gave them the earth for their inheritance.

Instead of preaching to encourage one part of mankind in insolence . . . it would be better that Priests employed their time to render the general condition of man less miserable than it is. Practical religion consists in doing good: and the only way of serving God is, that of endeavouring to make his creation happy. All preaching that has not this for its object is nonsense and hypocracy.

THOMAS PAINE.

Agrarian Justice

To preserve the benefits of what is called civilized life, and to remedy at the same time the evil which it has produced ought to be considered as one of the first objects of reformed legislation.

Whether that state that is proudly, perhaps erroneously, called civilization, has most promoted or most injured the general happiness of man, is a question that may be strongly contested. On one side, the spectator is dazzled by splendid appearances; on the other, he is shocked by extremes of wretchedness; both of which it has erected. The most affluent and the most miserable of the human race are to be found in the countries that are called civilized.

To understand what the state of society ought to be, it is necessary to have some idea of the natural and primitive state of man; such as it is at this day among the Indians of North America.[2] There is not, in that state, any of those spectacles of human misery which poverty and want present to our eyes in all the towns and streets in Europe. Poverty therefore, is a thing created by that which is called civilized life. It exists not in the natural state. On the other hand, the natural state is without those advantages which flow from agriculture, arts, science, and manufactures.

The life of an Indian is a continual holiday, compared with the poor of Europe; and, on the other hand it appears to be abject when

2. For much of his career, Paine showed little interest in or sympathy for the native peoples of North America, except insofar as he accused them of frontier massacres at the behest of Britain. Here he repeats a common eighteenth-century view of Indians as "natural" people and anticipates the nineteenth-century trope of the "noble savage."

compared to the rich. Civilization therefore, or that which is so called, has operated two ways to make one part of society more affluent, and the other more wretched, than would have been the lot of either in a natural state.

It is always possible to go from the natural to the civilized state, but it is never possible to go from the civilized to the natural state. The reason is, that man in a natural state, subsisting by hunting, requires ten times the quantity of land to range over to procure himself sustenance, than would support him in a civilized state, where the earth is cultivated. When, therefore, a country becomes populous by the additional aids of cultivation, art, and science, there is a necessity of preserving things in that state; because without it there cannot be sustenance for more, perhaps, than a tenth part of its inhabitants.[3] The thing, therefore, now to be done is to remedy the evils and preserve the benefits that have arisen to society by passing from the natural to that which is called the civilized state.

In taking the matter upon this ground, the first principle of civilization ought to have been, and ought still to be, that the condition of every person born into the world, after a state of civilization commences, ought not to be worse than if he had been born before that period. But the fact is, that the condition of millions, in every country in Europe, is far worse than if they had been born before civilization began, or had been born among the Indians of North-America at the present day. I will shew how this fact has happened.

It is a position not to be controverted that the earth, in its natural uncultivated state was, and ever would have continued to be, *the common property of the human race*. In that state every man would have been born to property. He would have been a joint life proprietor with the rest in the property of the soil, and in all its natural productions, vegetable and animal.[4]

But the earth in its natural state, as before said, is capable of supporting but a small number of inhabitants compared with what it is capable of doing in a cultivated state. And as it is impossible to separate the improvement made by cultivation from the earth itself, upon which that improvement is made, the idea of landed property arose from that inseparable connection; but it is nevertheless true,

---

3. This is the same rationale that John Locke, Emmerich Vattel, and many others used to justify the seizure of aboriginal lands: those who did not farm the earth did not truly occupy or productively use it and, therefore, should give way to those who did.

4. These lines echo a radical strain of English thought that dates back to the seventeenth century and before, when peasants and rural laborers were driven out of common lands and pastures. During the English Revolution and Civil War (1630–48), Gerrard Winstanly, a leader of the radical Diggers, declared: "In the beginning of time the great Creator, Reason, made the earth to be a common treasury. . . . The poorest man hath as true a title and just right to the land as the richest man. . . . True freedom lies in the free enjoyment of the earth."

that it is the value of the improvement only, and not the earth itself, that is individual property. Every proprietor, therefore, of cultivated land, owes to the community a *groundrent* (for I know of no better term to express the idea) for the land which he holds; and it is from this groundrent that the fund proposed in this plan is to issue.

It is deducible, as well from the nature of the thing as from all the histories transmitted to us, that the idea of landed property commenced with cultivation, and that there was no such thing as landed property before that time. It could not exist in the first state of man, that of hunters. It did not exist in the second state, that of shepherds: neither Abraham, Isaac, Jacob, nor Job, so far as the history of the Bible may be credited in probable things, were owners of land.[5] Their property consisted, as is always enumerated, in flocks and herds, and they travelled with them from place to place. The frequent contentions at that time, about the use of a well in the dry country of Arabia, where those people lived, also shew that there was no landed property. It was not admitted that land could be claimed as property.

There could be no such thing as landed property originally. Man did not make the earth, and, though he had a natural right to *occupy* it, he had no right to *locate as his property* in perpetuity any part of it; neither did the creator of the earth open a land-office, from whence the first title-deeds should issue. Whence then, arose the idea of landed property? I answer as before, that when cultivation began the idea of landed property began with it, from the impossibility of separating the improvement made by cultivation from the earth itself, upon which that improvement was made. The value of the improvement so far exceeded the value of the natural earth, at that time, as to absorb it; till, in the end, the common right of all became confounded into the cultivated right of the individual. But there are, nevertheless, distinct species of rights, and will continue to be so long as the earth endures.

It is only by tracing things to their origin that we can gain rightful ideas of them, and it is by gaining such ideas that we discover the boundary that divides right from wrong, and teaches every man to know his own. I have entitled this tract Agrarian Justice, to distinguish it from Agrarian Law.[6] Nothing could be more unjust than

---

5. Paine had already published *The Age of Reason*, a withering assault on biblical inconsistencies. Hence his qualifying phrase about the Bible's usefulness.
6. During the 1780s and 1790s, radical leaders and poverty-stricken rural dwellers in North America and in France sometimes called for an agrarian law that would encode the labor theory of value. Since all property derived from useful work, they argued, no one should be allowed to own more land than he could possibly "improve" himself. In a 1779 draft proposal of the Massachusetts constitution, for example, the General Court would confiscate estates larger than a thousand acres and redistribute them to landless farmers. Conservatives quickly buried this idea, and in the United States generally,

Agrarian Law in a country improved by cultivation; for though every man, as an inhabitant of the earth, is a joint proprietor of it in its natural state, it does not follow that he is a joint proprietor of cultivated earth. The additional value made by cultivation, after the system was admitted, became the property of those who did it, or who inherited it from them, or who purchased it. It had originally no owner. Whilst, therefore, I advocate the right, and interest myself in the hard case of all those who have been thrown out of their natural inheritance by the introduction of the system of landed property, I equally defend the right of the possessor to the part which is his.

Cultivation is at least one of the greatest natural improvements ever made by human invention. It has given to created earth a ten-fold value. But the landed monopoly that began with it has produced the greatest evil. It has dispossessed more than half the inhabitants of every nation of their natural inheritance, without providing for them, as ought to have been done, an indemnification for that loss, and has thereby created a species of poverty and wretchedness that did not exist before.

In advocating the case of the persons thus dispossessed, it is a right, and not a charity, that I am pleading for. But it is that kind of right which, being neglected at first, could not be brought forward afterwards till heaven had opened the way by a revolution in the system of government. Let us then do honour to revolutions by justice, and give currency to their principles by blessings.

Having thus in a few words, opened the merits of the case, I shall now proceed to the plan I have to propose, which is,

To create a National Fund, out of which there shall be paid to every person, when arrived at the age of twenty-one years, the sum of fifteen pounds sterling, as a compensation in part, for the loss of his or her natural inheritance, by the introduction of the system of landed property:

> And also, the sum of ten pounds per annum, during life, to every person now living, of the age of fifty years, and to all others as they shall arrive at that age.

Means by Which the Fund Is to Be Created

I have already established the principle, namely, that the earth, in its natural uncultivated state was, and ever would have continued to be, *the common property of the human race*, that in that state, every person would have been born to property; and that the system

---

such arguments dropped from political legitimacy after the ratification of the federal Constitution and establishment of a new national state in 1789.

of landed property, by its inseparable connection with cultivation, and with what is called civilized life, has absorbed the property of all those whom it dispossessed, without providing, as ought to have been done, an indemnification for that loss.

The fault, however, is not in the present possessors. No complaint is intended, or ought to be alleged against them, unless they adopt the crime by opposing justice. The fault is in the system, and it has stolen imperceptibly upon the world, aided afterwards by the agrarian law of the sword. But the fault can be made to reform itself by successive generations; and without diminishing or deranging the property of any of the present possessors, the operation of the fund can yet commence, and be in full activity, the first year of its establishment, or soon after, as I shall shew.

It is proposed that the payments, as already stated, be made to every person, rich or poor. It is best to make it so, to prevent invidious distinctions. It is also right it should be so, because it is in lieu of the natural inheritance, which, as a right, belongs to every man, over and above the property he may have created, or inherited from those who did. Such persons as do not choose to receive it can throw it into the common fund.

Taking it then for granted that no person ought to be in a worse condition when born under what is called a state of civilization, than he would have been had he been born in a state of nature, and that civilization ought to have made, and ought still to make, provision for that purpose, it can only be done by subtracting from property a portion equal in value to the natural inheritance it has absorbed.

Various methods may be proposed for this purpose, but that which appears to be the best (not only because it will operate without deranging any present possessors, or without interfering with the collection of taxes or emprunts necessary for the purposes of government and the revolution, but because it will be the least troublesome and the most effectual, and also because the subtraction will be made at a time that best admits it) is at the moment that property is passing by the death of one person to the possession of another. In this case, the bequeather gives nothing: the receiver pays nothing. The only matter to him is that the monopoly of natural inheritance, to which there never was a right, begins to cease in his person. A generous man would not wish it to continue, and a just man will rejoice to see it abolished.

My state of health prevents my making sufficient inquiries with respect to the doctrine of probabilities, whereon to found calculations with such degrees of certainty as they are capable of. What, therefore, I offer on this head is more the result of observation and reflection than of received information; but I believe it will be found to agree sufficiently with fact.

In the first place, taking twenty-one years as the epoch of maturity, all the property of a nation, real and personal, is always in the possession of persons above that age. It is then necessary to know, as a datum of calculation, the average of years which persons above that age will live. I take this average to be about thirty years, for though many persons will live forty, fifty, or sixty years after the age of twenty-one years, others will die much sooner, and some in every year of that time.

Taking, then, thirty years as the average of time, it will give, without any material variation one way or other, the average of time in which the whole property or capital of a nation, or a sum equal thereto, will have passed through one entire revolution in descent, that is, will have gone by deaths to new possessors; for though, in many instances, some parts of this capital will remain forty, fifty, or sixty years in the possession of one person, other parts will have revolved two or three times before those thirty years expire, which will bring it to that average; for were one half the capital of a nation to revolve twice in thirty years, it would produce the same fund as if the whole revolved once.

Taking, then, thirty years as the average of time in which the whole capital of a nation, or a sum equal thereto, will revolve once, the thirtieth part thereof will be the sum that will revolve every year, that is, will go by deaths to new possessors; and this last sum being thus known, and the ratio per cent. to be subtracted from it determined, it will give the annual amount or income of the proposed fund, to be applied as already mentioned.

In looking over the discourse of the English minister Pitt,[7] in his opening of what is called in England the budget, (the scheme of finance for the year 1796,) I find an estimate of the national capital of that country. As this estimate of a national capital is prepared ready to my hand, I take it as a datum to act upon. When a calculation is made upon the known capital of any nation, combined with its population, it will serve as a scale for any other nation, in proportion as its capital and population be more or less. I am the more disposed to take this estimate of Mr. Pitt, for the purpose of showing to that minister, upon his own calculation, how much better money may be employed than in wasting it, as he has done, on the wild project of setting up Bourbon kings. What, in the name of heaven, are Bourbon kings to the people of England? It is better that the people have bread.

7. William Pitt II (1759–1806) had become first lord of the treasury and chancellor of the exchequer in 1783, distinguishing himself for his command of public finance and opposition to the slave trade. In 1793, he organized the First Coalition (Britain, Portugal, Spain, Sardinia, Naples, Austria, Prussia, and Russia) against the revolutionary Republic and led a general crackdown on radicals within Britain.

Mr. Pitt states the national capital of England, real and personal, to be one thousand three hundred millions sterling, which is about one-fourth part of the national capital of France, including Belgia. The event of the last harvest in each country proves that the soil of France is more productive than that of England, and that it can better support twenty-four or twenty-five millions of inhabitants than that of England can seven or seven and a half millions.

The thirtieth part of this capital of 1,300,000,000£ is 43,333,333£ which is the part that will revolve every year by deaths in that country to new possessors; and the sum that will annually revolve in France in the proportion of four to one, will be about one hundred and seventy-three million sterling. From this sum of 43,333,333£ annually revolving, is to be subtracted the value of the natural inheritance absorbed in it, which, perhaps, in fair justice, cannot be taken at less, and ought not to be taken for more, than a tenth part.

It will always happen, that of the property thus revolving by deaths every year a part will descend in a direct line to sons and daughters, and the other part collaterally, and the proportion will be found to be about three to one; that is, about thirty millions of the above sum will descend to direct heirs, and the remaining sum of 13,333,333£ to more distant relations, and in part to strangers.

Considering, then, that man is always related to society, that relationship will become comparatively greater in proportion as the next of kin is more distant, it is therefore consistent with civilization to say that where there are no direct heirs society shall be heir to a part over and above the tenth part due to society. If this additional part be from five to ten or twelve per cent., in proportion as the next of kin be nearer or more remote, so as to average with the escheats that may fall, which ought always to go to society and not to the government (an addition of ten per cent. more), the produce from the annual sum of 43,333,333£ will be:

From 30,000,000£ at ten per cent..........................3,000,000£

From 13,333,333£ at ten per cent. with the addition of ten per cent.
    more 2,666,666£

From 43,333,333£ ....5,666,666£ 14

Having thus arrived at the annual amount of the proposed fund, I come, in the next place, to speak of the population proportioned to this fund, and to compare it with the uses to which the fund is to be applied.

The population (I mean that of England) does not exceed seven millions and a half, and the number of persons above the age of fifty will in that case be about four hundred thousand. There would not, however, be more than that number that would accept the proposed ten pounds sterling per annum, though they would be entitled to it. I have no idea it would be accepted by many persons who had a yearly income of two or three hundred pounds sterling. But as we often see instances of rich people falling into sudden poverty, even at the age of sixty, they would always have the right of drawing all the arrears due to them. Four millions, therefore, of the above annual sum of 5,666,666£ will be required for four hundred thousand aged persons, at ten pounds sterling each.

I come now to speak of the persons annually arriving at twenty-one years of age. If all the persons who died were above the age of twenty-one years, the number of persons annually arriving at that age, must be equal to the annual number of deaths, to keep the population stationary. But the greater part die under the age of twenty-one, and therefore the number of persons annually arriving at twenty-one will be less than half the number of deaths. The whole number of deaths upon a population of seven millions and an half will be about 220,000 annually. The number arriving at twenty-one years of age will be about 100,000. The whole number of these will not receive the proposed fifteen pounds, for the reasons already mentioned, though, as in the former case, they would be entitled to it. Admitting then that a tenth part declined receiving it, the amount would stand thus:

Fund annually
To 400,000 age@ persons at 10£ each ....4,000,000£
To 90,000 persons of 21 years, 15£ ster. each ....1,350,000£

There are, in every country, a number of blind and lame persons, totally incapable of earning a livelihood. But as it will always happen that the greater number of blind persons will be among those who are above the age of fifty years, they will be provided for in that class.

The remaining sum of 316,666£ will provide for the lame and blind under that age, at the same rate of 10£ annually for each person.

Having now gone through all the necessary calculations, and stated the particulars of the plan, I shall conclude with some observations.

It is not charity but a right, not bounty but justice, that I am pleading for. The present state of civilization is as odious as it is unjust. It is absolutely the opposite of what it should be, and it is necessary that a revolution should be made in it. The contrast of affluence and wretchedness continually meeting and offending the eye, is like dead and living bodies chained together. Though I care as little about riches, as any man, I am a friend to riches because they are capable of good. I care not how affluent some may be, provided that none be miserable in consequence of it. But it is impossible to enjoy affluence with the felicity it is capable of being enjoyed, whilst so much misery is mingled in the scene. The sight of the misery, and the unpleasant sensations it suggests, which, though they may be suffocated cannot be extinguished, are a greater drawback upon the felicity of affluence than the proposed 10 per cent upon property is worth. He that would not give the one to get rid of the other has no charity, even for himself.

There are, in every country, some magnificent charities, established by individuals. It is, however, but little that any individual can do, when the whole extent of the misery to be relieved is considered. He may satisfy his conscience but not his heart. He may give all that he has, and that all will relieve but little. It is only by organizing civilization upon such principles as to act like a system of pullies, that the whole weight of misery can be removed.

The plan here proposed will reach the whole. It will immediately relieve and take out of view three classes of wretchedness—the blind, the lame, and the aged poor; and it will furnish the rising generation with means to prevent their becoming poor; and it will do this without deranging or interfering with any national measures. To shew that this will be the case, it is sufficient to observe that the operation and effect of the plan will, in all cases, be the same as if every individual were voluntarily to make his will and dispose of his property in the manner here proposed.

But it is justice, and not charity, that is the principle of the plan. In all great cases it is necessary to have a principle more universally active than charity; and, with respect to justice, it ought not to be left to the choice of detached individuals whether they will do justice or not. Considering then, the plan on the ground of justice, it ought to be the act of the whole, growing spontaneously out of the principles of the revolution, and the reputation of it ought to be national and not individual.

A plan upon this principle would benefit the revolution by the energy that springs from the consciousness of justice. It would multiply also the national resources; for property like vegetation, increases by offsets. When a young couple begin the world, the difference is exceedingly great whether they begin with nothing or with fifteen pounds a piece. With this aid they could buy a cow, and implements to cultivate a few acres of land; and instead of becoming burdens upon society, which is always the case where children are produced faster than they can be fed, would be put in the way of becoming useful and profitable citizens. The national domains also would sell the better if pecuniary aids were provided to cultivate them in small lots.[8]

It is the practice of what has unjustly obtained the name of civilization (and the practice merits not to be called either charity or policy) to make some provision for persons becoming poor and wretched only at the time they become so. Would it not, even as a matter of economy, be far better to adopt means to prevent their becoming poor? This can best be done by making every person when arrived at the age of twenty-one years an inheritor of something to begin with. The rugged face of society, chequered with the extremes of affluence and want, proves that some extraordinary violence has been committed upon it, and calls on justice for redress. The great mass of the poor in all countries are become an hereditary race, and it is next to impossible for them to get out of that state of themselves. It ought also to be observed that this mass increases in all countries that are called civilized. More persons fall annually into it than get out of it.

Though in a plan of which justice and humanity are the foundation-principles, interest ought not to be admitted into the calculation, yet it is always of advantage to the establishment of any plan to shew that it is beneficial as a matter of interest. The success of any proposed plan submitted to public consideration must finally depend on the numbers interested in supporting it, united with the justice of its principles.

The plan here proposed will benefit all, without injuring any. It will consolidate the interest of the Republic with that of the individual. To the numerous class dispossessed of their natural inheritance by the system of landed property it will be an act of national justice. To persons dying possessed of moderate fortunes it will operate as a tontine[9] to their children, more beneficial than the sum of money paid into the fund: and it will give to the accumulation of riches a

8. One year after this essay appeared, Thomas Malthus (1766–1834), an Anglican priest, published *Essay on the Principle of Population as It Effects the Future Improvement of Society*. It employed some of the same assumptions about modern society and population trends found in Paine's essay. Yet Malthus drew harsh and reactionary conclusions—most notably about the need for cutthroat competition and low wages—from the observation that population growth often outpaced food supply. The great difference between the two men is that Paine believed justice, as discerned by reason and sympathy, should be the end of public life, whereas Malthus called for a social order that better reflected people as they generally were, as determined by recorded history.

9. Named for seventeenth-century Neapolitan banker Lorenzo Tonti. Refers to an investment plan in which members pool their money and receive annuities, the value of which increases with the death of each member. Tontine buildings, created with such funds, had become common in Britain and North America by the late eighteenth century. Tontine coffee houses were especially important places of elite and bourgeois socializing.

degree of security that none of the old governments of Europe, now tottering on their foundations, can give.

I do not suppose that more than one family in ten, in any of the countries of Europe, has, when the head of the family dies, a clear property left of five hundred pounds sterling. To all such the plan is advantageous. That property would pay fifty pounds into the fund, and if there were only two children under age they would receive fifteen pounds each, (thirty pounds,) on coming of age, and be entitled to ten pounds a-year after fifty. It is from the overgrown acquisition of property that the fund will support itself; and I know that the possessors of such property in England though they would eventually be benefited by the protection of nine-tenths of it, will exclaim against the plan. But without entering into any inquiry how they came by the property, let them recollect that they have been the advocates of this war, and that Mr. Pitt has already laid on more new taxes to be raised annually upon the people of England and that for supporting the despotism of Austria and the Bourbons against the liberties of France, than would pay annually all the sums proposed in this plan.

I have made the calculations stated in this plan, upon what is called personal, as well as upon landed property. The reason for making it upon land is already explained and the reason for taking personal property into the calculation is equally well founded though on a different principle. Land, as before said, is the free gift of the Creator in common to the human race. Personal property is *the effect of society*; and it is as impossible for an individual to acquire personal property without the aid of society, as it is for him to make land originally. Separate an individual from society, and give him an island or a continent to possess, and he cannot acquire personal property. He cannot be rich. So inseparably are the means connected with the end, in all cases, that where the former do not exist the latter cannot be obtained. All accumulation, therefore, of personal property, beyond what a man's own hands produce, is derived to him by living in society; and he owes on every principle of justice, of gratitude, and of civilization, a part of that accumulation back again to society from whence the whole came. This is putting the matter on a general principle, and perhaps it is best to do so; for if we examine the case minutely it will be found that the accumulation of personal property is, in many instances, the effect of paying too little for the labour that produced it; the consequence of which is, that the working hand perishes in old age, and the employer abounds in affluence. It is, perhaps, impossible to proportion exactly the price of labour to the profits it produces; and it will also be said, as an apology for the injustice, that were a workman to receive an increase of wages daily he would not save it against old age, nor be much better for it in the interim. Make, then, society the treasure to guard it for him in a common fund; for it is no reason that because he might not make a good use of it for himself another should take it.

The state of civilization that has prevailed throughout Europe, is as unjust in its principle, as it is horrid in its effects; and it is the consciousness of this, and the apprehension that such a state cannot continue when once investigation begins in any country, that makes the possessors of property dread every idea of a revolution. It is the hazard and not the principle of revolutions that retards their progress. This being the case, it is necessary as well for the protection of property, as for the sake of justice and humanity, to form a system that, whilst it preserves one part of society from wretchedness, shall secure the other from depredation.

The superstitious awe, the enslaving reverence, that formerly surrounded affluence, is passing away in all countries and leaving the possessor of property to the convulsion of accidents. When wealth and splendour, instead of fascinating the multitude, excite emotions of disgust; when, instead of drawing forth admiration, it is beheld as an insult upon wretchedness; when the ostentatious appearance it make serves to call the right of it in question, the case of property becomes critical, and it is only in a system of justice that the possessor can contemplate security.

To remove the danger, it is necessary to remove the antipathies, and this can only be done by making property productive of a national blessing, extending to every individual. When the riches of one man above another shall increase the national fund in the same proportion; when it shall be seen that the prosperity of that fund depends on the prosperity of individuals; when the more riches a man acquires, the better it shall be for the general mass; it is then that antipathies will cease, and property be placed on the permanent basis of national interest and protection.

I have no property in France to become subject to the plan I propose. What I have, which is not much, is in the United States of America. But I will pay one hundred pound sterling towards this fund in France, the instant it shall be established; and I will pay the same sum in England, whenever a similar establishment shall take place in that country.

A revolution in the state of civilization is the necessary companion of revolutions in the system of government. If a revolution in any country be from bad to good, or from good to bad, the state of what is called civilization in that country, must be made conformable thereto, to give that revolution effect. Despotic government supports itself by abject civilization, in which debasement of the human mind, and wretchedness in the mass of the people, are the chief criterions. Such governments consider man merely as an animal; that the exercise of intellectual faculty is not his privilege; that he has nothing to do with the laws but to obey them;[1] and they politically depend more upon breaking the spirit of the people by poverty, than they fear enraging it by desperation.

It is a revolution in the state of civilization that will give perfection to the revolution of France. Already the conviction that government by representation is the true system of government is spreading itself fast in the world. The reasonableness of it can be seen by all. The justness of it makes itself felt even by its opposers. But when a system of civilization, growing out of that system of government shall be so organized that not a man or woman born in the Republic but shall inherit some means of beginning the world, and see before them the certainty of escaping the miseries that under other governments accompany old age, the revolution of France will have an advocate and an ally in the heart of all nations.

An army of principles will penetrate where an army of soldiers cannot; it will succeed where diplomatic management would fail: it is neither the Rhine, the Channel, nor the Ocean that can arrest its progress: it will march on the horizon of the world, and it will conquer.

Means for Carrying the Proposed Plan into Execution, and to Render It at the Same Time Conducive to the Public Interest

I. Each canton shall elect in its primary assemblies, three persons, as commissioners for that canton, who shall take cognizance, and keep a register of all matters happening in that canton, conformable to the charter that shall be established by law for carrying this plan into execution.

II. The law shall fix the manner in which the property of deceased persons shall be ascertained.

III. When the amount of the property of any deceased person shall be ascertained, the principal heir to that property, or the eldest of the co-heirs, if of lawful age, or if under age the person authorized by the will of the deceased to represent him or them, shall give bond to the commissioners of the canton to pay the said tenth part thereof in four equal quarterly payments, within the space of one year or sooner, at the choice of the payers. One half of the whole property shall remain as a security until the bond be paid off.

IV. The bond shall be registered in the office of the commissioners of the canton, and the original bonds shall be deposited in the national bank at Paris. The bank shall publish every quarter of a

---

1. Expression of Horsley, an English bishop, in the English parliament.—Author [Paine's note].

year the amount of the bonds in its possession, and also the bonds that shall have been paid off, or what parts thereof, since the last quarterly publication.

V. The national bank shall issue bank notes upon the security of the bonds in its possession. The notes so issued shall be applied to pay the pensions of aged persons, and the compensations to persons arriving at twenty-one year of age. It is both reasonable and generous to suppose, that persons not under immediate necessity, will suspend the right of drawing on the fund, until it acquire, as it will do, a greater degree of ability. In this case, it is proposed, that an honorary register be kept, in each canton, of the names of the persons thus suspending that right, at least during the present war.

VI. As the inheritors of property must always take up their bonds in four quarterly payments, or sooner if they choose, there will always be *numéraire* [cash] arriving at the bank after the expiration of the first quarter, to exchange for the bank notes that shall be brought in.

VII. The bank notes being thus put in circulation, upon the best of all possible security, that of actual property, to more than four times the amount of the bonds upon which the notes are issued, and with *numéraire* continually arriving at the bank to exchange or pay them off whenever they shall be presented for that purpose, they will acquire a permanent value in all parts of the Republic. They can therefore be received in payment of taxes, or *emprunts* equal to *numéraire*, because the government can always receive *numéraire* for them at the bank.

VIII. It will be necessary that the payments of the ten per cent be made in *numéraire* for the first year from the establishment of the plan. But after the expiration of the first year, the inheritors of property may pay ten per cent either in bank notes issued upon the fund, or in *numéraire*. If the payments be in *numéraire*, it will lie as a deposit at the bank, to be exchanged for a quantity of notes equal to that amount; and if in notes issued upon the fund, it will cause a demand upon the fund, equal thereto; and thus the operation of the plan will create means to carry itself into execution.

THOMAS PAINE.

CONTEXTS

[SECOND CONTINENTAL CONGRESS]

A Declaration by the Representatives of the United Colonies of North-America, Now Met in Congress at Philadelphia, Setting Forth the Causes and Necessity of Their Taking Up Arms, July 1775[†]

If it was possible for men, who exercise their reason to believe, that the divine Author of our existence intended a part of the human race to hold an absolute property in, and an unbounded power over others, marked out by his infinite goodness and wisdom, as the objects of a legal domination never rightfully resistible, however severe and oppressive, the inhabitants of these colonies might at least require from the parliament of Great-Britain some evidence, that this dreadful authority over them, has been granted to that body. But a reverance for our Creator, principles of humanity, and the dictates of common sense, must convince all those who reflect upon the subject, that government was instituted to promote the welfare of mankind, and ought to be administered for the attainment of that end. The legislature of Great-Britain, however, stimulated by an inordinate passion for a power not only unjustifiable, but which they know to be peculiarly reprobated by the very constitution of that kingdom, and desparate of success in any mode of contest, where regard should be had to truth, law, or right, have at length, deserting those, attempted to effect their cruel and impolitic purpose of enslaving these colonies by violence, and have thereby rendered it necessary for us to close with their last appeal from reason to arms.—Yet, however blinded that assembly may be, by their intemperate rage for unlimited domination, so to slight justice and the opinion of mankind, we esteem ourselves bound by obligations of respect to the rest of the world, to make known the justice of our cause.[1]

Our forefathers, inhabitants of the island of Great-Britain, left their native land, to seek on these shores a residence for civil and

---

[†] From Yale Law School, "18th Century Documents: 1700–1799," *The Avalon Project: Documents in Law, History, and Diplomacy,* http://avalon.law.yale.edu/subject_menus/18th.asp.

1. This paragraph offers two important statements of principle: first, that government ought to "promote the welfare" of mankind and, second, that the creation of a new nation inherently involved the opinion of humanity in general. The first became a source of great controversy among the revolutionary and postrevolutionary generations, with most Americans—including Jefferson, one of the principal authors of this statement—arguing instead for a much more limited role for public institutions. The second was a commonplace among American leaders, who appealed habitually to the "eyes of mankind."

religious freedom. At the expense of their blood, at the hazard of their fortunes, without the least charge to the country from which they removed, by unceasing labour, and an unconquerable spirit, they effected settlements in the distant and unhospitable wilds of America, then filled with numerous and warlike barbarians.— Societies or governments, vested with perfect legislatures, were formed under charters from the crown, and an harmonious inter-course was established between the colonies and the kingdom from which they derived their origin. The mutual benefits of this union became in a short time so extraordinary, as to excite astonishment. It is universally confessed, that the amazing increase of the wealth, strength, and navigation of the realm, arose from this source; and the minister, who so wisely and successfully directed the measures of Great-Britain in the late war,[2] publicly declared, that these colonies enabled her to triumph over her enemies.—Towards the con-clusion of that war, it pleased our sovereign to make a change in his counsels.—From that fatal movement, the affairs of the British empire began to fall into confusion, and gradually sliding from the summit of glorious prosperity, to which they had been advanced by the virtues and abilities of one man, are at length distracted by the convulsions, that now shake it to its deepest foundations.—The new ministry finding the brave foes of Britain, though frequently defeated, yet still contending, took up the unfortunate idea of grant-ing them a hasty peace, and then subduing her faithful friends.

These devoted colonies were judged to be in such a state, as to present victories without bloodshed, and all the easy emoluments of statuteable plunder.—The uninterrupted tenor of their peace-able and respectful behaviour from the beginning of colonization, their dutiful, zealous, and useful services during the war, though so recently and amply acknowledged in the most honourable manner by his majesty, by the late king, and by parliament, could not save them from the meditated innovations.—Parliament was influenced to adopt the pernicious project, and assuming a new power over them, have in the course of eleven years, given such decisive speci-mens of the spirit and consequences attending this power, as to leave no doubt concerning the effects of acquiescence under it. They have undertaken to give and grant our money without our consent, though we have ever exercised an exclusive right to dis-pose of our own property; statutes have been passed for extending the jurisdiction of courts of admiralty and vice-admiralty beyond their ancient limits; for depriving us of the accustomed and inesti-

2. William Pitt the Elder, Earl of Chatham (1708–1778) led the British ministry during the Seven Years' War (1756–63), also known as the French and Indian Wars in North America.

mable privilege of trial by jury, in cases affecting both life and property; for suspending the legislature of one of the colonies; for interdicting all commerce to the capital of another; and for altering fundamentally the form of government established by charter, and secured by acts of its own legislature solemnly confirmed by the crown; for exempting the *"murderers"* of colonists from legal trial, and in effect, from punishment; for erecting in a neighbouring province, acquired by the joint arms of Great-Britain and America, a despotism dangerous to our very existence;[3] and for quartering soldiers upon the colonists in time of profound peace. It has also been resolved in parliament, that colonists charged with committing certain offences, shall be transported to England to be tried.

But why should we enumerate our injuries in detail? By one statute it is declared, that parliament can *"of right make laws to bind us in all cases whatsoever."* What is to defend us against so enormous, so unlimited a power?[4] Not a single man of those who assume it, is chosen by us; or is subject to our control or influence; but, on the contrary, they are all of them exempt from the operation of such laws, and an American revenue, if not diverted from the ostensible purposes for which it is raised, would actually lighten their own burdens in proportion, as they increase ours. We saw the misery to which such despotism would reduce us. We for ten years incessantly and ineffectually besieged the throne as supplicants; we reasoned, we remonstrated with parliament, in the most mild and decent language.

Administration sensible that we should regard these oppressive measures as freemen ought to do, sent over fleets and armies to enforce them. The indignation of the Americans was roused, it is true; but it was the indignation of a virtuous, loyal, and affectionate people. A Congress of delegates from the United Colonies was assembled at Philadelphia, on the fifth day of last September.[5] We

3. A reference to the Québec Act of October 1774, whereby the more than sixty-five thousand French-speaking and Catholic *habitants* claimed by the British Empire in 1763 were granted "the free Exercise of the Religion of the Church of Rome" along with considerable rights to regulate their civil affairs. American leaders feared a larger design to control the colonies through the presence of a large and powerful Catholic state to the north—a measure of how much they hated "papist" religion and how completely they distrusted the British government. In addition, the act expanded Québec's borders farther west into the Mississippi Valley than Pennsylvania, New York, and Virginia would have preferred.

4. This language comes from the Declaratory Act of March 1766, issued in response to colonial protests against the Stamp Act. Congress's reference to "so enormous, so unlimited a power" perfectly captures one of the premises of Whig thought throughout the English-speaking world: that power was inherently and endlessly expansionary, requiring constant containment by well-made law.

5. The First Continental Congress met in response to the alarming measures taken by Parliament after the Boston Tea Party. Besides drafting the conciliatory petition mentioned here, the delegates also organized a new embargo on British goods along with state committees to enforce these measures. During the winter of 1774–75, such committees assumed control of much of the day-to-day governance of the colonies, taking

resolved again to offer an humble and dutiful petition to the King, and also addressed our fellow-subjects of Great-Britain. We have pursued every temperate, every respectful measure; we have even proceeded to break off our commercial intercourse with our fellow-subjects, as the last peaceable admonition, that our attachment to no nation upon earth should supplant our attachment to liberty.— This, we flattered ourselves, was the ultimate step of the controversy: but subsequent events have shewn, how vain was this hope of finding moderation in our enemies.

Several threatening expressions against the colonies were inserted in his majesty's speech; our petition, tho' we were told it was a decent one, and that his majesty had been pleased to receive it graciously, and to promise laying it before his parliament, was huddled into both houses among a bundle of American papers, and there neglected. The lords and commons in their address, in the month of February, said, that *"a rebellion at that time actually existed within the province of Massachusetts-Bay; and that those concerned with it, had been countenanced and encouraged by unlawful combinations and engagements, entered into by his majesty's subjects in several of the other colonies; and therefore they besought his majesty, that he would take the most effectual measures to inforce due obediance to the laws and authority of the supreme legislature."*—Soon after, the commercial intercourse of whole colonies, with foreign countries, and with each other, was cut off by an act of parliament; by another several of them were intirely prohibited from the fisheries in the seas near their coasts, on which they always depended for their sustenance; and large reinforcements of ships and troops were immediately sent over to general Gage.

Fruitless were all the entreaties, arguments, and eloquence of an illustrious band of the most distinguished peers, and commoners, who nobly and strenuously asserted the justice of our cause, to stay, or even to mitigate the heedless fury with which these accumulated and unexampled outrages were hurried on.—equally fruitless was the interference of the city of London, of Bristol, and many other respectable towns in our favor. Parliament adopted an insidious manoeuvre calculated to divide us, to establish a perpetual auction of taxations where colony should bid against colony, all of them uninformed what ransom would redeem their lives; and thus to extort from us, at the point of the bayonet, the unknown sums that should be sufficient to gratify, if possible to gratify, ministerial rapacity, with the miserable indulgence left to us of raising, in our own mode, the

---

power from the royal governors and magistrates with remarkable speed and relative ease.

prescribed tribute. What terms more rigid and humiliating could have been dictated by remorseless victors to conquered enemies? in our circumstances to accept them, would be to deserve them.

Soon after the intelligence of these proceedings arrived on this continent, general Gage, who in the course of the last year had taken possession of the town of Boston, in the province of Massachusetts-Bay, and still occupied it a garrison, on the 19th day of April, sent out from that place a large detachment of his army, who made an unprovoked assault on the inhabitants of the said province, at the town of Lexington, as appears by the affidavits of a great number of persons, some of whom were officers and soldiers of that detachment, murdered eight of the inhabitants, and wounded many others. From thence the troops proceeded in warlike array to the town of Concord, where they set upon another party of the inhabitants of the same province, killing several and wounding more, until compelled to retreat by the country people suddenly assembled to repel this cruel aggression. Hostilities, thus commenced by the British troops, have been since prosecuted by them without regard to faith or reputation.—The inhabitants of Boston being confined within that town by the general their governor, and having, in order to procure their dismission, entered into a treaty with him, it was stipulated that the said inhabitants having deposited their arms with their own magistrate, should have liberty to depart, taking with them their other effects. They accordingly delivered up their arms, but in open violation of honour, in defiance of the obligation of treaties, which even savage nations esteemed sacred, the governor ordered the arms deposited as aforesaid, that they might be preserved for their owners, to be seized by a body of soldiers; detained the greatest part of the inhabitants in the town, and compelled the few who were permitted to retire, to leave their most valuable effects behind.[6]

By this perfidy wives are separated from their husbands, children from their parents, the aged and the sick from their relations and friends, who wish to attend and comfort them; and those who have been used to live in plenty and even elegance, are reduced to deplorable distress.

The general, further emulating his ministerial masters, by a proclamation bearing date on the 12th day of June, after venting the

6. The language used to describe the crisis in Boston is especially important because it suggests that the Americans already constituted a separate nation. The colonists now had their own magistrates and made treaties with the invading force. At the same time, the paragraph condemns the British—who considered the provincials as rebels, not foreign sovereigns—for breaking those treaties in a way that "even savage nations" would never think to do.

grossest falsehoods and calumnies against the good people of these colonies, proceeds to *"declare them all, either by name or description, to be rebels and traitors, to supersede the course of the common law, and instead thereof to publish and order the use and exercise of the law martial."*—His troops have butchered our countrymen, have wantonly burnt Charlestown, besides a considerable number of houses in other places; our ships and vessels are seized; the necessary supplies of provisions are intercepted, and he is exerting his utmost power to spread destruction and devastation around him.

We have rceived certain intelligence, that general Carelton [*Carleton*], the governor of Canada, is instigating the people of that province and the Indians to fall upon us;[7] and we have but too much reason to apprehend, that schemes have been formed to excite domestic enemies against us. In brief, a part of these colonies now feel, and all of them are sure of feeling, as far as the vengeance of administration can inflict them, the complicated calamities of fire, sword and famine. We are reduced to the alternative of chusing an unconditional submission to the tyranny of irritated ministers, or resistance by force.—The latter is our choice.—We have counted the cost of this contest, and find nothing so dreadful as voluntary slavery.—Honour, justice, and humanity, forbid us tamely to surrender that freedom which we received from our gallant ancestors, and which our innocent posterity have a right to receive from us. We cannot endure the infamy and guilt of resigning succeeding generations to that wretchedness which inevitably awaits them, if we basely entail hereditary bondage upon them.

Our cause is just. Our union is perfect. Our internal resources are great, and, if necessary, foreign assistance is undoubtedly attainable.—We gratefully acknowledge, as signal instances of the Divine favour towards us, that his Providence would not permit us to be called into this severe controversy, until we were grown up to our present strength, had been previously exercised in warlike operation, and possessed of the means of defending ourselves. With hearts fortified with these animating reflections, we most solemnly, before God and the world, declare, that, exerting the utmost energy

---

7. British emissaries had indeed met with many Indian nations at Montréal during the summer of 1775; similar meetings also took place in western Carolina. The substance of these meetings was largely a matter of rumor, and American rebels seized on this uncertainty to charge Britain with the most horrifying crime of all. According to General Philip Schuyler, a British agent at Montréal had invited the Canadian tribes to "Feast on a Bostonian and Drink His Blood." Most newspapers published this account in December 1775, and an early edition of Paine's *Common Sense* was bound together with a fictional dialogue between a dead American general (killed while attacking Québec on December 31, 1775) and a congressman. The general's ghost affirms that the British were inviting various foreigners and "savages," as well as slaves, to wage war without mercy on American men, women, and children. This accusation, along with the British army's offer of freedom to American slaves, may well have created more rebels during 1776 than all the previous arguments for independence.

of those powers, which our beneficent Creator hath graciously bestowed upon us, the arms we have been compelled by our enemies to assume, we will, in defiance of every hazard, with unabating firmness and perseverance, employ for the preservation of our liberties; being with one mind resolved to die freemen rather than to live slaves.

Lest this declaration should disquiet the minds of our friends and fellow-subjects in any part of the empire, we assure them that we mean not to dissolve that union which has so long and so happily subsisted between us, and which we sincerely wish to see restored.—Necessity has not yet driven us into that desperate measure, or induced us to excite any other nation to war against them.—We have not raised armies with ambitious designs of separating from Great-Britain, and establishing independent states. We fight not for glory or for conquest. We exhibit to mankind the remarkable spectacle of a people attacked by unprovoked enemies, without any imputation or even suspicion of offence. They boast of their privileges and civilization, and yet proffer no milder conditions than servitude or death.

In our own native land, in defence of the freedom that is our birthright, and which we ever enjoyed till the late violation of it—for the protection of our property, acquired solely by the honest industry of our fore-fathers and ourselves, against violence actually offered, we have taken up arms. We shall lay them down when hostilities shall cease on the part of the aggressors, and all danger of their being renewed shall be removed, and not before.

With an humble confidence in the mercies of the supreme and impartial Judge and Ruler of the Universe, we most devoutly implore his divine goodness to protect us happily through this great conflict, to dispose our adversaries to reconciliation on reasonable terms, and thereby to relieve the empire from the calamities of civil war.

[PENNSYLVANIA GENERAL ASSEMBLY]

Pennsylvania—An Act for the Gradual Abolition of Slavery, March 1, 1780[†]

SECTION 1. When we contemplate our abhorrence of that condition to which the arms and tyranny of Great Britain were exerted to reduce us; when we look back on the variety of dangers to which we

---

[†] From Yale Law School, "18th Century Documents: 1700–1799," *The Avalon Project: Documents in Law, History, and Diplomacy,* http://avalon.law.edu/subject_menus.18th .asp.

have been exposed, and how miraculously our wants in many instances have been supplied, and our deliverances wrought, when even hope and human fortitude have become unequal to the conflict; we are unavoidably led to a serious and grateful fence of the manifold blessings which we have undeservedly received from the hand of that Being from whom every good and perfect gift cometh. Impressed with these ideas, we conceive that it is our duty, and we rejoice that it is in our power to extend a portion of that freedom to others, which hath been extended to us; and a release from that state of thraldom to which we ourselves were tyrannically doomed, and from which we have now every prospect of being delivered. It is not for us to enquire why, in the creation of mankind, the inhabitants of the several parts of the earth were distinguished by a difference in feature or complexion. It is sufficient to know that all are the work of an Almighty Hand. We find in the distribution of the human species, that the most fertile as well as the most barren parts of the earth are inhabited by men of complexions different from ours, and from each other; from whence we may reasonably, as well as religiously, infer, that He who placed them in their various situations, hath extended equally his care and protection to all, and that it becometh not us to counteract his mercies. We esteem it a peculiar blessing granted to us, that we are enabled this day to add one more step to universal civilization, by removing as much as possible the sorrows of those who have lived in undeserved bondage, and from which, by the assumed authority of the kings of Great Britain, no effectual, legal relief could be obtained. Weaned by a long course of experience from those narrower prejudices and partialities we had imbibed, we find our hearts enlarged with kindness and benevolence towards men of all conditions and nations; and we conceive ourselves at this particular period extraordinarily called upon, by the blessings which we have received, to manifest the sincerity of our profession, and to give a Substantial proof of our gratitude.

SECT. 2. And whereas the condition of those persons who have heretofore been denominated Negro and Mulatto slaves, has been attended with circumstances which not only deprived them of the common blessings that they were by nature entitled to, but has cast them into the deepest afflictions, by an unnatural separation and sale of husband and wife from each other and from their children; an injury, the greatness of which can only be conceived by supposing that we were in the same unhappy case. In justice therefore to persons So unhappily circumstanced, and who, having no prospect before them whereon they may rest their sorrows and their hopes, have no reasonable inducement to render their service to society, which they otherwise might; and also in grateful commemoration of our own happy deliverance from that state of unconditional submission to which we were doomed by the tyranny of Britain.

SECT. 3. Be it enacted, and it is hereby enacted, by the representatives of the freeman of the commonwealth of Pennsylvania, in general assembly met, and by the authority of the same, That all persons, as well Negroes and Mulattoes as others, who shall be born within this state from and after the passing of this act, shall not be deemed and considered as servants for life, or slaves; and that all servitude for life, or slavery of children, in consequence of the slavery of their mothers,[1] in the case of all children born within this state, from and after the passing of this act as aforesaid, shall be, and hereby is utterly taken away, extinguished and for ever abolished.

SECT. 4. Provided always, and be it further enacted by the authority aforesaid, That every Negro and Mulatto child born within this state after the passing of this act as aforesaid (who would, in case this act had not been made, have been born a servant for years, or life, or a slave) shall be deemed to be and shall be by virtue of this act the servant of such person or his or her assigns, who would in such case have been entitled to the service of such child, until such child shall attain unto the age of twenty eight years, in the manner and on the conditions whereon servants bound by indenture for four years are or may be retained and holder; and shall be liable to like correction and punishment, and entitled to like relief in case he or she be evilly treated by his or her master or mistress, and to like freedom dues and other privileges as servants bound by indenture for four years are or may be entitled, unless the person to whom the service of any such child shall belong shall abandon his or her claim to the same; in which case the overseers of the poor of the city, township or district respectively, where such child shall be So abandoned, shall by indenture bind out every child so abandoned, as an apprentice for a time not exceeding the age herein before limited for the service of such children.

SECT. 5. And be it further enacted by the authority aforesaid, That every person, who is or shall be the owner of any Negro or Mulatto slave or servant for life or till the age of thirty one years, now within this state, or his lawful attorney, shall on or before the

---

1. During the mid-seventeenth century, slaveholders in North America had instituted the rule of *partus sequitur ventrum* regarding the children of slaves—their status was to follow that of their mother. This meant that the children of a free white master and a woman he owned became the property of that same man and master. This rule derived from Roman rather than English law; in all other respects, the Anglo-American colonies and later states followed patriarchal and patrilineal rules of property and authority.

said first day of November next deliver or claim to be delivered in writing to the clerk of the peace of the county, or to the clerk of the court of record of the city of Philadelphia, in which he or she shall respectively inhabit, the name and surname and occupation or profession of such owner, and the name of the county and township, district or ward wherein he or she resideth; and also the name and names of any such slave and slaves, and servant and servants for life or till the age of thirty one years, together with their ages and sexes severally and respectively set forth and annexed, by such person owned or statedly employed and then being within this state, in order to ascertain and distinguish the slaves and servants for life, and till the age of thirty one years, within this state, who shall be such on the said first day of November next, from all other persons; which particulars shall by said clerk of the sessions asked clerk of the said city court be entered in books to be provided for that purpose by the said clerks; and that no Negro or Mulatto, now within this state, shall from and after the said first day of November, be deemed a slave or servant for life, or till the age of thirty one years, unless his or her name shall be entered as aforesaid on such record, except such Negro and Mulatto slaves and servants as are herein after excepted; the said clerk to be entitled to a fee of two dollars for each slave or servant so entered as aforesaid from the treasurer of the county, to be allowed to him in his accounts.

SECT. 6. Provided always, That any person, in whom the ownership or right to the service of any Negro or Mulatto shall be vested at the passing of this act, other than such as are herein before excepted, his or her heirs, executors, administrators and assigns, and all and every of them severally shall be liable to the overseers of the poor of the city, township or district to which any such Negro or Mulatto shall become chargeable, for such necessary expence, with costs of suit thereon, as such overseers may be put to, through the neglect of the owner, master or mistress of such Negro or Mulatto; notwithstanding the name and other descriptions of such Negro or Mulatto shall not be entered and recorded as aforesaid; unless his or her master or owner shall before such slave or servant attain his or her twenty eighth year execute and record in the proper county a deed or instrument, securing to such slave or servant his or her freedom.

SECT. 7. And be it further enacted by the authority aforesaid, That the offences and crimes of Negroes and Mulattoes, as well slaves and servants as freemen, shall be enquired of, adjudged, corrected and punished in like manner as the offences and crimes of the other inhabitants of this state are and shall be enquired of, adjudged, corrected and punished, and not otherwise; except that a slave shall not be admitted to bear witness against a freeman.

SECT. 8. And be it further enacted by the authority aforesaid, That in all cases wherein sentence of death shall be pronounced against a slave, the jury before whom he or she shall be tried, shall appraise and declare the value of such slave; and in case such sentence be executed, the court shall make an order on the state treasurer, payable to the owner for the same and for the costs of prosecution; but case of remission or mitigation, for the costs only.

SECT. 9. And be it further enacted by the authority aforesaid, That the reward for taking up runaway and absconding Negro and Mulatto slaves and servants, and the penalties for enticing away, dealing with, or harbouring, concealing or employing Negro and Mulatto slaves and servants, shall be the same, and shall be recovered in like manner as in case of servants bound for four years.

SECT. 10. And be it further enacted by the authority aforesaid, That no man or woman of any nation or colour, except the Negroes or Mulattoes who shall be registered as aforesaid, shall at any time hereafter be deemed, adjudged, or holden within the territories of this commonwealth as slaves or servants for life, but as free men and free women; except the domestic slaves attending upon delegates in congress from the other American states,[2] foreign ministers and consuls, and persons passing through or sojourning in this state, and not becoming resident therein; and seamen employed in ships not belonging to any inhabitant of this state, nor employed in any ship owned by any such inhabitant. Provided such domestic slaves be not aliened or fold to any inhabitants nor (except in the case of members of congress, foreign ministers and consuls) retained in this state longer than six months.

SECT. 11. Provided always; And be it further enacted by the authority aforesaid, That this act or any thing in it contained shall not give any relief or shelter to any absconding or runaway Negro or Mulatto slave or servant, who has absented himself or shall absent himself from his or her owner, master or mistress residing in any other state or country, but such owner, master or mistress shall have like right and aid to demand, claim and take away his slave or servant, as he might have had in case this act had not been made: And that all Negro and Mulatto slaves now owned and heretofore resident in this state, who have absented themselves, or been clandestinely carried away, or who may be employed abroad as seamen and have not returned or been brought back to their owners, masters or mistresses, before the passing of this act, may within five years be registered as effectually as is ordered by this act concerning those

---

2. At the time of this act and up to 1801, when the federal government moved to the new capital of Washington, D.C., Philadelphia was the center of national politics. The status of the slaves whom southern delegates brought with them to the city was thus a matter of high concern.

who are now within the state, on producing such slave before any two justices of the peace, and satisfying the said justices by due proof of the former residence, absconding, taking away, or absence of such slaves as aforesaid; who thereupon shall direct and order the said slave to be entered on the record as aforesaid.

SECT. 12. And whereas attempts maybe made to evade this act, by introducing into this state Negroes and Mulatoes bound by covenant to serve for long and unreasonable terms of years, if the same be not prevented:

SECT. 13. Be it therefore enacted by the authority aforesaid, That no covenant of personal servitude or apprenticeship whatsoever shall be valid or binding on a Negro or Mulatto for a longer time than seven years, unless such servant or apprentice were at the commencement of such servitude or apprenticeship under the age of twenty one years; in which case such Negro or Mulatto may be holden as a servant or apprentice respectively, according to the covenant, as the cafe shall be, until he or she shall attain the age of twenty eight years, but no longer.

SECT. 14. And be it further enacted by the authority aforesaid, That an act of assembly of die province of Pennsylvania, passed in the year one thousand Seven hundred and five, intitled, "an Act for the trial of Negroes;" and another act of assembly of the said province, passed in the year one thousand seven hundred and twenty five, intitled, "An Act for the better regulating of Negroes in this province;" and another act of assembly of the said province, passed in the year one thousand seven hundred and sixty one, intitled, "An Act for laying a duty on Negro and Mulatto slaves imported into this province;" and also another act of assembly of the said province, passed in the year one thousand seven hundred and seventy three, intitled, "An Act making perpetual an Act laying a duty on Negro and Mulatto slaves imported into this province, and for laying an additional duty said slaves," shall be and are hereby repealed, annulled and made void.[3]

JOHN BAYARD, SPEAKER

Enabled into a law at Philadelphia, on Wednesday, the first day of March, A.D. 1780

---

3. These acts had established a separate and very unequal legal system for blacks and whites in colonial Pennsylvania. Whether slave or free, blacks were tried by two justices of the peace and six freeholders rather than by a jury. Penalties were harsher for convicted blacks than for whites; after 1706, for example, the attempted "ravishment" of a white woman by a black man brought the same penalty as theft, or thirty-nine lashes, a "R" or "T" branded into the forehead, and banishment from the province. The act "for the better regulating of Negroes" also required slaves to carry a pass.

QUOBNA OTTOBAH CUGOANO

From Thoughts and Sentiments on the Evil and Wicked Traffic of the Slavery and Commerce of the Human Species (1787)

In this advanced era, when the kings of Europe are become more conspicuous for their manly virtues, than any before them have been, it is to be hoped that they will not any longer suffer themselves to be imposed upon, and be beguiled, and brought into guilt and shame, by any instigations of the cunning craftiness and evil policy of the avaricious and the vile profligate enslavers of men. And as their wisdom and understanding is great, and exalted as their high dignity, it is also to be hoped that they will exert themselves, in the cause of righteousness and justice, and be like the wisest and the greatest monarchs of old, to hearken to the counsel of the wise men that know the times, and to the righteous laws of God, and to deliver the oppressed, and to put an end to the iniquitous commerce and slavery of men. And as we hear tell of the kings of Europe having almost abolished, the infernal invention of the bloody tribunal of the inquisition, and the Emperor and others making some grand reformations for the happiness and good of their subjects; it is to be hoped also that these exalted and liberal principles will lead them on to greater improvements in civilization and felicitation, and next to abolish that other diabolical invention of the bloody and cruel African slave trade, and the West Indian slavery.[1]

But whereas the people of Great Britain having now acquired a greater share in that iniquitous commerce than all the rest together, they are the first that ought to set an example, lest they have to repent for their wickedness when it becomes too late; lest some impending calamity should speedily burst forth against them, and lest a just retribution for their enormous crimes, and a continuance in committing similar deeds of barbarity and injustice should involve them in ruin. For we may be assured that God will certainly avenge himself of such heinous transgressors of his law, and of all those planters and merchants, and of all others, who are the authors

---

1. A reference to the abolition of serfdom and slavery in parts of central and eastern Europe. Frederick II (1712–1786) of Prussia declared an end to serfdom in his lands in 1773, and Joseph II (1741–1790) of Austria followed suit a decade later. Along with Catherine II (1729–1796) of Russia, these rulers typified Enlightened despotism, a statist version of the reform movement and revolutionary moments in the English- and French-speaking worlds.

of the African graves, severities, and cruel punishments and no plea of any absolute necessity can possibly excuse them. And as the inhabitants of Great Britain, and the inhabitants of the colonies, seem almost equally guilty of the oppression, there is great reason for both to dread the severe vengeance of Almighty God upon them, and upon all such notorious workers of wickedness; for it is evident that the legislature of Great Britain patronises and encourages them, and shares in the infamous profits of the slavery of the Africans. It is therefore necessary that the inhabitants of the British nation should seriously consider these things for their own good and safety as well as for our benefit and deliverance, and that they may be consible of their own error and danger, lest they provoke the vengeance of the Almighty against them. For what wickedness was there ever risen up so monstrous, and more likely to bring a heavy rod of destruction upon a nation, then the deeds committed by the West Indian slavery, and the African slave trade. And even in that part of it oarried on by the Liverpool and Bristol merchants, the many shocking and inhuman instances of their barbarity and cruelty are such that every one that heareth thereof has reason to tremble, and cry out, *Should not the land tremble for this, and every one mourn that dwelleth therein?*[2]

The vast carnage and murders committed by the British instigators of slavery, is attended with a very shocking, peculiar, and almost unheard of conception, according to the notion of the perpetrators of it; they either consider them as their own property, that they may do with as they please, in life or death; or that the taking away the life of a black man is of no more account than taking away the life of a beast. A very melancholy instance of this happened about the year 1780, as recorded in the courts of law; a master of a vessel bound to the Western Colonies, selected 132 of the most sickly of the black slaves, and ordered them to be thrown overboard into the sea in order to recover their value from the insurers, as he had perceived that he was too late to get a good market for them in the West Indies. On the trial, by the counsel for the owners of the vessel against the underwriters, their argument was that the slaves were to be considered the same as horses; and their plea for throwing them into the sea, was nothing better than that it might be more necessary to throw them overboard to lighten their vessel than goods of greater value or something to that effect. These poor creatures, it seems, were tied two and two together when they were thrown into the sea, lest some of them might swim a little for the last gasp of air, and, with the animation of their approaching exit, breathe their souls away to the gracious Father of spirits. Some of

2. Amos 8:8

the last parcel, when they saw the fate of their companions, made their escape from trying by jumping overboard, and one was saved by means of a rope from some in the ship. The owners of the vessel, I suppose (inhuman connivers of robbery, slavery, murder and fraud) were rather a little defeated in this, by bringing their villainy to light in a court of law; but the inhuman monster of a captain was kept out of the way of justice from getting hold of him.[3] Though such perpetrators of murder and fraud should have been sought after from the British Dan in the East Indies, to her Beershebah in the West.[4]

But our lives are accounted of no value, we are hunted after as the prey in the desert, and doomed to destruction as the beasts that perish. And for this, should we appeal to the inhabitants of Europe, would they dare to say that they have not wronged us, and grievously injured us, and that the blood of millions do not cry out against them? And if we appeal to the inhabitants of Great Britain, can they justify the deeds of their conduct towards us? And is it not strange to think, that they who ought to be considered as the most learned and civilized people in the world that they should carry on a traffic of the most barbarous cruelty and injustice, and that many even among them, are become so dissolute, as to think slavery, robbery and murder no crimes? But we will answer to this, that no man can, with impunity, steal, kidnap, buy or sell another man, without being guilty of the most atrocious villainy. And we will aver that every slave-holder that claims any property in slaves, or holds them in an involuntary servitude, are the most obnoxious and dissolute robbers among men; and that they have no more right, nor any better title to any of them than the most profligate and notorious robbers and thieves in the world, has to the goods which they have robbed and stolen from the right owners and lawful possessor thereof. But should the slave-holders say that they buy them; their title and claim is no better than that of the most notorious conniver, who buys goods from other robbers, knowing them to be stolen, and accordingly gives an inferior price for them. According to the laws of England, when such connivers are discovered, and the property of

3. In September 1781, the slave ship *Zong* sailed from west Africa to Jamaica, carrying 470 enslaved Africans. When the voyage dragged on and many Africans became ill, the captain ordered 133 of the sickest Africans to be cast into the Atlantic. In this way, he and the ship owners would be able to pass the costs of the dead slaves on to the insurance underwriters, citing the dead as "lost at sea." The insurers challenged the claim, and the case went to court—not over the murder of the slaves, but over the proper apportionment of cost. The *Morning Chronicle, and London Advertiser* printed a report on this case in March 1783, and abolitionist leaders, including Olaudah Equiano and Granville Sharp used the calamity to expose the profound evils of the traffic. The incident also inspired Joseph Turner's 1840 painting *Slave Ship*.
4. As throughout his essay, Cugoano relies on biblical references and metaphors to situate his own times into a larger narrative of redemption and wrath. Dan was the most northerly and Beershebah the most westerly cities of the Holy Land.

others unlawfully found in their possession the right owners thereof can oblige the connivers to restore back their property, and to punish them for their trespass.[5] But the slave-holders, universally, are those connivers, they do not only rob men of some of their property, but they keep men from every property belonging to them, and compel them to their involuntary service and drudgery; and those whom they buy from other robbers, and keep in their possession, are greatly injured by them when compared to any species of goods whatsoever; and accordingly they give but a very inferior price for men, as all their vast estates in the West Indies is not sufficient to buy one of them, if the rightful possessor was to sell himself to them in the manner that they claim possession of him. Therefore let the inhabitants of any civilized nation determine whether if they were to be treated in the same manner that the Africans are, by various pirates, kidnappers, and slave-holders, and their wives, and their sons and daughters were to be robbed from them, or themselves violently taken away to a perpetual and intolerable slavery; or whether they would not think those robbers, who only took away their property, less injurious to them than the other. If they determine it so, as reason must tell every man, that himself is of more value than his property; then the executors of the laws of civilization ought to tremble at the inconsistency of passing judgment upon those whose crimes, in many cases, are less than what the whole, legislature must be guilty of, when those of a far greater is encouraged and supported by it wherever *slavery* is tolerated by law, and consequently, that slavery can no where be tolerated with any consistency to civilization and the laws of justice among men; but if it can maintain its ground, to have any place at all, it must be among a society of barbarians and thieves, and where the laws of their society is, for every one to catch what he can. Then, when theft and robbery become no crimes, the man-stealer and the conniving slave-holder might possibly get free.

But the several nations of Europe that have joined in that iniquitous traffic of buying, selling and enslaving men, must in course have left their own laws of civilization to adopt those of barbarians and robbers, and that they may say to one another, *When thou sawest a thief, then thou consentest with him, and hast been partaker with all the workers of iniquity.*[6] But whereas every man, as a rational creature, is responsible for his actions, and he becomes not only guilty in doing evil himself, but in letting others rob and oppress their fellow-creatures with impunity, or in not delivering the

5. These references to British law suggest a basic familiarity, which Cugoano might have obtained from a variety of sources, including William Blackstone's authoritative *Commentaries on the Laws of England* (1765–69).
6. Psalms 50:18.

oppressed when he has it in his power to help them.[7] And likewise that nation which may be supposed to maintain a very considerable degree of civilization, justice and equity within its own jurisdiction, is not in that case innocent, while it beholds another nation or people carrying on persecution, oppression and slavery, unless it remonstrates against that wickedness of the other nation, and makes use of every effort in its power to help the oppressed, and to rescue the innocent. For so it ought to be the universal rule of duty to all men that fear God and keep his commandments, to do good to all men wherever they can; and when they find any wronged and injured by others, they should endeavour to deliver the ensnared whatever their grievances may be; and should this some-times lead them into war they might expect the protection and blessing of heaven. How far other motives may appear eligible for men to oppose one another with hostile force, it is not my business to enquire. But I should suppose the hardy veterans who engage merely about the purposes of envying one another concerning any different advantages of commerce, or for enlarging their territories and dominions, or for the end of getting riches by their conquest; that if they fall in the combat, they must generally die, as the fool dieth, vaunting in vain glory; and many of them be like to those who go out in darkness, never to see light; and should they come off alive, what more does their honour and fame amount to, but only to be like that antediluvian conqueror, *who had slain a man to his own wounding, and a young man to his hurt.*[8] But those mighty men of renown in the days of old, because of their apostacy from God, and rebellion and wickedness to men, were at last all swallowed up by an universal deluge for their iniquity and crimes.

But again let me observe, that whatever civilization the inhabit-ants of Great Britain may enjoy among themselves, they have seldom maintained their own innocence in that great duty as a Christian nation towards others; and I may say, with respect to their African neighbours, or to any other wheresoever they may go by the way of commerce, they have not regarded them at all. And when they saw others robbing the Africans, and carrying them into captivity and slavery, they have neither helped them, nor opposed their oppres-sors in the least. But instead thereof they have joined in combination against them with the rest of other profligate nations and people, to buy, enslave and make merchandize of them, because they found them helpless and fit to suit their own purpose, and are become the head carriers on of that iniquitous traffic. But the greater that any

7. One of the foundations of Christian ethics was the rationality of man—that is, his abil-ity to discern the laws of God, as revealed in the Old and New Testaments. This ability to know rendered humankind culpable for its sins.
8. Genesis 4:23

reformation and civilization is obtained by any nation, if they do not maintain righteousness, but carry on any course of wickedness and oppression, it makes them appear only the more inconsistent, and their tyranny and oppression the more conspicuous. Wherefore because of the great wickedness, cruelty and injustice done to the Africans, those who are greatest in the transgression give an evident and undubious warrant to all other nations beholding their tyranny and injustice to others, if those nations have any regard to their own innocence and virtue, and wish to maintain righteousness, and to remain clear of the oppression and blood of all men; it is their duty to chastize and suppress such unjust and tyrannical oppressors and enslavers of men. And should none of these be found among the enlightened and civilized nations, who maintain their own innocence and righteousness, with regard to their duty unto all men; and that there may be none to chastize the tyrannical oppressors of others; and it may be feared, as it has often been, that fierce nations of various insects, and other annoyances, may be sent as a judgment to punish the wicked nations of men. For by some way or other every criminal nation, and all their confederates, who sin and rebel against God, and against his laws of nature and nations, will each meet with some awful retribution at last, unless they repent of their iniquity. And the greater advantages of light, learning, knowledge and civilization that any people enjoy, if they do not maintain righteousness, but do wickedly, they will meet with the more severe rebuke when the visitations of God's judgment cometh upon them. And the prophecy which was given to Moses, is still as much in force against the enlightened nations now for their wickedness, in going after the abominations of heathens and barbarians, for none else would attempt to enslave and make merchandize of men, as it was when denounced against the Israelitish nations of old, when they departed, or should depart, from the laws and statutes of the Most High. *The Lord shall bring a nation against thee, from far, from the ends of the earth, as swift as the eagle flieth, a nation whose tongue thou shalt not understand, &c.* See Deut. xxviii.

But lest any of these things should happen to the generous and respectful Britons, who are not altogether lost to virtue and consideration; let me say unto you, in the language of a wise and eminent Queen,[9] as she did when her people were sold as a prey to their enemies: That it is not all your enemies (for they can he reckoned nothing else), the covetous instigators and carriers on of slavery and wickedness, that can in any way countervail the damage to

---

9. This is a reference to Queen Esther, who outwitted a conspirator seeking to destroy the Jewish people. See Esther 5–9.

yourselves, to your king, and to your country; nor will all the infamous profits of the poor Africans avail you anything if it brings down the avenging hand of God upon you. We are not saying that we have not sinned, and that we are not deserving of the righteous judgments of God against us. But the enemies that have risen up against us are cruel, oppressive and unjust; and their haughtiness of insolence, wickedness and iniquity is like to that of Haman the son of Hammedatha; and who dare suppose, or even presume to think, that the inhuman ruffians and ensnarers of men, the vile negotiators and merchandizers of the human species, and the ostensive combinations of slave-holders in the West have done no evil? And should we be passive, as the suffering martyrs dying in the flames, whose blood crieth for vengeance on their persecutors and murderers; so the iniquity of our oppressors, enslavers and murderers rise up against them. For we have been hunted after as the wild beasts of the earth, and sold to the enemies of mankind as their prey; and should any of us have endeavoured to get away from them, as a man would naturally fly from an enemy that waylaid him; we have been pursued after, and, by haughty mandates and laws of iniquity, overtaken, and murdered and slain, and the blood of millions cries out against them. And together with these that have been cruelly spoiled and slain, the very grievous afflictions that we have long suffered under, has been long crying for vengeance on our oppressors; and the great distress and wretchedness of human woe and misery, which we are yet lying under, is still rising up before that High and Sovereign Hand of Justice, where men, by all their oppression and cruelty, can no way prevent; their evil treatment of others may serve to increase the blow, but not to evade the stroke of His power, nor withhold the bringing down that arm of vengeance on themselves, and upon all their connivers and confederators, and the particular instigators of such wilful murders and inhuman barbarity. The life of a black man is of as much regard in the sight of God, as the life of any other man; though we have been sold as a carnage to the market, and as a prey to profligate wicked men, to torture and lash us as they please, and as their oaprice may think fit, to murder us at discretion.

And should any of the best of them plead, as they generally will do, and tell of their humanity and charity to those whom they have captured and enslaved, their tribute of thanks is but small; for what is it, but a little restored to the wretched and miserable whom they have robbed of their all; and only to be dealt with, like the spoils of those taken in the field of battle, where the wretched fugitives must submit to what they please. For as we have been robbed of our natural right as men, and treated as beasts, those who have injured us, are like to them who have robbed the widow, the orphans, the poor and the needy of their right, and whose children are rioting on the spoils of those who are begging at their doors for bread. And should they say, that their fathers were thieves and connivers with ensnarers of men, and that they have been brought up to the iniquitous practice of slavery and oppression of their fellow-creatures and they cannot live without carrying it on and making their gain by the unlawful merchandize and cruel slavery of men, what is that to us, and where will it justify them? And some will be saying, that the Black people, who are free in the West Indies are more miserable than the slaves;—and well they may; for while they can get their work and drudgery done for nothing, it is not likely that they will employ those whom they must pay for their labour. But whatever necessity the enslavers of men may plead for their iniquitous practice of slavery, and the various advantages which they get by it, can only evidence their own injustice and dishonesty. A man that is truly honest, fears nothing so much as the very imputation of injustice; but those men who dare not face the consequence of acting uprightly in every case are detestable cowards, unworthy the name of men; for it is manifest that such men are more afraid of temporal inconveniences than they are of God: *And I say unto you, my friends, be not afraid of them that kill the body, and after that have no more that they can do; but I will forewarn you whom you shall fear: Fear him, who, after he hath killed, hath power to cast into hell.* Luke xii. 4–5.

RICHARD PRICE

A Discourse on the Love of Our Country, delivered on Nov. 4, 1789, at the Meeting-House in the Old Jewry, to the Society for Commemorating the Revolution in Britain.

A Discourse, &c.

PSALM CXXII. 2D, AND FOLLOWING VERSES

Our feet shall stand within thy gates, O Jerusalem, whither the tribes go up; the tribes of the Lord unto the testimony of Israel. To give thanks to the name of the Lord, for there sit the thrones of judgment; the throne of the House of David. Pray for the peace of Jerusalem. They shall prosper that love thee. Peace be within thy walls, and prosperity within thy palaces. For my brethren and companions sake I will now say peace be within thee. Because of the House of the Lord our God, I will seek thy good.

In these words the Psalmist expresses, in strong and beautiful language, his love of his country, and the reasons on which he founded it; and my present design is, to take occasion from them to explain the duty we owe to our country, and the nature, foundation, and proper expressions of that love to it which we ought to cultivate.

I reckon this a subject particularly suitable to the services of this day, and to the Anniversary of our deliverance at the Revolution from the dangers of popery and arbitrary power; and should I, on such an occasion, be led to touch more on political subjects than would at any other time be proper in the pulpit, you will, I doubt not, excuse me.

The love of our country has in all times been a subject of warm commendations; and it is certainly a noble passion; but, like all other passions, it requires regulation and direction. There are mistakes and prejudices by which, in this instance, we are in particular danger of being misled.—I will briefly mention some of these to you, and observe,

First, That by our country is meant, in this case, not the soil or the spot of earth on which we happen to have been born; not the forests and fields, but that community of which we are members; or that body of companions and friends and kindred who are associated with us under the same constitution of government, protected by the same laws, and bound together by the same civil polity.

Secondly, It is proper to observe, that even in this sense of our country, that love of it which is our duty, does not imply any conviction of the superior value of it to other countries, or any particular preference of its laws and constitution of government. Were this implied, the love of their country would be the duty of only a very small part of mankind; for there are few countries that enjoy the advantage of laws and governments which deserve to be preferred. To found, therefore, this duty on such a preference, would be to found it on error and delusion. It is, however, a common delusion. There is the same partiality in countries, to themselves, that there is in individuals. All our attachments should be accompanied, as far as possible, with right opinions.—We are too apt to confine wisdom and virtue within the circle of our own acquaintance and party. Our friends, our country, and in short every thing related to us, we are disposed to overvalue. A wise man will guard himself against this delusion. He will study to think of all things as they are, and not suffer any partial affections to blind his understanding. In other families there may be as much worth as in our own. In other circles of friends there may be as much wisdom; and in other countries as much of all that deserves esteem; but, notwithstanding this, our obligation to love our own families, friends, and country, and to seek, in the first place, their good, will remain the same.

Thirdly, It is proper I should desire you particularly to distinguish between the love of our country and that spirit of rivalship and ambition which has been common among nations.—What has the love of their country hitherto been among mankind? What has it been but a love of domination; a desire of conquest, and a thirst for grandeur and glory, by extending territory, and enslaving surrounding countries? What has it been but a blind and narrow principle, producing in every country a contempt of other countries, and forming men into combinations and factions against their common rights and liberties? This is the principle that has been too often cried up as a virtue of the first rank: a principle of the same kind with that which governs clans of *Indians* or tribes of *Arabs*, and leads them out to plunder and massacre. As most of the evils which have taken place in private life, and among individuals, have been occasioned by the desire of private interest overcoming the public affections; so most of the evils which have taken place among bodies of men have been occasioned by the desire of their own interest overcoming the principle of universal benevolence: and leading them to attack one another's territories, to encroach on one another's rights, and to endeavour to build their own advancement on the degradation of all within the reach of their power—What was the love of their country among the *Jews,* but a wretched partiality to themselves, and a proud contempt of all other nations? What was the love of their country among the old *Romans?* We have heard much of it; but I cannot hesitate in saying that, however great it appeared in some of its exertions, it was in general no better than a principle holding together a band of robbers in their attempts to crush all liberty but their own. What is now the love of his country in a *Spaniard,* a *Turk,* or a *Russian?* Can it be considered as any thing better than a passion for slavery, or a blind attachment to a spot where he enjoys no rights, and is disposed of as if he was a beast?

Let us learn by such reflexions to correct and purify this passion, and to make it a just and rational principle of action.

It is very remarkable that the founder of our religion has not once mentioned this duty, or given us any recommendation of it; and this has, by unbelievers, been made an objection to Christianity. What I have said will entirely remove this objection. Certain it is, that, by inculcating on men an attachment to their country, Christianity would, at the time it was propagated, have done unspeakably more harm than good. Among the *Jews,* it would have been an excitement to war and insurrections; for they were then in eager expectation of becoming soon (as the favourite people of Heaven) the lords and conquerors of the earth, under the triumphant reign of the *Messiah.* Among the *Romans,* likewise, this principle had, as I have just observed, exceeded its just bounds, and rendered them enemies to the peace and happiness of mankind. By inculcating it, therefore, Christianity would have confirmed both Jews and Gentiles in one of the most pernicious faults. Our Lord and his Apostles have done better. They have recommended that universal benevolence which is an unspeakably nobler principle than any partial affections. They have laid such stress on loving all men, even our enemies, and made an ardent and extensive charity so essential a part of virtue, that the religion they have preached may, by way of distinction from all other religions, be called the Religion of Benevolence. Nothing can be more friendly to the general rights of mankind; and were it duly regarded and practised, every man would consider every other man as his brother, and all the animosity that now takes place among contending nations would be abolished. If you want any proof of this, think of our Saviour's parable of the good Samaritan.[1] The *Jews* and *Samaritans* were two rival nations that entertained a hatred of one another the most inveterate. The design of this parable was to shew to a *Jew,* that even a *Samaritan,* and consequently all men of all nations and religions, were included in the precept, Thou shalt love thy neighbour as thyself.

But I am digressing from what I had chiefly in view; which was, after noticing that love of our country which is false and spurious, to explain the nature and effects of that which is just and reasonable. With this view I must desire you to recollect that we are so constituted that our affections are more drawn to some among mankind than to others, in proportion to their degrees of nearness to us, and our power of being useful to them. It is obvious that this is a circumstance in the constitution of our natures which proves the wisdom and goodness of our Maker; for had our affections been determined alike to all our fellow-creatures, human life would have been a scene of embarrassment and distraction. Our regards, according to the order of nature, begin with ourselves; and every man is charged primarily with the care of himself. Next come our families, and benefactors, and friends; and after them our country. We can do little for the interest of mankind at large. To this interest, however, all other interests are subordinate. The noblest principle in our nature is the regard to general justice, and that good-will which embraces all the world.—I have already observed this; but it cannot be too often repeated. Though our immediate attention must be employed in promoting our own interest and that of our nearest connections; yet we must remember, that a narrower interest ought always to give way to a more extensive interest. In pursuing particularly the interest of our country, we ought to carry our views beyond

1. See Luke 10:25–37. The passage relates to the proper meaning of *neighbor.* Jesus argued for a universal application of that label and of the ethical duties it implied.

it. We should love it ardently, but not exclusively. We ought to seek
its good, by all the means that our different circumstances and abilities will allow; but at the same time we ought to consider ourselves as
citizens of the world, and take care to maintain a just regard to the
rights of other countries.

The enquiry by what means (subject to this limitation) we may
best promote the interest of our country is very important; and all
that remains of this discourse shall be employed in answering it,
and in exhorting you to manifest your love to your country, by the
means I shall mention.

The chief blessings of human nature are the three following:—
Truth—Virtue—and Liberty.—These are, therefore, the blessings
in the possession of which the interest of our country lies, and to
the attainment of which our love of it ought to direct our endeavours. By the diffusion of knowledge it must be distinguished from a
country of *Barbarians*: by the practice of religious virtue, it must be
distinguished from a country of *gamblers, Atheists,* and *libertines*:
and by the possession of liberty, it must be distinguished from a
country of *slaves*.—I will dwell for a few moments on each of these
heads:

Our first concern, as lovers of our country, must be to *enlighten*
it.—Why are the nations of the world so patient under despotism?—
Why do they crouch to tyrants, and submit to be treated as if they
were a herd of cattle? Is it not because they are kept in darkness,
and want knowledge? Enlighten them and you will elevate them.
Shew them they are *men,* and they will act like *men.* Give them just
ideas of civil government, and let them know that it is an expedient
for gaining protection against injury and defending their rights,[2]
and it will be impossible for them to submit to governments which,
like most of those now in the world, are usurpations on the rights of
men, and little better than contrivances for enabling the *few* to
oppress the *many.* Convince them that the Deity is a righteous and
benevolent as well as omnipotent being, who regards with equal eye
all his creatures, and connects his favour with nothing but an honest desire to know and do his will; and that zeal for mystical doctrines which has led men to hate and harass one another will be
exterminated. Set religion before them as a rational service, consisting not in any rites and ceremonies, but in worshipping God
with a pure heart and practising righteousness from the fear of his
displeasure and the apprehension of a future righteous judgment,
and that gloomy and cruel superstition will be abolished which has
hitherto gone under the name of religion, and to the support of

2. See the Declaration of Rights by the National Assembly of *France,* in the Appendix
   [Price's note].

which civil government has been perverted.—Ignorance is the parent of bigotry, intolerance, persecution and slavery. Inform and instruct mankind; and these evils will be excluded.—Happy is the person who, himself raised above vulgar errors, is conscious of having aimed at giving mankind this instruction. Happy is the Scholar or Philosopher who at the close of life can reflect that he has made this use of his learning and abilities: but happier far must he be, if at the same time he has reason to believe he has been successful, and actually contributed, by his instructions, to disseminate among his fellow-creatures just notions of themselves, of their rights, of religion, and the nature and end of civil government. Such were *Milton, Locke, Sidney, Hoadly,* &c. in this country; such were *Montesquieu, Fenelon, Turgot,*[3] &c. in France. They sowed a seed which has since taken root, and is now growing up to a glorious harvest. To the information they conveyed by their writings we owe those revolutions in which every friend to mankind is now exulting.—What an encouragement is this to us all in our endeavours to enlighten the world? Every degree of illumination which we can communicate must do the greatest good. It helps to prepare the minds of men for the recovery of their rights, and hastens the overthrow of priestcraft and tyranny.—In short, we may, in this instance, learn our duty from the conduct of the oppressors of the world. They know that light is hostile to them, and therefore they labour to keep men in the dark. With this intention they have appointed licensers of the press; and, in Popish countries, prohibited the reading of the Bible. Remove the darkness in which they envelope the world, and their usurpations will be exposed, their power will be subverted, and the world emancipated.

The next great blessing of human nature which I have mentioned is virtue. This ought to follow knowledge, and to be directed by it. Virtue without knowledge makes enthusiasts; and knowledge without virtue makes devils; but both united elevates to the top of human dignity and perfection.—We must, therefore, if we would serve our country, make both these the objects of our zeal. We must discourage vice in all its forms; and our endeavours to enlighten must have ultimately in view a reformation of manners and virtuous practice.

---

3. John Milton, John Locke, and Baron Charles Montesquieu were universally known among the political and cultural elite of the English-speaking world. Algernon Sidney was a Whig activist and anti-royalist philosopher who was executed for allegedly plotting to assassinate King Charles II in 1683. Benjamin Hoadly (1676–1761), François de Salignae de la Mothe Fénelon (1651–1715), and Anne-Robert-Jacques Turgot (1727–1781) were all critics of religious persecution and of the reckless abuse of power by monarchs and aristocratic governments. Turgot was also a friend of Adam Smith and a member of the so-called *physiocratic* school in France, which advocated liberal trade and the supremacy of agricultural production.

I must add here, that in the practice of virtue I include the discharge of the public duties of religion. By neglecting these we may injure our country essentially. But it is melancholy to observe that it is a common neglect among us; and in a great measure owing to a cause which is not likely to be soon removed: I mean, the defects (may I not say, the absurdities?) in our established codes of faith and worship. In foreign countries, the higher ranks of men, not distinguishing between the religion they see established and the Christian religion, are generally driven to irreligion and infidelity. The like evil is produced by the like cause in this country; and if no reformation of our established formularies can be brought about, it must be expected that religion will go on to lose its credit, and that little of it will be left except among the lower orders of people, many of whom, while their superiors give up all religion, are sinking into a barbarism in religion lately revived by Methodism,[4] and mistaking, as the world has generally done, the service acceptable to God for a system of faith souring the temper, and a service of forms supplanting morality.

I hope you will not mistake what I am now saying, or consider it as the effect of my prejudices as a Dissenter from the established church. The complaint I am making, is the complaint of many of the wisest and best men in the established church itself, who have been long urging the necessity of a revisal of its Liturgy and Articles.[5] These were framed above two centuries ago, when Christendom was just emerging from the ignorance and barbarity of the dark ages. They remain now much the same they were then; and, therefore, cannot be properly adapted to the good sense and liberality of the present times.—This imperfection, however, in our public forms of worship, affords no excuse to any person for neglecting public worship. All communities will have some religion; and it is of infinite consequence that they should be led to that which, by enforcing the obligations of virtue and putting men upon loving instead of damning one another, is most favourable to the interest of society.

4. The Methodists began as a movement within the Church of England, led by John Wesley and a small group of pious Oxford students during the late 1720s (they were derisively called "Methodists" because of their methodical forms of devotion and study.) By 1743, Wesley had published specific rules for Methodist societies, and the movement spread on both sides of the Atlantic during the evangelical revivals of the day. Methodists reinvigorated traditional Calvinism by stressing the possibility of salvation through faith and by embracing itinerant preaching and intimate fellowship. The emotional style of Methodist meetings and their apparent indifference to social hierarchies alarmed the more conservative elements of Anglo-American society.
5. See a pamphlet ascribed to a great name, and which would dignify any name, entitled, *Hints, &c. submitted to the serious Attention of the Clergy, Nobility, and Gentry, newly assembled. By a Layman, a Friend to the true Principles of the Constitution in Church and State, and to Civil and Religious Liberty.* The Third Edition, corrected; and printed for *White* and *Debrett,* 1789 [Price's note].

If there is a Governor of the world, who directs all events, he ought to be invoked and worshipped; and those who dislike that mode of worship which is prescribed by public authority, ought (if they can find no worship *out* of the church which they approve) to set up a separate worship for themselves; and by doing this, and giving an example of a rational and manly worship, men of weight, from their rank or literature, may do the greatest service to society and the world. They may bear a testimony against that application of civil power to the support of particular modes of faith, which obstructs human improvement, and perpetuates error; and they may hold out an instruction which will discountenance superstition, and at the same time recommend religion, by making it appear to be (what it certainly is when rightly understood) the strongest incentive to all that is generous and worthy, and consequently the best friend to public order and happiness.

Liberty is the next great blessing which I have mentioned as the object of patriotic zeal. It is inseparable from knowledge and virtue, and together with them completes the glory of a community. An enlightened and virtuous country must be a free country. It cannot suffer invasions of its rights, or bend to tyrants.—I need not, on this occasion, take any pains to shew you how great a blessing liberty is. The smallest attention to the history of past ages, and the present state of mankind, will make you sensible of its importance. Look round the world, and you will find almost every country, respectable or contemptible, happy or miserable, a fruitful field or a frightful waste, according as it possesses or wants this blessing. Think of *Greece,* formerly the seat of arts and science, and the most distinguished spot under heaven; but now, having lost liberty, a vile and wretched spot, a region of darkness, poverty, and barbarity.— Such reflexions must convince you that, if you love your country, you cannot be zealous enough in promoting the cause of liberty in it. But it will come in my way to say more to this purpose presently.

The observations I have made include our whole duty to our country; for by endeavouring to liberalize and enlighten it, to discourage vice and to promote virtue in it, and to assert and support its liberties, we shall endeavour to do all that is necessary to make it great and happy.—But it is proper that, on this occasion, I should be more explicit, and exemplify our duty to our country by observing farther, that it requires us to obey its laws, and to respect its magistrates.

Civil government (as I have before observed) is an institution of human prudence for guarding our persons, our property, and our good name, against invasion; and for securing to the members of a community that liberty to which all have an equal right, as far as they do not, by any overt act, use it to injure the liberty of others.

Civil laws are regulations agreed upon by the community for gaining these ends;[6] and civil magistrates are officers appointed by the
community for executing these laws. Obedience, therefore, to the
laws and to magistrates, are necessary expressions of our regard to
the community; and without this obedience the ends of government cannot be obtained, or a community avoid falling into a state
of anarchy that will destroy those rights and subvert that liberty,
which government is instituted to protect.

I wish it was in my power to give you a just account of the importance of this observation. It shews the ground on which the duty of
obeying civil governors stands, and that there are two extremes in
this case which ought to be avoided.—These extremes are adulation
and servility on one hand; and a and licentious contempt on the
other. The former is the extreme to which mankind in general have
been most prone; for it has oftener happened that men have been
too passive than too unruly; and the rebellion of Kings against their
people has been more common, and done more mischief, than the
rebellion of people against their Kings.

Adulation is always odious, and when offered to men in power it
corrupts *them,* by giving them improper ideas of their situation;
and it debases those who offer it, by manifesting an abjectness
founded on improper ideas of *themselves.* I have lately observed in
this kingdom too near approaches to this abjectness. In our late
addresses to the King, on his recovery from the severe illness with
which God has been pleased to afflict him,[7] we have appeared more
like a herd crawling at the feet of a master, than like enlightened
and manly citizens rejoicing with a beloved sovereign, but at the
same time conscious that he derives all his consequence from themselves. But, perhaps, these servilities in the language of our late
addresses should be pardoned, as only *forms* of civility and expressions of an overflow of good-nature. They have, however, a dangerous
tendency. The potentates of this world are sufficiently apt to consider
themselves as possessed of an inherent superiority, which gives them
a right to govern, and makes mankind *their own;* and this infatuation
is almost every where fostered in them by the creeping sycophants
about them, and the language of flattery which they are continually
hearing.

Civil governors are properly the servants of the public; and a
King is no more than the first servant of the public, created by it,

---

6. See Articles III. and VI. of the Declaration of Rights, by the National Assembly of
France, in the Appendix [Price's note].
7. King George III lapsed into insanity during 1788, after which he ceded much of his
authority to the extraordinarily energetic William Pitt the Younger. The king was widely
popular with the English people, remaining so even after further mental and physical
crises in 1804 and after 1810.

maintained by it, and responsible to it: and all the homage paid him, is due to him on no other account than his relation to the public. His sacredness is the sacredness of the community. His authority is the authority of the community; and the term Majesty, which it is usual to apply to him, is by no means *his own* majesty, but the majesty of the people. For this reason, whatever he may be in his private capacity; and though, in respect of personal qualities, not equal to, or even far below many among ourselves—For this reason, I say, (that is, as representing the community and its first magistrate), he is entitled to our reverence and obedience. The words most excellent majesty are rightly applied to him; and there is a respect which it would be criminal to withhold from him.

You cannot be too attentive to this observation. The improvement of the world depends on the attention to it: nor will mankind be ever as virtuous and happy as they are capable of being, till the attention to it becomes universal and efficacious. If we forget it, we shall be in danger of an idolatry as gross and stupid as that of the ancient heathens, who, after fabricating blocks of wood or stone, fell down and worshipped them.—The disposition in mankind to this kind of idolatry is indeed a very mortifying subject of reflexion.—In Turkey, millions of human beings adore a silly mortal, and are ready to throw themselves at his feet, and to submit their lives to his discretion.—In Russia, the common people are only a stock on the lands of grandees, or appendages to their estates, which, like the fixtures in a house, are bought and sold with the estates. In Spain, in Germany, and under most of the governments of the world, mankind are in a similar state of humiliation. Who, that has a just sense of the dignity of his nature, can avoid execrating such a debasement of it?

Had I been to address the King on a late occasion, I should have been inclined to do it in a style very different from that of most of the addressers, and to use some such language as the following:—
"I rejoice, Sir, in your recovery. I thank God for his goodness to you. I honour you not only as my King, but as almost the only lawful King in the world, because the only one who owes his crown to the choice of his people. May you enjoy all possible happiness. May God shew you the folly of those effusions of adulation which you are now receiving, and guard you against their effects. May you be led to such a just sense of the nature of your situation, and endowed with such wisdom, as shall render your restoration to the government of these kingdoms a blessing to it, and engage you to consider yourself as more properly the *Servant* than the *Sovereign* of your people."

But I must not forget the opposite extreme to that now taken notice of; that is, a disdainful pride, derived from a consciousness of equality, or, perhaps, superiority, in respect of all that gives true dignity to men in power, and producing a contempt of them, and a disposition to treat them with rudeness and insult. It is a trite observation, that extremes generally beget one another. This is particularly true in the present case. Persons justly informed on the subject of government, when they see men dazzled by looking up to high stations, and observe loyalty carried to a length that implies ignorance and servility: such persons, in such circumstances, are in danger of spurning at all public authority, and throwing off that respectful demeanor to persons invested with it which the order of society requires. There is undoubtedly a particular deference and homage due to civil magistrates, on account of their stations and offices; nor can that man be either truly wise or truly virtuous, who despises governments, and wantonly *speaks evil of his rulers;* or who does not, by all the means in his power, endeavour to strengthen their hands, and to give weight to their exertions in the discharge of their duty.—*Fear God,* says St. Peter. *Love the brotherhood. Honour all men. Honour the King.*—*You must needs,* says St. Paul, *be subject to rulers, not only for wrath* (that is, from the fear of suffering the penalties annexed to the breach of the laws), *but for conscience sake. For rulers are ministers of God, and revengers for executing wrath on all that do evil.*

Another expression of our love to our country is defending it against enemies. These enemies are of two sorts, internal and external; or domestic and foreign. The former are the most dangerous, and they have generally been the most successful. I have just observed, that there is a submission due to the executive officers of government, which is our duty; but you must not forget what I have also observed, that it must not be a blind and slavish submission. Men in power (unless better disposed than is common) are always endeavouring to extend their power. They hate the doctrine, that it is a trust derived from the people, and not a *right* vested in themselves. For this reason, the tendency of every government is to despotism; and in this the best constituted governments must end, if the people are not vigilant, ready to take alarms, and determined to resist abuses as soon as they begin. This vigilance, therefore, it is our duty to maintain. Whenever it is withdrawn, and a people cease to reason about their rights and to be awake to encroachments, they are in danger of being enslaved, and their *servants* will soon become their *masters.*

I need not say how much it is our duty to defend our country against foreign enemies. When a country is attacked in any of its rights by another country, or when any attempts are made by ambitious foreign powers to injure it, a war in its defence becomes necessary: and, in such circumstances, to die for our country is meritorious and noble. These *defensive* wars are, in my opinion, the only just wars. *Offensive* wars are always unlawful; and to seek the aggrandizement of our country by them, that is, by attacking other countries, in order to extend dominion, or to gratify avarice, is wicked and detestable. Such, however, have been most of the wars which have taken place in the world; but the time is, I hope, coming, when a conviction will prevail, of the folly[8] as well as the iniquity of wars; and when the nations of the earth, happy under just governments, and no longer in danger from the passions of Kings, will find out better ways of settling their disputes; and beat (as Isaiah prophecies) *their swords into plowshares, and their spears into pruning-hooks.*

Among the particulars included in that duty to our country, by discharging which we should shew our love to it, I will only further mention praying for it, and offering up thanksgivings to God for every event favourable to it. At the present season we are called upon to express, in this way, our love to our country. It is the business of this day, and of the present service; and, therefore, it is necessary that I should now direct your attention to it particularly.

We are met to thank God for that event in this country to which the name of The Revolution has been given; and which, for more than a century, it has been usual for the friends of freedom, and more especially Protestant Dissenters, under the title of the Revolution Society, to celebrate with expressions of joy and exultation.—My highly valued and excellent friend,[9] who addressed you on this occasion last year, has given you an interesting account of the principal circumstances that attended this event, and of the reasons we have for rejoicing in it. By a bloodless victory, the fetters which despotism had been long preparing for us were broken; the rights of the people were asserted, a tyrant expelled, and a Sovereign of our own choice appointed in his room. Security was given to our property, and our consciences were emancipated. The bounds of free enquiry were enlarged; the volume in which are the words of eternal life, was laid more open to our examination; and that *æra* of light and liberty was introduced among us, by which we have been made an example to other kingdoms, and became the instructors of the world. Had it not been for this deliverance, the probability is,

---

8. See a striking representation of the folly of wars, in the last sections of *Mr. Necker's Treatise on the Administration of the Finances of France.* There is reason to believe that the sentiments on this subject in that treatise, are now the prevailing sentiments in the court and legislature of France; and, consequently, that one of the happy effects of the revolution in that country may be, if not our own fault, such a harmony between the two first kingdoms in the world, strengthened by a common participation in the blessings of liberty, as shall not only prevent their engaging in any future wars with one another, but dispose them to unite in preventing wars every where, and in making the world free and happy [Price's note].

9. See Dr. Kippis's Sermon, preached on November 4th, 1788, to the Revolution Society, and printed for Mr. Cadell [Price's note].

that, instead of being thus distinguished, we should now have been a base people, groaning under the infamy and misery of popery and slavery. Let us, therefore, offer thanksgivings to God, the author of all our blessings. *Had he not been on our side, we should have been swallowed up quick, and the proud waters would have gone over our souls. But our souls are escaped, and the snare has been broken. Blessed then be the name of the Lord, who made heaven and earth.* cxxivth Psalm.

It is well known that King James was not far from gaining his purpose; and that probably he would have succeeded, had he been less in a hurry. But he was a fool as well as a bigot. He wanted courage as well as prudence; and, therefore, fled, and left us to settle quietly for ourselves that constitution of government which is now our boast. We have particular reason, as Protestant Dissenters, to rejoice on this occasion. It was at this time we were rescued from persecution, and obtained the liberty of worshipping God in the manner we think most acceptable to him. It was then our meeting-houses were opened, our worship was taken under the protection of the law, and the principles of toleration gained a triumph. We have, therefore, on this occasion, peculiar reasons for thanksgiving—But let us remember that we ought not to satisfy ourselves with thanksgivings. Our gratitude, if genuine, will be accompanied with endeavours to give stability to the deliverance our country has obtained, and to extend and improve the happiness with which the Revolution has blest us—Let us, in particular, take care not to forget the principles of the Revolution. This Society has, very properly, in its Reports, held out these principles, as an instruction to the public. I will only take notice of the three following:

First; The right to liberty of conscience in religious matters.

Secondly; The right to resist power when abused. And,

Thirdly; The right to chuse our own governors; to cashier them for misconduct; and to frame a government for ourselves.

On these three principles, and more especially the last, was the Revolution founded. Were it not true that liberty of conscience is a sacred right; that power abused justifies resistance; and that civil authority is a delegation from the people—Were not, I say, all this true; the Revolution would have been not an assertion, but an invasion of rights; not a Revolution, but a Rebellion. Cherish in your breasts this conviction, and act under its influence; detesting the odious doctrines of passive obedience, nonresistance, and the divine right of kings—doctrines which, had they been acted upon in this country, would have left us at this time wretched slaves—doctrines which imply, that God made mankind to be oppressed and plundered; and which are no less a blasphemy against him, than an insult on common sense.

I would farther direct you to remember, that though the Revolution was a great work, it was by no means a perfect work; and that all was not then gained which was necessary to put the kingdom in the secure and complete possession of the blessings of liberty.[1]—In particular, you should recollect, that the toleration then obtained was imperfect. It included only those who could declare their faith in the doctrinal articles of the church of England. It has, indeed, been since extended, but not sufficiently; for there still exist penal laws on account of religious opinions, which (were they carried into execution) would shut up many of our places of worship, and silence and imprison some of our ablest and best men.—The test laws are also still in force; and deprive of eligibility to civil and military offices, all who cannot conform to the established worship. It is with great pleasure I find that the body of Protestant Dissenters, though defeated in two late attempts to deliver their country from this disgrace to it, have determined to persevere. Should they at last succeed, they will have the satisfaction, not only of removing from themselves a proscription they do not deserve, but of contributing to lessen the number of our public iniquities. For I cannot call by a gentler name, laws which convert an ordinance appointed by our Saviour to commemorate his death, into an instrument of oppressive policy, and a qualification of rakes and atheists for civil posts.—I have said, *should* they succeed—but perhaps I ought not to suggest a doubt about their success.[2] And, indeed, when I consider that in

1. This critique of British politics dates at least to the 1720s and 1730s, when the so-called Commonwealthmen or Country Whigs argued that the British constitution had been corrupted by commercial interests, courtly intrigue, and a general absence of public spirit and involvement in civic life.
2. It has been unfortunate for the Dissenters that, in their late applications for a repeal of the Test Laws, they have been opposed by Mr. Pitt. He has contended that, on account of their not believing and worshipping as the Church of England does, they ought to be excluded from that eligibility to public offices which is the right of other citizens, and consequently denied a *complete* toleration; acknowledging, however, their integrity and respectableness, but reckoning it only the more necessary on that account to defend the national church against them. Such sentiments in these times can do no honour to any man, much less to a son of the late Lord Chatham, whose opinion of toleration and Protestant Dissenters may be learnt from the following account.
   In 1769 and 1772, the ministers among the Dissenters applied to Parliament for relief from the obligation they were then under to subscribe the doctrinal articles of the Church of England in order to be entitled to a toleration, and both times succeeded in the House of Commons, in consequence of Lord North's neutrality, but were defeated in the House of Lords, in consequence of an opposition from the Episcopal Bench. They persevered, however; the Bishops repented; and a third application proved successful in both Houses.—In the debate occasioned in the House of Lords by the *second* application, Dr. Drummond, the Archbishop of York, having called the Dissenting Ministers "men of close ambition," Lord Chatham said, that this was judging uncharitably; and that whoever brought such a charge against them, without proof, defamed. Here he paused; and then went on—"The Dissenting Ministers are represented as men of close ambition. They are so, my Lords; and their ambition is to keep *close* to the college of fishermen, not of cardinals, and to the doctrine of inspired

Scotland the established church is defended by no such test—that in Ireland it has been abolished—that in a great neighbouring country it has been declared to be an indefeasible right of all citizens to be equally eligible to public offices—that in the same kingdom a professed Dissenter from the established church holds the first office in the state[3]—that in the Emperor's dominions *Jews* have been lately admitted to the enjoyment of equal privileges with other citizens—and that in this very country, a Dissenter, though excluded from the power of *executing* the laws, yet is allowed to be employed in *making* them.—When, I say, I consider such facts as these, I am disposed to think it impossible that the enemies of the repeal of the Test Laws should not soon become ashamed, and give up their opposition.[4]

But the most important instance of the imperfect state in which the Revolution left our constitution, is the inequality of our representation. I think, indeed, this defect in our constitution so gross and so palpable, as to make it excellent chiefly in form and theory. You should remember that a representation in the legislature of a kingdom is the *basis* of constitutional liberty in it, and of all legitimate government; and that without it a government is nothing but an usurpation.[5] When the representation is fair and equal, and at the same time vested with such powers as our House of Commons possesses, a kingdom may be said to govern itself, and consequently to possess true liberty. When the representation is partial, a king-

---

apostles, not to the decrees of interested and aspiring bishops. They contend for a spiritual creed, and scriptural worship. We have a Calvinistic creed, a Popish liturgy, and an Arminian clergy. The Reformation has laid open the scriptures to all. Let not the Bishops shut them again. Laws in support of ecclesiastical power are pleaded for, which it would shock humanity to execute. It is said, that religious sects have done great mischief, when they were not kept under restraint: but history affords no proof that sects have ever been mischievous, when they were not oppressed and persecuted by the ruling church." See the Parliamentary Debates for 1772.

   In one of his letters to me, not long after this debate, dated Burton-Pynsent, January 16, 1773, he expresses himself in the following words: "In writing to you, it is impossible the mind should not go of itself to that most interesting of all objects to fallible man— Toleration. Be assured, that on this sacred and unalienable right of nature, and bulwark of truth, my warm wishes will always keep pace with your own. Happy, if the times had allowed us to add hopes to our wishes" [Price's note].

3. This seems to be a reference to very recent events in France. After the events of the summer of 1789 abolished the legitimacy of absolute monarchy, the Declaration of the Rights of Man and Citizen—which guaranteed religious liberty—was ratified by Louis XVI in October. Louis had already recalled the Protestant and Geneva-born finance minister, Jacques Necker (1732–1804) to the government.
4. Dissenters from the United Church of England and Ireland—the Anglican establishment—included Methodists, Presbyterians, Quakers, Baptists, Congregationalists, and Unitarians. All of them were free to preach and practice their faith, but they still had to pay for the support of the Anglican clergy and faced various exclusions from the institutions of British life. Catholics and Jews faced heavier restrictions, notably in voting and holding high office. For more on the Test Acts, which enforced Anglican orthodoxy, see Price's notes to this selection.
5. Except in states so small as to admit of a Legislative Assembly, consisting of all the members of the state [Price's note].

dom possesses liberty only partially; and if extremely partial, it only gives a *semblance* of liberty; but if not only extremely partial, but corruptly chosen, and under corrupt influence after being chosen, it becomes a *nuisance,* and produces the worst of all forms of government—a government by corruption—a government carried on and supported by spreading venality and profligacy through a kingdom. May heaven preserve this kingdom from a calamity so dreadful! It is the point of depravity to which abuses under such a government as ours naturally tend, and the last stage of national unhappiness. We are, at present, I hope, at a great distance from it. But it cannot be pretended that there are no advances towards it, or that there is no reason for apprehension and alarm.

The inadequateness of our representation has been long a subject of complaint. This is, in truth, our fundamental grievance; and I do not think that any thing is much more our duty, as men who love their country, and are grateful for the Revolution, than to unite our zeal in endeavouring to get it redressed. At the time of the American war, associations were formed for this purpose in London, and other parts of the kingdom; and our present Minister himself has, since that war, directed to it an effort which made him a favourite with many of us. But all attention to it seems now lost, and the probability is, that this inattention will continue, and that nothing will be done towards gaining for us this essential blessing, till some great calamity again alarms our fears, or till some great abuse of power again provokes our resentment; or, perhaps, till the acquisition of a pure and equal representation by other countries (while we are mocked with the shadow)[6] kindles our shame.

Such is the conduct by which we ought to express our gratitude for the Revolution.—We should always bear in mind the principles that justify it. We should contribute all we can towards supplying what it left deficient; and shew ourselves anxious about transmitting the blessings obtained by it to our posterity, unimpaired and improved.—But, brethren, while we thus shew our patriotic zeal, let us take care not to disgrace the cause of patriotism, by any licentious, or immoral conduct.—Oh! how earnestly do I wish that all who profess zeal in this cause, were as distinguished by the purity of their morals, as some of them are by their abilities; and that I could make them sensible of the advantages they would derive from a virtuous character, and of the suspicions they incur and the loss of consequence they suffer by wanting it.—Oh! that I could see in men who oppose tyranny in the state, a disdain of the tyranny of low passions in themselves; or, at least, such a sense of shame, and

---

6. A representation chosen principally by the Treasury, and a few thousands of the dregs of the people, who are generally paid for their votes [Price's note].

regard to public order and decency as would induce them to *hide* their irregularities, and to avoid insulting the virtuous part of the community by an open exhibition of vice!—I cannot reconcile myself to the idea of an immoral patriot, or to that separation of private from public virtue, which some think to be possible. Is it to be expected that— But I must forbear. I am afraid of applications, which many are too ready to make, and for which I should be sorry to give any just occasion.

I have been explaining to you the nature and expressions of a just regard to our country. Give me leave to exhort you to examine your conduct by what I have been saying. You love your country, and desire its happiness; and, without doubt, you have the greatest reason for loving it. It has been long a very distinguished and favoured country. Often has God appeared for it and delivered it. Let us study to shew ourselves worthy of the favour shewn us.—Do you practise virtue yourselves, and study to promote it in others? Do you obey the laws of your country, and aim at doing your part towards maintaining and perpetuating its privileges? Do you always give your vote on the side of public liberty; and are you ready to pour out your blood in its defence? Do you look up to God for the continuance of his favour to your country, and pray for its prosperity; preserving, at the same time, a strict regard to the rights of other countries, and always considering yourselves more as citizens of the world than as members of any particular community?—If this is your temper and conduct you are blessings to your country, and were all like you, this world would soon be a heaven.

I am addressing myself to Christians. Let me, therefore, mention to you the example of our blessed Saviour. I have observed, at the beginning of this discourse, that he did not inculcate upon his hearers the love of their country, or take any notice of it as a part of our duty. Instead of doing this, I observed that he taught the obligation to love all mankind, and recommended universal benevolence, as (next to the love of God) our first duty; and, I think, I also proved to you, that this, in the circumstances of the world at that time, was an instance of incomparable wisdom and goodness in his instructions. But we must not infer from hence, that he did not include the love of our country in the number of our duties. He has shewn the contrary by his example. It appears that he possessed a particular affection for his country, though a very wicked country. We read in Luke x. 42, that when, upon approaching *Jerusalem,* in one of his last journies to it, he beheld it, he wept over it, and said; *Oh! that thou hadst known (even thou, at least in this thy day) the things that belong to thy peace.*—What a tender solicitude about his country does the lamentation over *Jerusalem* imply, which is recorded in the same gospel, chap. xiii. and 34. *Oh! Jerusalem, Jerusalem, thou that killest the prophets, and stonest them who are sent to thee, how often would I have gathered thy children together, as a hen gathereth her brood under her wings, but ye would not.*

It may not be improper farther to mention the love St. Paul expressed for his country, when he declared, that, for the sake of his brethren and kinsmen, he could even wish himself *accursed from Christ.* (Rom. ix. 3.) The original words are an Anathema *from Christ;* and his meaning is, that he could have been contented to suffer *himself* the calamities which were coming on the Jewish people, were it possible for him, by such a sacrifice of himself, to save them.

It is too evident that the state of this country is such as renders it an object of concern and anxiety. It wants (I have shewn you) the grand security of public liberty. Increasing luxury has multiplied abuses in it. A monstrous weight of debt is crippling it. Vice and venality are bringing down upon it God's displeasure. That spirit to which it owes its distinctions is declining;[7] and some late events seem to prove that it is becoming every day more reconcileable to encroachments on the securities of its liberties.[8]—It wants, therefore, your patriotic services; and, for the sake of the distinctions it has so long enjoyed; for the sake of our brethren and companions, and all that should be dear to a free people, we ought to do our utmost to save it from the dangers that threaten it; remembering, that by acting thus, we shall promote, in the best manner, our own private interest, as well as the interest of our country; for when the community prospers, the individuals that compose it must prosper with it.—But, should that not happen, or should we even suffer in our secular interest by our endeavours to promote the interest of our country, we shall feel a satisfaction in our own breasts which is preferable to all this world can give; and we shall enjoy the transporting hope of soon becoming members of a perfect community in the heavens, and having *an entrance ministered to us, abundantly into the everlasting kingdom of our Lord and Saviour Jesus Christ.*

You may reasonably expect that I should now close this address to you. But I cannot yet dismiss you. I must not conclude without recalling, particularly, to your recollection, a consideration to which I have more than once alluded, and which, probably, your thoughts have been all along anticipating: A consideration with which my

7. One of these distinctions is, that being in possession of the forms of an excellent constitution of government, any changes or improvements necessary to correct abuses and to give perfect liberty, may be grafted upon them, without tumult or danger; whereas other countries, wanting these forms, and being under the necessity of erecting a new constitution on the ruins of an old one, cannot acquire liberty without setting every thing afloat, and making their escape from slavery through the dangers of anarchy [Price's note].

8. Among these encroachments I must reckon the extension of the Excise laws, the introduction of the custom of farming taxes, and the additional burdens lately thrown on the freedom of the press, and the circulation of intelligence [Price's note].

mind is impressed more than I can express. I mean, the consideration of the favourableness of the present times to all exertions in
the cause of public liberty.

What an eventful period is this! I am thankful that I have lived to
it; and I could almost say, *Lord, now lettest thou thy servant depart in
peace, for mine eyes have seen thy salvation.* I have lived to see a diffusion of knowledge, which has undermined superstition and
error—I have lived to see the rights of men better understood than
ever; and nations panting for liberty, which seemed to have lost the
idea of it.—I have lived to see Thirty Millions of people, indignant
and resolute, spurning at slavery, and demanding liberty with an
irresistible voice; their king led in triumph, and an arbitrary monarch surrendering himself to his subjects.—After sharing in the
benefits of one Revolution, I have been spared to be a witness to two
other Revolutions, both glorious.—And now, methinks, I see the
ardor for liberty catching and spreading; a general amendment
beginning in human affairs; the dominion of kings changed for the
dominion of laws, and the dominion of priests giving way to the
dominion of reason and conscience.

Be encouraged, all ye friends of freedom, and writers in its defence!
The times are auspicious. Your labours have not been in vain. Behold
kingdoms, admonished by you, starting from sleep, breaking their
fetters, and claiming justice from their oppressors! Behold, the light
you have struck out, after setting America free, reflected to France,
and there kindled into a blaze that lays despotism in ashes, and
warms and illuminates Europe!

Tremble all ye oppressors of the world! Take warning all ye supporters of slavish governments, and slavish hierarchies! Call no more
(absurdly and wickedly) Reformation, innovation. You cannot now
hold the world in darkness. Struggle no longer against increasing
light and liberality. Restore to mankind their rights; and consent to
the correction of abuses, before they and you are destroyed together.

FINIS.

JAMES MADISON

On Perpetual Peace, February 2, 1792[†]

Among the various reforms which have been offered to the world,
the projects for universal peace have done the greatest honor to the

---

† From *The Writings of James Madison, Comprising His Public Papers and His Private
Correspondence, Including His Numerous Letters and Documents Now for the First
Time Printed,* ed. Gaillard Hunt (New York: G.P. Putnam's Sons, 1900), vol. 6.

hearts, though they seem to have done very little to the heads of their authors. Rousseau,[1] the most distinguished of these philanthropists, has recommended a confederation of sovereigns, under a council of deputies, for the double purpose of arbitrating external controversies among nations, and of guaranteeing their respective governments against internal revolutions. He was aware, neither of the impossibility of executing his pacific plan among governments which feel so many allurements to war, nor, what is more extraordinary, of the tendency of his plan to perpetuate arbitrary power wherever it existed; and, by extinguishing the hope of one day seeing an end of oppression, to cut off the only source of consolation remaining to the oppressed.

A universal and perpetual peace, it is to be feared, is in the catalogue of events, which will never exist but in the imaginations of visionary philosophers, or in the breasts of benevolent enthusiasts. It is still however true, that war contains so much folly, as well as wickedness, that much is to be hoped from the progress of reason; and if any thing is to be hoped, every thing ought to be tried.

Wars may be divided into two classes: one flowing from the mere will of the government, the other according with the will of the society itself.

Those of the first class can no otherwise be prevented than by such a reformation of the government, as may identify its will with the will of the society. The project of Rousseau, was, consequently, as preposterous as it was impotent. Instead of beginning with an external application, and even precluding internal remedies, he ought to have commenced with, and chiefly relied on, the latter prescription.

He should have said, whilst war is to depend on those whose ambition, whose revenge, whose avidity, or whose caprice may contradict the sentiment of the community, and yet be uncontrouled by it; whilst war is to be declared by those who are to spend the public money, not by those who are to pay it; by those who are to direct the public forces, not by those who are to support them; by those whose power is to be raised, not by those whose chains may be riveted, the disease must continue to be *hereditary* like the government of which it is the offspring. As the first step towards a cure, the government itself must be regenerated. Its will must be

---

1. In 1761, Jean-Jacques Rousseau (1721–1778) revised earlier plans for a working peace in Europe by proposing a federal union or league of the various countries. Under this plan, each nation would submit to the decisions of a tribunal charged with brokering conflicts. This federation would have its own military power, so that it could enforce its resolves. Enlightenment figures often condemned militarism and mass violence. See, for example, Voltaire's bitterly sarcastic discussion of "Splendid Armies" in *Candide* (1759).

made subordinate to, or rather the same with, the will of the community.[2]

Had Rousseau lived to see the constitution of the United States and of France, his judgment might have escaped the censure to which his project has exposed it.

The other class of wars, corresponding with the public will, are less susceptible of remedy. There are antidotes, nevertheless, which may not be without their efficacy. As wars of the first class were to be prevented by subjecting the will of the government to the will of the society, those of the second class can only be controuled by subjecting the will of the society to the reason of the society; by establishing permanent and constitutional maxims of conduct, which may prevail over occasional impressions and inconsiderate pursuits.

Here our republican philosopher might have proposed as a model to lawgivers, that war should not only be declared by the authority of the people, whose toils and treasures are to support its burdens, instead of the government which is to reap its fruits: but that each generation should be made to bear the burden of its own wars, instead of carrying them on, at the expence of other generations. And to give the fullest energy to his plan, he might have added, that each generation should not only bear its own burdens, but that the taxes composing them, should include a due proportion of such as by their direct operation keep the people awake, along with those, which being wrapped up in other payments, may leave them asleep, to misapplications of their money.

To the objection, if started, that where the benefits of war descend to succeeding generations, the burdens ought also to descend, he might have answered; that the exceptions could not be easily made; that, if attempted, they must be made by one only of the parties interested; that in the alternative of sacrificing exceptions to general rules, or of converting exceptions into general rules, the former is the lesser evil; that the expense of *necessary* wars, will never exceed the resources of an *entire* generation; that, in fine the objection vanishes before the fact, that in every nation which has drawn on posterity for the support of its wars, the *accumulated interest* of its perpetual debts, has soon become more than a *sufficient principal* for all its exigencies.

2. In 1789, Madison had received a letter from Thomas Jefferson denouncing the influence of past generations over the living and arguing for a thorough change in all laws every few decades. Madison obviously disagreed—he had, after all, just designed a Constitution to secure a national government for posterity. In this passage, however, he seems to gesture to both the theory of generational sovereignty and the provision in the Constitution (Article I, Section 8) whereby Congress must approve war funding every two years.

Were a nation to impose such restraints on itself, avarice would be sure to calculate the expences of ambition; in the equipoise of these passions, reason would be free to decide for the public good; and an ample reward would accrue to the state, first, from the avoidance of all its wars of folly, secondly, from the vigor of its unwasted resources for wars of necessity and defence. Were all nations to follow the example, the reward would be doubled to each; and the temple of Janus might be shut, never to be opened more.[3]

Had Rousseau lived to see the rapid progress of reason and reformation, which the present day exhibits, the philanthropy which dictated his project would find a rich enjoyment in the scene before him. And after tracing the past frequency of wars to a will in the government independent of the will of the people; to the practice by each generation of taxing the principal of its debts on future generations; and to the facility with which each generation is seduced into assumption of the interest, by the deceptive species of taxes which pay it; he would contemplate, in a reform of every government subjecting its will to that of the people, in a subjection of each generation to the payment of its own debts, and in a substitution of a more palpable, in place of an imperceptible mode of paying them, the only hope of Universal and Perpetual Peace.

WILL CHIP, A COUNTRY CARPENTER
[HANNAH MORE]

Village Politics: Addressed to All the Mechanics, Journeymen, and Day-Labourers, in Great Britain (1793)

A DIALOGUE between JACK ANVIL the Blacksmith, and TOM HOD the Mason.

JACK.   WHAT's the matter, Tom? Why dost look so dismal?
TOM.   Dismal indeed! Well enough I may.
JACK.   What's the old mare dead? or work scarce?

---

3. The idea of opposing dangerous passions against one another had been an important part of Anglo-American thought since the seventeenth century, when economists theorized about the social motivations underpinning commerce. In *Federalist* #51, Madison argued that the best way, perhaps the only way, to give government power while still protecting the liberties of the governed was to make different power holders separate and independent: "Ambition must be made to counteract ambition."

TOM.   No, no, work's plenty enough, if a man had but the
heart to go to it.[1]

JACK.   What book art reading? Why dost look so like a
hang-dog?

TOM.   *(looking on his book)* Cause enough. Why I find here
that I'm very unhappy, and very miserable; which I should
never have known if I had not had the good luck to meet
with this book. O 'tis a precious book!

JACK.   A good sign tho'; that you can't find out you're unhappy
without looking into a book for it. What is the matter?

TOM.   Matter! Why I want Liberty.

JACK: Liberty! What has any one fetched a warrant for thee?
Come man, cheer up, I'll be bound for thee.—Thou art an
honest fellow in the main, tho' thou dost tipple and prate a
little too much at the rose and crown.

TOM.   No, no, I want a new constitution.

JACK.   Indeed! Why I thought thou hadst been a desperate
healthy fellow. Send for the doctor then.

TOM.   I'm not sick; I want Liberty and Equality, and the Rights
of Man.

JACK.   O now I understand thee. What thou art a leveller and
a republican, I warrant.

TOM.   I'm a friend to the people. I want a reform.

JACK.   Then the shortest way is to mend thyself.

TOM.   But I want a general reform.

JACK.   Then let every one mend one.

TOM.   Pooh! I want freedom and happiness, the same as they
have got in France.

JACK.   What, Tom, we imitate them? We follow the French!
Why they only begun all this mischief at first, in order to be
just what we are already. Why I'd sooner go to the Negers to
get learning, or to the Turks to get religion, than to the
French for freedom and happiness.

TOM.   What do you mean by that? ar'nt the French free?

JACK.   Free, Tom! aye, free with a witness. They are all so free,
that there's nobody safe. They make free to rob whom they
will, and kill whom they will. If they don't like a man's looks,
they make free to hang him without judge or jury, and the
next lamppost does for the gallows, so then they call themselves free, because you see they have no king to take them
up and hang them for it.

---

1. Arguments based on plenty became much harder to sustain in 1794, just after this
pamphlet appeared, when a very cold winter and high commodity prices brought hunger and food riots through much of Britain.

TOM.   Ah, but Jack, didn't their King formerly hang people for
nothing too? and besides, wer'n't they all Papists before the
Revolution?

JACK.   Why, true enough, they had but a poor sort of religion,
but bad is better than none, Tom. And so was the government bad enough too, for they could clap an innocent man
into prison, and keep him there too as long as they would,
and never say with your leave or by your leave, Gentlemen of
the Jury. But what's all that to us?

TOM,   To us! Why don't our governors put many of our poor
folks in prison against their will? What are all the gaols for?
Down with the gaols, I say; all men should be free.[2]

JACK.   Harkee, Tom, a few rogues in prison keep the rest in
order, and then honest men go about their business, afraid
of nobody; that's the way to be free. And let me tell thee,
Tom, thou and I are tried by our peers as much as a lord is.
Why the king can't send me to prison if I do no harm, and if
I do, there's reason good why I should go there. I may go to
law with Sir John, at the great castle yonder, and he no more
dares lift his little finger against me than if I were his equal.
A lord is hanged for hanging matter, as thou or I should be;
and if it will be any comfort to thee, I myself remember a
Peer of the Realm being hanged for killing his man, just the
same as the man would have been for killing him.[3]

TOM.   Well, that is some comfort.—But have you read the
Rights of Man?

JACK.   No, not I. I had rather by half read the *Whole Duty of
Man*.[4] I have but little time for reading, and such as I should
therefore only read a bit of the best.

TOM.   Don't tell me of those old fashioned notions. Why should
not we have the same fine things they have got in France? I'm
for a *Constitution* and *Organization,* and *Equalization*.

JACK.   Do be quiet. Now, Tom, only suppose this nonsensical
equality was to take place; why it would not last while one
could say Jack Robinson; or suppose it could— suppose, in

2 In Part II of *Rights of Man*, Paine noted that Britain's penal system was especially harsh
in dealing with property crimes (theft, larceny, and more seriously, counterfeiting).
During the course of the eighteenth century, the number of capital crimes increased
fourfold, to well over one hundred. In many counties, the overwhelming majority of
those executed had committed theft, often on a very small scale.
3. Lord Ferrers was hanged in 1760, for killing his steward [More's note].
4. Probably the work of the Anglican clergyman Richard Alestree (1619–1681), *The
Whole Duty of Man* was a devotional tract first published in 1658 and reprinted
throughout the eighteenth century. The complete title of the eighteenth-century editions is telling: *The Whole Duty of Man: Laid Down in a Plain and Familiar Way for the
Use of All, but Especially the Meanest Reader.* The book also billed itself as "Necessary
for all Families."

the general division, our new rulers were to give us half an acre of ground a-piece; we could to be sure raise potatoes on it for the use of our families; but as every other man would be equally busy in raising potatoes for *his* family, why then you see if thou was to break thy spade, I should not be able to mend it. Neighbour Snip would have *no* time to make us a suit of cloaths, nor the clothier to weave the cloth, for all the world would be gone a digging. And as to boots, and shoes, the want of someone to make them for us, would be a greater grievance than the tax on leather. If we should be sick, there would be no doctor's stuff for us; for doctor would be digging too. We could not get a chimney swept, or a load of coal from pit, for love or money.[5]

TOM.   But still I should have no-one over my head.

JACK.   That's a mistake: I'm stronger than; and Standish, the exciseman, is a better scholar; so we should not remain equal a minute. I would out-*Fight* thee, and he'd out-*wit* thee. And if such a sturdy fellow as I am, was to come and break down thy hedge for a little firing, or to take away the crop from thy ground, I'm not so sure that these new-fangled laws would see thee righted. I tell thee, Tom, we have a fine constitution already, and our fore-fathers thought so.

TOM.   They were a pack of fools; and had never read the Rights of Man.

JACK.   I'll tell thee a story. When Sir John married, my Lady, who is a little fantastical, and likes to do everything like the French, begged him to pull down yonder fine old castle, and build it up in her frippery way. No, says Sir John; what shall I pull down this noble building, raised by the wisdom of my brave ancestors; which outstood the civil wars; and only underwent a little needful repair at the Revolution; and which all my neighbours come to take a pattern by—shall I pull it all down, I say, only because there may be a dark closet of an inconvenient room or two in it? My lady mumpt and grumbled; but the castle was let stand, and a glorious building it is, though there may be a trifling fault or two and tho' a few decays may want stopping; so now and then they mend a little thing, and they'll go on mending I dare say, as they have

---

5. One of the most dreaded ideas to emerge from the French (and to a much lesser extent, the American) Revolution was that of limiting the size of private estates and of redistributing landed wealth. Such "agrarian laws" and the more general idea of equality sparked a massive conservative backlash in the Anglo-American world. More's language in this pamphlet echoes both the title and the declarations of the Association for Preserving Liberty and Property against Republicans and Levellers, formed in London after war broke out with France in 1793. Similar groups spread all over Britain during the 1790s.

leisure, to the end of the chapter, if they are let alone. But no
pull-me-down works. What is it you are crying out for, Tom?

TOM.   Why for a perfect government.

JACK.   You might as well cry for the moon. There's nothing
perfect in this world, take my word for it.

TOM.   I don't see why we are to work like slaves, while others
roll about in their coaches, feed on the fat of the land, and
do nothing.

JACK.   My little maid brought home a storybook from the
Charity-School t'other day, in which was a bit of a fable
about the Belly and the Limbs. The hand said, I won't work
any longer to feed this lazy belly, who sits in state like a lord,
and does nothing. Said the feet, I won't walk and tire myself
to carry him about; let him shift for himself; so said all the
members ; just as your Levellers and Republicans do now.
And what was the consequence? Why the belly was pinched
to be sure; but the hands and the feet, and the rest of the
members suffered so much for want of their old nourishment,
that they fell sick, pined away, and would have died, if they
had not come to their senses just in time to save their lives, as
I hope all you will do.[6]

TOM   But the times—but the taxes, Jack.

JACK.   Things are dear, to be sure: but riot and murder is not
the way to make them cheap. And taxes are high; but I'm
told there's a deal of old scores paying off, and by them who
did not contract; the debt neither, Tom. Besides things are
mending, I hope, and what little is done, is for us poor people; our candles are somewhat cheaper, and I dare say, if the
honest gentleman is not disturbed by you levellers, things will
mend every day. But bear one thing in mind: the more we riot,
the more we shall have to pay. Mind another thing too, that in
France the poor paid all the taxes, as I have heard 'em say, and
the quality paid nothing.

TOM.   Well, I know what's what, as well as another; and I'm as
fit to govern—

JACK.   No, Tom, no. You are indeed as good as another man,
seeing you have hands to work, and a soul to be saved. But are
all men fit for all kinds of things? Solomon says, "'How can he
be wise whose talk is of oxen ?' Every one in his way."[7] I am a
better judge of a horse-shoe than Sir John; but he has a deal

---

6. This story recalls a traditional theory of politics that understood the state, especially
the monarchy, as the organic representation of the people. In the new United States,
such bodily metaphors gave way to architectural images—the Constitution as a building or an edifice, with the various states represented as pillars.

7. The wisdom of Solomon, one of the ancient kings of Israel, is evoked in 1 Kings 4:30–
34. *The Whole Duty of Man* also makes frequent reference to Solomon's wisdom.

better notion of state affairs than I; and I can no more do without him than he can do without me. And few are so poor but they may get a vote for a parliament-man, and so you see the poor have as much share in the government as they well know how to manage.[8]

TOM.   But I say all men are equal. Why should one be above another?

JACK.   If that's thy talk, Tom, thou dost quarrel with providence and not with government. For the woman is below her husband, and the children are below their mother, and the servant is below is master.

TOM.   But the subject is not below the king; all kings are "crowned ruffians" and all governments are wicked. For my part, I'm resolved I'll pay no more taxes to any of them.

JACK.   Tom, Tom, this is thy nonsense; if thou didst go oftener to church, thou wouldest know where it is said, "Render unto Cæsar the things that are Cæsar's" and also, "Fear God, honour the king." Your book tells you that we need obey no government but that of the people, and that we may fashion and alter the government according to our whimsies; but mine tells me, "Let every one be subject to the higher powers, for all power is of God."[9] Thou sayst, thou wilt pay no taxes to any of them. Dost thou know who it was that worked a miracle, that he might have money to pay tribute with, rather than set you and me an example of disobedience to government?

TOM.   I say we shall never be happy, till we do as the French have done.

JACK.   The French and we contending for liberty, Tom, is just as if thou and I were to pretend to run a race; thou to set out from the starting post, when I am in already: why we've got it man, we've no race to run. We're there already. Our constitution is no more like what the French one was, than a mug of our Taunton beer is like a platter of their soup-maigre.[1]

---

8. This is not accurate. Only about one English man in five or six was even qualified by property requirements to vote, and the parliamentary seats were often controlled by small oligarchies that effectively selected candidates.

9. Here More blends together three separate New Testament injunctions. The first is from Jesus, taken from Matthew 22:20–22. The second is from St. Peter, in 1 Peter 2:17. (The complete injunction from the King James version is: "Honor all men. Love the brotherhood. Fear God. Honor the King." More pointedly and conveniently left out the first two parts of the quote.) The third is from St. Paul, in Romans 13:1

1. Eighteenth-century British nationalism often contrasted the hearty, healthy Englishman, who ate roast beef and drank good ale, with the supposedly starving and oppressed peasants of France. The *soup-maigre*, literally "thin soup," was made of various vegetables or fish and butter. References to Taunton beer occasionally appear in gentlemen's letters, apparently in reference to a strong ale.

GEORGE WASHINGTON

Farewell Address, September 19, 1796[†]

Friends and Citizens:

The period for a new election of a citizen to administer the executive government of the United States being not far distant, and the time actually arrived when your thoughts must be employed in designating the person who is to be clothed with that important trust, it appears to me proper, especially as it may conduce to a more distinct expression of the public voice, that I should now apprise you of the resolution I have formed, to decline being considered among the number of those out of whom a choice is to be made.

I beg you, at the same time, to do me the justice to be assured that this resolution has not been taken without a strict regard to all the considerations appertaining to the relation which binds a dutiful citizen to his country; and that in withdrawing the tender of service, which silence in my situation might imply, I am influenced by no diminution of zeal for your future interest, no deficiency of grateful respect for your past kindness, but am supported by a full conviction that the step is compatible with both.

The acceptance of, and continuance hitherto in, the office to which your suffrages have twice called me have been a uniform sacrifice of inclination to the opinion of duty and to a deference for what appeared to be your desire. I constantly hoped that it would have been much earlier in my power, consistently with motives which I was not at liberty to disregard, to return to that retirement from which I had been reluctantly drawn. The strength of my inclination to do this, previous to the last election, had even led to the preparation of an address to declare it to you; but mature reflection on the then perplexed and critical posture of our affairs with foreign nations,[1] and the unanimous advice of persons entitled to my confidence, impelled me to abandon the idea.

I rejoice that the state of your concerns, external as well as internal, no longer renders the pursuit of inclination incompatible with the sentiment of duty or propriety, and am persuaded,

---

[†] From Yale Law School, "18th Century Documents: 1700–1799," *The Avalon Project: Documents in Law, History, and Diplomacy,* http://avalon.law.edu/subject_menus.washpap.asp.

1. American relations with foreign nations were "perplexed and critical" throughout the 1790s, so it is difficult to know exactly what crisis Washington had in mind here. Most likely he meant the ongoing struggle with Britain over the terms of the 1783 Treaty of Paris along with the initial crises brought on by the French Revolution.

whatever partiality may be retained for my services, that, in the present circumstances of our country, you will not disapprove my determination to retire.

The impressions with which I first undertook the arduous trust were explained on the proper occasion. In the discharge of this trust, I will only say that I have, with good intentions, contributed towards the organization and administration of the government the best exertions of which a very fallible judgment was capable. Not unconscious in the outset of the inferiority of my qualifications, experience in my own eyes, perhaps still more in the eyes of others, has strengthened the motives to diffidence of myself; and every day the increasing weight of years admonishes me more and more that the shade of retirement is as necessary to me as it will be welcome. Satisfied that if any circumstances have given peculiar value to my services, they were temporary, I have the consolation to believe that, while choice and prudence invite me to quit the political scene, patriotism does not forbid it.

In looking forward to the moment which is intended to terminate the career of my public life, my feelings do not permit me to suspend the deep acknowledgment of that debt of gratitude which I owe to my beloved country for the many honors it has conferred upon me; still more for the steadfast confidence with which it has supported me; and for the opportunities I have thence enjoyed of manifesting my inviolable attachment, by services faithful and persevering, though in usefulness unequal to my zeal. If benefits have resulted to our country from these services, let it always be remembered to your praise, and as an instructive example in our annals, that under circumstances in which the passions, agitated in every direction, were liable to mislead, amidst appearances sometimes dubious, vicissitudes of fortune often discouraging, in situations in which not unfrequently want of success has countenanced the spirit of criticism, the constancy of your support was the essential prop of the efforts, and a guarantee of the plans by which they were effected. Profoundly penetrated with this idea, I shall carry it with me to my grave, as a strong incitement to unceasing vows that heaven may continue to you the choicest tokens of its beneficence; that your union and brotherly affection may be perpetual; that the free Constitution, which is the work of your hands, may be sacredly maintained; that its administration in every department may be stamped with wisdom and virtue; that, in fine, the happiness of the people of these States, under the auspices of liberty, may be made complete by so careful a preservation and so prudent a use of this blessing as will acquire to them the glory of recommending it to the applause, the affection, and adoption of every nation which is yet a stranger to it.

Here, perhaps, I ought to stop. But a solicitude for your welfare, which cannot end but with my life, and the apprehension of danger, natural to that solicitude, urge me, on an occasion like the present, to offer to your solemn contemplation, and to recommend to your frequent review, some sentiments which are the result of much reflection, of no inconsiderable observation, and which appear to me all-important to the permanency of your felicity as a people. These will be offered to you with the more freedom, as you can only see in them the disinterested warnings of a parting friend, who can possibly have no personal motive to bias his counsel. Nor can I forget, as an encouragement to it, your indulgent reception of my sentiments on a former and not dissimilar occasion.

Interwoven as is the love of liberty with every ligament of your hearts, no recommendation of mine is necessary to fortify or confirm the attachment.

The unity of government which constitutes you one people is also now dear to you. It is justly so, for it is a main pillar in the edifice of your real independence, the support of your tranquility at home, your peace abroad; of your safety; of your prosperity; of that very liberty which you so highly prize. But as it is easy to foresee that, from different causes and from different quarters, much pains will be taken, many artifices employed to weaken in your minds the conviction of this truth; as this is the point in your political fortress against which the batteries of internal and external enemies will be most constantly and actively (though often covertly and insidiously) directed, it is of infinite moment that you should properly estimate the immense value of your national union to your collective and individual happiness; that you should cherish a cordial, habitual, and immovable attachment to it; accustoming yourselves to think and speak of it as of the palladium of your political safety and prosperity; watching for its preservation with jealous anxiety; discountenancing whatever may suggest even a suspicion that it can in any event be abandoned; and indignantly frowning upon the first dawning of every attempt to alienate any portion of our country from the rest, or to enfeeble the sacred ties which now link together the various parts.

For this you have every inducement of sympathy and interest. Citizens, by birth or choice, of a common country, that country has a right to concentrate your affections. The name of American, which belongs to you in your national capacity, must always exalt the just pride of patriotism more than any appellation derived from local discriminations. With slight shades of difference, you have the same religion, manners, habits, and political principles. You have in a common cause fought and triumphed together; the independence and liberty you possess are the work of joint counsels, and joint efforts of common dangers, sufferings, and successes.

But these considerations, however powerfully they address themselves to your sensibility, are greatly outweighed by those which apply more immediately to your interest. Here every portion of our country finds the most commanding motives for carefully guarding and preserving the union of the whole.

The North, in an unrestrained intercourse with the South, protected by the equal laws of a common government, finds in the productions of the latter great additional resources of maritime and commercial enterprise and precious materials of manufacturing industry. The South, in the same intercourse, benefiting by the agency of the North, sees its agriculture grow and its commerce expand. Turning partly into its own channels the seamen of the North, it finds its particular navigation invigorated; and, while it contributes, in different ways, to nourish and increase the general mass of the national navigation, it looks forward to the protection of a maritime strength, to which itself is unequally adapted. The East, in a like intercourse with the West, already finds, and in the progressive improvement of interior communications by land and water, will more and more find a valuable vent for the commodities which it brings from abroad, or manufactures at home. The West derives from the East supplies requisite to its growth and comfort, and, what is perhaps of still greater consequence, it must of necessity owe the secure enjoyment of indispensable outlets for its own productions to the weight, influence, and the future maritime strength of the Atlantic side of the Union, directed by an indissoluble community of interest as one nation. Any other tenure by which the West can hold this essential advantage, whether derived from its own separate strength, or from an apostate and unnatural connection with any foreign power, must be intrinsically precarious.

While, then, every part of our country thus feels an immediate and particular interest in union, all the parts combined cannot fail to find in the united mass of means and efforts greater strength, greater resource, proportionably greater security from external danger, a less frequent interruption of their peace by foreign nations; and, what is of inestimable value, they must derive from union an exemption from those broils and wars between themselves, which so frequently afflict neighboring countries not tied together by the same governments, which their own rival ships alone would be sufficient to produce, but which opposite foreign alliances, attachments, and intrigues would stimulate and embitter. Hence, likewise, they will avoid the necessity of those overgrown military establishments which, under any form of government, are inauspicious to liberty, and which are to be regarded as particularly hostile to republican liberty. In this sense it is that your union ought to be considered as a main prop of your liberty, and that the love of the one ought to endear to you the preservation of the other.[2]

These considerations speak a persuasive language to every reflecting and virtuous mind, and exhibit the continuance of the Union as a primary object of patriotic desire. Is there a doubt whether a common government can embrace so large a sphere? Let experience solve it. To listen to mere speculation in such a case were criminal. We are authorized to hope that a proper organization of the whole with the auxiliary agency of governments for the respective subdivisions, will afford a happy issue to the experiment. It is well worth a fair and full experiment. With such powerful and obvious motives to union, affecting all parts of our country, while experience shall not have demonstrated its impracticability, there will always be reason to distrust the patriotism of those who in any quarter may endeavor to weaken its bands.

In contemplating the causes which may disturb our Union, it occurs as matter of serious concern that any ground should have been furnished for characterizing parties by geographical discriminations, Northern and Southern, Atlantic and Western; whence designing men may endeavor to excite a belief that there is a real difference of local interests and views. One of the expedients of party to acquire influence within particular districts is to misrepresent the opinions and aims of other districts. You cannot shield yourselves too much against the jealousies and heartburnings which spring from these misrepresentations; they tend to render alien to each other those who ought to be bound together by fraternal affection. The inhabitants of our Western country have lately had a useful lesson on this head; they have seen, in the negotiation by the Executive, and in the unanimous ratification by the Senate, of the treaty with Spain, and in the universal satisfaction at that event, throughout the United States, a decisive proof how unfounded were the suspicions propagated among them of a policy in the General Government and in the Atlantic States unfriendly to their interests in regard to the Mississippi; they have been witnesses to the formation of two treaties, that with Great Britain, and that with Spain, which secure to them everything they could desire, in respect to our foreign relations, towards confirming their prosperity. Will it not be

---

2. One of the strongest arguments for the federal Constitution was that it would spare the people of North America from the fate of Europe, where many different countries meant constant war and oppressive military establishments. As the historian and political scientist David Hendrickson has argued, the Constitution was a "peace pact," a breakthrough in international relations as well as domestic politics.

their wisdom to rely for the preservation of these advantages on the Union by which they were procured? Will they not henceforth be deaf to those advisers, if such there are, who would sever them from their brethren and connect them with aliens?[3]

To the efficacy and permanency of your Union, a government for the whole is indispensable. No alliance, however strict, between the parts can be an adequate substitute; they must inevitably experience the infractions and interruptions which all alliances in all times have experienced. Sensible of this momentous truth, you have improved upon your first essay, by the adoption of a constitution of government better calculated than your former for an intimate union, and for the efficacious management of your common concerns. This government, the offspring of our own choice, uninfluenced and unawed, adopted upon full investigation and mature deliberation, completely free in its principles, in the distribution of its powers, uniting security with energy, and containing within itself a provision for its own amendment, has a just claim to your confidence and your support. Respect for its authority, compliance with its laws, acquiescence in its measures, are duties enjoined by the fundamental maxims of true liberty. The basis of our political systems is the right of the people to make and to alter their constitutions of government. But the Constitution which at any time exists, till changed by an explicit and authentic act of the whole people, is sacredly obligatory upon all. The very idea of the power and the right of the people to establish government presupposes the duty of every individual to obey the established government.

All obstructions to the execution of the laws, all combinations and associations, under whatever plausible character, with the real design to direct, control, counteract, or awe the regular deliberation and action of the constituted authorities, are destructive of this fundamental principle, and of fatal tendency. They serve to organize faction, to give it an artificial and extraordinary force; to put, in the place of the delegated will of the nation the will of a party, often a

---

3. The people of the "Western country" had given Washington many anxious moments during his presidency. Farmers in western Pennsylvania had bitterly resented and sometimes violently opposed a new excise tax on whiskey; Washington personally led a large force to put down the insurrection in 1794, believing that the rebels might seek an alliance with Britain or Spain. To the south, in the new states of Kentucky and Tennessee, settlers furiously opposed the federal government's efforts to make peace with the Cherokee and Creek Indians. Above all, westerners complained that the federal government did not protect their right to send their goods down the Mississippi River and through the great depot of New Orleans. Hence Washington highlights the terms of the Treaty of San Lorenzo, signed in October 1795, in which Spain settled the boundaries of Florida and Louisiana and promised free navigation of the Mississippi to American citizens. The so-called Jay's Treaty with Britain, signed by Washington in August 1795, was far less favorable to American interests, although it did open some Caribbean ports to American trade.

small but artful and enterprising minority of the community; and, according to the alternate triumphs of different parties, to make the public administration the mirror of the ill-concerted and incongruous projects of faction, rather than the organ of consistent and wholesome plans digested by common counsels and modified by mutual interests.

However combinations or associations of the above description may now and then answer popular ends, they are likely, in the course of time and things, to become potent engines, by which cunning, ambitious, and unprincipled men will be enabled to subvert the power of the people and to usurp for themselves the reins of government, destroying afterwards the very engines which have lifted them to unjust dominion.

Towards the preservation of your government, and the permanency of your present happy state, it is requisite, not only that you steadily discountenance irregular oppositions to its acknowledged authority, but also that you resist with care the spirit of innovation upon its principles, however specious the pretexts. One method of assault may be to effect, in the forms of the Constitution, alterations which will impair the energy of the system, and thus to undermine what cannot be directly overthrown. In all the changes to which you may be invited, remember that time and habit are at least as necessary to fix the true character of governments as of other human institutions; that experience is the surest standard by which to test the real tendency of the existing constitution of a country; that facility in changes, upon the credit of mere hypothesis and opinion, exposes to perpetual change, from the endless variety of hypothesis and opinion; and remember, especially, that for the efficient management of your common interests, in a country so extensive as ours, a government of as much vigor as is consistent with the perfect security of liberty is indispensable. Liberty itself will find in such a government, with powers properly distributed and adjusted, its surest guardian. It is, indeed, little else than a name, where the government is too feeble to withstand the enterprises of faction, to confine each member of the society within the limits prescribed by the laws, and to maintain all in the secure and tranquil enjoyment of the rights of person and property.

I have already intimated to you the danger of parties in the State, with particular reference to the founding of them on geographical discriminations. Let me now take a more comprehensive view, and warn you in the most solemn manner against the baneful effects of the spirit of party generally.

This spirit, unfortunately, is inseparable from our nature, having its root in the strongest passions of the human mind. It exists under different shapes in all governments, more or less stifled, controlled, or repressed; but, in those of the popular form, it is seen in its greatest rankness, and is truly their worst enemy.

The alternate domination of one faction over another, sharpened by the spirit of revenge, natural to party dissension, which in different ages and countries has perpetrated the most horrid enormities, is itself a frightful despotism. But this leads at length to a more formal and permanent despotism. The disorders and miseries which result gradually incline the minds of men to seek security and repose in the absolute power of an individual; and sooner or later the chief of some prevailing faction, more able or more fortunate than his competitors, turns this disposition to the purposes of his own elevation, on the ruins of public liberty.

Without looking forward to an extremity of this kind (which nevertheless ought not to be entirely out of sight), the common and continual mischiefs of the spirit of party are sufficient to make it the interest and duty of a wise people to discourage and restrain it.

It serves always to distract the public councils and enfeeble the public administration. It agitates the community with ill-founded jealousies and false alarms, kindles the animosity of one part against another, foments occasionally riot and insurrection. It opens the door to foreign influence and corruption, which finds a facilitated access to the government itself through the channels of party passions. Thus the policy and the will of one country are subjected to the policy and will of another.

There is an opinion that parties in free countries are useful checks upon the administration of the government and serve to keep alive the spirit of liberty. This within certain limits is probably true; and in governments of a monarchical cast, patriotism may look with indulgence, if not with favor, upon the spirit of party. But in those of the popular character, in governments purely elective, it is a spirit not to be encouraged. From their natural tendency, it is certain there will always be enough of that spirit for every salutary purpose. And there being constant danger of excess, the effort ought to be by force of public opinion, to mitigate and assuage it. A fire not to be quenched, it demands a uniform vigilance to prevent its bursting into a flame, lest, instead of warming, it should consume.

It is important, likewise, that the habits of thinking in a free country should inspire caution in those entrusted with its administration, to confine themselves within their respective constitutional spheres, avoiding in the exercise of the powers of one department to encroach upon another. The spirit of encroachment tends to consolidate the powers of all the departments in one, and thus to create, whatever the form of government, a real despotism. A just estimate of that love of power, and proneness to abuse it, which predominates in the human heart, is sufficient to satisfy us of the truth of this position. The necessity of reciprocal checks in the exercise of political power, by dividing and distributing it into different depositaries, and constituting each the guardian of the public weal against invasions by the others, has been evinced by experiments ancient and modern; some of them in our country and under our own eyes. To preserve them must be as necessary as to institute them. If, in the opinion of the people, the distribution or modification of the constitutional powers be in any particular wrong, let it be corrected by an amendment in the way which the Constitution designates. But let there be no change by usurpation; for though this, in one instance, may be the instrument of good, it is the customary weapon by which free governments are destroyed. The precedent must always greatly overbalance in permanent evil any partial or transient benefit, which the use can at any time yield.

Of all the dispositions and habits which lead to political prosperity, religion and morality are indispensable supports. In vain would that man claim the tribute of patriotism, who should labor to subvert these great pillars of human happiness, these firmest props of the duties of men and citizens. The mere politician, equally with the pious man, ought to respect and to cherish them. A volume could not trace all their connections with private and public felicity. Let it simply be asked: Where is the security for property, for reputation, for life, if the sense of religious obligation desert the oaths which are the instruments of investigation in courts of justice? And let us with caution indulge the supposition that morality can be maintained without religion. Whatever may be conceded to the influence of refined education on minds of peculiar structure, reason and experience both forbid us to expect that national morality can prevail in exclusion of religious principle.[4]

It is substantially true that virtue or morality is a necessary spring of popular government. The rule, indeed, extends with more or less force to every species of free government. Who that is a sincere friend to it can look with indifference upon attempts to shake the foundation of the fabric?

Promote then, as an object of primary importance, institutions for the general diffusion of knowledge. In proportion as the structure of

---

4. What makes this defense of religion so interesting is that Washington himself was not a particularly pious man, even by the standards of Enlightenment-era gentlemen. Like many elite figures across the Atlantic world, though, he saw religion as a necessary check on the passions of the people—especially in light of the tumults emanating from the French Revolution. Together with the genuine piety of most Americans, this sensibility created a very harsh audience for works such as Paine's *Age of Reason*.

a government gives force to public opinion, it is essential that public opinion should be enlightened.

As a very important source of strength and security, cherish public credit. One method of preserving it is to use it as sparingly as possible, avoiding occasions of expense by cultivating peace, but remembering also that timely disbursements to prepare for danger frequently prevent much greater disbursements to repel it, avoiding likewise the accumulation of debt, not only by shunning occasions of expense, but by vigorous exertion in time of peace to discharge the debts which unavoidable wars may have occasioned, not ungenerously throwing upon posterity the burden which we ourselves ought to bear. The execution of these maxims belongs to your representatives, but it is necessary that public opinion should co-operate. To facilitate to them the performance of their duty, it is essential that you should practically bear in mind that towards the payment of debts there must be revenue; that to have revenue there must be taxes; that no taxes can be devised which are not more or less inconvenient and unpleasant; that the intrinsic embarrassment, inseparable from the selection of the proper objects (which is always a choice of difficulties), ought to be a decisive motive for a candid construction of the conduct of the government in making it, and for a spirit of acquiescence in the measures for obtaining revenue, which the public exigencies may at any time dictate.

Observe good faith and justice towards all nations; cultivate peace and harmony with all. Religion and morality enjoin this conduct; and can it be, that good policy does not equally enjoin it—It will be worthy of a free, enlightened, and at no distant period, a great nation, to give to mankind the magnanimous and too novel example of a people always guided by an exalted justice and benevolence. Who can doubt that, in the course of time and things, the fruits of such a plan would richly repay any temporary advantages which might be lost by a steady adherence to it? Can it be that Providence has not connected the permanent felicity of a nation with its virtue? The experiment, at least, is recommended by every sentiment which ennobles human nature. Alas! is it rendered impossible by its vices?

In the execution of such a plan, nothing is more essential than that permanent, inveterate antipathies against particular nations, and passionate attachments for others, should be excluded; and that, in place of them, just and amicable feelings towards all should be cultivated. The nation which indulges towards another a habitual hatred or a habitual fondness is in some degree a slave. It is a slave to its animosity or to its affection, either of which is sufficient to lead it astray from its duty and its interest. Antipathy in one nation against another disposes each more readily to offer insult and injury, to lay hold of slight causes of umbrage, and to be haughty and intractable, when accidental or trifling occasions of dispute occur. Hence, frequent collisions, obstinate, envenomed, and bloody contests. The nation, prompted by ill-will and resentment, sometimes impels to war the government, contrary to the best calculations of policy. The government sometimes participates in the national propensity, and adopts through passion what reason would reject; at other times it makes the animosity of the nation subservient to projects of hostility instigated by pride, ambition, and other sinister and pernicious motives. The peace often, sometimes perhaps the liberty, of nations, has been the victim.

So likewise, a passionate attachment of one nation for another produces a variety of evils. Sympathy for the favorite nation, facilitating the illusion of an imaginary common interest in cases where no real common interest exists, and infusing into one the enmities of the other, betrays the former into a participation in the quarrels and wars of the latter without adequate inducement or justification. It leads also to concessions to the favorite nation of privileges denied to others which is apt doubly to injure the nation making the concessions; by unnecessarily parting with what ought to have been retained, and by exciting jealousy, ill-will, and a disposition to retaliate, in the parties from whom equal privileges are withheld. And it gives to ambitious, corrupted, or deluded citizens (who devote themselves to the favorite nation), facility to betray or sacrifice the interests of their own country, without odium, sometimes even with popularity; gilding, with the appearances of a virtuous sense of obligation, a commendable deference for public opinion, or a laudable zeal for public good, the base or foolish compliances of ambition, corruption, or infatuation.

As avenues to foreign influence in innumerable ways, such attachments are particularly alarming to the truly enlightened and independent patriot. How many opportunities do they afford to tamper with domestic factions, to practice the arts of seduction, to mislead public opinion, to influence or awe the public councils. Such an attachment of a small or weak towards a great and powerful nation dooms the former to be the satellite of the latter.

Against the insidious wiles of foreign influence (I conjure you to believe me, fellow-citizens) the jealousy of a free people ought to be constantly awake, since history and experience prove that foreign influence is one of the most baneful foes of republican government. But that jealousy to be useful must be impartial; else it becomes the instrument of the very influence to be avoided, instead of a defense against it. Excessive partiality for one foreign nation and excessive dislike of another cause those whom they actuate to see danger only on one side, and serve to veil and even second the arts of influence on the other. Real patriots who may resist the intrigues of the favorite are liable to become suspected and odious, while its tools and dupes usurp the applause and confidence of the people, to surrender their interests.[5]

The great rule of conduct for us in regard to foreign nations is in extending our commercial relations, to have with them as little political connection as possible. So far as we have already formed engagements, let them be fulfilled with perfect good faith. Here let us stop. Europe has a set of primary interests which to us have none; or a very remote relation. Hence she must be engaged in frequent controversies, the causes of which are essentially foreign to our concerns. Hence, therefore, it must be unwise in us to implicate ourselves by artificial ties in the ordinary vicissitudes of her politics, or the ordinary combinations and collisions of her friendships or enmities.

Our detached and distant situation invites and enables us to pursue a different course. If we remain one people under an efficient government, the period is not far off when we may defy material injury from external annoyance; when we may take such an attitude as will cause the neutrality we may at any time resolve upon to be scrupulously respected; when belligerent nations, under the impossibility of making acquisitions upon us, will not lightly hazard the giving us provocation; when we may choose peace or war, as our interest, guided by justice, shall counsel.

Why forego the advantages of so peculiar a situation? Why quit our own to stand upon foreign ground? Why, by interweaving our destiny with that of any part of Europe, entangle our peace and prosperity in the toils of European ambition, rivalship, interest, humor or caprice?

It is our true policy to steer clear of permanent alliances with any portion of the foreign world; so far, I mean, as we are now at liberty to do it; for let me not be understood as capable of patronizing infidelity to existing engagements. I hold the maxim no less applicable to public than to private affairs, that honesty is always the best policy. I repeat it, therefore, let those engagements be observed in their genuine sense. But, in my opinion, it is unnecessary and would be unwise to extend them.

---

5. This is a clear rebuke of the opposition party led by Thomas Jefferson and James Madison. According to Washington, Hamilton, and other Federalists, these so-called Republicans were far too attached to revolutionary France to understand the problems and interests of the United States.

Taking care always to keep ourselves by suitable establishments on a respectable defensive posture, we may safely trust to temporary alliances for extraordinary emergencies.

Harmony, liberal intercourse with all nations, are recommended by policy, humanity, and interest. But even our commercial policy should hold an equal and impartial hand; neither seeking nor granting exclusive favors or preferences; consulting the natural course of things; diffusing and diversifying by gentle means the streams of commerce, but forcing nothing; establishing (with powers so disposed, in order to give trade a stable course, to define the rights of our merchants, and to enable the government to support them) conventional rules of intercourse, the best that present circumstances and mutual opinion will permit, but temporary, and liable to be from time to time abandoned or varied, as experience and circumstances shall dictate; constantly keeping in view that it is folly in one nation to look for disinterested favors from another; that it must pay with a portion of its independence for whatever it may accept under that character; that, by such acceptance, it may place itself in the condition of having given equivalents for nominal favors, and yet of being reproached with ingratitude for not giving more. There can be no greater error than to expect or calculate upon real favors from nation to nation. It is an illusion, which experience must cure, which a just pride ought to discard.

In offering to you, my countrymen, these counsels of an old and affectionate friend, I dare not hope they will make the strong and lasting impression I could wish; that they will control the usual current of the passions, or prevent our nation from running the course which has hitherto marked the destiny of nations. But, if I may even flatter myself that they may be productive of some partial benefit, some occasional good; that they may now and then recur to moderate the fury of party spirit, to warn against the mischiefs of foreign intrigue, to guard against the impostures of pretended patriotism; this hope will be a full recompense for the solicitude for your welfare, by which they have been dictated.

How far in the discharge of my official duties I have been guided by the principles which have been delineated, the public records and other evidences of my conduct must witness to you and to the world. To myself, the assurance of my own conscience is, that I have at least believed myself to be guided by them.

In relation to the still subsisting war in Europe, my proclamation of the twenty-second of April, 1793, is the index of my plan. Sanctioned by your approving voice, and by that of your representatives in both houses of Congress, the spirit of that measure has continually governed me, uninfluenced by any attempts to deter or divert me from it.

After deliberate examination, with the aid of the best lights I could obtain, I was well satisfied that our country, under all the circumstances of the case, had a right to take, and was bound in duty and interest to take, a neutral position. Having taken it, I determined, as far as should depend upon me, to maintain it, with moderation, perseverance, and firmness.[6]

The considerations which respect the right to hold this conduct, it is not necessary on this occasion to detail. I will only observe that, according to my understanding of the matter, that right, so far from being denied by any of the belligerent powers, has been virtually admitted by all.

The duty of holding a neutral conduct may be inferred, without anything more, from the obligation which justice and humanity impose on every nation, in cases in which it is free to act, to maintain inviolate the relations of peace and amity towards other nations.

The inducements of interest for observing that conduct will best be referred to your own reflections and experience. With me a predominant motive has been to endeavor to gain time to our country to settle and mature its yet recent institutions, and to progress without interruption to that degree of strength and consistency which is necessary to give it, humanly speaking, the command of its own fortunes.

Though, in reviewing the incidents of my administration, I am unconscious of intentional error, I am nevertheless too sensible of my defects not to think it probable that I may have committed many errors. Whatever they may be, I fervently beseech the Almighty to avert or mitigate the evils to which they may tend. I shall also carry with me the hope that my country will never cease to view them with indulgence; and that, after forty five years of my life dedicated to its service with an upright zeal, the faults of incompetent abilities will be consigned to oblivion, as myself must soon be to the mansions of rest.

Relying on its kindness in this as in other things, and actuated by that fervent love towards it, which is so natural to a man who views in it the native soil of himself and his progenitors for several generations, I anticipate with pleasing expectation that retreat in which I promise myself to realize, without alloy, the sweet enjoy-

6. After the French revolutionaries executed Louis XVI and declared war on Britain in early 1793, Washington asked Alexander Hamilton and Thomas Jefferson to render their opinions as to the legitimacy of the Franco-American treaties of 1778. Was the United States still bound to France despite the violent change in that nation's government? Hamilton argued no, while Jefferson insisted that treaties were agreements between the people of nations, regardless of their leaders. Washington shared Hamilton's view and in April 1793 declared the United States neutral in the European war.

ment of partaking, in the midst of my fellow-citizens, the benign influence of good laws under a free government, the ever-favorite object of my heart, and the happy reward, as I trust, of our mutual cares, labors, and dangers.

Geo. Washington.

INTERPRETATIONS

ROBERT A. FERGUSON

The Commonalities of *Common Sense*†

Historians always note the great impact of Thomas Paine's *Common Sense* in 1776, and critics generally agree in calling it "one of the most brilliant pamphlets ever written in the English language." Yet, despite the frequency of these claims, scholars rarely bring them together as mutually informing insights or controlling premises.[1] On the one side, the twin appeals of the pamphlet—the historical assertion of immediate impact and the literary assessment of timeless merit—make it an extraordinary source for gauging how Americans think about themselves and their country, then and now. On the other side, the same unique combination of instant effect and lasting influence welcomes rhetorical analysis, turning *Common Sense* into a seminal text for thinking about "the art of persuasion" in American life.[2] One can go further. Precisely how the pamphlet persuades its readers is an object lesson in the workings of modern democratic culture, and the way Americans have absorbed it into collective or national memory remains an untold story in ideological formations.

There is, in fact, no other written production in American culture quite like *Common Sense*. No other text by a single author can claim to have so instantly captured and then so permanently held the national imagination.[3] At a time when the largest colonial

---

† From *William and Mary Quarterly* 57.3 (2000): 465–504. Reprinted by permission of the Omohundro Institute of Early American History and Culture.

1. The divorce between historical claim and literary assessment is an interesting feature in the criticism of *Common Sense*. Historians emphasize its power as event, paraphrasing the language instead of analyzing it and tracing the presumed influences on Paine. Literary critics tend to ignore the implications and immediacy of a lost genre like the political pamphlet. Not surprisingly, then, the quoted literary assessment in the text comes from an historian who has studied the pamphlet tradition. See Bernard Bailyn, "Common Sense," *Fundamental Testaments of the American Revolution* (Washington, D. C., 1973), 7, and, more generally, Bailyn, ed., *Pamphlets of the American Revolution, 1750–1776* (Cambridge, Mass., 1965).

2. Rhetoric, defined broadly, is "the art of persuasion." Rhetorical analysis involves the study of the deliberate stylistic and narrative devices for persuading a reader or listener to believe or to do something. In classical terms, the emphasis is upon the formal strategies that try to teach, to please, or to move—an emphasis that sometimes distinguishes rhetoric from mere logic and that, in consequence, has given rise to pejorative connotations. A more modern definition, one that seeks to avoid negative implications, refers to rhetoric as "the science of human attention structures." See Richard A. Lanham, *A Handlist of Rhetorical Terms: A Guide for Students of English Literature*, 2d ed. (Berkeley, 1991), 131–35.

3. Jefferson's Declaration of Independence (1776), Harriet Beecher Stowe's *Uncle Tom's Cabin* (1851–1852), and Abraham Lincoln's Gettysburg Address (1863) are other obvious candidates. But the Declaration, a composite document, and Lincoln's "remarks" at Gettysburg were not instantly recognized as controlling expressions in their own times. *Uncle Tom's Cabin* did have a similar immediate impact, and it is still avidly read, but central aspects of its message have been rejected by later Americans. Compare, for

newspapers and most important pamphlets had circulations under 2,000, *Common Sense* reached between 120,000 and 150,000 copies in its first year alone. It was the first American best-seller. Hundreds of thousands of Americans, perhaps a fifth of the adult population in all, either read *Common Sense* or had it read to them during the course of the Revolution. Paine could credibly boast that his work had achieved "the greatest sale that any performance ever had since the use of letters."[4]

Other leaders of the Revolution were almost as extravagant in their own praise, and their comments convey another quality, the innate vitality in Paine's words. George Washington called *Common Sense* "unanswerable" and found it to be "working a wonderful change . . . in the minds of many men." Benjamin Franklin thought its effect "prodigious." Benjamin Rush wrote that "it burst from the press with an effect which has rarely been produced by types and papers in any age or country."[5] When modern scholars test these earlier assessments, they tend to agree that Paine "transformed the terms of political debate" and "forged a new political language."[6] Moreover, there are good reasons for such glowing appraisals. Much of the terminology of national discourse, including the very term "United States of America," can be traced to Paine's Revolutionary writings.[7] The rhetorical patterns initiated in *Common Sense* have become intrinsic to American political speech, and they are now permanently embedded in the expressions of identity on which the culture depends.

The originary powers of *Common Sense* remain crucial rhetorical ingredients for another reason: they have made the pamphlet all things to all people. Every brand of American politics seems to find

example, favorable contemporary usage of a phrase like "common sense" to pejorative evocations of "Uncle Tom."

4. In the scholarly disputes over numbers of copies printed, I accept the guarded assessment of Paine's most thorough, recent biographer. See John Keane, *Tom Paine: A Political Life* (New York, 1995), 108–11, and also A. J. Ayer, *Thomas Paine* (New York, 1988), 35, and Eric Foner, *Tom Paine and Revolutionary America* (New York, 1976), 79. Some scholars have followed the claim of up to half a million copies in 1776, or one for every four Americans then living. See Arthur M. Schlesinger, *Prelude to Independence: The Newspaper War on Britian 1764–1776* (New York, 1958), 253. For Paine's own comment, see Paine to Henry Laurens, January 14, 1779, in Philip S. Foner, ed. *The Complete Writings of Thomas Paine*, 2 vols. (New York, 1945), 2:1162–63 (hereinafter cited as *Complete Writings of Paine*). For a recent more conservative estimate of circulation, see Patricia Loughran, "Virtual Nation: Local and National Cultures of Print, 1776–1850" (Ph. D. diss., University of Chicago, 1999).
5. For Washington's evaluation of *Common Sense*, see his letters to Col. Joseph Reed in January and March of 1776 quoted in *Complete Writings of Paine*, 1:2. For the quotations from Franklin and Rush, as well as a good, balanced summary of the overall impact of *Common Sense*, see Isaac Kramnick, "Editor's Introduction," *Common Sense* (New York, 1976), 7–10 (all further references to *Common Sense*, unless otherwise noted, are to this readily available Penguin edition), and Keane, *Tom Paine*, 108–14.
6. Eric Foner, *Tom Paine and Revolutionary America*, 74, xvi.
7. Manfred Pütz and Jon-K Adams, "Preface," *A Concordance to Thomas Paine's* Common Sense *and The American Crisis* (New York and London, 1989), vii.

some justification in its pages, and the glass that Paine so beguilingly offers can, in consequence, be either half empty or half full as each occasion or cause commands. The bold hardihood of a continental union and the utter fragility of that union both receive first expression here: "now is the seed time of continental union," but also, "the least fracture now will be like a name engraved with the point of a pin on the tender rind of a young oak."[8] Here, as well for the first time, is the daring prediction of a legitimating national constitutional convention, but this optimism appears against a deliberately gloomy backdrop, "the precariousness of human affairs." *Common Sense* inaugurates both sides of a never-ending debate in American federalism. It demands a stronger union ("The Continental belt is too loosely buckled") while also recognizing the hold of local identities ("the force of local prejudice").[9]

Time and again, *Common Sense* succeeds in having it both ways on debates that will consume the later body politic. The pamphlet famously resists government and authority, making them necessary evils, but it simultaneously lauds both in its new plan ("the glorious union of all things") and in its exaltation of a proper order ("in America THE LAW IS KING").[1] Revolutionary Americans learn that, like Noah, "we have it in our power to begin the world over again," but they also receive the first in a whole series of stock political warnings: their house, when divided against itself, will not stand; their virtue, because not cultivated, will surely disappear; their common sense, as it becomes less vigilant, will tumble before "the mind of the multitude," and so on.[2] Not least, Paine's confident assertions of strength in unity must be read against a counter proposition: danger lurks everywhere from a hidden enemy within.[3]

A certain manic-depressive quality governs such prose—a quality that has become standard fare in American politics.[4] Paine, the pamphleteer, instinctively knew what the more philosophical thinkers of his day failed to grasp. He saw that material success in the secular state might be boring instead of dramatic, that the result might prove hollow or even comic rather than enlightened. In celebrating the unprecedented promise of America, he realized that communal well-being might best be appreciated in a context of crisis. Therefore, the presumed glory of America could be made to

8. *Common Sense*, 82, 94.
9. Ibid., 95–98, 118, 85.
1. Ibid., 65, 100, 98
2. Ibid., 118–20, 70.
3. Ibid., 100, 109–10, 88–89.
4. William L. Hedges was the first to document this tendency in early republican thought, in "Toward a Theory of American Literature, 1765–1800," *Early American Literature*, 4 (1970), 5–14, and "The Old World Yet: Writers and Writing in Post-Revolutionary America," ibid., 16 (1981), 3–18.

matter more if the country itself seemed to teeter on the edge of ruin and chaos. Danger, properly conveyed and then overcome, would carry mere prosperity toward the realms of higher accomplishment.[5]

These and other ambiguities shape the rhetorical stances as well as the themes of later generations. *Common Sense* insists that "the cause of America is in a great measure the cause of all mankind," but it also orders Americans to protect themselves from the rest of the world.[6] Paine blithely punctuates his claims of reasonableness and disinterestedness with other, disconcerting demands for revenge.[7] Sometimes a lofty civic virtue appears as the necessary linchpin of American endeavors; at other times, though, the practical world of commerce appears to dominate the writers expectations; and at still others, market forces are definitely the enemy. Greater wealth will help to defend the new republic, but Paine also warns that it will encourage "the trembling duplicity of a spaniel" in leaders who will have more to lose.[8]

The conflict of alternatives in *Common Sense* can be quite direct. Paine congratulates Americans for their "spirit of good order and obedience" on one page and condemns them for their dangerous lawlessness on another.[9] Even as he castigates his opponents for "mingling religion with politics," his own narrative constantly conflates biblical and secular imagery and explanations.[1] Thematically, the stakes on the table always seem to be at their highest when Paine pauses to claim that he writes to avoid exaggeration and hyperbole.[2]

Such extremes in theme and tone are everywhere in the pamphlet, and they are important beyond themselves. They help to explain how the widest range of readers could be pulled into Paine's orbit, and they identify the birth of a distinctively American voice in politics. But more immediately, they need to be incorporated into a larger philosophical and rhetorical frame of reference, for when they are not, they seem to be contradictions in terms, blocking awareness of the underlying consistencies and overall aesthetic

---

5. *Common Sense*, 88, 117–18.
6. Ibid., 63, 82, 86
7. Ibid., 81, 64, 90, 99, 113.
8. Ibid., 104–07, 120, 115, 86. For extended analyses of Paine's integrations of the ideals of civic virtue and material prosperity, see David Wootton, ed., "Introduction," *Republicanism, Liberty, and Commercial Society, 1649–1776* (Stanford, Calif., 1994), 32–41, and Peter C. Messer, "Stories of Independence: Eighteenth-Century Narratives" (Ph.D. diss., Rutgers University—New Brunswick, 1997).
9. *Common Sense*, 95, 117–18.
1. Ibid., 128. We see this conflation most famously in the long opening section that uses the First Book of Samuel to demonstrate that "original sin and hereditary succession are parallels"; ibid., 71–82.
2. For example, while insisting that he is "not inflaming or exaggerating matters," Paine also writes "the present winter is worth an age if rightly employed, but if lost or neglected the whole continent will partake of the misfortune"; ibid., 89.

integrity of *Common Sense*. J. G. A. Pocock conveys the frustrations that many readers experience when he claims that *Common Sense* "does not consistently echo any established radical vocabulary" and that Paine himself "remains difficult to fit into any kind of category."[3] Indeed, seeming inconsistencies in the work are often traced and verified through more apparent irregularities in the life.

Paine has been called a raucous haranguer (too embittered to think about style), a journalist shopping the ideas of others, a propagandist rather than an original thinker, and an opportunist of expression instead of a philosopher of thought. Even his most careful defenders tend to speak disparagingly of his weakness in argument and his deficiencies in intellectual originality.[4] But whereas many of these criticisms apply to the man, they divert attention from the actual text, and they tend to disregard the overarching craft of the writer. The impressive things about *Common Sense* are intrinsic to the rhetorical structure and narrative pace of the pamphlet. Paine orchestrated ideological unities out of fragments, and he knew how to wrap his readers in the sincerity of his claims.

The strength of the work can also be seen in an oddly compelling historical fact from 1776. Paine is the only figure in the pantheon of Revolutionary leaders who achieved his place entirely through authorship. Whatever they wrote, the other republican founders all owed something to their original station, their prowess in the field, their political accomplishments, their subsequent positions, their good fortune in events, their families, their regional affiliations, their wealth, their political alliances, or their location in some other grouping. Paine stood alone in this regard. Now a citizen of the world, he was then an isolated, impoverished immigrant who gained attention wholly through his writings. An embarrassment in every political position that he later filled, he possessed powers of expression that were clearer and bolder than those of his contemporaries, and, to their credit, they realized as much. In the words of Thomas Jefferson, "no writer has exceeded Paine in ease and familiarity of

---

3. Pocock, *Virtue, Commerce, and History: Essays on Political Thought and History* . . . (Cambridge, 1985), 276.
4. For the most popular version of the embroiled and thoughtless haranger, see Howard Fast, *Citizen Tom Paine* (New York, 1943), 18–19, 26–27, 47–48, 92–95. Eric Foner, *Tom Paine and Revolutionary America*, 79–80, among others, notes that Paine's originality lies not in his ideas, but in his innovative combination of others' ideas in an American context. More recently, Ayer, *Thomas Paine*, 36, finds that Paine achieved his results "more by rhetoric, of which he was a master, than by force of argument"; David A. Wilson, *Paine and Cobbett: The Transatlantic Connection* (Kingston and Montreal, 1988), 48, 25, suggests that "there was nothing particularly original about Paine's views" in placing him somewhere between philosopher and polemicist; and Jack T. Fruchtman, Jr., *Thomas Paine: Apostle of Freedom* (New York, 1994), 4, argues that "Paine's life as a journalist, which was something he came to quite by accident in 1775, imparted to him much of his character and style."

style, in perspicuity of expression, happiness of elucidation, and in simple and unassuming language."[5]

There is another level of complexity to be dealt with in the acknowledged power of this writer. Gifted beyond other Revolutionary propagandists, Paine nonetheless created far better than even he knew, and the language that he used quickly took on a life of its own. Significantly, the story that Americans have received is far more potent than the one Paine originally tried to tell, and here, once again, the embattled personality of the writer has gotten in the way of a deeper understanding. The political maverick who wrote can be deciphered readily enough, but that individual does not begin to explain the received written product that shattered the traditional Anglo-American mold for pamphleteering in 1776.

Paine gave many commonly available stories a new form and energy. The man who added the final "e" to his name only as he reached America wanted to see himself—and everything else—afresh. He strained to marshal affinities that he could only intuit, and he raised still vaguer proclivities toward the surface of conscious articulation. It is easy to suggest that the strengths, frustrations, and eccentricities of the writer tallied with the felt necessities of his times. But in another sense, Paine stimulated previously unforeseen possibilities, changing the very nature of the political reality that he saw around him. The uncanny aspect of Paine's creativity occurred in this area. He grasped, in recognizable literary form, the emerging ingenuities that the new politics would require.

To study all of these spheres of implication at once presents inevitable problems in analysis. How does one measure the overlapping but still concentric circles of production that have made *Common Sense* a seminal text? Separating the pamphleteer who knew what he was doing from the author of heightened magnitudes is to make an artificial distinction, but it reveals the craft in Paine's writing, and it clarifies the relation of ephemeral political pamphlet to timeless literary work. Accordingly, the following three sections adopt a tiered approach but with two synchronous aims always in mind. These twin aims might best be expressed as questions. How does *Common Sense* galvanize an enormous audience so quickly and so permanently? How do the different and often conflicting components in colonial understanding and imperial design generate a new form of communal understanding in consensual nationhood?

The first section explores the historical Paine, the disaffected member of the Anglo-American empire who knew many things

---

5. *The Writings of Thomas Jefferson*, ed. H. A. Washington, 12 vols. (Washington, D. C., 1853), 7:198.

about his various eighteenth-century audiences and who possessed a broad but explicable range of devices for persuading them of his own purposes and desires. In a famous comment from his Rhetoric, Aristotle observed "it is not hard to praise Athenians among Athenians." Paine comparably knew how to praise Americans in America and, thereby, to establish popular identifications with his arguments.[6] But more was at work for the disenchanted emigrant who carefully kept the identity of "an Englishman" in the first edition of *Common Sense*. In 1776, he was peculiarly situated to make the most of his disaffections, but he was able to do so without sacrificing either the identity or the rhetorical platform available to him as an Englishman with an Englishman's rights.[7] There is real genius in his manipulation of these combinations—a genius born of conscious risk and dislocation, the very elements that he had to convince British Americans to adopt.

A second section scrutinizes the pamphlet itself for its literary elements of tone, style, symbol, form, and metaphor and for the relation of literary import to political content. These factors, often referred to but rarely examined in detail, give *Common Sense* much of its practical punch with audiences of all periods. They explain why the pamphlet is such a complex performance despite the simplest of dictions and organizations. In their combined effect, these literary elements also force a dramatic reconsideration of a central debate in rhetorical theory. For manifestly, Paine finds his innermost power in his manipulation of an ancient rhetorical conundrum or uncertainty.

Classical and modern rhetoricians alike have always argued over the proper dimensions of their art. Is successful language, they want to know, about encouraging the recipients of that language to feel a given way or must that language necessarily go further and persuade an audience to act a certain way in order to be considered effective?[8] Paine solves this conundrum by stepping into the continuum of response between feeling and action. Feeling, properly claimed, becomes action in *Common Sense*. The pamphlet celebrates an orchestrated solidarity of the right-minded in a new type of participatory republic. This idea of the right-minded rests on its own excitement, sufficient unto the moment, but the potential discrepancy between political expediency and philosophical explanation

6. Kenneth Burke uses the Aristotle quotation in his discussion of the process of identification in rhetoric. See Burke, *A Rhetoric of Motives* (Berkeley, Calif., 1969), 55–59.
7. Paine acknowledged as much in 1780 when he wrote Maj. Gen. Nathanael Greene that "it was in great measure owing to my bringing a knowledge of England with me to America that I was enabled to enter deeper into politics, and with more success, than other people"; *Complete Writings of Paine*, 2:1189.
8. Lanham, *Handlist of Rhetorical Terms*, 2d ed., 131–35, and Burke, *Rhetoric of Motives*, 49–50.

remains great. Paine's account presents a troubling first image of the citizen en masse in the modern nation state.

A third section of the essay then carries the historical figure of the first section and the literary analysis of the second into another dimension, into the imaginative domain of storytelling. Paine seems to have deliberately sought a place and, hence, a rhetorical stance at the farthest edges of the Anglo-American empire, a world in which he had failed miserably until emigrating to America. Somehow, after a scant twelve months in colonial Philadelphia, the so-named city of brotherly love, he taught himself to write a previously unimagined story about a better and decidedly new world. The positive appeal of that story is clear enough to all—"we have it in our power to begin the world over again"—but much of its force comes from more unsettling and darker factors. Paine re-fashions a conventional, hackneyed political account into an electrifying tale of basic affections and even more primal hatreds. Americans easily forget that their republic began in feelings of fear, betrayal, anger, and self-righteousness—the feelings that the Revolution required of its participants. Half of a single sentence from *Common Sense* parades all four emotions at work: "there is no punishment which that man will not deserve, be he who, or what, or where he will, that may be the means of sacrificing a season so precious and useful."[9] Paine learned to wield these negative sentiments to stunning collective effect, and current Americans have been left with the patterns of his success.

Every culture has five or six stories that it tells itself over and over again as part of a pattern in self-recognition and sought-after cohesion. *Common Sense* clearly provides one of those stories in the United States of America. Recent theories of nationalism, with their recognition of the power of language in the ritualistic reiteration of national formations, permit an additional claim.[1] Paine's story of love and hatred constitutes an inexhaustible source in the reservoir of national energies, and when that story is used or repeated in all or in part, it demands of its participants some acceptance of its implications in the ritual performance of national consciousness. Is it an accident that succeeding generations of Americans always reach so promptly for the language of crisis that Paine helped to instill in their forebears? Should the search for internal enemies in times of

9. *Common Sense*, 120, 89.
1. Benedict Anderson discounts the notion of philosophical coherence as a basis of national thinking in favor of language repetition in a print culture that encourages "a deep, horizontal comradeship." A community is "imagined" in this process of reiteration. See Anderson, *Imagined Communities: Reflections on the Origin and Spread of Nationalism* (London, 1983), 13–16, 38–40.

trouble, whether those enemies are real or imagined, surprise any-one? Here, as well, are the commonalities in *Common Sense*.

I

Controversies about *Common Sense* abound in part because the facts about its author are tantalizingly scant.[2] Thomas Paine was born in 1737 at Thetford, a Whig stronghold in Norfolk, England. He grew up as the son of a Quaker father, a staymaker for the corset industry, and an Anglican mother, the daughter of a local attorney. Paine was raised in both faiths but confirmed in the Anglican church, though he rejected, by the age of eight, the basic tenet of Christianity, the sacrifice of the Son by the Father. As he would later summarize his youthful conclusions, "any system of religion that has anything in it that shocks the mind of a child cannot be a true sys-tem." An early freethinker, he was still raised in a solid denomina-tional setting; he knew the Bible well, better by far than any other writing.[3]

Into middle age Paine experienced "almost unrelenting failure."[4] The corset trade of his father, a life at sea, teaching, possibly the Methodist ministry, shopkeeping, and government service all attracted Paine, but he floundered in each vocation more than once. These experiences took him from town to town, including Dover, Sandwich, Lewes, and London as well as Thetford. By 1774, the year that he left for America at the age of thirty-seven, Paine had descended into bankruptcy with two dismissals for cause from gov-ernment service and two failed marriages behind him. The separa-tion settlement from his second wife paid for his voyage to America, during which he nearly died of typhoid fever. Notably, his first ambi-tions on arriving in America were neither political nor daring in scope. He hoped to open a school, and yet within thirteen months he had written *Common Sense* and emerged as the personage whom

---

2. Because of the controversies surrounding them, the biographical facts in the next 5 para-graphs are winnowed from a consensus in 5 basic sources, all of which tend to repeat the same information in slightly different ways: Philip Foner, "Introduction," *Complete Writ-ings of Paine*, i:ix-xii; Eric Foner, *Tom Paine and Revolutionary America*, 1–17; Ayer, *Thomas Paine*, 1–13; George Claeys, *Thomas Paine: Social and Political Thought* (Bos-ton, 1989), 20–24; and Keane, *Tom Paine*, 3–71.

3. For Paine's account of his education, including his Christian upbringing, in *The Age of Reason*, see *Complete Writings of Paine*, 1:496–98. Keane, *Tom Paine*, 18–19, suggests that the tension between Quakerism and Anglicanism in Paine's upbringing not only led to early toleration of all religion but freed him rhetorically "by establishing nonreligious spaces of compromise." Fruchtman, *Thomas Paine and the Religion of Nature* (Baltimore, 1993), 172–75, argues alternatively that the combination turned Paine into a secular preacher of sorts.

4. Eric Foner, *Tom Paine and Revolutionary America*, 3.

John Adams and other Revolutionary founders would marvel over, a man with "genius in his eyes."[5]

The intellectual background of these early events is just as vague and unprepossessing. Paine received a limited education from grammar school between the ages of eight and thirteen but no formal schooling thereafter. Newtonian science interested him more than politics as a young man, and he attended public lectures in London on the subject, meeting, among others, the writer and poet Oliver Goldsmith and making scientific connections that led him eventually to Benjamin Franklin.[6]

Even so, some formal political sentiments can be traced as early as 1772, when Paine wrote against administrative abuses in his earliest known composition, "Case of the Officers of Excise."[7] Between 1768 and 1774, Paine also learned something of the "Wilkes and Liberty" campaign when John Wilkes, a popular political figure who fled England after being convicted of seditious libel in 1763, returned to create new controversies by regaining his lost seat in Parliament. The Wilkes campaign focused on freedom of the press, ministerial corruption, and Parliamentary reform—all favorite subjects of the later writer—and it drew from the rapidly evolving public sphere of radical coffee houses that materialized in eighteenth-century England. Paine would have had some access to these institutions in the towns where he lived, especially in London and Lewes, but the extent of his involvement remains uncertain, and his poverty would have kept him a peripheral figure in their controversies.

Paine's personal readings from the period remain largely a mystery; they were certainly unsystematic and often superficial, with the possible exception of close newspaper reading. The deeper parallels that scholars like to draw among John Locke, other political theorists, and *Common Sense* falter in the face of Paine's admissions. "I have never read Locke nor even had the work in my hand," he wrote in 1807, "and by what I heard of it . . . I had no inducement to read it."[8] At the same time, Paine could brag of a perfect memory

5. Maj. Gen. Charles Lee, second in command of the Revolutionary army, described Paine as one who "has genius in his eyes"; Lee to Benjamin Rush, Feb. 25, 1776, in *The Lee Papers*, 4 vols., *Collections of the New-York Historical Society for the Year 1871* (New York, 1872), 1:325, 312. Adams, who introduced Paine to Lee in the first place as "a Citizen of the World," picked up and used Lee's phrase in his letters; Adams to Abigail Adams, Apr. 28, 1776, in Charles Francis Adams, ed., *Familiar Letters of John Adams and His Wife Abigail Adams during the Revolution* (Freeport, N. Y., 1970; orig. pub. 1875), 167. In each instance, the words and related commentary imply the sudden appearance of a prodigy.
6. For accounts of these meetings and the scientific circles that Paine entered, see Keane, *Tom Paine*, 42–43, 61, 75, 79, 111.
7. Philip Foner, *Complete Writings of Paine*, 2:3–15.
8. Paine to James Cheetham, Aug. 21, 1807, quoted in Fruchtman, "Nature and Revolution in Paine's *Common Sense*," *History of Political Thought*, 10 (1989), 427 n. 28. Scholars typically try to escape the dilemma of direct influence by arguing that "Paine was, consciously or unconsciously, in agreement with Locke"; Ayer, *Thomas Paine*, 41; see also Fruchtman, *Thomas Paine: Apostle of Freedom*, 64–70.

for everything he did read, and he frequently claimed prodigious intellectual capacities. "I seldom passed five minutes of my life, however circumstanced, in which I did not acquire some knowledge," ran a typical assertion.[9]

This mixture of dreary biographical fact and personal bombast has encouraged scholarly license when dealing with the intractable but endlessly fascinating problem of influence. If the boasts of the self-made man are allowed to dominate the paucity of actual data, the possibilities quickly become open-ended and conflicting. Historians in search of handy correlations have turned Paine into the consummate intellectual blotter. Whatever he touched, he can be seen to have absorbed; whomever he mentioned, he can be said to have mastered.

Virtually every fact just noted has been magnified to secure some interpretation of *Common Sense*. The Whig political orientations of towns like Thetford and Lewes and Paine's Quaker background have been variously tied to the writer's oppositional politics, antiestablishment courage, and moral fervor.[1] Just as the religious split between the Quaker father, whom Paine admired, and the Anglican mother, whom he never mentioned, has been offered to justify his later animosity toward an Anglican "mother country," so Paine's failures in marriage have been raised to explain the writer's frequent familial metaphors.[2] Predictably, the negative experiences of the excise officer have provided an especially convenient handle for interpreting the later Revolutionary's zeal in a righteous cause.[3]

The puzzle of Paine's sudden triumph in America has made such speculation unavoidable. Do the unhappy experiences of the corset maker and shopkeeper refine artisanal angers and class affiliations in the pamphleteer?[4] Can the young Englishman's interests in Newtonian science explain and justify his later optimism about human nature and natural rights?[5] Either way, the radicalism of the coffeehouses and Paine's presumed newspaper reading have emerged as favorite repositories for whatever philosophy one wants to find in

9. Quoted in Philip Foner, "Introduction," *Complete Writings of Paine*, 1:ix.
1. For Paine's Whig origins, see Claeys, *Thomas Paine*, 20, and Eric Foner, *Tom Paine and Revolutionary America*, 4–13. For different versions of the Quaker influence, see Moncure D. Conway, *The Life of Thomas Paine*, 2 vols. (New York, 1892), and Harry Hayden Clark, "Introduction," *Thomas Paine: Representative Selections* (New York, 1944), xii-xv.
2. For arguments that use Paine's parents and marriages to "stretch Paine out on the couch," see Winthrop D. Jordan, "Familial Politics: Thomas Paine and the Killing of the King, 1776," *Journal of American History*, 60 (1973), 302–03.
3. See Kramnick, "Editor's Introduction," *Common Sense*, 27.
4. For the formative interpretation of Paine's involvement in 18th-century artisanal culture, see Eric Foner, *Tom Paine and Revolutionary America*, xvii, 28–29, 32–43.
5. Joseph V. Metzgar, "The Cosmology of Thomas Paine," *Illinois Quarterly*, 37 (Sept. 1974), 47–63. See also Wilson's analysis that Paine's plain style can be traced directly to his interest in the scientific revolution in *Paine and Cobbett*, 20–29.

Common Sense, from Whig "country" or party rhetoric, to the Scottish moral sense school, to the social compact of Locke, to the denominational agenda of deism, to utilitarian notions of happiness and prosperity.[6] In the absence of hard evidence, any one of these distinct frames of reference can be found "in the air" of Paine's England.

But none of the particulars of influence—nor, for that matter, the sum total of them—produces the author who stunned the world. Even if the reductionism of a single or paramount claim is avoided, the alternative, a collation of relevant influences, still leaves us with the unoriginal thinker rather than the creative writer. Indeed, the distinction itself is worth a pause in rhetorical analysis. Rhetoric trades on the memorable utterance to achieve a peculiar kind of originality. The speaker or writer takes what is plausible to an immediate audience and turns that recognition into something unforgettable. The Massachusetts Whig, Joseph Hawley, captured the essence of this quality when describing his own reading experience of *Common Sense*. "Every sentiment," he wrote in 1776, "has sunk into my well prepared heart."[7] An anonymous contributor to the *New York Journal* found himself galvanized in the same way, explaining "you can scarce put your finger to a single page, but you are pleased, though it may be, startled, with the sparks of original genius. . . . It treats of the most important subjects to America . . . exciting and calling forth to public view, the thoughts of others."[8]

Put another way, rendition provides the potency in thought. Platonic ideas may epitomize the highest form of knowledge, but they are disembodied in their abstractness, and they lack two central ingredients for securing themselves in collective memory. They lack "the timing" that place or context supplies and "the agency" that individual people give to observable experience. Ideas, in short, require concrete expression, and the set of records that we hold about ourselves comes through the timing and agency that stories grant—"stories of all kinds, true, embellished, invented."[9] To tell such a story in 1776, Paine had to know how to comprehend and manipulate the milieu of his audience, and so the issue comes back again to the basic puzzle. How did Paine understand the hearts of

---

6. See, in order, Eric Foner, *Tom Paine and Revolutionary America*, 4–13; Fruchtman, "Nature and Revolution in Paine's *Common Sense*," 424–25; Ayer, *Thomas Paine*, 17–23; J.C.D. Clark, *The Language of Liberty, 1660–1832: Political Discourse and Social Dynamics in the Anglo-American World* (New York, 1994), 30–38, 244, 329–38; and Wootton, "Introduction," *Republicanism, Liberty, and Commercial Society*, 32–39.
7. Quoted in Eric Foner, *Tom Paine and Revolutionary America*, 86.
8. "Independent Whig" to "The Printer," *New York Journal*, Feb. 22, 1776.
9. I paraphrase and quote from Roger Shattuck, *Forbidden Knowledge: From Prometheus to Pornography* (New York, 1996), 9.

his new and still inchoate American auditors so quickly and what gave him the ability to express their sentiments so well?

For part of the answer, the admittedly scant record of biographical facts can be used but with more literary purposes in mind. There are patterns in the early life of Paine that clarify the transition of the transplanted Englishman. Note, for example, the degree of mobility that Paine enjoyed along a number of fronts—geographical, religious, vocational, and social. While his movements from town to town, from denominational affiliation to affiliation, from job to job, from oral protest to published dissent, and even from one familial context to another were all part of a record of failure, they also distinguished him from the earlier, more restricted world of an eighteenth-century Englishman of his class, and they gave him comparative frames of reference with which to work. Note, as well, that the obscure Paine managed to meet and mingle with such acknowledged great men as Oliver Goldsmith and Benjamin Franklin.

Paine in his mobility illustrated something fresh afoot.[1] The Anglo-American world of the eighteenth century did not discourage unlikely figures with "genius in their eyes." In fact, it expected them as part of its peculiar quest for knowledge, and its leaders, figures like Goldsmith and Franklin, kept themselves on the lookout. The Enlightenment motto—"*Sapere aude!!*"—"Have the courage to use your own understanding!"—meant that fresh knowledge might come from anywhere and anyone.[2] Meanwhile, the rapid spread of print technology in England and America dictated the logical avenues of communication for the dissemination of that knowledge. The linked result, any good writer with access to a printing press, made these innovations tangible and exhilarating. From the moment that Paine wrote his first essay, "Case of the Officers of Excise," in 1772, he became a member in good standing of what became "the republic of letters."[3]

---

1. Fruchtman, *Thomas Paine: Apostle of Freedom*, 4, also draws attention, though with different implications, to how Paine's political and social ideas "developed in ways that mirrored a wandering lifestyle."
2. The phrase came originally from the Latin poet Horace, but it was popularized by Immanuel Kant and other late 18th-century thinkers as the essential precondition in the spread of new knowledge or enlightenment. See, for example, Kant, "An Answer to the Question: 'What Is Enlightenment?'" in Hans Reiss, ed., *Kant: Political Writings*, trans. H. B. Nisbet (Cambridge, 1970), 54. See, as well, Robert A. Ferguson, "'What Is Enlightenment?' Some American Answers," *American Literary History*, 1 (1989), 245–72.
3. For the best analysis of the historical and literary ramifications of the republic of letters, one on which both the quoted terminology and the ideas of the following paragraph depend, see Lewis P. Simpson, *The Brazen Face of History: Studies in the Literary Consciousness in America* (Baton Rouge, 1980), 3–24. For the impact of the printing press on 18th-century Anglo-American culture, see Michael Warner, *The Letters of the Republic: Publication and the Public Sphere in Eighteenth-Century America* (Cambridge, Mass., 1990), and Larzer Ziff, *Writing in the New Nation: Prose, Print, and Politics in the Early United States* (New Haven, 1991).

The eighteenth-century version of the republic of letters gave Paine his basic stance in *Common Sense*. Its membership consisted of self-consciously equal or "classless," "world-historical men of letters." Its message involved a critique of Church and State, both of which it challenged by assuming an "autonomous order of mind" that could be liberated from custom, superstition, locality, and unwarranted hierarchy. Its medium was print, the very source of its existence, and its mode was the occasional essay or pamphlet, through which it took on "specific historical situations," often questioning the exercises of authority within them. Inasmuch as Paine reached maturity as the republic of letters became a "third realm" alongside the two more established realms of Church and State, his optimism and success become that much easier to see and explain. He wrote as a leading pamphleteer in the age of pamphleteering.

The self-confidence with which Paine rode the crest of this historical wave sustained *Common Sense*—a source of vitality easily overlooked because the same concatenation of historical ideas and events allowed Paine to ignore the ocean of history beneath him. The rising third realm of the republic of letters was a historical phenomenon that questioned previous interpretations of history and assumed that history itself might be made over or changed. Thus, the mantra of *Common Sense*, repeated in some form on almost every page, advised everyone to ignore the past by accepting the present. In its sharpest expression, it read: "a new æra for politics is struck; a new method of thinking hath arisen. All plans, proposals, &c. prior to the nineteenth of April, *i. e.* to the commencement of hostilities, are like the almanacks of the last year; which, though proper then, are superceded and useless now."[4]

Paine's ingenuity in refashioning already established or conventional themes took a similar form. He refurbished stories by removing, dismissing, or at least disarming the domineering pasts that controlled narrative development. Most political pamphlets of the period began with a tedious review of the history of government, and *Common Sense* followed the model in its own introduction, "Of the Origin and Design of Government in General."[5] Paine, however, recast the whole discussion by boldly challenging the legitimating histories of governments, all of which he pronounced to be false and bloody. His convenient tool of entry was a more optimistic prehistory in social contract theory. "Society in every state is a blessing," he

---

4. *Common Sense*, 82.
5. For a generic explanation of the standard rehearsals of legal philosophy and social contract theory in the introductions of Revolutionary pamphleteering, see Ferguson, "Writing the Revolution," in *The American Enlightenment, 1750–1820* (Cambridge, Mass., 1997), 80–123.

began, "but government even in its best state is but a necessary evil."[6]

While Paine also brought the biblical story of the Fall into this introduction, he did so to rob it of its customary constraining inflections. Governments did not protect the race from its own fallen nature, as the realms of Church and State would have it; instead, they represented the fall itself, and they actively repressed the human good that would otherwise flourish in social interaction. "Government, like dress, is the badge of lost innocence;" Paine warned, "the palaces of kings are built on the ruins of the bowers of paradise."[7] The implications for Americans choosing between their king and their independence were mesmerizing. You could be fallen and naturally depraved and, thereby, subject to the crown under previous historical conceptions of identity, or you could find yourself to be socially integrated in your natural goodness and, therefore, deserving of ever greater dimensions of freedom. These new dimensions of freedom could be disconcerting in scope but not if you accepted your place in the new order.

Consider, for a moment, the alternative rhetorical predicament of the American loyalists, who necessarily tied themselves to a more familiar but increasingly problematic old order. "When a Reconciliation is effected, and things return into the old channel," wrote the Episcopalian minister Charles Inglis, in direct response to *Common Sense*, "a few years of peace will restore everything to its pristine state." *Everything? What* pristine state? Were Inglis's conditional hopes for the past any easier to believe than Paine's aggressive predictions about the future?[8] In a master stroke, Paine grasped that Americans must be forced to choose between a brilliant future and a manifestly duller past, and for that choice to be made absolute, he saw that all of history had to be refigured and collapsed into a fresh sense of the present.

Paine accepted that assignment with unflagging energy and ingenuity in *Common Sense*. For while he clearly sanctioned the conventional Whig Theory of History, affirming a struggle for human rights since the Norman Conquest, he also rejected its backward-looking

---

6. *Common Sense*, 65.
7. Ibid., 65. The analogy of tyranny in government to original sin in humanity is kept afloat throughout the long section, "Of Monarchy and Hereditary Succession," where Paine concludes, "it unanswerably follows that original sin and hereditary succession are parallels" (p. 78).
8. Charles Inglis, "An American, The True Interest of America Impartially Stated" (1776), in Leslie F. S. Upton, ed., *Revolutionary Versus Loyalist: The First American Civil War, 1774–1784* (Waltham, Mass., 1968), 73. In a direct comparison of Paine and Inglis, Stephen Newman, "A Note on *Common Sense* and Christian Eschatology," *Political Theory*, 6 (1978), 101–08, argues that Paine's predictions were indeed considerably easier to believe for many Americans because they tallied with the eschatological framework of New World Calvinism.

assumption of an ancient Anglo-Saxon golden age.[9] There must be no pristine past to reach for! The present and the future had to be the only keys to an effective understanding. True, William the Conqueror had been singular—"a very paltry rascally original," "a French bastard landing with an armed banditti, and establishing himself king of England against the consent of the natives"—but every other king in history, no matter how benevolent, helped the Conqueror to put "the world in blood and ashes." Exalting monarchy in any of its forms contributed to false history and an equally dangerous psychological confusion about liberty.[1]

Paine, the disenchanted Englishman, knew what American colonials could never quite admit to themselves as imperial subjects in need of a usable past. He saw that a belief in monarchy was the mortal enemy of common sense in representative government and that it had to be answered directly. This insight turned the whole long second section of *Common Sense*, "Of Monarchy and Hereditary Succession," into a battle over the true nature of sovereignty, and it put basic ideas about history up for grabs in the process. When Paine attacked the accepted notion of "an honorable origin" for kingliness, he reduced all of the intricacies of Anglo-American debate about the king and his ministers to a more elemental level. Contention was no longer about failures in policy but rather "the natural disease of monarchy."[2]

To be sure, the world was still absolutely geared to royal sway. To break this orientation, *Common Sense* had to show not just that monarchy had grown evil, but that it had always been so: "it is more than probable, that could we take off the dark covering of antiquity, and trace them to their first rise, that we should find the first of them nothing better than the principal ruffian of some restless gang, whose savage manners or pre-eminence in subtilty obtained him the title of chief among plunderers." Here, in a nutshell, was a conversion experience for the enlightened citizen. Only with such a bold claim could Paine turn his readers away from the familiar past and toward an uncomfortable but promising present. Paine's conclusion to the section drove the point home. "Of more worth is one honest

9. The Whig Theory of History assumed that all of English history could be interpreted as a struggle to recover the lost rights of Anglo-Saxon times after they had been swept away by the Norman Conquest in 1066. Magna Carta, the legal reforms of Edward the First, and the Glorious Revolution of 1688 became so many stepping-stones along that path of recovery. For the most complete 18th-century version of this theory, one with which Americans were thoroughly familiar, see William Blackstone, "Chapter 33: Of the Rise, Progress, and Gradual Improvements, of the Laws of England," *Commentaries on the Laws of England*, 4 vols. (Oxford, 1765–1769), 4:400–36.

1. *Common Sense*, 69, 72, 78, 80. "It is the pride of kings," wrote Paine, "which throw mankind into confusion."

2. Ibid., 77, 80–81, 69. "Why is the constitution of E——d sickly," Paine concluded the section, "but because monarchy hath poisoned the republic, the crown hath engrossed the commons?"

man to society, and in the sight of God," he declared, "than all the crowned ruffians who ever lived."[3]

Paine employed similar revisionist strategies to guide the remaining sections of *Common Sense*, "Thoughts on the present State of American Affairs" and "Of the present ability of America, with some miscellaneous Reflexions." Everywhere the message was the same: the past could not be allowed to determine the present. If Paine could argue that "the nearer any government approaches to a republic the less business there is for a king," he could also add "there is something very absurd, in supposing a continent to be perpetually governed by an island. . . . They belong to different systems: England to Europe, America to itself." Geography and the force of gravity were no different from republican politics when it came to transforming the past. "In no instance hath nature made the satellite larger than its primary planet," Paine contended. Why, then, should America revolve around England? Something had to be terribly wrong when the course of history "reverses the common order of nature."[4]

These arguments may seem merely glib today, but they were trumps in an integrated pattern of rhetorical play in 1776. With the formal discourses of eighteenth-century political science, cartography, Newtonian physics, and natural law in place, Paine inserted a separate but unifying flourish, one that domesticated all of knowledge in the blink of an eye. Permeating everything, in a trope that appeared with ever increasing frequency in *Common Sense*, was the eighteenth-century paradigm of the household, and once again, the pamphleteer wrote transgressively. Rooted patriarchal authority was a dangerous symbol for Paine with its obvious, traditional parallels to absolute monarchy. Since he could hardly leave these familiar associations in place, he attacked head-on with a narrative based on the increasingly popular ideas of sentiment and nurture. What, after all, was authority without love? Loyalty without a reciprocating consideration? The traditional sway of the parent meant nothing when, instead of "tender embraces," one encountered "the cruelty of the monster." England was an "unnatural," even a "false" progenitor. In Paine's elaboration, "the phrase parent or mother country hath been jesuitically adopted," and anyone who still so approached England stood condemned, "unworthy the name of husband, father, friend, or lover."[5]

The relationships so named—husband, father, friend, and lover— forged a new family. Sequentially, the term "husband" led Paine's catalogue precisely because it subsumed and codified the succeeding

---

3. Paine's criticism of monarchy, with this point as his probe, is his longest sustained discussion in the pamphlet. See ibid., 69–81.
4. Ibid., 77, 80–81, 91.
5. Ibid., 84, 89.

roles. Husband led to father, friend to lover, or all in one, and all four categories bespoke the paramount goal of parenting and nurturing a new republic. Not the distant and disinterested parent in Europe but the American child in a united family was Paine's preeminent subject—so much so that childhood, and especially the vulnerability of childhood, operates as a constitutive metaphor in *Common Sense*.[6] Repeatedly, Paine forced his reader back on "the intimacy which is contracted in infancy" but always with a twist.[7] For if the truest reader was still at least symbolically the child of a European, the act of reading was calculated to resolve the dependency of that child in an acceptance of adult responsibility, and that new accountability could mean only one thing in context: parenting in a logically independent America.

Rhetorically, every theme held in common the erasure of a previous history. A government without kings, the timeless sanction of nature, the cruelty of forebears, the separate nuclear family, the innocent child—none of the images in question welcomed a return to the past. Of course, Paine was temperamentally suited and historically poised for just such a rejection. The successful immigrant kept only those elements of the past that were of immediate use to the present, calmly dismissing even his own former self. As he would later describe the attitude of 1776:

> Our style and manner of thinking have undergone a revolution more extraordinary than the political revolution of the country. We see with other eyes; we hear with other ears; and think with other thoughts, than those we formerly used. We can look back on our own prejudices, as if they had been the prejudices of other people.[8]

It is impossible to underestimate the psychological importance of "see[ing] with other eyes" as a project in *Common Sense*. Without this ideological jump, without dismissing conventional history altogether, no revolution could have been accomplished by the colonial mind in America. Ordinary wisdom, realpolitik, and the undergirding philosophy of the times all confirmed colonial attachment, loyalty, and imperial design in 1776. The greatest pamphleteer from the English side of the controversy proves the point nicely. Just a year before *Common Sense*, in 1775, Samuel Johnson had torn all the

---

6. For the best reading of late 18th-century obsessions with childhood and childrearing, one that sees a Lockean transformation from nature toward nurture, see Jay Fliegelman, *Prodigals and Pilgrims: The American Revolution against Patriarchal Authority, 1750–1800* (Cambridge, 1982).

7. *Common Sense*, 108, but also 87, 89, 99–100, 109, 114–15.

8. "Letter to the Abbé Raynal" (1782), in *Complete Writings of Paine*, 2:243. This pamphlet gives Paine's most detailed account of the American Revolution.

arguments for independence to shreds, and he had managed the feat by keeping his own eyes carefully on received history.

Johnson's memorable jibe—"how is that we hear the loudest yelps for liberty among the drivers of negroes?"—was only an aside in *Taxation No Tyranny: An Answer to the Resolutions and Address of the American Congress* (1775). His more telling maneuver separated natural law from the standard history of English rights. In Johnson's devastating account, either the Americans were "naked sons of Nature," in which case their particular historical claims on the crown as Englishmen became nonsense, or, in claiming English rights, they accepted the time-bound legal obligations that went with those rights, including the premises of taxation. The choice was theirs, but by resorting to the history of English rights in the first place, "these lords of themselves, these kings of Me, these demigods of independence, sink down to colonists, governed by a charter." Assertions to the contrary were "airy boasts of malevolence"; to claim them meant either "interested faction" or, in a more withering thrust, "honest stupidity."[9]

The sting in Johnson's words was unavoidable unless the recipient learned "to see with other eyes," "hear with other ears," and "think with other thoughts." To answer *Taxation No Tyranny* and other writings like it, a very different conception of the basic issues had to be found, and Paine showed his recognition of the problem with a series of opening instructions in *Common Sense*. Through "preliminaries to settle with the reader," he demanded that the latter "generously enlarge his views beyond the present day"; nothing less than the removal of all "prepossession" was required, a stipulation that clearly asked for more than the stock suspension of "prejudice."[1] These "preliminaries" reach for another level of aesthetic coherence. They show that Paine understood better than anyone else in America that "style and manner of thinking" might dictate the difficult shift from loyalty to rebellion.

II

Three constitutive or controlling metaphors dominate the writing of *Common Sense*. The first, already encountered, is "childhood," with the accompanying idea of maturation. The second and third involve more elemental abstractions, ones that allow Paine to manipulate the parameters of childhood for political effect. The second metaphor emphasizes "time present," and it emerges most frequently

9. Johnson, *Taxation No Tyranny: An Answer to the Resolutions and Address of the American Congress*, in Donald J. Greene, ed. *Samuel Johnson: Political Writings* (New Haven, 1977), 411–55, esp. 454, 428–29, 443, 417–18.
1. *Common Sense*, 81–82.

in Paine's reiterated use of the temporal adverb "now." The third dwells on the virtue that can be assigned to "simplicity." These stylistic devices ride the surfaces of Paine's prose, but they reinforce each other at deeper levels and in much more subtle ways.

Taken together, the metaphors in question enact a dramatic coordination of status, context, and aesthetic form in the overall narrative of *Common Sense*. Youthfulness (status) becomes dramatic in the myriad urgencies of "now" (context), and that basic drama, in turn, is sharpened in a redaction of the plain, the new, the common, the innocent, the fundamental, the direct, the simple, the peremptory—an aesthetic form that dominates both style and substance. Separately, the metaphors are devices on the page. Jointly, they produce "a strategy of intimacy" or identification between author and reader, a near prerequisite for communication in the print medium of a rapidly evolving democratic culture.[2]

The essential dynamic at work appears in a single sentence. Deploring the failure of "repeated petitioning" for peace with England, Paine fastens his reader with a simple imperative: "Wherefore since nothing but blows will do, for God's sake, let us come to a final separation, and not leave the next generation to be cutting throats, under the violated unmeaning names of parent and child." Political negotiation, he continues, has become "too weighty, and intricate," and further attempts "will in a few years be looked upon as folly and childishness," literally a regression in adult thinking.[3] Timeliness, simplicity, and proper domestic nurture all require separation. Anything else, anything but the stark urgency of physical retaliation—"nothing but blows will do"—ruptures the American family, leaving it to cope with "the violated unmeaning names of parent and child." A proper conception of the parent's role commands action now by reading the future in the name of the still innocent child. "In order to discover the line of our duty," Paine writes, "we should take our children in our hand, and fix our station a few years farther into life; that eminence will present a prospect, which a few present fears and prejudices conceal from our sight."[4]

Insistence on the present moment in *Common Sense* compels interest and drama by demanding that the reader make a choice immediately. Paine, in fact, reserves a special wrath for "men of passive tempers" and anyone else who hesitates through "ill-judged deliberation."[5] To grant the urgency in Paine's claims is to enter a sequence. If "now is the seed time of continental union," it follows

---

2. Both the quoted phrase and the premise that "in the Age of Print a successful style involves a strategy of intimacy" are from Simpson, *Brazen Face of History*, 10–11.
3. *Common Sense*, 90.
4. Ibid., 87–88.
5. Ibid., 88–89. See, as well, 82.

that "Britain, being now an open enemy, extinguishes every other name and title." The proposition that "Reconciliation is *now* a fala- cious dream" translates easily into "reconciliation *now* is a danger- ous doctrine," into "it is *now* the interest of America to provide for herself," into "We ought not now to be debating whether we shall be independant or not."[6] Each successive formulation binds the reader to a firmer acceptance of separation "now." Thus, "the present winter is worth an age if rightly employed" becomes "the present time is preferable to all others," becomes "the *present time* is the *true time*," becomes "the present time, likewise, is that peculiar time, which never happens to a nation but once." In this hectoring fashion, Paine turns the reader's choices into group decisions. We read "to find out the *very* time," but we soon learn "the *time hath found us*."[7]

The vital importance of time present also contains an open threat for the reader. If history begins "now," then the reader of the moment is responsible for it. " 'Tis not the concern of a day, a year, or an age," Paine asserts; "posterity are virtually involved, in the contest, and will be more or less affected, even to the end of time, by the proceed- ings now."[8] This definition of history through current event has fun- damental psychological consequences. Although the past is dead, a sentient future watches over the living present. In effect, the future becomes a censorious audience of the present, and any American who tries to wait out the crisis of 1776 will figure as an enemy in this impending view of history. "Should a thought so fatal and unmanly possess the colonies in the present contest," Paine admonishes, "the name of ancestors will be remembered by future generations with detestation."[9]

The rhetorical creativity of *Common Sense* becomes apparent in the endlessly rich and varied tones of these threats. When all of his- tory appears at risk, all of its registers can be brought to bear in a cautionary tale. Typically, in making a shift from "the present state" to "the present ability" of America, Paine inserts a remarkable gloss on present inability. Those readers who cannot act against England become the soldiers who crucified Christ. "Ye that oppose indepen- dence now," Paine intones, "ye know not what ye do."[1] Earlier colo- nials would have found blasphemy in this appropriation of the voice of Jesus, and today the association seems a bizarre one, but eighteenth-century Americans were steeped in a bible culture even

6. Ibid., 82, 85, 90, 93, 114, 121. All of the emphases on the word "now" in the quotations in the text are Paine's.

7. Ibid., 89, 107, 108, 100. The emphases in these quotations are Paine's.

8. Ibid., 82.

9. Ibid., 82, 120–21. Paine makes this point both early and late for those who think they can "neglect the present favorable and inviting period."

1. Ibid., 99. The biblical allusion is to Jesus speaking as he is crucified, Luke 23:34. "Then said Jesus, Father, forgive them; for they know not what they do."

as they were concurrently obsessed with their place on the cutting edge of the Enlightenment. Caught up in secular-religious associations, they were neither surprised nor intimidated to find their independence presented as part of God's plan. Few Americans in 1776 questioned a comparable parallel in *Common Sense*: "The reformation was preceded by the discovery of America, as if the Almighty graciously meant to open a sanctuary to the persecuted in future years."[2]

Paine knew that a country of radical reform Protestants would be willing to pay a price for an acknowledgment of its centrality in history; also that this price might transcend the raging debate over colonies versus nation. *Common Sense* cleverly manipulates the political dispute without running afoul of religious or philosophical differences. There is a warning for every ear in the following passage:

> Ye that tell us of harmony and reconciliation, can ye restore to us the time that is past? Can you give to prostitution its former innocence? Neither can you reconcile Britain and America. . . . There are injuries which nature cannot forgive; she would cease to be nature if she did. As well can the lover forgive the ravisher of his mistress, as the continent forgive the murderers of Britain. The Almighty hath implanted in us these unextinguishable feelings for good and wise purposes. They are the guardians of his image in our hearts.[3]

The Almighty of this text is both more and less than the angry, inscrutable God of Puritan theology.[4] Paine retains the emotion but reverses the flow of anger and, hence, the direction of revealed design. Without losing sight of divine wrath altogether, he concentrates on a justifiable, collective anger in the human world (also figured as "popular rage").[5] History and nature are the mediate forms of Paine's deity, and they dictate a coherent or continental resentment in response to British abuses. Those abuses anger everyone because, as Paine's questions indicate, they violate everything, the domestic sphere as well as historical time: "can the lover forgive the ravisher of his mistress?" intensifies "can ye restore us to the time that is past?"

---

2. *Common Sense*, 87.
3. Ibid., 99–100.
4. For an extended treatment of Paine's conflation of revealed and natural religion, see Fruchtman, *Thomas Paine and the Religion of Nature*, 8ff.
5. *Common Sense*, 121. In the second section, "Of Monarchy And Hereditary Succession," Paine provides an interesting prefiguration of originating anger in the people. Even here, in the biblical context, Paine's emphasis remains a human one. When the misguided Israelites ask the prophet Samuel to place a king over them in Paine's version, God's reluctant and benevolent response to Samuel consists mostly of the refrain "*Hearken unto the voice of the people*"; ibid., 72–76.

Orthodox colonial readers could still reach their Calvinist God through Paine's construct, but just as available were a Quaker God (an image in the human heart), a deistic God (at work in nature's design), and a Scottish moral-sense God (instilling inextinguishable feelings for good and wise purposes). The Supreme Being remains scrupulously abstract in the pages of *Common Sense*. No denominational flags fly, and Paine's inner conception grows out of one basic, reiterated, external premise, "above all things the free exercise of religion."[6] This elemental trait guarantees the acceptability of Paine's multifaceted deity. Simplicity of design invites alternative approaches to the divine, allowing each worshiper to fill in the relevant blanks.

This virtue in simplicity is Paine's third constitutive metaphor, and it shapes his writing in decisive and volatile ways. "I offer nothing more than simple facts, plain arguments, and common sense," Paine avers.[7] The claim is disarmingly rudimentary, deliberately so in its thematic and rhetorical thrusts, but despite the disavowal ("I offer nothing more"), it contains an underlying complexity of purpose and effect that is all the harder to grasp in a text that turns complexity into the symbol of evil. Stylistically, Paine's insistence on simplicity is as unambiguous as it is daring for the time. Eighteenth-century pamphleteering thrived on self-conscious erudition, incorporating constant asides to previous thinkers and a profusion of references to other works. Paine, by way of contrast, gives just three short sentences in fifty pages to the words of other writers (choosing to recognize only Milton and Dragonetti), and he alludes to just one other book in all of *Common Sense*, the Bible.[8]

As Paine's avoidance of other sources implies, his use of "the plain style" has as much to do with ideology as it does with diction. *Common Sense* eschews arch circumlocutions, latinates, elevated tones, and sophisticated nuances. The alternatives are common language, easy alliteration, balanced phraseology, and verbal antitheses in short, memorable sentences.[9] The rationale for these choices is apparent: closer association with the common people. Paine believed that anyone who understood basic English should comprehend his argument and, in one of his great optimistic leaps, that the goal of writing was to make everyone eager to do so. When his opponents complained of a "vulgar style," they had this appeal to the lowest common denominator in mind, and their pejorative use changed the meaning of the term. For Paine, "vulgar" meant "common," "of the

---

6. Ibid., 97, but also 84, 108–09.
7. Ibid., 81.
8. Pütz and Adams, eds., *Concordance to Thomas Paine's* Common Sense, 159, 331.
9. For the best detailed discussion of Paine's "plain style" in *Common Sense*, see Elaine K. Ginsberg, "Style and Identification in *Common Sense*," *Philological Papers: West Virginia University Bulletin*, 23 (1977), 26–36.

people." For his opponents, it suggested that which was boorish or debased.[1]

We are on the brink of a great ideological divide with Paine's seemingly guileless but actually manipulative simplicity in style. Writing to enlist universal involvement in politics frightened Paine's contemporaries. It led a figure like John Adams to deplore *Common Sense* as "so democratical, without any restraint or even an Attempt at any Equilibrium or Counterpoise, that it must produce confusion and every Evil Work." The debate between Paine and Adams raised a fundamental philosophical question. Would general participation in government introduce greater clarity or only confusion in the body politic? Answers to this query could only be conjectural in 1776. Adams published his own pamphlet, *Thoughts on Government*, in quick response to *Common Sense*, and he wrote to insure that government be left "to a few of the most wise and good."[2]

Years later, knowing that he had lost the battle over participatory democracy, Adams vented his frustrations in a splenetic summary:

> I know not whether any Man in the World has had more influence on its inhabitants or affairs for the last thirty years than Tom Paine. There can be no severer Satyr on the Age. For such a mongrel between Pigg and Puppy, begotten by a wild Boar on a Bitch Wolf, never before in any Age of the World was suffered by the Poltroonery of mankind, to run through such a Career of Mischief. Call it then the Age of Paine.[3]

How promiscuous should the role of the people be in a people's government? Despite his rage, Adams saw clearly that the spontaneous vitality of the mongrel came from below. The monstrous lineage that he ascribed to Paine evoked the grotesque, but his fusion of wildness, youth, and transgressive procreation contained an admission. Paine's writings were the catalyst for something new in the world.

Common Sense fosters "the Age of Paine" by insisting on an alliance between common expression and the common in politics. Americans in 1776 were alarmed and many were confused by a world that seemed to be changing out from under them.[4] Paine cut through

---

1. For a discussion of this distinction, see James T. Boulton, *The Language of Politics in the Age of Wilkes and Burke* (London, 1963), 138–39.
2. L. H. Butterfield, ed., *The Diary and Autobiography of John Adams*, 4 vols. (Cambridge, Mass., 1961), 3:333, and Adams, *Thoughts on Government*, in Charles S. Hyneman and Donald S. Lutz, eds., *American Political Writing during the Founding Era, 1784–1822*, 2 vols. (Indianapolis, 1983), 1:403.
3. Adams to Benjamin Waterhouse, Oct. 29, 1805, in Worthington Chauncey Ford, ed., *Statesman and Friend: Correspondence of John Adams with Benjamin Waterhouse, 1784–1822* (Boston, 1927), 31.
4. All sides in the American controversy foresaw a cultural collapse if the wrong choices were made in 1776. The one thing that Charles Inglis shared with Paine in his attack on *Common Sense* was his acceptance of a presumed threat to all of posterity: "But if

that alarm and confusion for anyone who was willing to reduce the world to common principle. There is, he claims, "a principle in nature which no art can overturn." Yes, "our eyes may be dazzled with show, or our ears deceived by sound," "prejudice may warp our wills, or interest darken our understanding," but everything becomes clear again when we return to a primary source: "the simple voice of nature and reason." And what did nature have to tell Americans in their mounting political crisis? In a formula that encompasses every argument in *Common Sense,* nature advises "the more simple any thing is, the less liable it is to be disordered."[5]

If you imbibe the plain style, you are susceptible to every subsequent declaration of "plain truth."[6] In a remarkable series of rhetorical strokes, Paine uses "the simple voice of nature and reason" to reverse the familiar and the strange in Anglo-American culture. He replaces the comfort of the historically commonplace with what would be a blatant oxymoron except for his management of the unfolding reading process. The willing reader must accept a *new familiarity*, everyday reason, from a friendly and colloquial but progressively importunate narrator: "I offer *nothing more* than simple facts, plain arguments, and common sense."[7] The qualification *"nothing more"* represents a stock exercise in humility, but it also strips away a whole series of other intellectual dimensions. Conventional associations of continuing loyalty to England turn into complicating disorders; the originally more frightening prospects of treason and separation become, instead, the easy manifestations of a simpler order.

The force of this transformation can only be fully appreciated in the movement of Paine's narrative. *Common Sense* opens with the plainest version of social contract theory imaginable: "let us suppose a small number of persons settled in some sequestered part of the earth, unconnected with the rest, they will then represent the first peopling of any country." This group, "four or five united," raise "a tolerable dwelling in the midst of a wilderness." The necessity of cooperation among them operates "like a gravitating power," and its influence moves "our newly arrived emigrants into society, the reciprocal blessing of which, would supercede, and render the obligations of law and government unnecessary while they remained

---

[the sons of] America should now mistake her real interest. . . . They will dismember this happy country—make it a scene of blood and slaughter and entail wretchedness and misery on millions yet unborn"; quoted in Upton, ed., *Revolutionary versus Loyalist*, 83.

5. *Common Sense*, 68.

6. Ibid., 71, 79. Similar phraseology, also at crucial moments in Paine's argument, abounds: "in plain terms," "plain arguments," "a plain method of argument," and the like. See ibid., 78, 81, 87.

7. Ibid., 81. Emphasis added for the following discussion in the text.

perfectly just to each other." For an undetermined period of time, "the first difficulties of emigration" keep this "colony" together "in a common cause," but soon the complexity of their undertaking undermines "their duty and attachment to each other," and government, "the badge of lost innocence," must be accepted as "a necessary evil" and "punisher." Notably, this first attempt at government includes everyone. "In this first parliament every man, by natural right will have a seat."[8]

In the technical literary sense, Paine has written a parable. The extended metaphor of an original and happy social simplicity awakens Americans to the moral of their own imaginary founding; everyone is involved but with *the least* government.[9] The story works at several levels. Most obviously, its phraseology evokes a presumed narrative about new world beginnings. Americans in 1776 would have recognized their own ancestors in these "newly arrived emigrants" who settle in a "sequestered part of the earth," who build homes "in the midst of a wilderness," and who overcome "the difficulties of emigration" to form a "colony." But Paine also uses these recognitions to create a philosophical counter narrative to Samuel Johnson's sharp division between natural law and the history of English common law. *Common Sense* demonstrates that "natural right" and English legality ("this first parliament") met in colonial origins and that, in coming together, they created a unique felicity in early America.

Like other parables, this one compels additional reflection through a concluding twist of the metaphor. The appearance of political complexity, figured also as original sin, pollutes the happy origins of the social contract in America, and the reader must muse over both the religious analogy and the historical contrast. An available simplicity in society, which "promotes our happiness positively by uniting our affections," must be balanced against a tangled and unhappy political present, in which Americans feel disenfranchised. And the cause of this confusion and unhappiness? "The constitution of England is so exceedingly complex, that the nation may suffer for years together without being able to discover in which part the fault lies."[1]

Paine employs the bifurcation between happy origins and the present crisis to introduce his long dissection of the British constitution and monarchical government; both are historically debased and intricate sources of evil. Not surprisingly, these first two historical sections of the pamphlet conclude with a rhetorical question that is its own answer. "Why is the constitution of E[nglan]d sickly,"

---

8. Ibid., 65–67.
9. In rhetorical terms, a parable involves "teaching a moral by means of an extended metaphor." See Lanham, *Handlist of Rhetorical Terms,* 2d ed., 106–07.
1. *Common Sense,* 65–68.

Paine wonders, "but because monarchy hath poisoned the republic, the crown hath engrossed the commons?" Again, it is the complication of the combination that is important. Constitutional divisions and monarchical brutality compound each other; together, they portend a spreading corruption that must be stopped. Rhetorically, Paine has moved more than halfway to his central premise: "reconciliation and ruin are nearly related."[2]

"RECONCILIATION OR INDEPENDENCE?" screams the headlined final version of the recurring inquiry. The narrator has replied many times by this stage of the argument, but his last answer provides an aesthetic resolution beyond politics. The shift is from Europe to America and from the complexity and sin of history to the simplicity and virtue of nature as the controlling frame of reference. Paine is especially blunt about the importance of this philosophical change in perspective. Only "he who takes nature for his guide" can hope to see the crisis of 1776 with sufficient clarity to reach intellectual certainty. Through nature, the reader enters a more systematic and mediate universe, one that will sustain *"the answer without doubt."* To express his appreciation of this certainty in design, Paine gives his own version of the answer in geometric terms. "INDEPENDANCE" forms *"a* SINGLE SIMPLE LINE, *contained within ourselves,"* leaving *"reconciliation, a matter exceedingly perplexed and complicated."*[3] Reconciliation has become so perplexing and complicated that it cannot even be rendered in a discernible geometric form. Only independence can be made visible in meaningful action. Proving the point in his peroration, Paine beseeches all Americans to "unite in drawing a line, which, like an act of oblivion, shall bury in forgetfulness every former dissension."[4]

There are problems with Paine's strategy of virtue in simplicity, and some of them are implied when his simile of separation requires "an act of oblivion." To the extent that independence dictates the removal of previous intellectual affinities, it can leave the reader of *Common Sense* feeling terribly alone.[5] In an unguarded moment of the opening parable, Paine reveals that "the strength of one man is so unequal to his wants, and his mind so unfitted for perpetual solitude, that he is soon obliged to seek assistance and relief of another, who in his turn requires the same."[6] This identified human craving

2. Ibid., 68–80, 81, 94.
3. Ibid., 115, 117. Paine falls back on the geometric device again in "The American Crisis, No. V," when he claims "what we have now to do is as clear as light, and the way to do it is as straight as a line"; *Complete Writings of Paine*, 1:125.
4. *Common Sense*, 122.
5. For an excellent analysis of the significance of loneliness in *Common Sense*, one on which this paragraph depends, see Martin Roth, "Tom Paine and American Loneliness," *EAL*, 22 (1987), 175–82.
6. *Common Sense*, 66.

for social relief and comfort does not necessarily welcome a revolution. Paine's separating Americans can achieve the enlarged view of their national situation only by divesting themselves of all of the previous connections, loyalties, and thoughts on which their colonial society has been based. Then, too, Paine's alternative of continental attachment is painfully abstract, antilocal, nonexperiential even artificial in 1776.[7] To become newly sufficient unto themselves, Paine's first readers must turn away from everything they know and face the void.

The final component in Paine's argument is his manipulation of these fears. American forebodings must be turned into something more empowering, and Paine's solution involves a singular conversion. In *Common Sense*, anxious thought becomes righteous feeling. Anger provides the cohesive social force that mere misgivings cannot. Methodologically, the reader is asked to "examine the passions and feelings of mankind," always remembering that this exercise will require an explanation "by those feelings and affections which nature justifies." To perform this examination in the colonial context—to "bring the doctrine of reconciliation to the touchstone of nature"—means to arouse hatred instead of love. Paine is quite clear on the point: "'never can true reconcilement grow where wounds of deadly hate have pierced so deep.'"[8]

Anger supplies the emotional force to bring Americans together in a formative act of self-recognition. "Men read by way of revenge," Paine declares.[9] *Common Sense* is that reading. It fuels itself with images of blood, ashes, suffering, cruelty, corruption, monstrosity, hellishness, and villainy. When critics of *Common Sense* called its author "furious," Paine welcomed the accusation. "There are men too," he responded, "who have not virtue enough to be angry."[1] This conjunction of anger and simplicity, under the rubric of virtue, was hardly accidental. Among other things, it supplied the perfect counter to a loyalist rhetoric that asked Americans to rest in the familiar calm of complex colonial associations.[2]

---

7. "It is pleasant to observe," Paine writes in a typical passage, "by what regular gradations we surmount the force of local prejudice, as we enlarge our acquaintance with the world." The particular gradations in the ensuing passage carry us from street, to town, to county, to country, to continent—each bringing a desirable change in perspective away from loyalty to England—but it remains unclear what Paine's "continental minds" are to use for an identity that connects with actual experience. See ibid., 85.

8. Ibid., 88–90. Paine quotes from Milton without revealing that it is Satan who is speaking in this passage from *Paradise Lost*. Roth, "Tom Paine and American Loneliness," 179, summarizes the importance of anger to *Common Sense* in general: "Despite the surface optimism of Paine's program of Americanization, his images and plots are always angry and ultimately bitter, whether they depict a heroic or a slavish America."

9. *Common Sense*, 113.

1. "The Forester's Letters: No. III," Apr. 22, 1776, in *Complete Writings of Paine*, 2:74.

2. Daniel Leonard, Adams's leading opponent as "Massachusettensis" in 1775, supplies perhaps the best example of this call for calm in loyalist rhetoric: "Be calm, my friends," was his litany in "To The Inhabitants of the Province of the Massachusetts-

Paine used the combination of anger and simplicity as a funneling device. Of all of the emotions, anger is the most difficult to control, and Paine's triumph in this regard is the great master stroke in his rhetorical plan. His "uncanny ability to articulate the emotions of the mob" allowed him to objectify colonial unrest as patriotism.[3] Only Paine really harnessed these forces in 1776. He alone, of all the writers of the Revolution, fathomed the depths of "popular rage" in America, and he plied that resentment to construct a vital identification between narrator and reader. It is this perception, more than any other, that carries *Common Sense* from story toward spellbinding myth.

III

A distinction must be drawn between the anger of colonial Americans in 1776 and their ability to express that anger in formal prose. Modern scholarship on the Revolution has puzzled over this paradox: pre-Revolutionary Americans were more fearful and angry than their circumstances warranted, but their "literature of revolution" appeared more decorous and less angry than English literary productions of the same period. *Common Sense* represented the exception that proves the rule. Written by a transplanted Englishman who brought his "daring impudence" with him, it rejected the "everyday, business-like sanity" of most colonial writings on politics.[4]

Anger, as such, surfaces most visibly in the frequency of popular uprisings throughout colonial America. Mob behavior was an intrinsic part of colonial life as well as an extralegal arm in important communal decisions. At different moments, rioting paralyzed each of the major colonial cities, and violent uprisings in the countryside periodically destroyed property and brought government to a halt—sometimes pitting whole regions against each other, as in the Paxton Boys riot of Western Pennsylvania in 1763.[5] Moreover, mob violence

---

Bay," as part of a complex description of "the bands of society cut asunder" and "civil government dissolved." His emphasis, as well as those of other loyalists, was on the circumspection that was required to appreciate the advantages in the many, still sustaining ties between England and America. See Upton, ed. *Revolutionary Versus Loyalist*, 36–38, 42, 46–48.

3. For an analysis of these qualities in Paine and for the quotation in this sentence, see Evelyn J. Hinz, "Thomas Paine," in Everett Emerson, ed., *American Literature, 1764–1789: The Revolutionary Years* (Madison, 1977), 48, 55–56.

4. Bailyn, *The Ideological Origins of the American Revolution* (Cambridge, Mass., 1967), 25, 94–143, 17–19. Bailyn speculates that Paine brought his "daring impudence" and "uncommon frenzy" with him from England.

5. For treatments of the prevalence and general unruliness of mob behavior in 18th-century America, see Gordon S. Wood, "A Note on Mobs in the American Revolution," *William and Mary Quarterly*, 3d Ser., 23 (1966), 635–42; Jesse Lemisch, "Jack Tar in the Streets: Merchant Seamen in the Politics of Revolutionary America," ibid., 25 (1968), 371–407; Pauline Meier, "Popular Uprisings and Civil Authority in Eighteenth-Century America," ibid., 27 (1970), 3–35; and Merrill Jensen, "The American People and the American Revolution," *JAH*, 57 (1970), 5–35.

increased exponentially after 1765, the year in which rioting through-out the colonies nullified the Stamp Act, and recognition of this change has led historians to assign "mass violence a dominant role at every significant turning point of the events leading up to the War for Independence."[6]

Even so, there is little commentary about mob behavior in the formal literature of the period, and when it does appear it is to maintain restraints on that behavior. The second most popular propaganda piece of the Revolutionary era, John Dickinson's *Letters from a Farmer in Pennsylvania* (1768), offers a good case in point. Dickinson began his long pamphlet by distinguishing between "inflammatory measures," which he "detests," and "a firm, modest exertion of a free spirit," which alone gave the proper tone to public protest. "The cause of liberty," he wrote, "is a cause of too much dignity, to be sullied by turbulence and tumult." On the face of it, unrest in America was almost as great a concern in colonial pamphleteering as British intransigence.[7] Rhetorical restraint and elevation were not just ploys to demonstrate rationality and accountability while petitioning the king; they were essential strategies for keeping the lower orders in line.

The many differences between Dickinson and Paine as pamphleteers flowed from as many historical factors, but the rhetorical contrast in their writing styles came down to an agenda of calm restraint against a program of deliberate emotional excess, cautionary balance versus fervent assertion. Psychologically, Paine was closer to the mob than Dickinson ever could be, and he knew how to manipulate its spiritual proclivities.[8] The artistry of *Common Sense*, like the animus of the mob, builds solidarity out of hatred. Paine engages his readers by promising them a final metamorphosis from anger to "the hearty hand of friendship," setting aside the question of whether rabble-rousing can ever achieve such a transformation.[9]

But if the ultimate price of fanning hatred remains unplumbed in *Common Sense*, the rhetorical pay-off was great in 1776. Paine's

---

6. Arthur M. Schlesinger, "Political Mobs and the American Revolution, 1765–1776," *Proceedings of the American Philosophical Society,* 99 (1955), 244.

7. John Dickinson, "Letter I," "Letter III," *Letters from a Farmer in Pennsylvania, to the Inhabitants of the British Colonies* (New York, 1903), 11, 29–30. See also Marc Egnal, *A Mighty Empire: The Origins of the American Revolution* (Ithaca, 1988), 213–14.

8. Paine's affinity with the mob can be expressed in either temperamental or class terms. By 1771, close to 30% of the adult male population in cities like Boston and Philadelphia were neither property owners nor the dependents of tax-paying members of the community. This large propertyless group of itinerant laborers, seamen, and artisans—men more-or-less in Paine's own first situation as an immigrant—constituted the rampaging mobs of the 1770s. Obviously, the corset maker from Thetford would have had more ties to these elements than Dickinson, the Philadelphia lawyer. For the class implications, see James Henretta, *The Evolution of American Society, 1700–1815* (Lexington, Mass., 1973), 96–97.

9. *Common Sense,* 122.

substitution of assertion and excess for Dickinsonian prudence and reserve worked in his favor. Held back for years by the restraining influence and decorum of leaders such as Dickinson and Adams, radical segments of the reading public welcomed the release of psychic energy that *Common Sense* offered.[1] Paine managed this release by discarding the historical colonial self-image of decorous self-restraint and by replacing it with an abstract process of reasoning that made anger compelling. His chain of postulates ran like this: anger is the natural and appropriate emotional reaction to an intensifying pattern of British tyranny; it is politically necessary to express this natural and appropriate feeling; communal health (often expressed as "manliness") also depends on it; therefore, anger is the legitimate precursor of virtuous civic action.

This chain of logic is reinforced by a parallel sequence of identifications that either saves or damns the reader, depending on that reader's reaction to *Common Sense*. The psychological movement of the narrative is from general outrage over British attacks, to an explicit anger against the person of the king, to a demonstration that such anger must foster an irreconcilable hatred against the mother country, to the conclusion that individuals who remain loyal to England must share the reception of that hatred as traitors "against the natural rights of all Mankind."[2] This final level of hatred knows no real limits. It encompasses "all those who espouse the doctrine of reconciliation," but it also extends to "moderate men, who think better of the European world than it deserves." Anyone who remains unreceptive to immediate independence should be despised. In saying so, Paine espouses what will later become a central recognition in crowd theory: you are either for the mob or it is against you.[3]

The most impressive dimension in this spiral of hatred is the rhetorical administration of its growth. Paine begins simply enough by claiming "the Power of feeling" against those who have attacked America. Feeling, in this sense, moves in one continuum from a distaste for kingliness, to anger at the British monarchy, to "an universal hatred" of George III. Paine understood—as his colonial counterparts did not—that it would be easier to loathe an identifiable person, King George, than any abstract collectivity, whether of Parliament, the ministry, or the people of England. As he puts this realization, "it is scarcely worth our while to fight against a

1. As Jensen has claimed, "the popular upheaval after 1773 demonstrated that some of the ordinary people in every colony were far ahead of their leaders in opposition to Britain"; Jensen, "American People and the American Revolution," 23.
2. *Common Sense*,, 63–64, 72–81, 88–89, 99–100, 114–15.
3. Ibid., 88. Elias Canetti, *Crowds and Power*, trans. Carol Stewart (New York, 1984; orig. pub. 1962), 19–20.

contemptible ministry only."[4] Significantly, there is a second and far nastier continuum of abhorrence in *Common Sense*. Paine reserves his ultimate vituperation for the unworthy American. It is not enough to expose those "who are not to be trusted" or even "prejudiced men who *will not* see." Paine, at the outset, says "I would carefully avoid giving unnecessary offense." By the end, however, the American who sympathizes with England in any way has devolved into something considerably less than human. This American has fallen farther than even "the royal brute of Great Britain." He has "sunk himself beneath the rank of animals" and must "contemptibly crawl through the world like a worm."[5]

It would be hard to imagine a more devastating loneliness than the state Paine reserves for his American opponents. What natural rights, if any, remain to those placed below even a subhuman category, "beneath the rank of animals"? Since the closest emotion to anger is revenge, Paine is unstinting in his exercise of it.[6] There will be no forgiveness for those who dare to deviate from the republican norm. Paine's parting shot at any "Tories" who remain in America takes the form of a threat. If they fail to support a republican form of government, they should expect to lose the security that has previously "protected them from popular rage." Paine is vehemently part of that rage. As he has already noted, "there is no punishment which that man will not deserve, be he who, or what, or where he will."[7]

The anger in these words is important because it is responsible for a political solidarity that would otherwise be lacking. After all, the corollary to Paine's isolation of unworthy Americans is an unsettling one: "Independance is the only BOND that can tye and keep us together."[8] The *only* bond? But if so, why should it work? Why should the untested prospect of independence guarantee the political fabric of a vast and heterogeneous continental republic? How are the separate liberties of each and every citizen going to accomplish "the glo-

---

4. *Common Sense*, 72, 81, 114, 91, 93. Unlike Paine, colonial American pamphleteers remained squeamish about assailing their king, preferring to blame British abuses on his ministers. As late as 1774, Thomas Jefferson, who goes further than other Americans, still kept his *A Summary View of the Rights of British America* "an humble and dutiful address to be presented to his Majesty." The *Summary View* is an extraordinary challenge of the king for a colonial thinker, but it still calls George III "chief officer of the people," whereas Paine, two years later in *Common Sense*, 93, makes him "the greatest enemy this continent hath." Jefferson attacked the king directly only after learning the value of this lesson from *Common Sense*. By July 4, 1776, the explicit accusations of the Declaration of Independence are all leveled against George III in order to demonstrate "every act which may define a tyrant." See Adrienne Koch and William Peden, eds., *The Life and Selected Writings of Thomas Jefferson* (New York, 1944), 22–26, 293.
5. *Common Sense*, 88, 98, 114. See also *Complete Writings of Paine*, 1:29.
6. In the first of the "American Crisis" pamphlets, also written in 1776, Paine justifies revenge and the right to exercise it as "the soft resentment of a suffering people"; *Complete Writings of Paine*, 1:55.
7. *Common Sense*, 89, 99, 121, 89.
8. Ibid., 121.

rious union of all things" that Paine so confidently predicts for the American strand?[9]

Realizing that there are no philosophical or political solutions to such questions, Paine responds on a series of distinct rhetorical levels. First, he creates a cohesive or corporate American self out of first-person, plural, pronominal forms. The ever-present "we" of *Common Sense* comprises neither colonies, nor voting citizens, nor leaderships of any kind. This ubiquitous "we" is literally everyone—every reading self who has been arranged by the acceptance of Paine's language into a collective but equal audience capable of receiving and (through identification) of giving speech.

Both the collective and the egalitarian flavors of this American audience are calculated effects. Collectivity carries the presumption of truth within it. "Could the straggling thoughts of individuals be collected," writes Paine, "they would frequently form materials for wise and able men to improve to useful matter."[1] Equality, in turn, provides a comparable safeguard; it joins "the equal rights of nature" and benevolent social origins ("all men being originally equal") with plans for the new government ("a large and equal representation"). Equality and collectivity thus become the sources of all social agreement. "Where there are no distinctions there can be no superiority, perfect equality affords no temptation," Paine observes in claiming that equal states will always retain "a spirit of good order."[2] "Perfect equality" in the union of states is, in this sense, the political equivalent of the rhetorical "we" in *Common Sense*.

But Paine's language holds another meaning and a second rhetorical device for bringing separate Americans together. The absence of hierarchy in "perfect equality" marks an intended audience, the mob. Paine uses anger, the natural emotion of the mob, to urge the people as mob to express the general will of a republican citizenry. Noting that "the mind of the multitude is left at random," he writes to give it direction through the act of independence, and his facilitating tool is the "unexampled concurrence of sentiment" in an angry people. There are two steps in this process: the admittedly temporary emotion of the people must be recognized and celebrated; and next, the people's anger must be harnessed to the more permanent political end of independence.[3]

Common Sense then identifies three ways for gaining that independence: "by the legal voice of the people in Congress; by a military power; or by a mob." Paine's hope for an amalgamation of these compelling forces leads to his greatest expressions of urgency. He

9. Ibid., 100.
1. Ibid., 96.
2. Ibid., 72, 76, 109, 95.
3. Ibid., 117–18.

begs for immediate action because he believes that Congress, the soldiery, and the mob have a rare opportunity to act as one in 1776. In this moment, and perhaps in no other, "our soldiers are citizens, and the multitude a body of reasonable men." Poignantly, this moment also provides the context for Paine's most famous claim, "we have it in our power to begin the world over again."[4]

Popular acceptance of this appeal emanates from the mob's discovery of its own assigned purpose and dignity. After a decade of pamphleteering on the rationality of moderate opposition, Paine's different, freewheeling endorsement of the people's emotions converts the mob from shameful by-product into a legitimate vehicle of colonial identity and cultural salvation. This shift, while superficial, is not without its subtleties. The mob responds initially to the narrator's buoyant inclusiveness ("we have it in our power"), but it remains engaged through an intricate arrangement of psychological ingredients. Unmistakably, there is real acumen in Paine's comprehension of these ingredients and a master's craft in his applications.

Contemporary theories of crowd psychology suggest that the mob feeds on five qualities: it wants to grow; it seeks equality within itself; it loves density, it needs direction, and its most conspicuous activity lies in its destructiveness.[5] The rhetoric of *Common Sense* plays itself out along these axes: first, in its attacks on monarchy and its call to arms, which seek to destroy all linkage with Britain, next in its language of equality, then in its plans for solidarity or density through union, and last in its explicit insistence upon the continental growth of the republic.[6]

After strengthening the character of the mob in this manner, Paine cunningly leaves it with a preordained choice, one that will either confirm or rob it of all identity. The mob can either declare for independence, with the life-giving violence that this will require of it, or it can hesitate, dwindle, and forever forfeit independence, leaving itself "continually haunted with the thoughts of its necessity."[7] That the mob easily imbibes the careful structures that we have identified— hatred of authority, outrage against wronged innocence, sympathy for domestic distress, identification with simplicity of design, and the acceptance of natural reason over historical experience—is a given. More arresting are the hidden patterns of deep threat that guarantee

4. Ibid., 120.
5. Canetti, *Crowds and Power*, 19–20, 29–30. See also J. S. McClelland, *The Crowd and the Mob: From Plato to Canetti* (Boston, 1989), 1–33, 327–35.
6. For a parallel description of the same phenomenon with a different vocabulary, see Jack P. Greene's understanding of Paine's contribution to "the *modernization* of political consciousness" through "two crucial developments: the mobilization of large segments of society theretofore politically inert, and the desacralization of the traditional political order," in *Understanding the American Revolution: Issues and Actors* (Charlottesville, 1995), 285–86.
7. *Common Sense*, 112.

these investments. In the end, neither the thoughtful individual nor the emotionally driven mob have choices to make if they are to survive on anything like their own terms as willing readers. The wrath that Paine has raised has been primed to turn inward if it fails to reach designated external targets.

The potential viciousness in this trajectory gives one more proof of Paine's rhetorical power in 1776; his language convinced an unprecedented number of Americans to accept his arguments on his terms, and the result was a revolution against colonial rule. But seeing this rhetoric for what it is, in all of its angry impetuses and accusatory denouement, makes *Common Sense* a disquieting text in national formations. Only a zealous convert can ignore the ugly impulses in Paine's pamphlet. The unleashing and manipulation of group hatreds do not make for a pretty sight, and the success of *Common Sense* depends on them. What is to be done with such levels of hatred and how susceptible do present Americans remain to their influence? These questions are especially relevant for a people that can no longer embrace the intellectual safety valve of natural reason—the source that made common sense such a comfort for Paine and his first readers.

Conclusion

If the angers of *Common Sense* are recognized for what they have become, national angers, they can be arranged and perhaps even curbed to serve a modern understanding. Nationalism in general thrives on two basic emotions, satisfaction raised by fulfillment and anger provoked by violation.[8] Paine is the first modern writer to grapple knowingly with these contrasting impulses in a revolutionary-minded state. What is more, his inspired exploitation of these satisfactions and angers contains the beginnings of a solution to the problems he has raised.

In contemporary theory, nations are not so much natural creations as they are invented constructs; nationalisms in such an understanding are not intrinsic ideas but cultural artifacts best recognized in the way language is used. National communities, in consequence, are known less by fixed or concrete conceptions and more by the flexible mode in which they are imagined.[9] Similarly, in most cultures an ethnocentric view of the nation as a natural, prepolitical entity made up of the folk with an inherited form of life competes with a more modern, more cosmopolitan conception of the nation

---

8. This bipolar anatomy of nationalist sentiment is the first premise in Ernest Gellner, *Nations and Nationalism* (Ithaca, 1983), 1.
9. Anderson, *Imagined Communities*, 140, 12–15. See also E. J. Hobsbawm, *Nations and Nationalism since 1780: Programme, Myth, Reality* (Cambridge, 1990), 1–45.

as a legal entity made up of citizens with constitutionally defined rights.[1] Thomas Paine, as an eighteenth-century figure steeped in natural law, would not have agreed with these assessments, but ironically, he began to make them conceivable for others when he articulated a design for the American nation in 1776. In fact, *Common Sense* marks the divide between the two understandings of the nation as folk entity and legal entity. It privileges the first in the notion of an originally happy society without government, but it constructs the latter. For it is only through the nation as legal entity that republicanism receives a guarantee of its operations, and Paine is dedicated first and foremost to a republican ideal based on law.

The narrator of *Common Sense* assumes that everything will collapse without the swift implementation of a republic of laws. When he argues that "the Continental belt is too loosely buckled," he means that America is "without law" and must rectify the situation immediately.[2] As Paine would later write of 1776, "we had no other law than a kind of moderated passion; no other civil power than an honest mob," and he also saw that if these conditions had been allowed to continue "this continent would have been plunged into irrecoverable confusion." The situation is saved, in his understanding, by the introduction of republican institutions for "a regular people," but it is Paine's admission of an alternative danger that should catch our attention. Without law, he warns, no passion stays moderate, and no mob remains honest.[3]

Paine clearly believes in the control that republican institutions will engender. Under their influence, the mob somehow turns itself into "a regular people." Unfortunately, the underlying theoretical basis of this transmutation is never fully articulated in *Common Sense*; as its author was the first to admit, he merely "threw out a few thoughts . . . for I only presume to offer hints, not plans."[4] Nonetheless, even if there is no mature plan, there is definitely a process in the "few thoughts" that are given.[5] Paine offers a story to register the transition from the mob to a regular people, and that story characteristically contains a multitude of complexities in the simplest of narratives. For all of these reasons, it is worth quoting in full:

1. For the terminology in this paragraph and a discussion of the ethnocentric against the cosmopolitan view of nationhood, see Jürgen Habermas, "The European Nation-State—Its Achievements and Its Limits: On the Past and Future of Sovereignty and Citizenship," in Gopal Balakrishnan, ed., *Mapping the Nation* (London, 1986), 281–82, 286–88.
2. *Common Sense*, 118.
3. "The American Crisis III," *Complete Writings of Paine*, 1:81.
4. *Common Sense*, 109.
5. Wilson, *Paine and Cobbett*, 52–53, goes further when he argues that "it was characteristic of Paine not to leave things hanging; where there was room for concrete proposals, he would supply them," though the result might look like "a trail of contradictions."

But where says some is the King of America? I'll tell you Friend, he reigns above, and doth not make havock of mankind like the Royal [Brute] of Britain. Yet that we may not appear to be defective even in earthly honors, let a day be solemnly set apart for proclaiming the charter; let it be brought forth placed on the divine law, the word of God; let a crown be placed thereon, by which the world may know, that so far as we approve of monarchy, that in America THE LAW IS KING. For as in absolute government the King is law, so in free countries the law *ought* to be King; and there ought to be no other. But lest any ill use should afterwards arise, let the crown at the conclusion of the ceremony be demolished, and scattered among the people whose right it is.[6]

The calculated indirections in this curious tale blend Paine's rhetorical methods with his political solutions. There can be no better concluding demonstration of his appeal as a writer, and the story itself gives an uncanny glimpse of the future, the republic as modern nation state.

Many of the standard rhetorical devices of *Common Sense* are present in this passage: exhortation, repetition, hyperbole, inversion, anaphora (using the same word at the beginning of successive clauses), hypophora (asking questions and immediately answering them), and frequent hectoring of the obedient reader ("I'll tell you friend"). Also familiar, thematically, are the conflations of divine and secular frames of reference, the contrasts between England and America, the parallel distinction between monarchical and republican forms of government, the display of villainy ("the Royal Brute"), the avowals of freedom found ("so in free countries"), and the casual assumption of an enormous, expectant audience ("by which the world may know"). And yet the story that Paine gives here is so much greater in the telling than the sum of its parts and devices might indicate.

Although a king is killed and metaphorically cannibalized in this passage, the violence involved has been stylized. Neither blood nor anguish ripples the surfaces of what has been "demolished." All "havock" has been relegated to the other side. God reigns more benevolently in America because unmediated by intervening kings. The people, like any pious tribe left to its own social devices, seek that benevolence by courting divine favor through "earthly honors." Above all, there is a saving sense of ceremony that is half biblical

---

6. *Common Sense*, 98. The Kramnick edition of *Common Sense* leaves a blank space with a dash after the word "Royal" to indicate an unspoken pejorative noun for "King" in the quotation. I have substituted "Brute" for that dash, placing the word in brackets, relying on the use of that term in the Philip Foner edition of *Common Sense* in *Complete Writings of Paine*, 1:29.

saga (a crown is placed on "the word of God") and half colonial politics ("proclaiming the charter"). Here Paine uses the decorum of ritual to subsume revolutionary angers. A day has been "solemnly set aside" to make the law king, and the people are justified and dignified in their actions by partaking of that authority, which is then "scattered" in their midst. The obvious parallel is to the Christian sacrament of communion in a parataxis that points toward civil religion in the modern nation state.[7]

More is at stake for the citizen than meets the eye in this ceremony of legal proclamation. Ritual in general promotes participation over contest. It welcomes performers instead of designating winners over losers, and it tries to bring everyone into the fold through an exercise in consent. To participate is to belong, and the participant usually engages with cooperation in mind.[8] Notably, there is little room for anger in such a ceremony, particularly when it assumes the form of a national celebration. The other or twin emotion of national sentiment—not anger from violation but satisfaction in fulfillment—tends to rule in this situation. So when Paine follows the configuration of ritual in his fanciful version of national ceremony, it represents an important variation. *Common Sense* is a text given over largely to American resentments, but anger suddenly becomes unseemly in this one ceremonial context, "solemnly set apart." The final scattering of a symbolic crown enacts a legal shift in empowerment and understanding rather than another act of rage. It is tellingly designed to avoid further "ill use."

A whimsical, even jocular, celebration of the law as king may seem no more than that. Even a profound day "set apart" is but one day, and Paine's rather offhand account of national ceremony reads a little like a minimalist's attempt to quell the Furies that he has aroused. Even so, if there is a saving difference, it lies in the controlling prescriptive language of the passage: "so in free countries the law *ought* to be King; and there ought to be no other." A national readership is being told that appropriate action should always take place through a recognition and acceptance of law, and the many deferrals in this aspiration do not make it any less real or compelling. Here, in effect, is an early rendition of the modern rule of law. In Paine's understanding, given in the last two sections of *Common Sense*, the process of law represents the stabilizing backbone for every other communal virtue in an advanced society, including free elections, a constitutional convention, an annual Congress, the security of property, the efficient use of bountiful resources, a strong

7. See Robert N. Bellah, "Civil Religion in America," *Daedalus*, 96 (1967), 1–21, and *The Broken Covenant: American Civil Religion in Time of Trial*, 2d ed. (Chicago, 1992).
8. These distinctions between ritual and contest are elucidated by Claude Lévi-Strauss, *The Savage Mind* (Chicago, 1966; orig. pub. 1962), 32.

navy, the growth of commerce, and the management of a national debt.

This rule of law is modern because accepted by all rather than imposed from above. Law always contains an element of imposition, but the modern rule of law, by definition, turns hierarchical intrusiveness into a penetrating force at work on every level of society, thus providing a structure accessible to the ruled as well as the ruler. As both typological superstructure and social infrastructure, this rule of law merges with the underlying basis of all productive relations. It becomes an unavoidable consideration for all concerned, whether in thought or in action. Rulers must turn to the logic of the rule of law to understand their own behavior; the ruled learn to keep power within constitutional limits and to insist on its applications. For everyone, the language of the rule of law stands for a cultural achievement of universal significance.[9]

Thomas Paine brings all of these elements to bear in *Common Sense*. He then welds the aspiration of the rule of law to the act of revolution. Using a typically reductionist tactic, he announces that "independancy means no more, than, whether we shall make our own laws." The quiet corollary to noisy independence is legality. As Paine tells his newly forming national readership, independence must be brought about by "the legal voice of the people in Congress"; only in this manner can "we have every opportunity and every encouragement before us, to form the noblest, purest constitution on the face of the earth."[1] *Common Sense* insists that a legal revolution will cap the angers that made independence possible. The crown of law will be scattered among the people, "whose right it is," and the exercise of that right will restore calm.

The optimism in such language functions as an intrinsic necessity in a rule of law. A people have to believe in the logic and the criteria of the law for it to work. The language and acts of the law must establish an expectation of justice in a receptive community.[2] Paine aims all of the solidarity that he has created in *Common Sense* in this direction. He is the first to predict that "the noblest, purest constitution on the face of the earth" will be made on a continental scale. Independence is the first step in such a legal framework. "We shall then see our object," Paine concludes in his last paragraph, "and our ears will be legally shut against the schemes of an intriguing, as well as a cruel enemy."[3] Seeing the object clearly stages an overriding

---

9. For a balanced definition of the rule of law, one on which this paragraph depends, see E. P. Thompson, "The Rule of Law," *Whigs and Hunters: The Origin of the Black Acts* (New York, 1975), 258–69.
1. *Common Sense*, 93, 120.
2. Thompson, *Whigs and Hunters*, 263.
3. *Common Sense*, 121.

enlightenment norm, the restoration of calm through proper sight. No other sense is allowed to disrupt this primal and prescriptive clarity of light. With their ears "legally shut against . . . a cruel enemy," Paine's readers use the law positively to channel their understanding. To the extent that they see clearly, they exchange the shouts of the mob for the more measured voice of a people.

The peculiar juxtaposition of aroused anger and law-giving calm means that *Common Sense* resists a simple reading. The pamphlet is there for the revolutionary mind; it is also there for the transcendent lawgiver. But rhetorically the writer has turned the combination into a vital sequence, and this affirmation is the key to a national text worth permanent scrutiny. Over and over again, Thomas Paine insists that a procedurally minded republic will find the forms that it needs in his pages and that a knowing people must use those forms to participate intelligently in their own governance. These words and others like them come out of crisis but succeed in the solution rendered. They reach for the common reader as useful citizen. They say *Common Sense* is a source book for a deserving people—if, or when, things go badly wrong.

NATHAN R. PERL-ROSENTHAL

The "Divine Right of Republics": Hebraic Republicanism and the Debate over Kingless Government in Revolutionary America[†]

British American patriots had a difficult time accepting kingless government. Though royal government was already a dead letter in much of the American colonies by 1775, replaced by committees and the Continental Congress, the patriot leadership remained attached to the idea of monarchy, at least in public. In late 1775, mere months before Congress finally abjured its allegiance to George III, Georgia delegate J. J. Zubly declared to his fellow representatives that the alternative, "Republican Government," would be "little better than Government of Devils." The first months of 1776 saw a dramatic repudiation of this view by the patriot leadership, culminating in the Declaration of Independence's searing indictment of the king. Though scholars have extensively studied this early 1776 discussion, they have not yet examined one of its important components: the argument, first developed at length by Thomas Paine in *Common Sense*, that monarchy was "a form of government which the word of

† From *William and Mary Quarterly* 66.3 (2009): 535–64. Reprinted by permission of the Omohundro Institute of Early American History and Culture.

God bears testimony against." Paine's assertion became a topic of vigorous debate, discussed by writers for and against independence in pamphlets, newspaper articles, and sermons.[1] Reconstructing this component of the 1776 debate and its roots in the English republican tradition can contribute to our understanding of the patriot movement's embrace of kingless government and to a fuller mapping of Anglo-American republicanism in the eighteenth century.

The argument Paine first made in 1776 grew out of a "Hebraic" strand in English republicanism that first took shape in the seventeenth century. This tradition claimed, on the basis of the putative account of a "Hebrew Republic" in the Bible, that God condemned monarchy, making it illegitimate, and that only kingless governments enjoyed divine approval. John Milton supplied the first English-language formulation of this complex of ideas as a way to justify England's new republican government at the beginning of the interregnum. It continued to be an important component of English republican thought through the 1680s: Algernon Sidney, most notably, made it a centerpiece of his celebrated *Discourses Concerning Government* (published posthumously in 1698). But in the eighteenth century, whig thinkers who took up the republican banner suppressed the Hebraic strand.[2] As supporters of Britain's mixed monarchic constitution and Protestant succession, these men selectively and unfaithfully read seventeenth-century texts such as *Discourses*

1. J. J. Zubly to Congress, Oct. 12, 1775, in L. H. Butterfield, Leonard C. Faber, and Wendell D. Garrett, eds., *Diary and Autobiography of John Adams* (Cambridge, Mass., 1961), 2: 204 ("Republican Government"); Thomas Paine, *Common Sense*, in Bruce Kuklick, ed., *Political Writings*, rev. ed. (Cambridge, Mass., 2000), 1–45 ("form of government," 15). On the collapse of royal authority, see Jack N. Rakove, *The Beginnings of National Politics: An Interpretive History of the Continental Congress* (New York, 1979), 42–62, esp. 52; Jerrilyn Greene Marston, *King and Congress: The Transfer of Political Legitimacy, 1774–1776* (Princeton, N.J., 1987), 35–63; Brendan McConville, *The King's Three Faces: The Rise and Fall of Royal America, 1688–1776* (Chapel Hill, N.C., 2006), 281–311, esp. 300–311. See also the local studies cited in footnote 9, pp. 230–31. The standard studies of the early 1776 debate are still Pauline Maier, *From Resistance to Revolution: Colonial Radicals and the Development of American Opposition to Britain, 1765–1776* (London, 1973), chap. 9; Maier, *American Scripture: Making the Declaration of Independence* (New York, 1997). See also Gordon S. Wood, *The Creation of the American Republic, 1776–1787* (Chapel Hill, N.C., 1969), 46–124, esp. 91–114; Richard L. Bushman, *King and People in Provincial Massachusetts* (Chapel Hill, N.C., 1985), chap. 6. For older but still valuable perspectives, see Louise Burnham Dunbar, *A Study of "Monarchical" Tendencies in the United States from 1776 to 1801* (Urbana, Ill., 1922), chap. 1; W. Paul Adams, "Republicanism in Political Rhetoric before 1776," *Political Science Quarterly* 85, no. 3 (September 1970): 397–421, esp. 420–21 nn. 67–70.
2. Readers should distinguish the term "Hebraic" from the broader concept of "political Hebraism," which refers to any uses of the Hebrew Republic in political thought. For definitions of that usage, see Kalman Neuman, "Political Hebraism and the Early Modern 'Respublica Hebraeorum': On Defining the Field," *Hebraic Political Studies* 1, no. 1 (Fall 2005): 57–70; Fania Oz-Salzberger, "The Political Thought of John Locke and the Significance of Political Hebraism," *Hebraic Political Studies* 1, no. 5 (Fall 2006): 568–92. For more on Hebraic republicanism, see footnote 9, pp. 224–25. Following the lead of recent scholarship, I lowercase "whig" because the term covers an ideologically diverse group of people who often did not see eye to eye on a variety of political and religious questions.

Concerning Government to elide their antimonarchist elements. They were so successful that Hebraic republican arguments, though still present in those books, were effectively hidden in plain sight.

Paine's *Common Sense* returned Hebraic republican arguments to the center of public discussion in 1776. In attacking monarchy's legitimacy, a main goal of his pamphlet, Paine drew heavily on the Hebraic republican tradition. Indeed he devoted more space in his pamphlet to Hebraic republican arguments than to almost any of his other lines of attack against monarchy. These arguments helped persuade at least some patriots to reject monarchy. Hebraic republican arguments also became a significant part of the broader public debate over the merits of monarchy and a kingless form of government. The major rebuttals to *Common Sense*, which, like Paine's pamphlet, circulated throughout the colonies, devoted a considerable part of their space to countering Paine's biblical attack on monarchy, helping to spread Hebraic republican arguments throughout the future United States. The discussion continued even after 1776, albeit in an attenuated form, as New England ministers employed the Hebrew Republic into the 1780s as a model for the new republican governments then being formed.

On a broader scale, recovering the Hebraic republican tradition reveals a few new wrinkles in the well-worn story of Anglo-American republicanism in the eighteenth century. The tradition's persistence and reappearance in the 1770s demonstrates that some thinkers, notwithstanding the dominance of classical republicanism in the eighteenth century, continued to regard a state's liberty as depending as much on the form of its government as on the virtue of its citizens. Hebraic republicanism's disappearance from public view after the Glorious Revolution, at the same time, confirms scholarship that has emphasized the monarchical tendencies of republican thought in England and America. Finally, the prominence of Hebraic republican discourse in 1776 shows that biblical mythology, used in a noneschatological fashion, underpinned the arguments of some secular political writers. This finding suggests that scholars need to revisit the role of the Bible in the political thought of the American Revolution.

The English Hebraic republicanism that first emerged in the seventeenth century had its roots in a sixteenth-century tradition of scholarship on the Hebrew Republic. This earlier tradition had taken shape in Continental universities around important students of Hebrew, such as Pieter van der Cun (Cunaeus), Johannes van den Driesche (Drusius), and Wilhelm Schickard, who studied the government of the ancient Israelites—the *respublica Hebraeorum* (Hebrew Republic), as they called it—in large part through postbiblical Jewish commentaries. (These scholars, like other seventeenth-

and eighteenth-century writers, used "Hebrew," "Jew," and "Israelite" interchangeably.) Though in one sense purely antiquarian, their scholarship had a definite political purpose as well: the Hebraists' accounts of the Israelite republic were intended to serve as models for modern polities. The Hebraists, like most early modern Christians, were supercessionists who believed that they, not modern Jews, were the true heirs of the biblical Israelites. In this narrative the Hebrew Republic stood as the ancestor of modern (Christian) states and, in their reading, offered a divinely instituted model for the organization of political power.[3]

John Milton, seeking to vindicate the kingless government created by the execution of Charles I, drew on this scholarly tradition to sketch out an argument for republican exclusivism. He first made the argument that kingless republics were the only (or exclusive) legitimate type of government in a 1651 polemic, *A Defence of the People of England* (originally published in Latin as *Pro populo anglicano defensio*). The crux of Milton's case was an account of the Hebrew Republic drawn from new interpretations of two chapters of the Bible: Deuteronomy 17 (which contains a list of laws for Israelite kings) and 1 Samuel 8 (the account of God's angry response to the Israelites' request for a king). Scholars had long interpreted both chapters, the latter against its plain sense, as proof that God commanded or at least permitted kingly government in Israel. Drawing on the opinions of a minority group of rabbis quoted in a Jewish

---

3. This paragraph and the next two are heavily indebted to Eric Nelson's excellent article. See Nelson, "'Talmudical commonwealthsmen' and the Rise of Republican Exclusivism," *Historical Journal* 50, no. 4 (December 2007): 809–35. This loose use of "Hebrew," "Jew," and "Israelite" as synonyms is at odds with the practice of modern scholarship and (to a lesser extent) of the Bible itself. Modern scholars, following the example of Jewish historian Flavius Josephus, generally use Israelite only for the preexilic period and Jew for the postexilic period. A thorough discussion of the use of these three terms in the Bible, which shows just how close they were to one another, is in Graham Harvey, *The True Israel: Uses of the Names Jew, Hebrew and Israel in Ancient Jewish and Early Christian Literature* (Leiden, Netherlands, 1996), esp. 267–73. See also the discussion of the term Judaean in relationship to these three terms in Shaye J. D. Cohen, *The Beginnings of Jewishness: Boundaries, Varieties, Uncertainties* (Berkeley, Calif., 1999), 71–78. For a discussion of leading Hebraist Pieter van der Cun (Cunaeus), see Arthur Eyffinger's introduction to Cunaeus, *The Hebrew Republic*, trans. Peter Wyetzner (Jerusalem, Israel, 2006), ix–lxx, esp. xxvii–xxx, xliv–xlvii. Cunaeus uses Hebrew and Jew interchangeably. For a general discussion of Hebraic republicanism in Europe, see Lea Campos Boralevi, "Classical Foundational Myths of European Republicanism: The Jewish Commonwealth," in *Republicanism: A Shared European Heritage, Volume I: Republicanism and Constitutionalism in Early Modern Europe*, ed. Martin van Gelderen and Quentin Skinner (Cambridge, 2002), 247–61. For political uses of the Hebrew Republic in the Netherlands, see Simon Schama, *The Embarrassment of Riches: An Interpretation of Dutch Culture in the Golden Age* (New York, 1987), 51–125, esp. 97; Boralevi, "La *Respublica hebraeorum* nella tradizione olandese," *Il pensiero politico* 35, no. 3 (2002): 431–63; Miriam Bodian, "The Biblical 'Jewish Republic' and the Dutch 'New Israel' in Seventeenth-Century Dutch Thought," *Hebraic Political Studies* 1, no. 2 (Winter 2006): 186–202. On political uses in England, see the introd. to Anna Strumia, *L'immaginazione repubblicana: Sparta e Israele nel dibattito filosofico-politico dell'età di Cromwell* (Florence, Italy, 1991), ix–xx.

commentary, *Devarim Rabbah*, which Schickard had recently published in Latin translation, Milton reinterpreted these chapters as a divine condemnation of kingship. After a series of complex exegetical moves, Milton declared that "this evidence all proves that the Israelites were given a king by God in his wrath."[4]

Following the lead of the Hebraists, Milton extended his conclusion about the ancient Israelites to modern Christians and their states. His reinterpretation of Deuteronomy 17 and 1 Samuel 8, he declared, demonstrated that "it is a form of idolatry to ask for a king . . . He who sets an earthly master over him and above all the laws is near to establishing a strange god for himself." Choosing monarchy was a sin not just when the Jews did it but when anybody did it. God, the evidence of the ancient Israelites' government showed, disapproved of monarchy in general. Milton repeated these exegeses and the strongly antimonarchical conclusions he drew from them in another pamphlet, *Readie and Easie Way to establish a free Commonwealth*, nearly a decade later.[5]

Algernon Sidney expanded Milton's Hebraic republicanism in his magnum opus, *Discourses Concerning Government*. He added depth to Milton's attack on the legitimacy of monarchy and enunciated a supplemental argument, the idea that republics enjoyed divine favor, at which Milton had only hinted. *Discourses Concerning Government*, like John Locke's nearly contemporaneous *Two Treatises of Government*, originated as a rebuttal to an extreme royalist tract, Sir Robert Filmer's *Patriarcha* (first published posthumously in 1680). Filmer asserted that kings ruled by right of descent from Adam and that royal power was divinely sanctioned and absolute. One of his major arguments to that effect—for which he offered extensive citations from Deuteronomy, Samuel, and the New Testament—was that God had ordained an absolute monarchy for the Jews.[6]

The three chapters of *Discourses Concerning Government* move from a refutation of Filmer toward the elaboration of a new system, turning Filmer's biblical evidence against him. The first two chap-

---

4. John Milton, *A Defence of the People of England*, 1651, in Don M. Wolfe et al., eds., *Complete Prose Works of John Milton* (New Haven, Conn., 1966), 4: 285–537 (quotation, 4: 370). Milton's exegeses are described and analyzed in Nelson, *Historical Journal* 50: 813–17.

5. Milton, *Defence of the People of England*, in Wolfe et al., *Complete Prose Works of John Milton*, 4: 369–70 (quotation). For Milton's veiled endorsement of republics over monarchies, ibid., 4: 365–66, 370. See the analysis of Milton's arguments in Nelson, *Historical Journal* 50: 809–10. For his later statement of the argument, see Milton, *Readie and Easie Way to establish a free Commonwealth*, 1660, in Wolfe et al., *Complete Prose Works of John Milton*, 7: 407–63, esp. 449–50.

6. See Peter Laslett, ed., *Patriarcha and Other Political Works of Sir Robert Filmer* (New York, 1984), 57–61, 83–126, esp. 84–86. For discussion of Sir Robert Filmer and his political context, see Gordon J. Schochet, *Patriarchalism in Political Thought: The Authoritarian Family and Political Speculation and Attitudes Especially in Seventeenth-Century England* (New York, 1975), chap. 8; James Daly, *Sir Robert Filmer and English Political Thought* (Toronto, Ontario, 1979), chap. 4.

ters, with a few exceptions, prove a series of claims against Filmer's position, which can be summed up as "God leaves to Man the choice of Forms in Government." Sidney showed that there was insufficient evidence to trace the line of kings from the Creation down to the Flood, as Filmer had tried to do. He then argued that God had not (as Filmer claimed) ordained a monarchical government for the Jews because neither the patriarchs nor the various judges or prophets had been kings. The first chapters of *Discourses Concerning Government*, in other words, largely paralleled Locke's *First Treatise*, which also used biblical passages to attack Filmer's monarchic exclusivist claim that political power had descended from Adam only to present-day kings[7]

Using sacred history and a selective account of Europe's past, the second half of *Discourses Concerning Government* advanced a fully fledged republican exclusivist argument. Though Sidney's exclusivism rested on Milton's exegeses of 1 Samuel and Deuteronomy, his account modified that of *A Defence of the People of England* in three ways. He sharpened Milton's attack on monarchy as "hateful to God." Samuel's condemnation of kingship, Sidney claimed, had specifically included "free monarchy": any king was "not only displeasing to the prophet, but declared by God to be a rejection of him." This distinction placed even an idealized limited monarchy beyond the pale. Sidney also reinforced the idea that God actively favored kingless governments by emphasizing (as Milton had not explicitly done in *A Defence of the People of England*) that the government God originally ordained for the Israelites had been a kingless republic. Ancient historian Flavius Josephus, Sidney wrote, had called the Israelite republic a "theocracy, by reason of God's presence with his people." But, he commented, "in relation to man" it was a three-part aristocratic republic: "They had a chief magistrate, who was called judge or captain, as Joshua, Gideon, and others, a council of seventy chosen men, and the general assemblies of the people . . . [and] whereas the Sanhedrin, which was the aristocratical part, was permanent, the whole might rightly be called an aristocracy, that part

---

7. Algernon Sidney, *Discourses Concerning Government*, ed. Thomas G. West (Indianapolis, Ind., 1996), 20 (quotation, chap. 1, sec. 6), 24–25 (chap. 1, sec. 7), 36–39 (chap. 1, sec. 13). The major exception to the rule that Algernon Sidney does not make exclusivist arguments in the first half of the book is chap. 2, sec. 9: "The Government instituted by God over the Israelites was Aristocratical" (ibid., 124). The relevant part of Sidney's refutation of *Patriarcha* is ibid., 36–46 (chap. 1, secs. 13–15). Because the first two chapters of *Discourses Concerning Government* (unlike John Locke's *Two Treatises of Government*) consist entirely of a refutation of Robert Filmer, they have at best "a limited coherence" as a system. See Jonathan Scott, *Algernon Sidney and the Restoration Crisis, 1677–1683* (Cambridge, 1991), 213–14 (quotation, 213). Nonetheless the third chapter of *Discourses Concerning Government* contains more elements of a new system than do the first two. On the distinct functions of the two treatises, see Peter Laslett's introduction to Locke, *Two Treatises of Government*, ed. Laslett (Cambridge, 1988), esp. 79–122.

prevailing above the others."[8] This kingless republic was God's original design for civil government. Finally, Sidney's account of the Hebrew Republic was uneschatological. His goal was not to propose a theocracy to his fellow subjects or to suggest that creating a republic would bring about the end days. Rather he sought to use the best textual authority available, the scriptures, to demonstrate the legitimacy of his preferred form of civil government.

Hebraic republicanism stands apart as a distinct stream within seventeenth-century republican thought. Much of the research on republicanism over the past generation has focused on the classical or civic republican tradition. Yet even James Harrington, a key figure in the classical tradition, recognized Hebraic republicanism as a separate set of ideas. In one 1658 treatise, he referred to its proponents as a discrete group of "Talmudical commonwealthsmen." More striking, given his key place in the pantheon of classical republicans, Harrington suggested in a later passage in the same work that he shared their principles. Classical and Hebraic republicanisms, though distinct, were not contradictory. The central problem of the classical, or civic, republican tradition was how to sustain virtue and thus liberty in a modern society. By contrast Hebraic republicanism was first and foremost a constitutional republicanism: its core concern was the form of government rather than the means to foster civic virtue.[9]

---

8. Sidney, *Discourses Concerning Government*, 336–39 ("hateful to God," 337, chap. 3, sec. 3), 124–31 ("theocracy," 128). I give strong emphasis to the Hebraic/biblical elements in this account of *Discourses Concerning Government*, partly to compensate for the neglect of the same by many scholars writing about it. James Conniff, for instance, focuses entirely on Algernon Sidney's uses of the history of England. See Conniff, "Reason and History in Early Whig Thought: The Case of Algernon Sidney," *Journal of the History of Ideas* 43, no. 3 (July-September 1982): 397–416. Jonathan Scott hardly discusses Sidney's extensive citations from the Bible, though he admits that Sidney's "favoured model republics [were] Israel and Rome." See Scott, *Algernon Sidney and the Restoration Crisis*, 236. Alan Craig Houston also virtually secularizes Sidney. See Houston, *Algernon Sidney and the Republican Heritage in England and America* (Princeton, N.J., 1991), 102. For a more balanced reading, see Blair Worden, "Republicanism and the Restoration, 1660–1683," in *Republicanism, Liberty, and Commercial Society, 1649–1776*, ed. David Wootton (Stanford, Calif., 1994), 139–93, esp. 165–68. See also J. G. A. Pocock, "England's Cato: The Virtues and Fortunes of Algernon Sidney," *Historical Journal* 37, no. 4 (December 1994): 915–35, esp. 929–30. John Milton noted that the original form of government given by God to the Israelites was a kingless republic but did not develop the point. See Milton, *Defence of the People of England*, in Wolfe et al., *Complete Prose Works of John Milton*, 4: 344. For Milton on Flavius Josephus, ibid., 4: 370.

9. Nelson, *Historical Journal* 50: 833–34 (quotation, 50: 834). The agenda of the literature on republican thought, especially its focus on civic virtue, was substantially set in the 1970s by J. G. A. Pocock and Quentin Skinner. See Pocock, *The Machiavellian Moment: Florentine Political Thought and the Atlantic Republican Tradition* (Princeton, N.J., 1975); Skinner, *Visions of Politics, Volume 2: Renaissance Virtues* (Cambridge, 2002). Zera S. Fink and Caroline Robbins were important in its early development. See Fink, *The Classical Republicans: An Essay in the Recovery of a Pattern of Thought in Seventeenth Century England* (Evanston, Ill., 1945); Robbins, *The Eighteenth-Century Commonwealthman: Studies in the Transmission, Development and Circumstance of English Liberal Thought from the Restoration of Charles II until the War with the Thirteen Colonies* (Cambridge, Mass., 1959). Another study in this vein,

The renewed enthusiasm for limited monarchy after the Glorious Revolution helped efface Hebraic republican exclusivism from public political debate in England and, eventually, the American colonies. The key individuals in this process were a loosely knit group of "radical" whig publicists, which included Thomas Gordon; Robert Molesworth, 1st Viscount Molesworth; John Toland; and John Trenchard. The radicals, most of whom had come of age politically after the Restoration, admired midcentury republican thinkers a great deal and shared their fear of royal prerogative and power. Yet they faced a different set of ideological circumstances from the ones that their forebears had confronted. The Glorious Revolution had placed on the throne a monarch who had sworn himself to defend English liberties and Protestantism and who, until the end of his reign, faced substantial threats to his throne and realm. Though the whigs resented many of William III's policies, they could not but choose to support him because the alternative was a likely Stuart restoration. During the following decades, therefore, the whigs sought to demonstrate their loyalty to the Augustan regime and to modify republicanism to make it acceptable and relevant in the post-1688 world. In pursuit of these linked ends, they transformed republican thought from a program of resistance and revolution into Country ideology, a republicanism that, though critical of court corruption, was fundamentally comfortable with limited monarchy.[1]

---

which attempts the valuable project of seeing the seventeenth-century republican corpus whole, is Jonathan Scott, *Commonwealth Principles: Republican Writing of the English Revolution* (Cambridge, 2004). My distinction between civic republicanism (meaning ideas of virtue and balance) and constitutional republicanism (kingless models of government) is drawn from Michael P. Winship, "Godly Republicanism and the Origins of the Massachusetts Polity," *William and Mary Quarterly*, 3d ser., 63, no. 3 (July 2006): 427–62, esp. 428–30. Winship draws on Blair Worden, "Republicanism, Regicide and the English Experience," in Van Gelderen and Skinner, *Republicanism*, 307–27. I have chosen to use Hebraic rather than Talmudic to describe this constitutional republican tradition based on the Bible, in keeping with scholarly practice in seventeenth- and eighteenth-century intellectual history, which has long used modern names for early modern ideologies. Two further considerations make Hebraic a particularly attractive name for this tradition. First, most of the growing number of scholars interested in the model of the Hebrew Republic have adopted this terminology. Second, by invoking the Hebrew Republic, it serves to remind us (as Talmudic does not) that the tradition's greatest strength as an argument for kingless government was its claim to be based on the authority of scripture.

1. On the ideological context of the 1690s and the radical whig response to it, see J. P. Kenyon, *Revolution Principles: The Politics of Party, 1689–1720* (Cambridge, 1977), chap. 4; Blair Worden, "The Revolution of 1688–9 and the English Republican Tradition," in *The Anglo-Dutch Moment: Essays on the Glorious Revolution and Its World Impact*, ed. Jonathan I. Israel (Cambridge, 1991), 241–77, esp. 261–67; Worden, "Republicanism and the Restoration," 175–93. The stain of antimonarchism nonetheless continued to adhere to the radical whigs. As late as 1721, Robert Molesworth still felt the need to insist in print that monarchical Britain was the true "commonwealth." Only "foolish People," he wrote, incorrectly associated the concept with the "*Anarchy* and *Confusion*" of the midcentury republic, "*falsly* called a *Commonwealth*." See Molesworth's introd. to François Hotoman [Hotman], *Franco-Gallia; Or, An account of the ancient free state of France, and most other parts of Europe, before the loss of their liberties*, [trans. Molesworth] (London, 1721), viii.

Algernon Sidney exemplified the challenge and opportunity whig publicists faced in trying to recast their intellectual idols according to revolution principles. Before the posthumous publication of *Discourses Concerning Government*, Sidney was renowned not as a political thinker but as a "martyr to English liberty." Accused of participating in the so-called Rye House Plot to kill the king, Sidney was tried and executed for treason in 1683. Many believed that his trial had exposed to public view the dangerously tyrannical tendencies of the late Stuart regime, thus helping to end it. As Toland explained in the preface to the first edition of *Discourses Concerning Government*, Sidney was "well known in the world" and "universally esteemed" for his personal sacrifice against tyranny. The radicals were eager to harness Sidney's sterling reputation and intellectual legacy to their agenda, yet his vociferous denunciations of monarchy in *Discourses Concerning Government* posed a giant obstacle to these efforts. They could not be assimilated into any respectable monarchist discourse (as were, for instance, his defenses of popular sovereignty).[2]

The radicals adopted two strategies, both varieties of dissimulation, for dealing with Sidney's antimonarchism: they denied that he had been an opponent of monarchy (or that this stance mattered), and they laid an "unfaithful stress on Sidney's scorn for . . . corruption." In his preface to Sidney's *Discourses Concerning Government*, Toland cast Sidney as an "Assertor . . . of Liberty," like Cicero, whose words were entirely appropriate for the "Reign of a Prince [William], whose Title is founded upon the principle of Liberty." Sidney's particular attitudes toward monarchy, he implied, did not matter because he and William stood for "liberty." Some twenty years later, in their famous *Cato's Letters*, Trenchard and Gordon elided Sidney's antimonarchism by focusing exclusively on his more classical republican remarks. They quoted a long passage from the second book of *Discourses Concerning Government*, for example, that began, "Lib-

---

2. Peter Karsten, *Patriot-Heroes in England and America: Political Symbolism and Changing Values over Three Centuries* (Madison, Wis., 1978), 32 ("martyr to English liberty"); preface to Algernon Sidney, *Discourses Concerning Government* (London, 1698), 2 ("well known"). My attribution of the preface to John Toland comes from Blair Worden, "The Commonwealth Kidney of Algernon Sidney," *Journal of British Studies* 24, no. 1 (January 1985): 1–40, esp. 39. On the Rye House Plot and trial, see Richard L. Greaves, *Secrets of the Kingdom: British Radicals from the Popish Plot to the Revolution of 1688–1689* (Stanford, Calif., 1992), 139–60, esp. 154. On Sidney's reputation and the early whigs' use of it, see Karsten, *Patriot-Heroes in England and America*, 25–28, 32–34; Worden, *Journal of British Studies* 24: 28–30; Melinda S. Zook, "The Restoration Remembered: The First Whigs and the Making of Their History," *Seventeenth Century* 17, no. 2 (October 2002): 213–34, esp. 216–17. My approach to the early whigs bears some similarity to Isaac Kramnick's notion of the commonwealthmen as ambivalent, though I do not agree with him that their ambivalence toward monarchy was necessarily backward looking. See Kramnick, *Bolingbroke and His Circle: The Politics of Nostalgia in the Age of Walpole* (Cambridge, Mass., 1968), chap. 9.

erty cannot be preserved, if the manners of the people are corrupted."[3] In both the quotation and their comments on it, Sidney appeared not as a republican exclusivist but rather as a moderate advocate of civic virtue.

The erasure of Sidney's antimonarchism extended even to his analysis of the Hebrew Republic. *The Judgment of Whole Kingdoms and Nations*, a 1710 whig tract, included an extended discussion of "the Government which God ordained over the Children of *Israel.*" Its analysis of the original form of the Hebrew Republic closely followed that of *Discourses Concerning Government*, even emphasizing the lack of any kingly figure through the time of Joshua. Yet, unlike Sidney, the author of *The Judgment of Whole Kingdoms* did not conclude that monarchy was displeasing to God. Instead he argued on the basis of the stories of the Israelite kings that the "Law of God" held merely that these kings be selected "by the People" and that they should "Rule the People according to Justice and Laws" rather than "by their own Will."[4] The Hebrew Republic, in the hands of this author, seemed to firmly support the ideal of limited monarchy that had emerged from the Glorious Revolution.

Most striking of all was the positive link that some whigs, such as Trenchard and Gordon, claimed Sidney had posited between monarchy and liberty, thus turning his republican exclusivism on its head. "Mr. Sidney's book, for the main of it," Trenchard and Gordon wrote, "is . . . agreeable to our own constitution, which is the best republick in the world, *with a prince at the head of it.*" They assured their readers that they "hope[d] in God never to see any other form of government in England than that which is now in England." They then

3. Worden, *Journal of British Studies* 24: 29 ("unfaithful stress"); preface to *Discourses Concerning Government*, 1 ("Assertor"); John Trenchard and Thomas Gordon, *Cato's Letters; Or, Essays on Liberty, Civil and Religious, and Other Important Subjects*, ed. Ronald Hamowy (Indianapolis, Ind., 1995), 1: 188–94 ("Liberty cannot be preserved," 1: 189, letter no. 26). John Toland's attempt to monarchize Sidney was entirely consonant with his own political situation, which required him to accommodate whigs and tories. See Stephen H. Daniel, *John Toland: His Methods, Manners, and Mind* (Kingston, Ontario, 1984), 8–14, esp. 9. A fascinating parallel in a later period to the neglect of Algernon Sidney's biblicism by his immediate disciples is recounted by T. H. Breen, who notes that the popular edition of Locke's *Two Treatises of Government* published in Boston in 1773 omitted the heavily biblical *First Treatise* altogether. See Breen, *The Lockean Moment: The Language of Rights on the Eve of the American Revolution* (Oxford, 2001), 3.

4. *The Judgment of Whole Kingdoms and Nations, Concerning the Rights, Power, and Prerogative of Kings, and the Rights, Priviledges, and Properties of the People . . . Written by a true lover of the Queen and Country . . .* (London, 1710), 13 ("Government which God ordained"), 14 ("Law of God"). The book was attributed by many contemporaries to John Somers, 1st Baron Somers, a leading whig. Modern scholars strongly doubt his authorship. See Richard Ashcraft and M. M. Goldsmith, "Locke, Revolution Principles, and the Formation of Whig Ideology," *Historical Journal* 26, no. 4 (December 1983): 773–800, esp. 796–97. William Warburton also retraced the history of the Hebrew Republic, though with quite a different purpose from that of *The Judgment of Whole Kingdoms*. See Warburton, *The Divine Legation of Moses Demonstrated, On the Principles of a Religious Deist . . .* , 2 vols. (London, 1738–41).

quoted a passage from *Discourses Concerning Government* that, in light of their introduction, strongly implied the prince was central to protecting virtue: "The good magistrate," Sidney had written, "thinks it a great part of his duty . . . to educate the youth in a love of virtue . . . In leading them to virtue, he increases their strength." In Trenchard and Gordon's hands, Sidney had become a "respectable country party M.P.," a supporter of monarchy. This sleight of hand placed the king at the center of the eighteenth-century republican project and made the institution of monarchy seem essential to sustaining virtue and liberty.[5]

Educated British Americans gradually adopted variants of Country ideology during the first half of the eighteenth century. As these principles spread, they encountered almost everywhere a highly monarchist culture that dovetailed neatly with their own celebration of limited monarchy. John Adams's "A Dissertation on the Canon and Feudal Law," one of the most celebrated Country tracts of the early revolutionary period, illustrates how deeply monarchism had settled in the mentality of leading thinkers even in Massachusetts, "reputedly the most independent colony." Though writing to criticize ministerial actions, Adams celebrated the "balanced" British constitution and carefully disavowed any hint of antimonarchism. By getting the "popular powers" to check those of "the monarch and the priest," the constitution protected the people's "rights . . . eternal and inviolable." In this way, Adams suggested, British subjects enjoyed the benefits of a monarchy without its attendant dangers. At one point, narrating the settlement of New England as the culmination of the Protestant English struggle for liberty, Adams went out of his way to note that the original settlers "were very far from being enemies to monarchy." Rather they were firm devotees of the balanced British constitution, as were, he implied, their descendants.[6]

---

5. Trenchard and Gordon, *Cato's Letters*, 1: 262–66 ("Mr. Sidney's book," 1: 262, my emphasis, "good magistrate," 1: 262–63); Worden, *Journal of British Studies* 24: 28 ("respectable country party M.P."). On the persistence of Sidney's reputation later in the eighteenth century, see Robbins, *Eighteenth-Century Commonwealthman*, 45; Houston, *Algernon Sidney and the Republican Heritage*, chap. 6. On the new representation of the king as protector of British liberty, see [Henry St. John, Viscount] Bolingbroke, *The Idea of a Patriot King*, 1738, in David Armitage, ed., *Political Writings* (Cambridge, 1997), 217–94; Linda Colley, *Britons: Forging the Nation, 1707–1837* (New Haven, Conn., 2005), 43–54. Hannah Smith emphasizes the element of Protestant soldier-monarch as key to the "rhetoric of Georgian monarchism." See Smith, "The Idea of a Protestant Monarchy in Britain, 1714–1760," *Past and Present*, no. 185 (November 2004): 91–118 (quotation, 94). On George III's internalization of the patriot-king role, see Jeremy Black, *George III: America's Last King* (New Haven, Conn., 2006), 10–12. For an account that puts the monarchism of Country thought in European context, see Jonathan Israel, *Enlightenment Contested: Philosophy, Modernity, and the Emancipation of Man, 1670–1752* (New York, 2006), 352–56.

6. Charles Francis Adams, ed., *The Works of John Adams, Second President of the United States . . .* (1851; repr., Freeport. N.Y., 1969), 3: 445 ("Dissertation"), 453 ("balanced"), 452 ("popular powers," "very far from being"), 461 ("eternal and inviolable"); Bushman, *King and People in Provincial Massachusetts*, 8 ("most independent colony"). Thomas

Interest in the Israelite constitution also made its way to the American colonies and occupied a prominent place in the public discourse of the New England clergy. Almost without exception they employed the Israelite constitution model as a support for monarchy. Charles Chauncy, for example, observed in his celebrated 1747 sermon *Civil Magistrates Must Be Just, Ruling in the Fear of God* that "the supreme authority in Israel . . . from which, of course, all subordinate power in that state was derived, was settled by God himself on David." Indeed the "civil millennialism" that the New England clergy fashioned in the eighteenth century, which melded Country ideology with Christian eschatology, went even further, using the Hebrew Republic model to praise and even sanctify the British constitution as liberty's bulwark. Ministers drew parallels between the Hanoverians and the just King David and offered complex analogies between the Hebrew and British constitutions to illustrate the latter's perfection.[7]

In one of history's great ironies, it was the monarchist Country ideology shared by the ministers that paradoxically helped to lead America down the road toward revolution. Country writers had

---

Hollis was one of the leading figures in the transmission of Country thought, and John Trenchard and Thomas Gordon's *Cato's Letters* was one of its most crucial texts. On Hollis and America, see Caroline Robbins, "The Strenuous Whig: Thomas Hollis of Lincoln's Inn," *WMQ* 7, no. 3 (July 1950): 406–53; Karsten, *Patriot-Heroes in England and America*, 34–56. See also, in the Anglicization literature, John M. Murrin, "Anglicizing an American Colony: The Transformation of Provincial Massachusetts" (Ph.D. diss., Yale University, 1966), esp. 259–67. On the appeal of Country principles in different regions, see in general Bernard Bailyn, *The Origins of American Politics* (New York, 1968). For the Tidewater, see T. H. Breen, *Puritans and Adventurers: Change and Persistence in Early America* (New York, 1980), chap. 6; Breen, *Tobacco Culture: The Mentality of the Great Tidewater Planters on the Eve of Revolution* (Princeton, N.J., 1985), 15, 160–203. For New England, see Breen, *The Character of the Good Ruler: A Study of Puritan Political Ideas in New England, 1630–1730* (New Haven, Conn., 1970), chap. 7; Nathan O. Hatch, *The Sacred Cause of Liberty: Republican Thought and the Millennium in Revolutionary New England* (New Haven, Conn., 1977). On the monarchism of British America at midcentury, see esp. Bushman, *King and People in Provincial Massachusetts*, 8, 11–54, esp. 13, 21–23, 52–54; Breen, "Ideology and Nationalism on the Eve of the American Revolution: Revisions Once More in Need of Revising," *Journal of American History* 84, no. 1 (June 1997): 13–39, esp. 27–29; McConville, *King's Three Faces*, 7.

7. Ellis Sandoz, *Political Sermons of the American Founding Era, 1730–1805*, 2d ed. (Indianapolis, Ind., 1998), 1: 144. On the origins and characteristics of civil millennialism, see Hatch, *Sacred Cause of Liberty*, 44–54. See also Alan Heimert, *Religion and the American Mind: From the Great Awakening to the Revolution* (Cambridge, Mass., 1966), 242–93; Mark A. Noll, *Christians in the American Revolution* (Washington, D.C., 1977), 57–58; Harry S. Stout, *The New England Soul: Preaching and Religious Culture in Colonial New England* (New York, 1986), 9, 169, 240–44. For more examples of monarchist uses of the Israelite constitution, see the introd. and many of the sermons in A. W. Plumstead, ed., *The Wall and the Garden: Selected Massachusetts Election Sermons, 1670–1775* (Minneapolis, Minn., 1968). A vivid example, not in Plumstead, is Samuel Langdon, *Joy and Gratitude to God for the Long Life of a Good King, and the Conquest of Quebec* . . . (Portsmouth, [N.H.], 1760), 8. The few allusions to the Hebrew Republic in sermon literature that were not explicitly monarchist were, at best, neutral. Massachusetts divine Samuel Checkley, for example, preaching on the occasion of George I's death in 1727, used mentions of the Israelite government in Proverbs and Psalms to show merely that God had instituted civil government. See Checkley, *The Duty of a People, to Lay to Heart and Lament the Death of a Good King* . . . (Boston, [1727]), 5–6.

taught educated colonists that liberty was fragile and that it would always be threatened by the forces of corruption. It taught them as well that the British constitution was the safeguard of liberty. So when patriots began to think a plot was afoot in England to rob them of their liberty, they quite naturally sought protection in the British constitution itself. During the decade from 1765 to 1775, patriots petitioned for redress from ministers and Parliament and sought to recruit allies among the people of England. As it became clear that help would not come from these quarters, they engaged in a "constitutional flight to the king," appealing to George III to fulfill his role as patriot-king by rising above the fray and rescuing them from oppression. But the king repeatedly turned a deaf ear to their entreaties and instead actively supported a policy of coercion.[8]

As the de facto split between the colonies and Britain widened in late 1775, a gap also grew between the reality of warfare and the persistence of monarchist rhetoric. Even in the face of open conflict, few patriot leaders were willing to publicly reject their king or even the monarchic constitution. John Dickinson, the most famous exemplar of this position, was far from the only one. Presbyterian minister John Carmichael, while preaching to colonial troops, exhorted them to "still continue to revere royalty, and observe [their] allegiance to the King, on the true principles of the constitution." The delegates of Maryland, who were on the radical wing of the patriot movement, expressed their loyalty in an address approved in December 1775. The members of the Maryland Convention assured the world that Marylanders were "strongly attached to the English constitution, and truly sensible of the blessings they have derived from it, warmly impressed with . . . loyalty to . . . the house of Hanover"; they declared themselves convinced that "to be free subjects of the king of Great-Britain . . . is to be the freest members of any civil society in the known world."[9]

8. McConville, *King's Three Faces*, 256–59 (quotation, 259). This story is well known; I draw here on accounts in Edmund S. Morgan and Helen M. Morgan, *The Stamp Act Crisis: Prologue to Revolution*, rev. ed. (New York, 1962); William D. Liddle, "A Patriot King, or None: American Public Attitudes towards George III and the British Monarchy, 1754–1776" (Ph.D. diss., Claremont Graduate School, 1970), 379–83; Maier, *From Resistance to Revolution*, 198–208; Bushman, *King and People in Provincial Massachusetts*, 212–26; Bernard Bailyn, *The Ideological Origins of the American Revolution*, enlarged ed. (Cambridge, Mass., 1992). On George III's role in the road to the Revolution, see Andrew Jackson O'Shaughnessy, "'If Others Will Not Be Active, I Must Drive': George III and the American Revolution," *Early American Studies* 2, no. 1 (Spring 2004): 1–46, esp. 9–16.

9. John Carmichael, *A Self-Defensive War Lawful, Proved in a Sermon . . . June 4th, 1775* (Lancaster, Pa., 1775), 23 ("still continue"); *Proceedings of the Convention of the province of Maryland, held at the city of Annapolis, on Thursday the seventh of December, 1775* (Annapolis, Md., 1775), 62 ("strongly attached"). For a discussion of the Maryland patriot leadership's radicalism, see David Ammerman, *In the Common Cause: American Response to the Coercive Acts of 1774* (Charlottesville, Va., 1974), 28–30, 143–44. For

At about the same time that the Maryland delegates were protesting their allegiance to king and constitution, Congress approved a resolution that rejected Parliament's sovereignty but expressed continued loyalty to the king. Writing after they received news of George III's August proclamation declaring the colonists outside his protection, the representatives responded: "We are accused of 'forgetting the allegiance which we owe to the power that has protected and sustained us' . . . What allegiance is it that we forget? Allegiance to Parliament? We never owed—we never owned it. Allegiance to our King? *Our words have ever avowed it,—our conduct has ever been consistent with it.*"[1] The representatives thus drew a stark contrast between their allegiance to Parliament, which they totally disavowed, and their loyalty to the king, which they vigorously reaffirmed.

Thomas Paine's *Common Sense*, first published in Philadelphia in January 1776, launched a public debate that was instrumental in bringing to an end the patriot leadership's lingering monarchism. The spark of the debate was Paine's fierce assault on monarchical government in the first two sections of the pamphlet. A main line of this attack was the dual claim, which he drew from the Hebraic republican tradition, that God "expressly disapprove[d]" of monarchy and favored republics.[2] Paine devoted a substantial amount of

---

similar examples from about the same time in Virginia and Pennsylvania, see Marston, *King and Congress*, 33–34; Benjamin L. Carp, *Rebels Rising: Cities and the American Revolution* (New York, 2007), 204. Even scholars who argue that the colonists' allegiance was essentially gone earlier do not dispute that patriot leaders remained for the most part publicly loyal until early 1776. For this view, see McConville, *King's Three Faces*, 286–87; Eran Shalev, "Empire Transformed: Britain in the American Classical Imagination, 1758–1783," *Early American Studies* 4, no. 1 (Spring 2006): 112–46, esp. 140–45. Gordon S. Wood's argument that monarchism was republicanized during the eighteenth century makes it difficult to pinpoint the moment when allegiance collapsed, but he strongly implies that it happened well before 1776. See Wood, *The Radicalism of the American Revolution* (New York, 1992), 95–99, 169–71. On John Dickinson, see Milton E. Flower, *John Dickinson: Conservative Revolutionary* (Charlottesville, Va., 1983), 62–64, 143. For other individual patriots who shared Dickinson's ambivalence, see Maier, *From Resistance to Revolution*, 270; William D. Liddle, "'A Patriot King, or None': Lord Bolingbroke and the American Renunciation of George III," *Journal of American History* 65, no. 4 (March 1979): 951–70.

1. Worthington Chauncey Ford, ed., *Journals of the Continental Congress, 1774–1789* (Washington, D.C., 1905), 3: 410 (my emphasis). There was a similar reluctance at the state level to throwing off allegiance to the king, for which see Larry R. Gerlach, *Prologue to Independence: New Jersey in the Coming of the American Revolution* (New Brunswick, N.J., 1976), chap. II; Richard Alan Ryerson, *The Revolution Is Now Begun: The Radical Committees of Philadelphia, 1765–1776* (Philadelphia, 1978), 4, 39–64, 89–115; Bushman, *King and People in Provincial Massachusetts*, 211–26, esp. 218–19; Edward Countryman, *A People in Revolution: The American Revolution and Political Society in New York, 1760–1790* (New York, 1989), chap. 4.

2. Paine, *Common Sense* [2000], 9 (quotation). The literature on *Common Sense* is voluminous and, by and large, excellent. The most influential older interpretations of *Common Sense* have been A. Owen Aldridge, *Thomas Paine's American Ideology* (Newark, Del., 1984); Eric Foner, *Tom Paine and Revolutionary America*, rev. ed. (New York, 2005). See also Bernard Bailyn, "The Most Uncommon Pamphlet of the American Revolution: Common Sense," *American Heritage* 25, no. 1 (December 1973): 36–41, 91–93. Jack Fruchtman Jr. frames his arguments within Paine's "religion of nature." See Fruchtman, *Thomas Paine and the Religion of Nature* (Baltimore, 1993), ix, 1–15.

Common Sense to making these Hebraic arguments, and they became major topics of discussion in the public debate over Paine's pamphlet and the legitimacy of kingly government in early 1776.

The first two sections of *Common Sense* offer a panoply of objections to the British constitution and in particular its monarchical component. In the first section, titled "On the Origin and Design of Government in General, with Concise Remarks on the English Constitution," Paine's main objection is that the constitution is "complex" to the point of "ridiculous[ness]." Its three-part structure of king, lords, and commons, he writes, is "farcical" and full of "flat contradictions." Moreover it does not work as described: the king, as "the remains of monarchical tyranny," in fact rules over the other two parts. In the second section of *Common Sense*, "Of Monarchy and Hereditary Succession," Paine moves to a two-part attack on the principle of kingly government. He argues first that "the Almighty hath . . . entered his protest against monarchical government" and then that any form of hereditary power is illegitimate and likely to lead to civil conflict. Together, he sums up at the end of the section, "monarchy and succession have laid . . . the world in blood and ashes."[3]

Paine's argument that monarchy is contrary to God's will forms one of the largest parts of the first two sections of *Common Sense*. It takes up roughly one-quarter (seven pages) of the twenty-eight pages constituting those sections in the pamphlet's first Philadelphia printing. Of those seven pages, four are almost completely given over to quoting from and commenting on the Bible. By contrast Paine's discussion of the complexity of the English constitution occupies about

---

Robert A. Ferguson examines the pamphlet as a contribution to the creation of a democratic culture. See Ferguson, "The Commonalities of *Common Sense*," *WMQ* 57, no. 3 (July 2000): 465–504. Edward Larkin and Nicole Eustace have offered fresh analyses of Paine's pamphlet that attend closely to its emotional and affective dimensions. See Larkin, *Thomas Paine and the Literature of Revolution* (Cambridge, 2005); Eustace, *Passion Is the Gale: Emotion, Power, and the Coming of the American Revolution* (Chapel Hill, N.C., 2008), chap. 9. I disagree, however, with Larkin's assertion that the "central argument of [Paine's] pamphlet" is the third section (Larkin, *Thomas Paine*, 56). For earlier discussions of *Common Sense* that focus on Paine's Hebraic republican argument, though with little attention to its seventeenth-century roots or its function in the political context of early 1776, see Stephen Newman, "A Note on *Common Sense* and Christian Eschatology," *Political Theory* 6, no. 1 (February 1978): 101–8; Maria Teresa Pichetto, "La 'Respublica Hebraeorum' nella Rivoluzione americana," *Il Pensiero politico* 35, no. 3 (2002): 481–500, esp. 495–500. Most scholars have emphasized the arguments in the first section. See for example Isaac Kramnick, "Religion and Radicalism: English Political Theory in the Age of Revolution," *Political Theory* 5, no. 4 (November 1977): 505–34, esp. 526–27; Jack P. Greene, "Paine, America, and the 'Modernization' of Political Consciousness," *Political Science Quarterly* 93, no. 1 (Spring 1978): 73–92, esp. 80–83.

3. Paine, *Common Sense* [2000], 3 ("Origin and Design"), 5 ("complex"), 6 ("ridiculous[ness]"), 8 ("Monarchy and Hereditary Succession"), 11 ("Almighty hath"), 15 ("monarchy and succession"). Other, briefer arguments for republican government appear elsewhere in the pamphlet, such as the observation that non-monarchical committee government had already been working well for several years.

four and one-half pages; his famous preamble ("Government . . . is but a necessary evil"), a mere two pages; and his description of the origin of government, about three and one-half pages. Indeed the only discussion in the first two sections that is as long as that of Hebraic republicanism is the argument against hereditary authority. Though length does not necessarily imply importance, the space Paine devoted to arguing that monarchy was contrary to God's will suggests he considered it a particularly significant aspect of his case against the British constitution. The fullness of Paine's account stands out even more sharply when compared with the earlier discussions of the Hebrew Republic during the 1770s, the longest of which, in a 1775 sermon by Samuel Langdon, ran a paragraph.[4]

The assault on kingship in "Of Monarchy and Hereditary Succession" closely followed the model supplied by the seventeenth-century English Hebraic republican thinkers. Like them Paine argued first on the evidence of the Bible that monarchy was hateful to God and thus illegitimate ipso facto: "The will of the Almighty," he wrote, "as declared by Gideon, and the prophet Samuel, expressly disapproves of government by kings." To the contrary, Paine claimed with his seventeenth-century forebears, the Israelites' original, divinely granted government was specifically nonmonarchical. "Near three thousand years passed away, from the Mosaic account of the creation, till the Jews under a national delusion requested a king. Till then their form of government . . . was a kind of republic, administered by a judge and the elders of the tribes. Kings they had none, and it was held sinful to acknowledge any being under that title but the Lord of Hosts."[5]

The subsequent pages of the section narrate the story of the Israelites' requests for a king in the books of Judges and 1 Samuel, interleaving quotations from the Bible with Paine's own commentary. Throughout these pages he consistently interprets these biblical passages, in good Hebraic republican fashion, to be an indictment of monarchy as a sin. He concludes, echoing Sidney, by reaffirming the biblical basis for these claims. "These portions of scripture," he sums up, referring to his pages of quotations, "are direct and positive. They

4. Paine, *Common Sense* (n.p., 1776 [Evans no. 43122]), iii ("but a necessary evil"); Samuel Langdon, *Government Corrupted by Vice, and Recovered by Righteousness: A Sermon Preached Before the Honorable Congress of the Colony of Massachusetts Bay in New England* . . . (Watertown, Mass., 1775), 11–12. This paragraph-long discussion in a twenty-nine-page pamphlet is the only known public discussion of the constitution of the Hebrew Republic in the revolutionary period before the publication of *Common Sense*. There were also a few scattered allusions before 1775 to monarchy as a sin. See for example William Palfrey's comment on an antimonarchical passage in Nehemiah in Maier, *From Resistance to Revolution*, 291. These passing mentions, however, do not show that any significant discussion of Hebraic republican ideas took place in the American colonies prior to 1776, and suggest how ready Thomas Paine's audience was for someone to offer an antimonarchist argument based on the Bible.
5. Paine, *Common Sense* [2000], 9.

admit of no equivocal construction. That the Almighty hath here entered his protest against monarchical government is true, or the scripture is false." Indeed, in words that could have been Sidney's, Paine writes that monarchy cannot "be defended on the authority of Scripture."[6] Like Sidney's, too, Paine's use of the Hebrew Republic is firmly noneschatological. His goal is to demonstrate, using the authority of the Bible, the validity and legitimacy of a kingless civil government.

Despite their unmistakable Hebraic republican pedigree, it is not clear which writers Paine used as sources. Scholars can immediately dismiss Paine's claim that the exegeses were purely his own invention. Hebraic republican arguments went against the plain sense of the Bible, and, in any case, Paine lacked the skills in Hebrew and Latin to reconstruct them from scratch. He may have drawn them directly from Milton's and Sidney's works or from their interpreters. John Adams offered some support for this latter hypothesis when he claimed that Paine himself had admitted that his "Reasoning from the Old Testament" in *Common Sense* had come "from Milton." Yet it is just as likely, as some scholars have suggested, that Paine absorbed Hebraic republican ideas from the English radical circles in which he moved before coming to America. (Despite his well-known deism in the 1790s, moreover, there is no good reason to think that the reverence for the Bible Paine expressed in *Common Sense* was insincere.)[7]

---

6. Ibid., 9–11 (quotations, 9). Thomas Paine calls monarchy the "sin of the Jews," yet the rest of the discussion makes clear that he believes that this sin is not particular to modern Jews (as some monarchical writers had claimed before John Milton) but had in fact come to inhere in Christian society as well, through supercession. Taking 1 Samuel to be an indictment of kingship generally, rather than just among the Israelites, was a move first made by Milton in *A Defence of the People of England*. See Nelson, *Historical Journal* 50: 825.

7. Butterfield, Faber, and Garrett, *Diary and Autobiography of John Adams*, 3: 333 (quotations). For evidence that Thomas Paine knew of and had probably read *Discourses Concerning Government*, see Caroline Robbins, "The Lifelong Education of Thomas Paine (1737–1809): Some Reflections upon His Acquaintance among Books," *Proceedings of the American Philosophical Society* 127, no. 3 (June 1983): 135–42, esp. 137. On Paine in English radical circles, see Jack Fruchtman Jr., *Thomas Paine: Apostle of Freedom* (New York, 1994), chaps. 2–3; John Keane, *Tom Paine: A Political Life* (Boston, 1995), pt. 1; Foner, *Tom Paine and Revolutionary America*, chap. 1. Contemporary observers also noted the connection between Paine's Hebraic republican arguments and the seventeenth-century tradition, though without much accuracy. One response to *Common Sense*, for example, cited "Of Monarchy and Hereditary Succession" as proof of Paine's "Leveller" agenda: "saints of his disposition . . . have a thousand times recited the same texts by which he attempts to level all distinctions." See *Reason in Answer to a Pamphlet Entitled Common Sense*, in Aldridge, *Thomas Paine's American Ideology*, 96. James Chalmers called Paine "our Cromwell" and asserted that he was a stalking horse for a New England Leveller party. See Candidus [Chalmers], *Plain Truth; Addressed to the Inhabitants of America, Containing, Remarks on a Late Pamphlet, Entitled Common Sense . . .* (Philadelphia, 1776 [Evans no. 43000]), 64. Though Paine's later criticisms of the Bible have led some to doubt his sincerity, there is virtually no evidence to show that Paine was anything but a believing (albeit nonconformist) Christian in the 1770s. Some scholarship has even argued that his religious views were integral to his political pro-

Common Sense began to spread Hebraic republican arguments throughout the colonies in the first months of 1776. Even admitting that the readership of *Common Sense* was not as universal as some of its more extravagant admirers have claimed, there can be no doubt that Paine's pamphlet had a print run of at least seventy-five thousand and that copies reached thousands of patriots. There is evidence that the arguments it contained helped persuade some of these patriots to embrace kingless government. As scholars have shown, a number of factors contributed to the patriots' rejection of monarchy from around 1774, particularly the revolutionary committees' effective seizure of power and the king's intransigence. But *Common Sense* played a role as well. As the former president of the Continental Congress, Henry Laurens, put it, "the Author's reasoning" against monarchy—which rested largely on Hebraic arguments— was "strong & captivating & will make many converts to Republican principles." Massachusetts divine Peter Whitney offered a concrete example. In a 1776 sermon titled *American Independence Vindicated*, he employed Hebraic republican arguments to justify abandoning monarchy: "It is a natural inference," he wrote, echoing Paine, "that kingly government is not agreeable to the divine will." He then quoted verbatim the passage from *Common Sense* on the original republican form of the Israelite commonwealth. The story of the Hebrew Republic and its fall, Whitney concluded, demonstrated that "kingly or monarchical" government was a sin.[8]

As a New England minister, Whitney was perhaps uniquely well prepared to accept and even adopt Hebraic republican arguments. Ministers' training in civic millennialism made them comfortable with using the Bible as a basis for political arguments and gave them an intimate familiarity with the key texts of the Hebraic republican tradition. Yet according to David Ramsay, a participant in the

gram in the 1770s. See Fruchtman, *Paine and the Religion of Nature*; Nathalie Caron, *Thomas Paine contre l'imposture des prêtres* (Paris, 1998).

8. Henry Laurens to John Laurens, Feb. 22, 1776, in David R. Chestnut et al., eds., *The Papers of Henry Laurens* (Columbia, S.C., 1988), 11: 114–21 ("Author's reasoning," 11: 115); Peter Whitney, *American Independence Vindicated. A Sermon Delivered September 12, 1776. At a Lecture Appointed for Publishing the Declaration of Independence Passed July 4, 1776* . . . (Boston, 1776), 43 ("natural inference"), 44 ("kingly or monarchical"). The most typical estimate holds that more than one hundred thousand copies of *Common Sense* were printed in 1776 alone, which does not count serialization in newspapers. For this figure, see Richard Gimbel, *Thomas Paine: A Bibliographical Check List of* Common Sense *with an Account of Its Publication* (New Haven, Conn., 1956); Aldridge, *Thomas Paine's American Ideology*, 45. Trish Loughran has rightly questioned these estimates, suggesting that the distribution of *Common Sense* was not as wide as some have claimed. Even by her own account, *Common Sense* still had by far the largest print run of any revolutionary pamphlet, in the tens of thousands of copies. See Loughran, "Disseminating *Common Sense*: Thomas Paine and the Problem of the Early National Bestseller," *American Literature* 78, no. 1 (March 2006): 1–28, esp. 17; Loughran, *The Republic in Print: Print Culture in the Age of U.S. Nation Building, 1770–1870* (New York, 2007), chap. 2. On the factors involved in the rejection of monarchy, see footnotes 1 and 18.

Revolution and one of its first historians, the appeal of Hebraic republican arguments was by no means limited to highly educated New Englanders. In his *History of the American Revolution*, Ramsay reported that *Common Sense*'s Hebraic republican arguments had a strong and widespread effect. "With the view of operating on the sentiments of a religious people, scripture was pressed into [Paine's] service, and the powers, and even the name of a king was rendered odious in the eyes of the numerous colonists who had read and studied the history of the Jews, as recorded in the Old Testament. The folly of that people in revolting from a government, instituted by Heaven itself . . . afforded an excellent handle for prepossessing the colonists in favour of republican institutions, and prejudicing them against kingly government." Ramsay's testimony suggests that Hebraic republican arguments convinced more than a few individuals to reject kingly government. Many colonists, in his estimation, found Hebraic republicanism useful in coming to terms with the idea of kingless government. Ramsay also offers some insight into the appeal of Hebraic republicanism. As he noted, colonists of all stations in life across North America had read and studied the biblical story of the Jews. Hebraic republican ideas based on that story thus had, at least in principle, a well-prepared and even receptive audience awaiting them throughout the colonies.[9]

Even those within the patriot camp who did not adopt Hebraic republicanism took note of it and added their voices to the public discussion of Hebraic arguments in the months leading up to independence. Adams, who wrote prolifically about *Common Sense* in his correspondence from Philadelphia, mentioned Paine's "old Testament Reasoning against Monarchy" to a correspondent. The reasoning made such an impression that he returned to it years later. In Virginia, meanwhile, Landon Carter obsessively read and reread *Common Sense*, grumbling over its reinterpretation of "the Scriptures about Society, Government, and what not."[1] Hebraic republi-

---

9. David Ramsay, *The History of the American Revolution*, ed. Lester H. Cohen (Indianapolis, Ind., 1990), 1: 315 (quotation). On knowledge of the Bible, see Patricia U. Bonomi, *Under the Cope of Heaven: Religion, Society, and Politics in Colonial America* (New York, 1986). For New England, see footnote 16. On Virginia, see Edward L. Bond, "Religion in Colonial Virginia: A Brief Overview," in Bond, ed., *Spreading the Gospel in Colonial Virginia: Sermons and Devotional Writings* (Lanham, Md., 2004), 1–64. Amazingly, given its prominent place in narratives of the Revolution, there is still no systematic study or the reception of *Common Sense* either in the patriot movement or more broadly.

1. See John Adams to William Tudor, Apr. 12, 1776, in Taylor, Lint, and Walker, *Papers of John Adams*, 4: 118–19 ("old Testament Reasoning," 4: 118); Landon Carter to George Washington, May 9, 1776, in Philander D. Chase, ed., *The Papers of George Washington, Revolutionary War Series* (Charlottesville, Va., 1991), 4: 234–42 ("Scriptures about Society," 4: 238). Adams came back to *Common Sense* in his *Autobiography*. See Butterfield, Faber, and Garrett, *Diary and Autobiography of John Adams*, 3: 333. For Landon Carter's comments on *Common Sense*, see Jack P. Greene, ed., *The Diary of Colonel Landon Carter of Sabine Hall, 1752–1778* (1964; repr., Richmond, Va., 1987), 2: 986–88, esp. 986–87 (Feb. 24, 1776), 1042–43, esp. 1042 (May 23, 1776). The Apr. 13, 1776,

canism, after decades of obscurity, was once again on the public agenda.

The major pamphlet and newspaper rebuttals of *Common Sense*, though written to urge continued loyalty to Britain, added considerably to the public discussion and dissemination of Hebraic republican arguments. The first extended published rebuttal of *Common Sense*, under the pseudonym "Rationalis," appeared in Philadelphia newspapers in late February 1776. The author of this relatively short piece (twelve pages in pamphlet form) concentrated his attention on what he took to be the core arguments of *Common Sense*. He summarized them as: "1st. That the English form of government has no wisdom in it . . . 2d. That monarchy is a form of government inconsistent with the will of God. 3d. That now is the time . . . to declare an independence of the Colonies." Among these elements of Thomas Paine's pamphlet, Rationalis gave particular attention to its Hebraic arguments. Approximately four pages—one-third of the pamphlet—went to refuting these arguments, whereas less than two pages concerned Paine's attack on the English constitution and barely one page debated the timing of independence.[2]

Rationalis's feeble rebuttal of Paine's Hebraic republican arguments suggests the particular difficulty that a biblical argument posed to its opponents. Paine had argued forcefully that the original Israelite government was a republic sanctioned by God and that God had expressed his opposition to monarchy when he consented to give the Jews a king. To dispute these points, Rationalis proposed to meet Paine's "scripture quotations" with countercitations from the Bible. This strategy led the author immediately to concede Paine's first point: unable to find an opposing proof text showing that the Jews had had a monarchy first, Rationalis dissimulated by saying that the Jews had been "under divers governments at divers times." To the second point, Rationalis offered a few countercitations from 1 Samuel and Proverbs, most of which he drew from *The Judgment of Whole Kingdoms*. But even Rationalis admitted that these citations demonstrated at best that monarchy was "not inconsistent" with God's will. They proved only that monarchy was "as pleasing to the Almighty . . . as any other form of government, even the author's beloved republic."[3] This weak conclusion hardly refuted Paine's powerful claim that the Bible proved that God disapproved of monarchical government.

---

entry indicates that he followed the subsequent pamphlet controversy as well (ibid., 2: 1016–17, esp. 1016).

2. Rationalis, appended to Chalmers, *Plain Truth*, 76–77.

3. Ibid., 80 ("scripture quotations"), 81 ("under divers governments"), 83 ("not inconsistent").

The True Interest of America Impartially Stated, a far longer and more astute reply to *Common Sense*, focused just as much as Rationalis on rebutting Paine's Hebraic republican thesis. Published under the pseudonym "An American," it was the work of Anglican minister Charles Inglis. Like his predecessor, Inglis viewed Paine's attack on "the English constitution and monarchy" as central to Paine's "beloved scheme of Independent Republicanism." In mapping out his systematic refutation of *Common Sense*, Inglis carefully highlighted what he regarded as the strongest points of Paine's argument against the constitution and monarchy in general. He entirely dismissed Paine's nonbiblical case against hereditary succession as a series of "crudities," which he felt he could safely ignore. He focused instead on what he admitted was a "formidable host of arguments" from scripture that Paine marshaled to support his attack on monarchy. Inglis devoted some twelve pages, about one-fifth of the total pamphlet, to refuting them.[4] Moreover Inglis, unlike Rationalis, quoted Paine's arguments at length before presenting his rebuttal. These citations were yet another vehicle that diffused Hebraic republican arguments in the colonies in the first months of 1776.

Inglis's rebuttal attacked both the key points in "Of Monarchy and Hereditary Succession": Paine's contention that God disapproved of monarchy in 1 Samuel and his argument that the Jews had a republic before a monarchy. Inglis reread Samuel, as other respondents would do, as evidence that the prophet was in fact "rather in favour of monarchy than against it." His exegesis showed "plain[ly]," he asserted, that neither 1 Samuel nor any other part of scripture testified "in the least against government by Kings." But Inglis, like Rationalis, was unable to find scriptural evidence to contradict Paine's claim that the Jews' original government had been republican. Instead Inglis adopted the strategy of dismissing the whole subject: it is "needless, at present," he wrote, "to determine how early kings began to reign." Yet this approach does not seem to have satisfied him because a few pages later he returned to the topic, asserting this time that the origins of monarchy, whatever they may have been, did not signify: "If a thing is good in itself, I conceive it to be a matter of very little moment, who it was that first introduced it."[5] This response, like the first, sought essentially to circumvent the issue. Faced with a scriptural argument for republics to which he could offer no countercitations, Inglis proved unable to give a convincing refutation.

---

4. An American [Charles Inglis], *The True Interest of America Impartially Stated in Some St[r]ictures on a Pamphlet Entitled Common Sense* (Philadelphia, 1776), 10 ("English constitution and monarchy"), 22 ("crudities").
5. Ibid., 25 ("rather in favour"), 30 ("plain[ly]"), 22 ("needless"), 24 ("thing is good").

"Cato"—the Reverend William Smith, first provost (president) of the University of Pennsylvania—wrote the most widely reprinted of the newspaper replies to *Common Sense*. It appeared in Connecticut, New York, Philadelphia, and Virginia, among other locations. Like the other writers, he devoted a considerable amount of space—one and one-half of his eight letters—to restating and refuting Paine's Hebraic republican arguments. Cato justified his decision by observing that Americans, because they believed in the authority of the Bible, were particularly susceptible to these arguments. In a country "in which (God be thanked) the Scriptures are read and regarded with that reverence which is due to a revelation from Heaven," a political argument based on the Bible could easily mislead good "Protestants." Cato therefore regarded himself as duty bound to "rescue out of our author's hands, that portion of the sacred history, which he has converted into a lible against the civil constitution of Great Britain" and a celebration of the "divine right of republics."[6]

Cato devoted his sixth letter to this ambitious refutation of Paine's biblical antimonarchism, which went far beyond the countercitations produced by Rationalis or Inglis. He set out to demonstrate that Paine had misread the biblical evidence and that, in fact, the passages in 1 Samuel condemned not monarchy in particular but governments instituted by human beings in general. Cato first argued that the original government of the Jews, contrary to Paine's assertion, had been a *"Theocracy,"* by which he meant direct government by God through the medium of prophecy. He then asserted that God's displeasure in 1 Samuel resulted not from the Jews' wish to institute a monarchy in place of a putative republic but from their rejection of his direct rule. Cato proved this contention by carefully reexamining all the biblical passages cited in *Common Sense* and comparing them with passages in Kings, Psalms, and Deuteronomy. He stressed that his interpretations were based on the works of reliable "commentators," in contrast to Paine's "far-fetch'd" views. In his eyes this more careful examination of the evidence led to the conclusion that "the Almighty would have as strongly expressed his displeasure against the Jews, had they rejected his government for one of their own appointment, whether it had been *Monarchical* or *Democratical*."[7] God, that is, was not a republican exclusivist at all but simply a partisan of direct divine governance.

In addition to trying to refute Paine's antimonarchical interpretation of the Bible directly through exegesis, Cato adopted two other strategies. He drew from alternative authorities to shore up support

6. "Cato" [Rev. William Smith], "To the People of Pennsylvania. Letter VI," [Philadelphia] *Pennsylvania Ledger*, Apr. 13, 1776, 1 ("God be thanked"); [Smith], "To the People of Pennsylvania. Letter V," *Pennsylvania Ledger*, Mar. 30, 1776, 2 ("divine right").
7. [Smith], "To the People of Pennsylvania. Letter VI," 1.

for monarchism. In his eighth letter, Cato cited a litany of writers who he claimed advocated monarchy, from Polybius and Plato to Montesquieu. He emphasized the monarchism of "Whig, nay . . . Independent Whig" authors, offering long quotations from John Trenchard and Thomas Gordon as proof. Cato also tried to get Algernon Sidney on his side. "The great Sidney," he wrote, "never meant more, by his celebrated work, than to reform the abuses of mixt government . . . But he did not write against kings generally." At the same time, Cato sought to blunt the force of Paine's Hebraic republican arguments by asserting that one should "leave scripture out of the institution of modern governments."[8] Whether Cato really believed that scripture was irrelevant to modern government (he was, after all, a minister), his argument was a canny effort to set aside what he saw as one of the strongest parts of *Common Sense*'s assault on the English constitution.

Paine, probably recognizing the strength of Cato's arguments, responded systematically in a series of letters under the pseudonym "Forester." In his third letter, Paine observed that "from this part of his fifth letter to the end of his seventh, he [Cato] . . . sets up the proud standard of Kings, in preference to a Republican form of government." Paine responded with a long paragraph citing a miscellany of arguments in favor of republican government. In addition to repeating some of the Hebraic arguments he had already made in *Common Sense*, Paine sought to reinforce them by emphasizing that they rested on the self-sufficient authority of the Bible plainly interpreted. Paine criticized Cato in particular for having "shelter[ed] himself chiefly in quotations from other authors" in his exegesis. Cato's sophisticated interpretations, Paine mocked, twisted the Bible's meaning and "turned the scripture into a jest." *Common Sense*'s arguments, by contrast, were "drawn from the nature of things, without borrowing from any one."[9]

James Chalmers, whose rebuttal of *Common Sense* otherwise ignored Paine's attacks on monarchy, also went to the trouble of trying to refute his Hebraic republican arguments. Chalmers, unlike most of the other authors, did not seriously dispute Paine's basic claims that the Jews' original government was a republic and that God had given the Jews a monarchy as punishment. Rather, he argued, these truths were irrelevant. Because "the Mosaic Law, gives

---

8. [Smith], "To the People of Pennsylvania. Letter VIII," *Pennsylvania Ledger*, Apr. 27, 1776, 2 ("Whig"), 1 ("great Sidney"); [Smith], "To the People of Pennsylvania. Letter VI," *Pennsylvania Ledger*, Apr. 13, 1776, 4 ("leave scripture"). Rationalis made a similar argument. See Rationalis, appended to Chalmers, *Plain Truth*, 80. On the secularization—or at least anticlerical deism—of whig thought in the eighteenth century, see Worden, "Revolution of 1688–9," 252.

9. "Forester" [Thomas Paine], "Letter III. To Cato," [Philadelphia] *Pennsylvania Gazette*, Apr. 24, 1776, 1.

way to the Gospel Dispensation," modern European states were not in fact the heirs of the ancient Israelite commonwealth. Evidence drawn from the "anti-philosophical story of the Jews" thus had no bearing on the ideal constitution of a modern government. True, he conceded, God had established the Israelite monarchy in his wrath, but he did so only to show that he hated the Jews, those "abhorred" social outcasts who "hated all mankind." The Hebrew Republic, indeed nothing in the "Old Testament," could legitimately serve as evidence for Paine's "indecent attack" on monarchy in general and "the English constitution" in particular.[1] In sum Chalmers accepted the exegetical moves of the Hebraic republican tradition and merely denied their relevance to modern governments.

The responses to *Common Sense* turned Hebraic republican ideas, which Paine's pamphlet had already spread across most of the colonies, into a focus of the debate over the legitimacy of kingly government. With the exception of the contractarian thesis, which held that the colonies were released from allegiance to the king because he had not done his duty, no other argument against monarchy took up so much of the public debate. The discussions of Hebraic republicanism, moreover, extended across the colonies. Rationalis's work, in addition to appearing in Philadelphia and Virginia newspapers, was reprinted as an appendix to Chalmers's *Plain Truth*, which had six printings in 1776 and circulated throughout the middle colonies. Inglis's *True Interest of America Impartially Stated* appeared in two Philadelphia versions, and there is evidence that it also circulated in New York. And Cato's letters, along with Paine's responses, were published in newspapers from Connecticut to Virginia.[2]

Hebraic republicanism disappeared from political discourse in most colonies after mid-1776. The coming of independence and a kingless republic naturally made its arguments less relevant to most political writers. New England proved to be an exception. A series of sermons, delivered by influential ministers in Connecticut, Massachusetts, and New Hampshire, used and adapted the model of the Hebrew Republic to respond to the changing political needs of the patriot movement and the new nation through the end of the 1780s.

1. Chalmers, *Plain Truth*, 13–14 ("Mosaic Law"), 13 ("anti-philosophical story"), 11 ("indecent attack"). James Chalmers's *Plain Truth* focused on Thomas Paine's practical case for independence, including arguments about military readiness and the effectiveness of kingless government. For a full discussion, see Aldridge, *Thomas Paine's American Ideology*, chap. 13.
2. Cato's letters were reprinted in newspapers in virtually every colony. The *Virginia Gazette* printed Rationalis's rebuttal shortly after its first appearance in the *Pennsylvania Gazette*. Numerous revolutionaries in Philadelphia and elsewhere in the middle colonies referred to *Plain Truth* in their correspondence, giving strong grounds to believe that it circulated widely. And Charles Inglis's *True Interest of America Impartially Stated* was offered for sale in New York.

All told, five sermons published from 1777 to 1788 employed the model as a substantial part of their argumentative structure. Several of these sermons were by important ministers, such as Samuel Cooper and Samuel Langdon, and became quite well known. Though scholars have discussed these sermons in the literature on the New England clergy in the Revolution, they have only recently linked the sermons to the broader Hebraic republican tradition.[3]

The most original of the five sermons was delivered by Samuel Cooper on the occasion of the "commencement" of the new Massachusetts state constitution in 1780. Cooper devoted fifteen pages, about one-quarter of the printed sermon's total length, to arguing the case for kingless government. After describing the "tyranny" of monarchs, Cooper turned to the Hebrew Republic, a "constitution, twice established by the hand of Heaven," to outline the "kind of government infinite wisdom and goodness would establish." The government "originally established in the Hebrew nation by a charter from Heaven," he wrote, "was that of a free republic." Its leadership consisted of a "council of seventy chosen men, and the general assemblies of the people," aided by the "occasional" appointment of a "judge or leader, such as Joshua." A citation to *Discourses Concerning Government* later in Cooper's printed sermon strongly suggests that he drew this account of the Hebrew Republic whole cloth from Algernon Sidney's volume. Other ministers echoed this view. James Dana wrote in his 1779 sermon that "the only form of government expressly instituted by heaven was that of the Hebrews." It was "a confederate republic with Jehovah at the head . . . most friendly to public liberty."[4]

3. For a full discussion of these sermons in context, see Eran Shalev, "'A Perfect Republic': The Mosaic Constitution in Revolutionary New England, 1775–1788," *New England Quarterly* 82, no. 2 (June 2009): 235–63. Several of them figure, without any connection to the Hebraic republican tradition, in Alice M. Baldwin, *The New England Clergy and the American Revolution* (Durham, N.C., 1928), 130–47; Ruth H. Bloch, *Visionary Republic: Millennial Themes in American Thought, 1756–1800* (Cambridge, 1985), chap. 4; Stout, *New England Soul*, 293–96. There is probably more evidence to be discovered of Hebraic republican ideas percolating among ministers and even ordinary people in New England. See for example the mention of the Sanhedrin in the town of Gorham's election returns on a "mode of government" for Massachusetts in Oscar Handlin and Mary Handlin, *The Popular Sources of Political Authority: Documents on the Massachusetts Constitution of 1780* (Cambridge, Mass., 1966), 429–30 (quotation, 430).
4. Samuel Cooper, *A Sermon Preached Before His Excellency John Hancock, Esq; Governour, the honourable the Senate, and the House of Representatives of the Commonwealth of Massachusetts, October 25, 1780. Being the Day of the Commencement of the Constitution, and Inauguration of the new Government* (Boston, [1780]), 13 ("tyranny"), 13–14 ("constitution, twice established"), 8 ("kind of government"); James Dana, *A Sermon Preached Before the General Assembly of the State of Connecticut, at Hartford, on the Day of the Anniversary Election, May 13, 1779* (Hartford, Conn., 1779), 17–18 ("expresly instituted by heaven," 17). Cooper's sermon was regarded as quite important. Benjamin Franklin complimented the author, and the sermon was translated into multiple foreign languages and apparently bound with copies of the Massachusetts constitution itself. See Baldwin, *New England Clergy*, 146–47 n. 35. See also Zabdiel Adams's 1782 Massachusetts election sermon, in which he asserted that "in the time of the judges

Though Cooper's basic description of the kingless Hebrew Republic closely followed that of Sidney and meshed with that of Paine, his sermon added an important new twist by emphasizing the utility of this model for the post-1776 period. By 1780 the burning political challenge was no longer how to justify republican government but the more complex question of how exactly to assemble one. Cooper argued that the Hebrew Republic could shed light on two important aspects of this problem: the correct extent of popular sovereignty and the role of popular consent. He emphasized that the Israelites accepted the law "framed" by God "by their own voluntary and express consent." They did so first when Moses offered it to them at Sinai and then confirmed their assent to this "covenant" repeatedly thereafter, always by their own "free determination." Cooper likewise presented fresh evidence from *Discourses Concerning Government* to demonstrate (more fully than Paine had) the popular character of the Israelite state. "To mention all the passages in sacred writ which prove that [in] the Hebrew government . . . the sovereignty resided in the people," he grandly observed, would require reciting "a large part of it's history." Nonetheless Cooper offered several illustrations of the point, most notably from Joshua. By emphasizing the democratic character of the Hebrew Republic, Cooper adapted the model to the new ideological needs of the post-1776 environment.[5]

None of the New England sermons after 1776 made direct reference to *Common Sense*, as Peter Whitney's *American Independence Vindicated* had. Indeed the ministers who penned the later sermons probably drew directly on the works of Sidney, John Milton, or the eighteenth-century whigs. Their use of the model of the Hebrew Republic nonetheless shows that Hebraic republicanism was not simply a phenomenon of early 1776. The sermons by New England ministers show that the tradition survived and was adapted to new situations for at least another decade and a half after its 1776 high-water mark.

---

the administration of their government was in the hands of God; and hence by the learned it is frequently called a *theocracy*." See Adams, *A Sermon . . . May 29, 1782, Being the Day of General Election* ([Boston], 1782), 7. Adams's use of the Hebrew Republic is somewhat confused. At times he appears to be arguing a republican exclusivist position; at others, he seems to use it to justify the idea that there is no single, ideal form of government. Similar arguments appeared in a 1781 Connecticut sermon by Joseph Huntington. See Huntington, *A Discourse, Adapted to the Present Day, on the Health and Happiness, or Misery and Ruin, of the Body Politic, in Similitude to that of the Natural Body . . .* (Hartford, Conn., 1781).

5. Cooper, *Sermon Preached Before His Excellency*, 8 ("framed"), 9 ("by their own"), 10 ("free determination"), 11 ("To mention all"). The standard treatment of popular sovereignty and consent in the critical period is Wood, *Creation of the American Republic*, pt. 2. The adaptation Samuel Cooper had begun would reach its fullest development in Samuel Langdon, *The Republic of the Israelites an Example to the American States: A Sermon, Preached at Concord, . . . before the honorable general court at the annual election* (Exeter, N.H., 1788).

Recovering the Hebraic republican tradition from the mid-seventeenth to the end of the eighteenth centuries reopens a few doors in the spacious mansion of Anglo-American republican thought. Since the 1950s scholars have strongly emphasized the importance of civic virtue as a central category of republicanism. There is some justification for this focus: republican thinkers consistently argued that a virtuous citizenry, not a particular form of government, offered the best guarantee of liberty. As Rationalis put it, "the best governments and the wisest laws" alone were no security for liberty "among a corrupt, degenerate people."[6] The eventual resurgence of Hebraic republicanism, which argued that a kingless government was the freest government, makes clear that the opposite notion—that the key to freedom was a particular form of government—never died out. When the moment was right, as in 1776, it could again become an important stream in republican thought.

The occultation of Hebraic republicanism earlier in the century also demonstrates the need to rethink somewhat the relationship between monarchism and the republican tradition at the end of the eighteenth century. It is true, as scholars have long argued, that the persistence of civic virtue as a central category of analysis created some degree of continuity between pre- and post-Glorious Revolution republicanism. But the early whigs' erasure of the Hebraic republican tradition from their canon in creating eighteenth-century Country thought was not merely a cosmetic change. It entailed deleting an entire branch of seventeenth-century republican thought that had sources and arguments distinct from the classical strand. Eighteenth-century Country thought, in that sense, represented a substantial monarchist departure from the seventeenth-century republican tradition. This account of Country thought, in turn, supports revisionist narratives of the coming of the American Revolution. Revolutionary republicanism, far from being the triumphant long-term culmination of a long-term republicanizing process, was in fact a sharp turnabout in political philosophy for many colonists.[7]

---

6. Rationalis appended to Chalmers, *Plain Truth*, 78 (quotations). On civic virtue as a central category, see Wood, *Creation of the American Republic*, 65–70, 610–11; Pocock, *Machiavellian Moment*, chap. 15. For a good, brief discussion of the different meanings of virtue to these two authors, see Daniel T. Rodgers, "Republicanism: The Career of a Concept," *Journal of American History* 79, no. 1 (June 1992): 11–38, esp. 19.

7. Of the new literature on the ideological origins of the Revolution, see particularly T. H. Breen, *The Marketplace of Revolution: How Consumer Politics Shaped American Independence* (New York, 2004), chap. 3; McConviile, *King's Three Faces*. The culminating view is found in Wood, *Radicalism of the American Revolution*, 95–109, esp. 109. A similar approach is in Jack P. Greene, "The American Revolution," *American Historical Review* 105, no. 1 (February 2000): 93–102.

The prominence of Hebraic republicanism in the 1776 debate, finally, shows that biblical mythology penetrated deeply, and in ways that have not been studied, into ostensibly secular revolutionary discourse. In contrast to the attention lavished on the role of classical sources in nonreligious discourse, scholars have paid little attention to its biblical origins. *Common Sense* and the responses to it, which fit squarely in the genre of the secular political pamphlet, offer an illustration of how biblical sources were present and could matter a great deal in nonreligious political writing. And it would be surprising indeed, given the cultural cachet of the Bible in revolutionary America, if this phenomenon did not extend well beyond this pamphlet debate. At the same time, the debate exemplifies a way, not yet adequately explored in the literature, in which revolutionaries employed biblical mythology. The bulk of the scholarship on biblical sources in revolutionary America has naturally focused on patriot ministers, emphasizing the theological and specifically the eschatological uses to which they put the Bible.[8] But biblical myth could also have a noneschatological function. For Thomas Paine and his opponents in early 1776, the Bible, like classical authors, functioned as an authoritative source of political wisdom. Such uses of the scriptures to make arguments very much of this world were surely more prevalent than we now know. Recovering the role that the Hebrew Republic played in the early 1776 debate is just a first step toward a fuller understanding of how the scriptures shaped revolutionary America.

8. See Bailyn, *Ideological Origins of the American Revolution*, 32–33; Rodgers, *Journal of American History* 79: 17. On classical sources, see Eran Shalev, *Rome Reborn on Western Shores: Historical Imagination and the Creation of the American Republic* (Charlottesville, Va., forthcoming). Part of scholars' hesitation about looking at religious sources is justified, given the dangers of arguing that the Founders' personal faith can explain their politics. For a good discussion of this problem, see Gordon S. Wood, "Praying with the Founders," *New York Review of Books*, May 1, 2008, 52–56. Excellent discussions of eschatological uses of the Bible in revolutionary thought can be found in Bloch, *Visionary Republic*, pt. 2; Stout, *New England Soul*, chap. 14; Mark A. Noll, *America's God: From Jonathan Edwards to Abraham Lincoln* (Oxford, 2002), 462 n. 7.

GARY KATES

From Liberalism to Radicalism: Tom Paine's *Rights Of Man*†

> In a fundamental sense, we are today all Paine's children. It was not the British defeat at Yorktown, but Paine and the new American conception of political society he did so much to popularize in Europe that turned the world upside down.
>
> —Jack P. Greene[1]

Thomas Paine's pamphlet, *Rights of Man*, stands as one of the fundamental texts of modern democracy. Written during the stormy days of the French Revolution, the pamphlet became an instant success throughout the European world, selling some 200,000 copies in two years, making Paine the era's best-known revolutionary writer. "I know not," John Adams wrote in 1805, "whether any man in the world has had more influence on its inhabitants or affairs for the last thirty years than Tom Paine."[2]

One of Paine's most cherished purposes was to convince readers that the various political changes affecting late eighteenth-century Europe and America were all part of a coherent and rational development towards a better world. "It has been my fate to have borne a share in the commencement and complete establishment of one revolution (I mean the Revolution of America)," he wrote to his French constituents in 1792. "The principles on which that Revolution began, have extended themselves to Europe." Despite obvious differences, Paine's vision unified Philadelphia merchants, British artisans, French peasants, Dutch reformers, and radical intellectuals from Boston to Berlin into one great movement: "it is the great cause of all; it is the establishment of a new era, that shall blot despotism from the earth and fix, on the lasting principles of peace and citizenship, the great Republic of Man."[3]

In his person as well, Paine seemed to embody the unity of an era of universal revolution. Born in England, where he lived the first half of his life and later sought radical change, Paine was, with Lafayette,

† From *Journal of the History of Ideas* 50.4 (1989): 569–87. Reprinted by permission of the University of Pennsylvania Press.

1. Jack P. Greene, "Paine, America, and the 'Modernization' of Political Consciousness," *Political Science Quarterly*, 93 (1978), 92. I wish to thank John Martin, Char Miller, Linda Salvucci, Dena Goodman, Lynn Hunt, Tom Cragin, Gayle Pendleton, and Lloyd Kramer for their helpful suggestions. An early version of this paper was presented to the Consortium on Revolutionary Europe, Atlanta, 1986. Funds for research were generously provided by the Faculty Development Committee of Trinity University.
2. John Adams to Benjamin Waterhouse, 29 October 1805, quoted in David Freeman Hawke, *Paine* (New York, 1974), 7.
3. "Address to the People of France," *The Complete Writings of Thomas Paine*, Ed. Philip S. Foner (2 vols.; New York, 1945), II, 538–39 (here cited as *Complete Writings*).

one of the very few activists to have played significant roles in both the American and French Revolutions. On the laurels of his writings, Paine was the only Anglo-American elected to the National Convention. More important, Paine himself later insisted that his entire life was devoted to the same democratic principles. If we believe Paine, he brought his ideas for representative democracy with him from England in 1774 and his ideas changed little during his tumultuous political career. "It was to bring forward and establish the representative system of Government," he wrote a year before his death, "That was the leading principle with me in writing that work [*Common Sense*], and all my other works during the progress of the revolution. And I followed the same principle in writing the *Rights of Man*. . . ."[4]

Paine's biographers have accepted his claim at face value. R. R. Fennessey, for example, asserts that Paine's "political ideas were completely *a priori*, and he was incapable of modifying them to suit the facts."[5] Obviously this is what Paine wanted readers to believe. But it is far from an accurate picture of Paine's ideological development. A more critical review of Paine's French Revolutionary writings, particularly *Rights of Man*, reveals fundamental change in his ideas. Tom Paine's radicalism was not prefabricated, but grew out of his own participation in France during the early years of the Revolution. As a result, his ideology was not simply modified, it was transformed.

Any analysis of *Rights of Man* must begin with the observation that it was written and published in two separate sections. Part One was completed in early 1791 and was in London bookshops by February of that year. Its purpose was to refute Edmund Burke's *Reflections on the Revolution in France*, published four months earlier. Part Two was written during the second half of 1791 and published in February, 1792. Even before Part Two appeared Paine's public expected it to be a sequel to Part One. "Its title is to be a repetition of the former 'Rights of Man,'" announced one London newspaper, "of which the words, 'Part the Second' will show that it is a continuation."[6] Indeed, Paine himself emphasized this connection between the two parts in his preface to Part Two: "When I began the chapter entitled the 'Conclusion' in the former part of the Rights of Man, published last year, it was my intention to have extended it to a greater length. . . ."

4. *Complete Writings*, II, 1491.
5. R. R. Fennessey, *Burke, Paine, and the Rights of Man* (The Hague, 1963), 31. Paine himself made virtually the same claim in 1802: "The principles of that work [*Rights of Man*] were the same as those in 'Common Sense'" (*Complete Writings*, II, 910). See also Eric Foner, *Tom Paine and Revolutionary America* (New York, 1976), 216; Harry Hayden Clark, ed., *Thomas Paine: Representative Selections* (New York, 1961), xxxiii-lviii; and, for a helpful introduction to Paine scholarship, A. O. Aldridge, "Thomas Paine: A Survey of Research and Criticism Since 1945," *British Studies Monitor*, 5 (1975), 3–27.
6. *The Gazetteer*, 25 January 1792, quoted in Monroe D. Conway, *Thomas Paine* (2 vols.; New York, [1892] 1980), I, 335.

Later in the same preface Paine offered "another reason for deferring the remainder of the work . . . that Mr. Burke promised in his first publication to renew the subject at another opportunity. . . . I therefore held myself in reserve for him."[7]

Biographers have taken Paine's remarks at face value and assume that the two parts deliver essentially the same message. Paine's Part Two, they agree, "went on with the belabouring of Burke and was equally successful."[8] At best, the more sensitive of Paine scholars believe that while Paine's rhetoric in Part Two may have become more militant, exhibiting "a 'jovial ferocity' toward sacred institutions," his ideas did not really change. "The shibboleths are the same," notes David Freeman Hawke, "but the tone of the attack has changed."[9]

But a careful examination of *Rights of Man* reveals that much more changed than simply rhetorical tone. In fact Part Two is not a sequel to Part One. The two parts have little in common, each espousing contradictory ideologies. The first fits squarely with what later came to be known as (nineteenth-century European) Liberalism, which argued for a constitutional monarchy based upon political freedom but an unequal electoral system. The other ideology found in *Rights of Man* is properly known as (nineteenth-century European) Radicalism: democratic republicanism based upon universal manhood suffrage and a commitment to the amelioration of the lower classes through significant social and economic legislation. Today the distinction between Liberalism and Radicalism may have become somewhat blurred. But from 1789 to at least 1848 these two ideological systems stood in as much opposition to each other as Socialism and Communism would after 1917. Some of the last century's most famous political struggles, such as English Chartism or the French Bloody June Days of 1848, suggest the potency of the conflict between Liberals and Radicals. During the French Revolution and the first part of the nineteenth century, therefore, Radicalism was not simply a more progressive variant of Liberalism (just as Communism was not simply a more progressive variant of Socialism), but rather Radicalism constituted a profound critique of Liberalism's anti-democratic features.[1] Paine's *Rights of Man* is a work at odds with itself.

---

7. Thomas Paine, *Rights of Man*, ed. Eric Foner (Harmondsworth, 1984), 153. All citations will be from this Penguin Books edition, referred to as *RoM*.
8. J. Hampden Jackson, "Paine" in David Thomson, *Political Ideas* (New York, 1966), 108. Foner describes Part Two as "a companion volume" to Part One in *Tom Paine*, 216.
9. Hawke, *Paine*, 241–42. See also Conway, *Thomas Paine*, I, 332; and Alfred Owen Aldridge, *Man of Reason: The Life of Thomas Paine* (Philadelphia, 1959), 157.
1. On these ideologies see Guido de Ruggiero, *The History of European Liberalism*, tr. R. G. Collingwood (Boston, 1959), 66–77, 99–108, 370–80, and, for the nineteenth century, Benedetto Croce, *History of Europe in the Nineteenth Century*, tr. Henry Furst (New York, 1963).

There is one curious fact about Part One that has eluded Paine scholars. In an essay that defends the principles and events of the early Revolution, it is remarkable that Paine chose to discuss only one revolutionary leader: the Marquis de Lafayette. Incredibly, neither Sieyès nor Mirabeau, neither the Lameths nor Barnave, neither Robespierre nor any other politician or revolutionary writer was ever discussed in Part One. Still, Paine returned to Lafayette at five different points in the essay. For Tom Paine—at least for the Paine of 1790—the French Revolution belonged to Lafayette.[2]

The portrayal of Lafayette in Part One is highly significant, and it illustrates Paine's own political position within French Revolutionary politics. Lafayette was certainly among the most powerful and influential revolutionary politicians in France. Indeed, the early years of the Revolution (1789–91) are often called "The Years of Lafayette."[3] As a member of the Constituent Assembly, founder of political clubs in Paris, and head of the capital's newly-established local militia, the Paris National Guard, Lafayette wielded enormous power.

Under Lafayette and his followers, usually called the Fayettists or Patriot Party, the National Assembly accomplished a great deal during the period between the passage of the Declaration of the Rights of Man and Citizen in August 1789 and the publication of *Rights of Man* Part One in March 1791. They nationalized church lands, abolished various "feudal" laws and taxes, established a suspensive royal veto, reorganized the country into eighty-three departments, and approved plans for a unicameral legislature. But that was as far as Lafayette wanted the Revolution to go.

The Fayettists believed in a liberal constitutional monarchy in which the power of king, church, and corporate bodies was severely limited; but like their Whig counterparts in Britain, they also tried to exclude the populace from participating directly in political affairs. In October 1789 the Fayettists easily maneuvered the Constituent Assembly to pass a decree restricting those eligible to vote in elections to taxpayers who paid direct taxes worth three days' labor; and at the same time they got the Assembly to pass a law that restricted those voters eligible for national political office to men who paid annual direct taxes equivalent to a *marc d'argent* (silver mark), worth about fifty-four days' labor. These new electoral laws effectively split

---

2. *RoM*, 45, 53, 62, 95, 115, and 121. Only two French Revolutionary leaders are even mentioned in passing in the text: Bailly (63) and Sieyès (105).

3. For example, Owen Connelly, *French Revolution/Napoleonic Era* (New York, 1979), chapter 3. On Lafayette's career, Louis Gottschalk and Margaret Maddox, *Lafayette in the French Revolution* (2 vols.; Chicago, 1969–73), and more generally, C. McClelland, "The Lameths and Lafayette: The Politics of Moderation in the French Revolution" (Ph.D. dissertation, University of California, Berkeley, 1942), and G. Michon, *Essai sur le parti Feuillant, Adrien Duport* (Paris, 1924).

the nation into active and passive citizens, the latter having full civil rights but limited political rights.

This repudiation of French democracy did not go unchallenged. Robespierre strongly objected to the new laws from the floor of the Constituent Assembly. But his views were soundly defeated by the Fayettist majority. The real struggle for democracy did not occur there but in the new Paris municipal institutions, the communal and district assemblies, where Paine's future "Girondin" allies, including politicians such as Condorcet and Brissot, were trying to establish a democratic municipality. Brissot, for example, was thrilled when Condorcet became the president of the Paris Communal Assembly because it meant that "the democratic party will always dominate it."[4]

Thus beginning in the fall of 1789 a democratic movement composed of well-known politicians and writers rose to challenge the Fayettist hegemony of the Revolution. Among the democrats were men who would soon become Paine's closest French allies. For two years they would wage a cold war against the Fayettists for control of national politics, a struggle that became violent after the king's infamous flight to Varennes in June 1791, when any hope for a liberal constitutional monarchy was put in serious jeopardy. My point is not simply that until 1791 Paine had been a Fayettist supporter; even more significantly, his support for Lafayette had much to do with *Rights of Man*. No one has ever doubted that Part One was an attack upon Burke's conservative ideas; but what has been less clear is that it also signified a repudiation of Parisian radicalism.

Far from exporting democratic republicanism from America to France in 1789, Paine ignored the democratic aspirations of Paris radicals. As early as September 1789 he had privately endorsed Thomas Jefferson's belief that "a tranquility is well established in Paris and tolerably well throughout the countryside," which would allow the Constituent Assembly to establish "a good constitution which will in its principles and merits be about a middle term between that of England and America."[5] It is hard to justify calling

---

4. For Robespierre's activities see P. J. B. Buchez and P. L. Roux, *Histoire parlementaire de la Révolution française* . . . (40 vols.; Paris, 1834), III, 213; Jacques-Pierre Brissot, *Correspondance et papiers*, ed. Claude Perroud (Paris, 1911), 241. On the rise of a Paris democratic movement see R. B. Rose, *The Making of the Sans-Culottes: Democratic Ideas and Institutions in Paris, 1789–1792* (Manchester, 1983); Jack Richard Censer, *Prelude to Power: The Parisian Radical Press, 1789–1791* (Baltimore, 1976); M. Genty, "Mandataires ou représentants: une problème de la démocratic municipale, Paris 1789–90," *Annales historiques de la Révolution française*, No. 207 (1972), 1–27; Gary Kates, *The Cercle Social the Girondins, and the French Revolution* (Princeton, 1985), 17–71.
5. Paine to Thomas Walker, September 19, 1789, reprinted in W. H. G. Armytage, "Thomas Paine and the Walkers:, An Early Episode in Anglo-American Cooperation," *Pennsylvania History*, 18 (1951), 23; *The Correspondence of Edmund Burke, Vol. VI, July 1789-December 1791*, eds. Alfred Cobban and Robert A. Smith (Chicago, 1967), 68 (letter of 17 January 1790).

Paine a democrat given his acceptance of this "middle term," when radicals were pressing for significant political changes.

In January 1790 tension mounted between Fayettists and radicals. When the Constituent Assembly reiterated its support for the *marc d'argent*, Condorcet attacked the Assembly, charging that this legislation was "dangerous for liberty." Condorcet predicted that its inclusion into the constitution would "establish a legal inequality against those you have declared equal in rights."[6]

More dangerously, on 22 January Lafayette took 3000 troops into the Cordeliers district, the headquarters of democratic radicalism, to arrest the notorious journalist Jean-Paul Marat. The President of the district, soon-to-be famous Georges-Jacques Danton, refused to surrender Marat to the authorities. While street violence was avoided, the confrontation was not forgotten. Never against would the radicals trust the political leadership of the Fayettists.[7]

Curiously, it was at this very moment that we catch the first glimpse of *Rights of Man*. (Paine had come to Paris in November 1789 and would return to London in March 1790.) On 12 January (some nine months before Burke's *Reflections* appeared) Lafayette wrote to George Washington that Paine was "writing for you a brochure in which you will see a portion of my adventures."[8] Since Part One was dedicated to Washington, scholars agree that Lafayette was here referring to an early draft of *Rights of Man*. This means that *Rights of Man* was begun in January 1790 as an apology for Lafayette at the very instant when that statesman was under attack for his anti-democratic policies. It is even more interesting that on 17 January 1790 Paine had written a friendly letter from Paris to none other than Edmund Burke. "If we distinguish the Revolution from the Constitution," Paine commented, "we may say that the first is compleat, and the second is in a fair prospect of being so."[9] The constitution Paine refers to here would have prevented most of the adult male population from holding seats in the national assembly. The "we" in Paine's remark may have been an indirect reference to Lafayette, but it never could have included Condorcet and the rest of the Paris radicals.

6. The manuscript for Condorcet's speech is in the Archives de la Seine, VD12, 48–57. It was first published in Bonneville's *Cercle Social* [February 1790], letter 8, 57–75. See also Marecel Dorigny, "Les Girondins et le droit de propriété," *Bulletin de la Commission d'histoire économique et sociale de la Révolution française* (1980–81), 15–31.
7. *Actes de la Commune de Paris pendant la Révolution. Première série, 25 juillet 1789 à 8 octobre 1790*, ed. Sigismond Lacroix (7 vols.; Paris, 1894–98), III, 520–60. For the reactions of democratic activists later associated with the Girondins, see also Marcel Dorigny, "La Presse Girondine et les movements populaires: necessité et limites d'une alliance," *Movements populaires et conscience sociale* (Paris, 1985), 519–27.
8. Quoted in Aldridge, *Man of Reason*, 126–33.
9. *Correspondence of Edmund Burke*, 68. On the relationship between Paine and Burke see Thomas W. Copeland, *Our Eminent Friend Edmund Burke. Six Essays* (New Haven, 1949), 146–82.

By January 1790, then, Paine envisioned *Rights of Man* to be a vindication of the Revolution won by Lafayette. No wonder he ignored all other leaders, including the radicals, and focused exclusively upon his hero. Only when he caught wind in April that Burke was about to publish a complete renunciation of the Revolution did Paine shrewdly decide to change rhetorical strategies and turn the pamphlet into a response to Burke. The point, however, is that this change marked no similar transformation in Paine's ideas; if anything, his loyalty to Lafayette was intensified.

Thus *Rights of Man* Part One does not belong to the burgeoning democratic movement that surfaced between 1789–91 in opposition to the leaders of the Constituent Assembly. Instead, it belongs to that vast outpouring of literature which defended the Fayettist interpretation of the French Revolution. What that literature suggests is that the essential difference between a Fayettist Patriot and a democrat before 1792 was the latter's faith in the ability of the ordinary citizen to participate fully in political affairs.

In *Rights of Man* Part One Paine's Fayettism is nakedly revealed in at least three places: first, his defense of the *marc d'argent*; second, his criticism of the popular executions of Bertier and Foulon; and finally, his discussion of the march to Versailles during the October Days.

Given the sharp criticism of the *marc d'argent* by 1791, it is significant that Paine did not attack it in *Rights of Man*, but replied to Burke's ironic attack upon the electoral laws by endorsing them, albeit in a twisted and opaque language: "The Constitution of France says, That every man who pays a tax of sixty sous per annum . . . is an elector. What article will Mr. Burke place against this? Can anything be more limited, and at the same time more capricious, than the qualifications of electors in England?"[1] Courting primarily an Anglo-American readership, Paine pointed out that at least the French laws were still more progressive than the English. But this weak defense of Lafayette's policies ignored the large and noisy groups of Paris radicals who argued that the electoral laws of both countries were anti-democratic. Thus his arguments should not simply be interpreted as a defense against Burke; they also reveal Paine's own anti-democratic attitudes.

Perhaps it is unfair to judge a foreigner according to the same standards we might judge Paris politicians. After all, what more could be expected from a British reformer in 1791? That question, however, is easily answered by glancing at another British pamphlet that appeared within a month of Paine's. In James Mackintosh's *Vindiciae Gallicae*, the laws restricting suffrage were passionately

1. *RoM*, 73.

attacked and the leaders of the Constituent Assembly were sharply criticized:

> Here I must cordially agree with Mr. Burke in reprobating the impotent and preposterous qualification by which the Assembly have *disenfranchised* every citizen who does not pay a direct contribution equivalent to the price of three days' labour. Nothing can be more evident than its inefficacy for any purpose but the display of inconsistency, and the violation of justice.... [It] stained the infant constitution with this absurd usurpation.[2]

Here in Mackintosh one finds a democratic ideology that is simply absent in Paine.

Louis-Benigne Bertier de Savigny, the last royal intendent of Paris, was arrested within days of the Bastille's fall. Under intense pressure from the Paris crowd, municipal authorities agreed to an immediate trial. But when Lafayette tried to delay the trial and have Bertier imprisoned, the crowd intervened. Bertier was dragged into the streets and hung on a lamppost.

Coincidentally, Bertier's father-in-law, the financier and former Controller-General Joseph-François Foulon, had been arrested at the same time on an unrelated charge. When the crowd learned that he was in the vicinity of the Bertier execution, someone shot him. Lafayette, who as Commander of the Paris National Guard was in charge of maintaining law and order in the capital, resigned over the episodes. But neither the mayor nor the Paris Communal Assembly accepted his resignation.[3]

The immediate response of the popular press helps to put Paine's later reaction into proper perspective. Within a week of the murders one of the capital's most popular papers, the *Révolutions de Paris*, edited by the staunch democrat, Elisée Loustalot, offered a lengthy description and analysis of the executions in the radical language of popular sovereignty. For Loustalot, both Bertier and Foulon had got what was coming to them. While Bertier had been a "slave to the great" and a "vicious courtisan," Foulon "was hated and even despised" for the "obnoxious monopolies hid from an angry public." Describing the murders in terms that were shockingly graphic even for that age, Loustalot nonetheless believed that the actions demonstrated "the terrible vengeance of a people justly upset." In these murders Loustalot saw the essence of the Revolution: a just people overthrowing a despotic regime in their own popular way. "Your

---

2. James Mackintosh, *Vindiciae Gallicae* (London, 1791), 224. For a somewhat opposing interpretation see William Christian, "James Mackintosh, Burke, and the Cause of Reform," *Eighteenth-Century Studies*, 7 (1973–74), 193–212.
3. Gottschalk and Maddox, *Lafayette*, I, 145–54.

hatred is revolting, it is terrifying," Loustalot admitted to his readers, "but remember how shameful it is to live in slavery!"[4]

Edmund Burke had a very different reaction to these murders. The "old Parisian ferocity has broken out in a shocking manner," he wrote to a friend on 9 August 1789.

> It is true, that this may be no more than a sudden explosion: If so no indication can be taken from it. But if it should be character rather than accident, then that people are not fit for Liberty, and must have a Strong hand like that of their former masters to coerce them. . . . To form a constitution requires wisdom as well as spirit.[5]

This view is sharply opposed to Loustalot's. For a radical democrat like Loustalot, politics must embody the will of the people; for a Whig like Burke, politics must embody wisdom and deference. Thus even if Burke approved of the Revolution in general—he was still making up his mind in August 1789—he could never justify the actions of a popular lynch mob. By the time Burke published the *Reflections*, he used these types of crowd actions to demonstrate the complete chaos and lawlessness inherent in the Revolution.

When Tom Paine sat down fifteen months later to write *Rights of Man* Part One, he thus had at least two ideologies available to him when he came to the section analyzing the Foulon and Bertier murders. Significantly, Paine rejected the language of the Paris democrats and chose a discourse that was remarkably close to Burke's. "There is in all European countries," he wrote, "a large class of people of that description which in England is called the 'mob,'" who,

> incensed at the appearance of Foulon and Bertier, tore them from their conductors before they were carried to the Hotel de Ville, and executed them on the spot. Why then does Mr. Burke charge outrages of this kind on a whole people? . . . These outrages were not the effect of the principles of the Revolution, but of the degraded mind that existed before the Revolution, and which the Revolution is calculated to reform.[6]

Compared to Loustalot, Paine displayed a self-conscious disagreement with Burke that seems superficial. Paine might have defended the crowd's actions on the grounds of revolutionary justice; certainly, neither Lafayette nor the Paris government had any doubts regard-

---

4. *Révolutions de Paris*, no. 2, 18–25 July 1789, 55–62. We know that Paine had read this paper from his footnote on p. 64 of *RoM*: "An account of the expedition to Versailles may be seen in No. 13 of the *Révolution de Paris*, containing the events from the 3rd to the 10th of October 1789." On Loustalot and his newspaper see Censer, *Prelude to Power*.
5. Burke, *Correspondence*, 10.
6. *RoM*, 58–59. For a more general discussion of these ideas see George Rudé, *The Crowd in the French Revolution* (New York, 1959).

ing the guilt of the two men. After all, the incidents occurred during the first days of a revolution; what better symbol of the old order
was there than the capital's intendent and a financier who had taken
advantage of the nation's fiscal problems? Paine might at least have
excused crowd actions as zealotry, thereby demonstrating the public's intense approval for the new regime.

But he did not. Instead, Paine largely sided with Burke in seeing
the crowd as an irrational "mob," which had no sense of justice or
patriotism. Burke argued that the crowd typified the revolution
because it embodied anarchy; Paine agreed with Burke's views on
mobs and this position forced him into the slippery argument that
the activities of the Paris crowd did not belong to the Revolution.
Apparently, therefore, the mark of a great revolutionary, such as
Lafayette, lay in his ability to manage the populace. "In the commencement of a Revolution," Paine wrote of the street activists,
"those men are rather the followers of the camp than the standard
of liberty, and have yet to be instructed how to reverence it."[7]

That Paine shared Lafayette's obsession for the restoration of
order is again demonstrated when the Marquis was once more pit-
ted against "the mob" during the October Days. Describing the popular women's march to Versailles as essentially "mischief," Paine
praised Lafayette for saving the king from "the mob" and thus preserving the Revolution from anarchy: "As soon therefore as a sufficient force could be collected, M. de Lafayette, by orders from the
civil authority of Paris, set off after them at the head of twenty
thousand of the Paris militia. The revolution could derive no benefit
from confusion, and its opposers might."[8] Here is the essence of the
Fayettist ideology: Lafayette embodied the Revolution in its difficult task of constructing a new order. The people are not really vil-
lainous but submissive actors, no doubt misguided partly by their own
ignorance and partly by the machinations of counter-revolutionaries.
In Paine's rhetoric the people who brought the king and queen back
to Paris were certainly not heroes.

Again, we need to emphasize, if only because the myth of Paine's
democratic ideas remains so pervasive among Paine scholars, that
there were other reformers writing at the same time, such as Mackintosh, who rejected this Fayettist rhetoric. In the *Vindiciae Gallicae*, for example, the patriotic common sense of "the people" has
replaced Paine's violent "mob": "A degree of influence exerted by the
people . . . must be expected in the crisis of a Revolution which the
people have made . . . that, therefore, the conduct of the populace

---

7. *RoM*, 59. Incidentally, years after the Revolution Lafayette admitted that Foulon had
been a corrupt statesmen who had earned the "people's hatred." See the *Mémoires, correspondance et manuscrits du Général Lafayette* (6 vols.; Paris, 1837–38), II, 274.
8. *RoM*, 62.

of Paris should not have been the most circumspect . . . was, in the nature of things, inevitable." In contrast to Paine, Mackintosh expected the crowd to enact their own style of popular politics in the streets.

Likewise, Mackintosh was not offended by the October Days but saw in them the expression of popular justice. "The march to Versailles," Mackintosh wrote, "seems to have been the spontaneous movement of an alarmed populace" who had good reasons to demand "the king to change his residence to Paris." What made Mackintosh's rhetoric democratic was that in his interpretation, the people do not follow the politicians, but were rather the driving force of the Revolution; they and not their leaders controlled political affairs.[9]

Rights of Man Part One, of course, was written in English for an Anglo-American audience. Its purpose was to stimulate a peaceful Fayettist revolution in Britain. Thus while Paine disagrees sharply with Burke over political principles, there is no real debate over the extent to which "the people" ought to participate in political affairs. Paine's focus is rather on the nature of monarchy in France, and here too Paine is more moderate than republicans might expect. Against Burke's prediction that the French Revolution would destroy monarchy, Paine came dangerously close to defending Louis XVI:

> It was not against Louis the XVIth, but against the despotic principles of the government, that the nation revolted. . . . The monarch and the Monarchy were distinct and separate things; and it was against the established despotism of the latter, and not against the person or principles of the former, that the revolt commenced. . . . [1]

Against the background of traditional Enlightenment views of despotism, such as the one found in Montesquieu's *Spirit of Laws*, Paine's argument sounds strange. How could there be despotism without a despot? How could despotism be attacked without the despot himself receiving the first blow? Nonetheless, Paine insisted that pre-revolutionary France was, in fact, a despotism without a despot. Displaying an attitude toward monarchy that was very different from the one found in *Common Sense*, Paine portrayed Louis XVI as a passive and neutral king, even "known to be a friend of the nation."[2] The despotism begun during the reign of Louis XIV had simply expanded beyond the control of the despot. Louis XVI could not have reformed the system even if he had wanted to.

---

9. Mackintosh, *Vindiciae Gallicae*, 181, 193–94.
1. *RoM*, 47.
2. *Ibid.* Compare with *Common Sense*: "There is something exceedingly ridiculous in the composition of monarchy . . ." (*Complete Writings*, I, 8).

For the Paine of Part One the French Revolution was above all against despotism but not monarchy itself. Since the key attribute of despotism was that it lacked a constitution, the prime objective of the French Revolution was not to overthrow the monarchy, but rather to make the monarchy constitutional. "Mr. Burke said in a speech last winter in parliament," Paine remarked,

> that when the National Assembly first met in three Orders . . . France had then a good constitution. This shows, among numerous other instances, that Mr. Burke does not understand what a constitution is. The persons so met were not a *constitution*, but a *convention*, to make a constitution.[3]

Thus the central distinction found in *Rights of Man* Part One is not between aristocracy and democracy or between monarchy and republic but between absolute monarchy (which Paine called "hereditary despotism of the monarchy"[4]) and constitutional monarchy.

It must be emphasized that in this first part of *Rights of Man*, Paine went no further than this relatively moderate position. There was no call to make France a republic; nor was there any insistence that the French Revolution become democratic.

As soon as *Rights of Man* Part One was published in February 1791, Paine returned to France. When he arrived in Paris, he found that the political climate in the capital was more polarized and embittered than at any time since the taking of the Bastille. Although a democratic movement had been developing since the fall of 1789, it was only now receiving support from large segments of the Paris public. A series of small but significant events had made Parisians realize that the Constituent Assembly had no real commitment to making France democratic. The activists with whom Paine made friends, and would be associated with for the rest of his political career in France—politicians such as Condorcet, Brissot, Bonneville, and the Rolands—had become thoroughly frustrated with the Fayettists and no longer had faith in their ability to lead the Revolution forward. For example, Paine's French translator, François Lanthenas, reported that his good friend Madame Roland "has been to the National Assembly" and "is now convinced that liberty and the constitution will not belong to and do not belong to, the men who have given the most to the Revolution." And a few days later Madame Roland herself scolded the Fayettists for holding views that were "false" and "dangerous."[5]

3. *Ibid.*, 72.
4. *Ibid.*, 47.
5. *Lettres de Madame Roland*, ed. Claude Perroud (2 vols.; Paris, 1900–1902), II, 206, 240. The best survey of this period is Marcel Reinhard, *La Chute de la royauté, 10 août*

Louis XVI's infamous flight to Varennes was the final step that converted Paine and his friends to the view that only a democratic republic could save the French Revolution. Behind the king's betrayal the Brissotins saw Lafayette's Machiavellian designs. "It is virtually impossible that Lafayette is not involved," wrote Madame Roland after learning of the flight. Immediately Brissot, Condorcet, and Paine became "the recognized chiefs of a republican party." They put out a journal, *Le Républicain ou Le Défenseur du gouvernement représentatif*, whose influence among Paris clubs was important. Yet despite their efforts Madame Roland did not believe that Lafayette's grip on the government could be broken: "Lafayette is more powerful than ever. His game is more developed and better received than we had supposed . . . he has the force of the army; he has a reserve of blind partisans; he has allied himself closely with the group of opportunists in the Assembly."[6]

Paine is often given credit for educating his friends in the new radical ideology.[7] But considering Paine's previous lack of commitment to the radical movement, there is much evidence that it was French radicals who helped convert Paine to democracy and republicanism in June 1791. For example, in *Rights of Man* Part Two there is an important section in which Paine defined a republic as a "res-publica, the public affairs, or the public good, or literally translated, the public thing." This section was lifted practically verbatim from his friend Bonneville's daily newspaper, *Bouche de fer*. "En definissant le mot *ré-publique*," wrote Bonneville four days after the king's flight, "et le traduissant litteralement dans notre langue, car c'est un mot latin *res-publica*, toute obscurité va disparoitre . . . La république, n'est autre chose litteralement que la chose commune, la chose publique, la grande communauté nationale, LE GOUVERNE-MENT NATIONAL."[8] Likewise, there is no evidence that Paine had progressed very far in writing Part Two until after his return to England. For commentators like Fennessey to suggest that Paine had always been a pronounced democrat and had never learned anything "from his extensive experience of American and French politics" is grossly mistaken:[9] however much he would later deny it, Paine's democratic republicanism developed and matured because of what he and his friends witnessed in the streets of Paris during the tumultuous period surrounding the king's flight to Varennes.

1792 (Paris, 1969). On the deterioration of Lafayette's reputation among Paris democrats see also Kates, *Cercle Social*, 138–51; Censer, *Prelude to Power*, 100–107, 144.

6. *Lettres de Madame Roland*, II, 302, 312–13.
7. For example, Foner, *Tom Paine*, 211–34; and A. O. Aldridge, "Condorcet et Paine. Leur rapports intellectuels," *Revue de litterature comparée*, 32 (1958), 47–65.
8. *RoM*, 178; *Bouche de fer*, 25 June 1791, 1–4.
9. Fennessey, *Burke, Paine*, 63.

Any further movement towards a democratic republic was soon repressed by Lafayette and his supporters in the Constituent Assembly. They refused to abolish the monarchy, forgave the king for all misdeeds as long as he professed support for the constitution, and prepared plans for liquidating the democratic movement. The climax of this anti-democratic campaign was the Massacre at the Champ de Mars, where on 17 July 1791 Lafayette's troops fired on a crowd of Parisians holding a peaceful republican rally. The suppression of the democrats was successful from Lafayette's viewpoint, insofar as order was restored in the city and Louis XVI and the Assembly were able to ratify the new constitution. "Yes, the National Guards are the instruments of oppression, the satellites of an abominable man," cried Madame Roland on the day of the Massacre. "We can say that the counter-revolution is being made at Paris by the majority of the National Assembly and the armed forces with Lafayette at the head."[1]

Nevertheless, Lafayette's victory was ephemeral. Unable to run for office in the new Legislative Assembly (months earlier all members of the Constituent Assembly had disqualified themselves), he and his allies quickly lost their power base. Into the political void stepped Brissot, Condorcet, and their supporters. These Girondins were frustrated by a monarchical constitution that was too conservative for their tastes. They looked to a new war to help minimize the influence of the king and maximize possibilities for French democracy. By January, 1792, the Girondins controlled both the Jacobin Club and the Legislative Assembly. In February they forced the king to replace his Fayettist ministers (who opposed any war) with Roland and Etienne Clavière, Brissot's close allies. A few weeks later, France declared war upon Austria. In the midst of these developments appeared *Rights of Man* Part Two.[2]

The schism between Paine and the Fayettists is dramatically displayed in the bizarre and awkward dedication "To M. Lafayette," that makes up the first pages of Part Two.[3] Paine acknowledged his break with Lafayette. But he claimed that the essential differences between them had to do not with "principles" but with "time." In brief but pungent prose, Paine argued that Lafayette was a misguided patriot, but he refused to call him a counter-revolutionary. Paine's attitude towards Lafayette was condescending but not hostile. Paine viewed Liberalism as only a temporary phase, with Radicalism's victory inevitable. "I wish you to hasten your principles, and overtake me," he urged Lafayette. Paine desperately needed to

1. *Lettres de Madame Roland*, II, 336.
2. M. J. Sydenham, *The Girondins* (London, 1961).
3. *RoM*, 151–52.

explain the relationship between Liberalism and Radicalism as developmental rather than oppositional, if the fiction of a "sequel" was to make any sense. Otherwise, he would leave the door open to charges that he and his hero had been opposed to progress and perhaps were even traitors to the cause of democracy.

The first pages of Part Two, therefore, announced that Paine and his hero had gone their separate ways. Nonetheless, the next few pages go over territory covered in Part One, repeating "the belabouring of Burke," until suddenly Paine comes clean with his readers, letting them know that unlike Part One, Part Two was not a response to Burke's *Reflections*: "Mr. Burke has talked of old and new whigs. If he can amuse himself with childish names and distinctions, I shall not interrupt his pleasure. It is not to him, but to the Abbé Sieyès, that I address this chapter."[4] If we take this statement together with Paine's dedication to Lafayette, it becomes clear that *Rights of Man* Part Two was never intended as an attack upon Burke, but rather a serious challenge to the leadership of Lafayette and Sieyès. This point—often ignored by Paine scholars still obsessed with the Burke/Paine debate—is the key to understanding the real purpose and ideology of Part Two.[5]

Why Sieyès? Between 1789 and 1791 Sieyès was an ally (though sometimes a strained one) of Lafayette. But while Lafayette was primarily a soldier and a statesman, Sieyès's most important contribution was as a thinker. His *What is the Third Estate?* (January 1789) became the most important French pamphlet of the period, inspiring the Declaration of the Rights of Man and Citizen. And as a member of the Constituent Assembly's Constitution Committee, Sieyès had considerable opportunity to translate his ideas into legislation. Under the direct influence of Adam Smith's *Wealth of Nations*, Sieyès argued that only those citizens who contributed to the national economy ought to participate in political life. Those citizens not able to become productive workers would be protected by the laws, but would have no right to make the laws. This idea, outlined in *What is the Third Estate?*, became the germ for the anti-democratic laws establishing the *marc d'argent*, which were, not surprisingly, written by Sieyès.[6]

Rights of Man Part Two was not the first battle in print between Paine and Sieyès. Immediately following the king's flight to Varennes in June-July 1791, Sieyès published an article in the *Moniteur*, the most important French daily, challenging anyone to defend republi-

4. *RoM*, 171.
5. Only Conway comes close to recognizing Sieyès's role. See his *Thomas Paine*, I, 328–29.
6. Paul Bastid, *Sieyès et sa pensée* (Paris, [1939] 1970), 89, 369–70; and Murray Forsyth, *Reason and Revolution: The Political Thought of the Abbé Sieyès* (New York, 1987).

canism over monarchy. Paine accepted the challenge, and he published a short response in *Le Républicain*. Thus *Rights of Man* Part Two should be viewed within the context of an ongoing debate with Sieyès over republican principles. In that sense *Rights of Man* is something of a paradox: where Part One defended the Fayettist Revolution, Part Two repudiated Fayettist ideology.[7]

If Paine was a spokesman for Lafayette in *Rights of Man* Part One, *Rights of Man* Part Two echoed the Girondins. The new element in Part Two was Paine's emphasis on "the representative system." Although Paine had mentioned representative government in passing in Part One, he now developed the concept of representative democracy into a mature theoretical framework. Paine acknowledged the debt modern democracies owed to ancient Greece. But he, like many thinkers during the Enlightenment, also recognized that it was impossible for large nation-states to imitate the Athenian model. Paine wanted a system in which representation would become the keystone for democratic political institutions. "By ingrafting representation upon democracy," Paine said, "we arrive at a system of government capable of embracing and confederating all the various interests and every extent of territory and population."[8]

This new kind of political system had no place for monarchy. "Every government that does not act on the principle of a Republic," he wrote, "is not a good government." Although a democratic monarchy was a theoretical possibility (one toyed with by several Revolutionary leaders, including Mirabeau and Robespierre), the Paine of Part Two viewed it as "eccentric government" and realized that only a representative democratic republic could provide the kind of freedom he desired. Consequently, Paine's model of an admirable state changed from Part One to Part Two: because France in February 1792 was not yet a democratic republic, Paine advised his readers to look towards the United States: "It is on this system that the American government is founded. It is representation ingrafted upon democracy." In Part One, in spite of his focus upon Lafayette, Paine had rarely mentioned the United States. Since he was defending a constitutional monarchy the example of 1776 was somewhat irrelevant. Ironically, America only became central to Paine's arguments when he dropped Lafayette in Part Two.[9]

---

7. On this exchange between Sieyès and Paine, see Aldridge, "Condorcet et Paine," 51–57. Aldridge makes a persuasive case that the debate was staged, suggesting that after the king's flight Sieyès himself had at least secretly become a republican. But more recently, Murray Forsyth (*Reason and Revolution*, 176–79) has reconfirmed Sieyès's commitment to monarchy.
8. *RoM*, 180.
9. *RoM*, 178–80. See also 125, where America is praised largely for its inexpensive government.

Paine's understanding of the nature of revolutionary change also changed from Part One to Part Two. In the first pamphlet Paine had hoped that other nations would choose to imitate the French in a short, peaceful, and above all rational transfer of sovereignty. But when Paine called for revolution to become "the order of the day" in Part Two, he meant something else. In Part One Paine expressed the belief that some kings, such as Louis XVI, were decent enough to hold national office. But Part Two returns to the view he espoused in *Common Sense* in which all kings were criminals, since all monarchies were "originally a tyranny, founded on an invasion and conquest of the country." That is why, Paine asserted, monarchies were inherently expansionist and militaristic. "War is their trade, plunder and revenue their objects." This kind of government, so different from the possibility of the kind of pacifist constitutional monarchy suggested in Part One, was unable to reform itself.[1]

In Part One, Paine hoped that the French Revolution would lead the world by example. But in Part Two that leadership took a more direct and more violent form: the French were expected to wage war on the rest of Europe, liberating the peoples of Europe from their old regimes. The first step was "the extinction of German despotism." But Germany was not enough. Only "when France shall be surrounded with revolutions" will she "be in peace and safety." And only through war could that goal be achieved quickly and efficiently. In Part One, the revolutionary process was described as pacifist and piecemeal. But now, reflecting Girondin foreign policy, Paine envisioned a war that would create a string of democratic republics from England to the Russian border, a war that led him to predict the death of monarchy: "I do not believe," Paine declared, "that monarchy and aristocracy will continue seven years longer in any of the enlightened countries in Europe."[2]

In contrast to Part One, then, Part Two was indeed radical; clearly without Part Two, *Rights of Man* would not have become the bible among nineteenth-century working-class Radicals.[3] Part Two, for example, advocates the abolition of all monarchy and the establishment of democratic republics based upon universal manhood suffrage. More importantly, its fifth chapter includes a social component, in which Paine argued for a graduated income tax, as well as health and old-age insurance, foreshadowing the idea of the welfare state. Obviously nothing in Part One had even hinted at these new and daring proposals.

1. *RoM*, 161, 192–93.
2. *RoM*, 151–52, 156.
3. E. P. Thompson, *The Making of the English Working Class* (New York, 1963), 104–11.

The Girondins themselves were aware of the inconsistency between the two parts. Brissot's close friend, François Lanthenas, did not translate the work until after Part Two was complete. His edition appeared in April or May 1792 and was published by the most significant Girondin publishing house, the Imprimerie du Cercle Social. Nonetheless, Lanthenas edited the work in a curious fashion. First, he eliminated the preface to Part Two because, as he put it,

> Owing to the prejudices that still govern *that nation*, the author has been obliged to condescend to answer Mr. Burke. He has done so more especially in an extended preface which is nothing but a piece of very tedious controversy, in which he shows himself very sensitive to criticisms that do not really affect him. To translate it seemed an insult to the *free French people*. . . . [4]

Clearly Paine's French friends did not see *Rights of Man* as primarily a response to Burke. The French version also eliminated the dedication to Lafayette. Not only did Lanthenas admonish Paine for addressing himself before Burke, but he refused to allow Paine to humble himself before Lafayette. "Paine, that uncorrupted friend of freedom," wrote Lanthenas, "believed too in the sincerity of Lafayette," a naiveté which Lanthenas believed proved that Paine had much to learn from the French. "Bred at a distance from courts, that austere American does not seem any more on his guard against the artful ways and speech courtiers than some Frenchmen who resemble him." By deleting the preface against Burke and the dedication to Lafayette, which had linked the two parts rhetorically, if not substantively, Lanthenas not only firmly established Part Two as an anti-Fayettist text, but he also drew attention to the problematic relationship between the two parts. This may explain why French reviews of *Rights of Man* were relatively cool and even critical, a fact that has perplexed Paine's biographers.[5]

Lanthenas' editorial efforts make clear that Paine united two works whose ideologies were contradictory. Why did Paine not renounce Lafayette more sharply in 1792, as Brissot and his colleagues were willing to do, and simply publish Part Two as a kind of Girondin manifesto? Insofar as Paine refused to attack Lafayette, he allowed his own political theory to decline into a cult of personality. His relationship with Lafayette also explains why Paine retreated from the

staunch republicanism of *Common Sense* and endorsed the constitutional monarchy of Louis XVI.

During the 1770s Lafayette had become the best known European supporter of the American Revolution. And Americans were
deeply proud that this young liberal nobleman admired their new
state. When Lafayette took a leading role in the French Revolution,
Anglo-American supporters naively supposed that he was offering
France the lessons that he had learned in America. "He took a practical existing model, in operation here," commented John Quincy
Adams speaking for American public opinion, "and never attempted
or wished more than to apply it faithfully to his own country."[6] Perhaps we can forgive the American president for this naive interpretation, but certainly Paine ought to have known better. Nonetheless,
Paine was keenly aware that representing Lafayette as this kind of a
symbol could enhance his own star as well.

Paine wanted readers to see the entire era characterized by the
universal progress of human rights, a process whose unity was best
embodied by Lafayette and himself. By 1792 only Lafayette and
Paine had played a major role in *both* the American and French
Revolutions; both of them could be used to represent a linkage
among the American and French Revolutions that would make British parliamentary reform appear urgent and inevitable.

For us *Rights of Man* reveals an ideologue's desperate search to
maintain some shred of intellectual consistency during a period of
intense revolutionary change. So long as the Revolution constituted
a united Third Estate against an entrenched and privileged aristocracy, Paine's ideas could be endorsed by all reformers. But the
moment that the Third Estate began to argue among itself—a process that began as early as the fall of 1789, Paine's ideology could no
longer represent the entire Revolution but only the dominant faction. As the gap between Fayettists and radicals widened between
1789 and 1791 over fundamental issues regarding democracy and
republicanism, Paine's ideological frame became even more problematic. By the time *Rights of Man* Part One was published in
March 1791 its ideology had already moved far to the right on the
spectrum of French Revolutionary politics. Within four months he
dropped his Fayettist endorsements and wrote Part Two as if it were
a sequel. But what the Girondins chose to minimize, their Monta-
gnard rivals later sought to exploit: Paine spent the year of the Terror

6. Quoted in Lloyd S. Kramer, "Lafayette and the Historians: Changing Symbol, Changing
Needs, 1834–1934," *Historical Reflections/Réflections historiques*, 11 (1984), 373–401.
See also his "America's Lafayette and Lafayette's America: A European and the Ameri-
can Revolution," *William and Mary Quarterly*, 3rd Series, 38 (1981), 233–41; and Anne
Loveland, *Emblem of Liberty: The Image of Lafayette in the American Mind* (Baton
Rouge, 1971), 16–34. Paine praises Lafayette for his American heroism in *RoM*, 46.

in prison, and while he would go on to write works of major importance, his political career was over.

GREGORY CLAEYS

From The Origins of the Rights of Labor:
Republicanism, Commerce, and the Construction
of Modern Social Theory in Britain, 1796–1805[†]

It has long been recognized that the 1790s constituted a watershed
in European thinking about the relations between government,
commerce, and property rights. There were material as well as
intellectual reasons for this transformation. In Britain, the period
commencing with the Napoleonic wars witnessed dramatically swift
economic growth, which augmented considerably the social and economic power of the commercial and manufacturing middle classes in
particular. The era nonetheless also experienced a recurrent threat
of famine worse than any seen in the preceding century, and with
the publication of Malthus's *Essay on Population* (1798) in particular
the modern debate about poverty commenced. These developments
became the more momentous by being coupled to an intense debate
about the nature and implications of the French Revolution itself.
This in turn coincided with a massive outburst of radical agitation
in which widespread plebeian participation first occurred and that
some have thought might also have instigated a revolution in Britain.[1] The result was one of the most turbulent periods in modern
British history.

Consequently, this era is usually taken as the starting point of
socialist economic thought;[2] of both radical and liberal conceptions of the welfare state originating in particular with Painite
republicanism;[3] of modern conservatism (given the impact and

---

[†] Parts of this article were first presented to the seminar "Power and Responses to
Power" at the Shelby Cullom Davis Center, Princeton University, Princeton, N.J., April
1990, and to the meeting of the Conference for the Study of Political Thought titled
"Images of the Enlightenment" at the City University of New York in April 1990. I am
grateful to Istvan Hont, John Pocock, Alan Ryan, Lawrence Stone, Dorothy Thompson, Edward Thompson, and the referees of this journal for their comments and criticisms. Reprinted by permission of the author and the University of Chicago Press.

1. The case for the threat of revolution is restated in Roger Wells, *Insurrection: The Brit-
ish Experience, 1795–1803* (London, 1983). The evidence favoring stability is given in
Ian Christie, *Stress and Stability in Late Eighteenth-Century Britain: Reflections on the
British Avoidance of Revolution* (Oxford, 1985).

2. Commencing with Anton Menger's influential *The Right to the Whole Produce of Labor*
(London, 1899).

3. For example, in my *Thomas Paine: Social and Political Thought* (London, 1989). See
also the introduction to my edition of Thomas Paine, *Rights of Man* (Indianapolis,
1992). On the origin of the modern idea of poverty, see esp. J. R. Poynter, *Society and*

principles of Burke's *Reflections on the Revolution in France,* 1790);
and, as Adam Smith's reputation grew rapidly, of post-Smithian
Whig theories of modern laissez-faire commercial society.[4] Already
by the mid-1790s, I have argued elsewhere, much of the tradition-
ally Whig discourse on natural rights and an original social contract
had been ceded by more moderate reformers, after considerable
struggle, to the rhetoric of working-class radicalism, which retained
such themes until well into the nineteenth century. Middle-class
reformers instead moved quickly toward a new liberal ideal dominated by classical political economy (which had many Tory adherents by 1815 as well) which was attended by several forms of
utilitarianism.[5] The growing prominence of economic laws in liberal
political thought was ensured by the end of the decade with the
thoroughgoing assault on the poor's right to charity and the rejection of "speculative" social theory in Malthus's *Essay.* Much of the
spectrum of modern political thought, with its familiar if often mis-
leading sweep from "right" to "left," thus emerged in this period.
And it is usually conceded, correspondingly, that the central opposition between "republican" or civic humanist virtue-based, and "liberal" rights–based discourses on society, commerce, and politics,
which it is often assumed had dominated much of later eighteenth-
century British political thought, either disappeared in this period
or adopted quite different forms.[6]

Attitudes toward property were clearly central to many of these
transformations. Yet while the origins of nineteenth-century political and economic liberalism are now quite well documented, few
close readings of the chief radical texts of this era have focused on
theories of property, especially in light of the now considerable and
complex scholarship on late eighteenth-century republicanism and
the now much enriched literature on the revolutionary debates in
Britain during the 1790s.[7] This involves consideration of some

---

Pauperism: English Ideas on Poor Relief, 1795–1834 (London, 1969); and Gertrude Him-
melfarb, *The Idea of Poverty: England in the Early Industrial Age* (London, 1984).

4. See especially John Burrow, *Whigs and Liberals: Continuity and Change in English
Political Thought* (Oxford, 1988); and Stefan Collini, Donald Winch, and John Burrow,
That Noble Science of Politics: A Study in Nineteenth Century Intellectual History
(Cambridge, 1983).

5. See my "The French Revolution Debate and British Political Thought," *History of
Political Thought* 11, no. 1 (Spring 1990): 59–80.

6. The "republican" or civic humanist view is best represented by J. G. A. Pocock (most
recently, *Virtue, Commerce and History* [Cambridge, 1985], pp. 215–310), the "liberal"
on the American side by Joyce Appleby (e.g., "Liberalism and the American Revolution,"
New England Quarterly 49 [1976]: 3–26), and the British, Isaac Kramnick ("Religion
and Radicalism: English Political Theory in the Age of Revolution," *Political Theory* 5
[1977]: 505–34, and "Republican Revisionism Revisited," *American Political Science
Review* 87 [1982]: 629–64, both now reprinted in his *Republicanism and Bourgeois
Radicalism: Political Ideology in Late Eighteenth-Century England and America* [Ithaca,
N.Y., 1990]).

7. Recent works of importance include H. T. Dickinson, ed., *Britain and the French Revolution* (London, 1989); Stephen Pritchett, *England and the French Revolution* (London,

themes that have tended to be ignored in recent controversies in this area. A more careful reconstruction of the evolution of plebeian radicalism will show us, among other things, that focusing on an opposition of "liberal" to "republican" thought does not take us very far in explaining some of the crucial intellectual shifts of this period. As in the preceding century, there were many different types of republicans writing in this period, and the more radical among them, in particular, freely mixed rights- and virtue-based theories in support of popular sovereignty. They also adopted many different conceptions of economic freedom and intervention. Moreover, the term "liberal" had not yet achieved any recognizable political status, though many of the concepts often associated with it were in use. My aim here is to explore how attitudes toward commerce, in particular, divided the radicals and revealed crucial differences in their republicanism. I want to show, however, that despite these disagreements radicals came in this period to accept as increasingly central claims for the just reward of the laboring classes. (Such pleas on the basis of justice and humanity had also been shared by writers like Smith.)[8] More innovatively, they linked such demands with an account of the poverty of the laboring classes. This in turn generated a strikingly new description of the relationship between wage laborers and their employers that would become crucial for nineteenth-century radicalism and socialism. I will summarize my main arguments before turning to a more detailed examination of the relevant texts.

My focus here is mainly on four key "representative" works from this period: two procommercial republican tracts—Thomas Paine's *Agrarian Justice* (1796) and John Thelwall's *The Rights of Nature against the Usurpations of Establishments* (1796)—and two more hostile to trade—William Godwin's *The Enquirer: Reflections on Education, Manners and Literature* (1797) and Charles Hall's *The Effects of Civilization on the People in European States* (1805). Desultory treatments of these texts, among the best-known works of contemporary radicalism, abound in the now mostly elderly histories of the radical and socialist thought of this period.[9] But they have not hitherto been treated as exemplifying two main types of radical republican response to claims about the superiority of modern commercial society, on the one hand; and the growth of famine and poverty in

---

1989); Mark Philp, ed., *The French Revolution and British Popular Politics* (Cambridge, 1991); Seamus Deane, *The French Revolution and Enlightenment in England* (Cambridge, Mass., 1988); and Ceri Crossley and Ian Small, eds., *The French Revolution and British Culture* (Oxford, 1989).

8. For example, Adam Smith, *The Wealth of Nations* (Oxford, 1976), 1:86, 91.

9. For example, Max Beer, *A History of British Socialism* (London, 1919), 1:101–32. Godwin and Hall are also the starting point of Menger's *The Right to the Whole Produce of Labour.*

Britain during the 1790s, on the other. It was these two impulses that transformed the doctrines of eighteenth-century radicalism, which were much (though by no means exclusively) indebted to the civic humanist tradition, into a very different account of society. The pervasiveness of Machiavellian or neo-Harringtonian republicanism in eighteenth-century Britain, as well as the gradual accommodation of many of its strands to the demands of a trading society, has been established thoroughly by J. G. A. Pocock in particular.[1] Though its popularity is sometimes denied, some contemporaries supposed that "the republican spirit," at least in the sense of a general hostility toward monarchy, had gained ground steadily since the accession of George III and was "principally prevalent among the subordinate and most numerous classes."[2] This was certainly still widely true in the early 1790s, though claims for the strength of popular loyalism cannot be discounted.[3] But little attention has been paid to the ways in which the republican paradigm, as opposed to attitudes toward kingship, was transformed in light of the events and debates of the 1790s. Though some had taken a much more radical view of property rights in particular, most previous republicans in seeking to avoid tyranny and preserve popular control had stressed the superiority of virtuous, independent, and civic-minded landowners to corrupt courtiers, speculative merchants, and dissolute city-dwellers generally. Concerned to emphasize the value of the civic participation of the virtuous few to the cause of liberty, they were very rarely either democratic or receptive to the claims of the poor to more than Christian charity. In the early 1790s, however, parts of this theory were forged into a distinctive form of plebeian radicalism, in particular by extending the notion of the desirability of independence to the laboring classes generally. This much is widely accepted by historians. During the decade considered here, however, the new democratic radicalism of the early 1790s was in turn transformed by a novel, sharp focus on the condition and means of livelihood of the laboring classes, never before carefully scrutinized by radical republican writers. It is this second transformation, which would prove central to nineteenth-century radical and socialist thought, that is my chief concern here.

The differing reactions to commerce treated here represent the working out of two quite different tendencies in British republicanism in the face of rapidly shifting economic developments and the

---

1. J. G. A. Pocock, *The Machiavellian Moment: Florentine Political Thought and the Atlantic Republican Tradition* (Princeton, N.J., 1975).
2. John Andrews, *An Essay on Republican Principles, and On the Inconveniences of a Commonwealth in a Large Country or Nation* (London, 1783), p. 7.
3. See, e.g., H. T. Dickinson, "Popular Conservatism and Militant Loyalism," in Dickinson, ed., pp. 103–25.

debate over the French revolution itself. To distinguish these strands, we need briefly to delineate the varieties of republicanism in this period. Though they were all indebted in varying degrees to the traditions of Machiavelli and Harrington, and more recently to those of Algernon Sidney, Walter Moyle, and Henry Neville, there were at least four kinds of republicans writing in late eighteenth-century Britain.[4] Most republicans in principle did not seek so much to abolish the monarchy as to reinforce the popular component in government. The more moderate embraced a republic in theory as the best guarantee of liberty, but they were resigned to a constitutional monarchy as more immediately practical and hoped that existing corruption could be curtailed and the Commons strengthened against both monarchical and governmental interference (e.g., the historian Catherine Macaulay, and, at his most speculative, David Hume).[5] In face of the growing democratic movement of the 1790s, they still often insisted that Britain was a republic.[6] A second group sought to abolish the monarchy, widen parliamentary representation, and revive civic virtue through an agrarian law. Condemning luxury as the main cause of corruption, these writers also sought to restrict commerce and regulate prices (e.g., James Burgh).[7] More concerned with virtue than greater participation, especially by the laboring classes, most republicans in this period, as in the seventeenth century, were thus, as Caroline Robbins has stressed, "in no sense democratic."[8] A number gave greater stress instead to, for example, the need to limit the size of cities (e.g., Andrew Fletcher).[9] A third, more extreme and more Utopian group extended this program further toward various

4. On eighteenth-century British republicanism, see also Caroline Robbins, *The Eighteenth Century Commonwealthman* (Cambridge, Mass., 1959); and, most recently, Alan Houston, *Algernon Sidney and the Republican Heritage in England and America* (Princeton, N.J., 1991). That "country party" views, which overlapped with many republican themes, could also be Tory is emphasized in Linda Colley, *In Defiance of Oligarchy: The Tory Party, 1714–60* (Cambridge, 1982). The connections between republicanism and millenarianism are explored in Jack Fruchtman, Jr., *The Apocalyptic Politics of Richard Price and Joseph Priestley* (Philadelphia, 1983). There are also useful comments in Patrice Higonnet, *Sister Republics: The Origins of French and American Republicanism* (Cambridge, Mass., 1988); and Thomas Pangle, *The Spirit of Modern Republicanism: The Moral Vision of the American Founders and the Philosophy of Locke* (Chicago, 1988).

5. In David Hume, "The Idea of a Perfect Commonwealth," reprinted in *Utopias of the British Enlightenment*, ed. Gregory Claeys (Cambridge, 1994). On Macaulay, see Bridget Hill, *The Republican Virago: The Life and Times of Catherine Macaulay* (Oxford, 1992).

6. Sir William Jones, *The British Constitution of Government, Compared with That of a Democratic Republic*, 2d ed. (London, 1793), p. 18.

7. James Burgh, *An Account of the First Settlement, Laws, Form of Government, and Police, of the Cessares, A People of South America* (London, 1764), p. 96 (reprinted in *Utopias of the British Enlightenment*, ed. Gregory Claeys [Cambridge, 1994], pp. 71–136).

8. Caroline Robbins, ed., *Two English Republican Tracts* (Cambridge, 1969), p. 49. Catherine Macaulay's "Sketch of a Democratical Form of Government," e.g., does not appear to aim at a very wide franchise (see her *Loose Remarks to Be Found in Mr. Hobbes' Rudiments of Government and Society* [London, 1767], pp. 29–39).

9. Andrew Fletcher of Saltoun, *Selected Political Writings and Speeches*, ed. David Daiches (Edinburgh, 1979), p. 111.

forms of Platonic and Christian republicanism. These included plans for the collective ownership of property (Robert Wallace); the management, in addition, of land revenues by parishes (Thomas Spence);[1] and even proposals for restricting labor to four hours daily and for abolishing money.[2]

Against many of these trends, however, a fourth group, which was ultimately the most influential, sought a modern representative republic with near-universal manhood suffrage and virtually unlimited commerce, with perhaps some variation on an agrarian law (e.g., Thomas Paine). This last, far more democratic and procommercial form of republicanism, while anticipated by the views of men like Joseph Priestley, was widely popularized during the early 1790s by the extraordinary controversy over Paine's much more stridently antimonarchical *Rights of Man* (1791–92).[3] All eighteenth-century republicans had sought greater public virtue, agreeing with Montesquieu and others that this was the basis of popular government.[4] But very few believed that a pure republic could embrace a large or relatively advanced state, preferring with Rousseau to presume that a small, poor country like Corsica was better suited to a republican constitution. By contrast, Paine's *Rights of Man*, building on the model of the young United States, promoted a republic of virtually any extent, to be achieved by universal male suffrage; a written constitution emanating from a convention along American lines; representative institutions governing through an elected executive; the abolition of aristocratic and Anglican monopolies; and the unlimited expansion of commerce. Even those republicans close to Paine who counseled considerably greater regulation of commerce, like the London doctor William Hodgson, did not doubt that a democratic commercial republic along modified American lines was the best form of government.[5] By the mid-1790s this group frequently termed themselves "democrats."[6]

---

1. Robert Wallace, *Various Prospects of Mankind, Nature and Providence* (Glasgow, 1758), p. 101. On Spence, see below, pp. 27–28.
2. For example, *Equality—a Political Romance* (Philadelphia, 1802), the utopian tract by John Lithgow first published in the United States, though it owed much to contemporary Anglo-Scottish property debates.
3. Priestley's enthusiasm for commercial liberty predated the *Wealth of Nations* (see, e.g., Joseph Priestley, "Lectures on History and General Policy," in *The Works of Joseph Priestley*, 25 vols. [London, 1803], 24:305). His preference for a republican form of government was given in the same lectures (pp. 338–39).
4. Baron de Montesquieu, *Political Writings*, ed. Melvin Richter (Indianapolis, 1990), p. 126.
5. See Hodgson's *The Commonwealth of Reason* (1795), reprinted in Claeys, ed., pp. 199–248.
6. *A Political Dictionary for the Guinea-less Pigs* (London, n.d.), one of Daniel Isaac Eaton's productions, defined, e.g., "democrat" as "one who favours that form of *Government*, wherein the supreme power is lodged with the people, who exercise the same by persons of their own order, deputed for that purpose" (p. 1).

From this period onward, however, mounting evidence served to cast doubt on the forecasts of the most optimistic, procommercial, and democratic republicans. For several reasons, a shift now began to take place among radical republicans from an analysis that centrally attributed working-class deprivation to governmental corruption, especially overly heavy taxation to support placemen and pensioners, to a new concern with wage labor as one, if not the main, source of poverty. This change of focus was by no means complete, for Cobbettite and various other forms of radicalism continued to inveigh against "Old Corruption" well into the 1830s. Some varieties of Chartism took up a similar cry, as did some sections of the Anti–Corn Law League.[7] Nonetheless, a novel concern with wages as a source of poverty was to become, through early socialism, Marxism, and anarchism, one of the most incisive developments in radical thought in the modern era, and this represents a fundamental reassessment of the implications of economic power for society and politics. It is argued here that to trace the emergence of this shift accurately we need to understand how parts of the republican inheritance, and particularly the notion of independence, were recrafted in light of radical debates about commerce in the 1790s. Earlier republicans had often worried that extensive commerce corroded the civic virtue or patriotism upon which the republican form depended.[8] By 1789, however, such anxieties were no longer so widespread, and many republicans were willing, with Paine, to accept commerce more or less on its own terms. Coincidentally, many artisans and shopkeepers were involved in popular radicalism, and they saw little sacrifice in exchanging a measure of civic virtue for a modicum of commercial sociability and the promise of both opulence and greater social equality. Despite such prejudices, however, the radical reformers were subjected to a massive hostile propaganda campaign, peaking in 1792–94, in which some hundreds of titles were dedicated to foiling their aims. Many of these "anti-Jacobin" tracts insisted that the attainments of commerce rested on the existing class structure and would disappear in the face of the social equality that the democrats seemingly expected would accompany their new constitution and greatly expanded electorate. An opulent commercial society and a republican form of government were, in the eyes of loyalist defenders of the British constitution, simply incompatible.

By and large the radicals did not counter this charge very successfully, though the war against France and the subsequent tainting of the principles of reform by association with the enemy rather

7. See W. R. Rubinstein, "The End of Old Corruption in Britain, 1780–1860," *Past and Present*, no. 101 (1983), pp. 55–86.
8. For example, Montesquieu, pp. 140–41.

loaded the dice against them. Their cause lost considerable ground
as a consequence. Out of the debate of the early 1790s, however,
there arose a more procommercial as well as a more anticommercial republican alternative that built upon similar trends in prerevo-
lutionary republicanism, and it is their shaping that I will concentrate
on here. Unwilling either to concede that trade required considerable social inequality or to relinquish commerce and return to
more classical, agrarian forms of republicanism, some democrats in
the mid-1790s instead sought to diffuse the benefits of trade more
widely and to ascertain more precisely how the laboring classes
could benefit most from its increase. Both Thomas Paine, who was
also responding to developments in France, and John Thelwall thus
contended (and this was for both a new argument by 1796) that the
laboring classes ought to be ensured a *proportionate* right to
increases in society's wealth generally. Moreover, after the famine
year of 1795 the problem of poverty began to loom ever larger, as it
would for most of the next century. But Paine and Thelwall argued
not only that the poor should be provided with a safety net to save
them from indigence, but also that demands of justice now sup-
planted those of charity. The key problem was therefore establishing
and securing these claims, which constituted an essential shift
toward that focus on rights not to charity, but to the produce of
labor that was to be central to socialism and that moved distinctively away from most previous radical emphases on historical, civil,
and constitutional rights. Nonetheless, older rights conceptions—
especially in relation to the notion of an original contract—would,
as we will see, prove crucial to establishing these new rights claims,
which are central to our understanding of the legacy of the French
Revolution in Britain.

This new range of concerns was not confined to the procommercial republicans, for some who were less optimistic about commerce
also sought to redefine their ideals in light of changing circumstances and the intense debate of the early 1790s. They particularly
sought to preserve civic virtue and individual independence by urging the right of the laboring poor to greater intellectual and personal
independence and leisure. While the strategy of the procommercial
republicans was, as we will see, rooted more in law and moral philosophy, that of the anticommercial republicans was, ironically,
more heavily indebted to political economy. Using a new definition
of wealth as the power to command labor drawn chiefly from
Adam Smith, William Godwin and Charles Hall in particular contended accordingly that the growth of commerce and manufactures,
especially luxury goods, merely compelled further labor from the
poor. This, Godwin emphasized, deprived the latter of leisure and
learning. For Hall, manufacturing, by forcing laborers into urban

employment, diminished their opportunity to obtain a basic subsistence from the land. Thus, though their motives diverged, Godwin and Hall alike advocated a return to a society of largely agricultural labor and greater personal independence and equality. (Godwin, initially much indebted to Rousseau's conception of the virtues of early societies, came however to doubt the advantages of some kinds of simplicity.) Like Paine and Thelwall, both consequently helped to redefine an older republican language of corruption and virtue by extending its application to the laboring classes. For both, the greater labor of the poor was itself an indication of corrupt dependence rather than, as previous republicans had believed, natural to a society of ranks. If the modern republicans thus aimed to equalize the benefits of commerce, Hall and Godwin, among others, sought to abolish all unnecessary dependence by returning to a largely precommercial society. Both the pro- and anticommercial strands of radical republicanism, however, demonstrated a heightened awareness of the problem of poverty and the claims of the working classes that had not been present in British radicalism prior to the early 1790s. Their redefinition of the sources of poverty and the claims of labor, then, constitutes one of the main turning points toward modern social and political thought.

Thomas Paine and John Thelwall: Simplicity, Luxury, and Commercial Society

Although Paine and most of his followers were "modern" republicans seeking free trade in a democratic representative republic, the accusation that such proposals, encapsulated in the bogey word "equality," would undermine modern agricultural and commercial opulence proved central to the ideological debates of the early 1790s. Crucial to the success of the massive loyalist propaganda campaign of 1791–94 was the allegation, prominently publicized by John Reeves's Association for Preserving Liberty and Property against Republicans and Levellers, that republicanism inevitably implied the restoration of society to its primitive natural state and, in particular, Paine's appeal to natural rights alone entailed returning to natural society because "leveling" existing inequalities would also subvert the opulence they supported.[9] This argument succeeded partly because of a widespread and willful misunderstanding of Paine's proposed substitution—and this was in a sense the heart of the modern republican argument—of considerable commercial sociability for much of the role played by civic virtue in Harringtonian republicanism. In effect, Paine was simply tarred as a primitivist republican because of the strength of

9. See Claeys, *Thomas Paine* (n. 3, p. 265), pp. 153–64, upon which the present account draws.

his appeal to natural rights and its potential reception in light of the swiftly growing popular radical movement of the early 1790s.

This was not a fair statement of Paine's intentions. The *Rights of Man*, part 2, had indeed proposed aiding children, the aged, and the poor through a progressive inheritance tax. This right to relief was defended on the basis of taxes already paid and the government's duty to provide "for the instruction of youth, and the support of old age." Paine's chief aim, certainly, was to undermine the landed aristocracy and to redistribute the tax burden more fairly. But he did not wish to limit property justly earned, only that derived from little or no effort. Only incomes from landed property "beyond the probable acquisition to which industry can extend" were to be prohibited, as well as "the accumulation of it by bequest."[1] For our purposes, it is crucial to emphasize that Paine was here almost exclusively concerned with great landed estates as the chief instance of the "robbery" that caused poverty. The basis for his taxation claims was both traditional and innovative. One of the main goals of the *Rights of Man* was to extend, harden, and institutionalize the duties toward the poor enjoined by natural law writers, transforming rights to charity that were usually imperfect or voluntary into hard or perfect rights to justice enforceable by government. But despite this variation on an agrarian law, Paine worried less than most republicans about the threat of luxury to virtue, terming himself "no enemy to genteel or fashionable dress, or to the moderate enjoyment of those articles of indulgence we are furnished with from abroad" if they were also taxed like agriculture. In a thousand years, America might "be what Europe is now," its liberties despoiled. In the meantime this was not a cause for concern.[2]

"Old countries" like Britain and France were another matter, however. By 1796 Paine came to believe that their poverty was endemic and had to be countered by a still greater redistribution of existing tax revenues and of returns from the largest landed estates. But compared to the *Rights of Man*, *Agrarian Justice Opposed to Agrarian Law and to Agrarian Monopoly* made far more sweeping claims for the poor's right to what Paine now contended was common wealth, especially agricultural improvements, doubtless partly inspired by the French egalitarian communist Gracchus Babeuf's views, which became widely known after his abortive conspiracy in 1795–96.[3] Crucially, Paine now saw poverty as originating partly in inadequate wages and an economic oppression in which all employers, not merely corrupt courts and aristocrats, participated, and less

1. Thomas Paine, *Complete Writings*, ed. Philip Foner, 2 vols. (New York, 1945), 1:434.
2. Ibid., pp. 387, 355, and 2:350, 358, 1348–49.
3. For Babeuf's views, see R. B. Rose, *Gracchus Babeuf: The First Revolutionary Communist* (Stanford, Calif., 1978), esp. pp. 230–32.

in the heavy taxation he had chiefly stressed earlier. This shift advertised a growing concern with the laboring classes generally and not only the poor; the delineation of its consequences for republicanism is my main concern here.

Central to *Agrarian Justice*'s new claims was Paine's discussion of the original community of property ordained by God. Here he distinguished for the first time between "natural property" bequeathed by the maker of the universe, "such as the earth, air, water," and "artificial property" created by mankind. Equality in the latter was "impossible; for to distribute it equally it would be necessary that all should have contributed in the same proportion, which can never be the case; and this being the case, every individual would hold on to his own property, as his right share." But of "equality of natural property . . . the subject of this little essay," Paine insisted that "every individual in the world is born therein with legitimate claims on a certain kind of property, or its equivalent."[4] This "natural birthright" Paine thought was still recognized among primitive societies like the North American Indians. But while early societies were blissfully unaware of "those spectacles of human misery which poverty and want present to our eyes in all the towns and streets of Europe," they had also lacked "those advantages which flow from agriculture, arts, science and manufactures." To retain these benefits while avoiding the evils of progress, it was necessary to acknowledge "the first principle of civilization . . . that the condition of every person born into the world, after a state of civilization commences, ought not to be worse than if he had been born before that period."[5] Thus Paine proposed that landowners pay a lump sum as well as an annuity to all deprived of their birthright. Much of his new plan to tax landed property seemingly hinged upon conceding this right of restitution.

Paine's next proposition was highly contentious given his skeptical deism, but he still used it to underpin a new notion of property rights.[6] This was the claim that "the earth, in its natural, uncultivated state was, and ever would have continued to be, *the common property of the human race*," with every man being "born to property" in the land. If this was true, only "the value of the improvement," not the earth itself, was "individual property," even though it was admittedly "impossible to separate the improvement made by cultivation" from what the earth itself provided. Paine could have argued that at some point not industry but inheritance generated unacceptable

---

4. Paine, *Complete Writings*, 1:606–7.
5. Ibid., pp. 609–10, 619.
6. In *The Age of Reason* he had dismissed as unhistorical the account of the Creation in Genesis, which was the source of natural law speculation about divine intentions (see Claeys, *Thomas Paine*, pp. 196–208).

inequalities in wealth. That was where the *Rights of Man* had left the matter hanging. Or he could have simply defined "a limit to property, or the accumulation of it by bequest." Instead he now justified a tax upon all landed wealth, without having to measure "improvement," by arguing that every landed proprietor owed the community a "ground-rent." Upon this, rather than the mere condemnation of the excessive "luxury" of great estates, Paine's new taxation plan was to be based.[7]

It was not merely the claim that land historically had once been held in common but also the original *intentional* bequest of the whole earth to all by God at the Creation which was vital here. This supported rights claims that merely acknowledging a historical state of nature with common use rights did not necessarily imply (and of course there were disagreements about what rights had existed then). Moreover, invoking the Deity lent Paine's case an important pedigree. For this strategy was central to natural jurisprudence accounts of property, which developed the biblical assertion that, at the Creation, dominion over the earth was vested in the first man and woman and all their descendants. By the 1790s, however, most Christians—and the chief natural jurists Paine probably read, Grotius and Pufendorf—believed that God gave the earth to all in common only negatively, that is, to develop individually as the need arose (principally from the pressure of population). From this interpretation there emerged in the eighteenth century the four-stages account of the progress of property to which most of the leading Scottish social theorists adhered. This usually observed that God had not intended a positive community of property where goods remained in common in perpetuity.[8]

Agrarian Justice clearly echoed such authoritative accounts without, similarly, reaching a communist conclusion. But Paine, continuing the trend by which, as Mirabeau observed, the American

---

7. Paine *Complete Writings*, 1:610–11.
8. See, e.g., Hugo Grotius, *De Jure Belli et Pacis* (1625) (Oxford, 1925), 2:186; and Samuel Pufendorf, *De Jure Naturae et Gentium* (1672) (Oxford, 1934), p. 537. Only a few late eighteenth-century writers contested the "negative community" conclusion, namely, William Ogilvie and, to some extent, Robert Wallace, Thomas Reid, and Thomas Spence. See W. Ogilvie, *An Essay on the Right of Property in Land* (Glasgow, 1781), p. 11 ("the earth having been given to mankind in common occupancy, each individual seems to have by nature a right to possess and cultivate an equal share"); Wallace (n. 1, p. 270), pp. 38–40, 66; Thomas Spence, *The Rights of Man*, 4th ed. (London, 1793), pp. 21–22, and *The Rights of Infants* (London, 1797). See generally my *Machinery, Money and the Millennium: From Moral Economy to Socialism, 1815–1860* (Princeton, N.J., 1987), pp. 1–33; and on the four-stages theory, Ronald Meek, *Social Science and the Ignoble Savage* (Cambridge, 1976). On discussions of property prior to this period generally, see also Paschal Larkin, *Property in the Eighteenth Century* (Cork, 1930); Thomas Horne, *Property Rights and Poverty: Political Argument in Britain, 1605–1834* (Chapel Hill, N.C., 1990), which focuses mainly on rights to charity rather than to the produce of labor; Alan Ryan, *Property and Political Theory* (Oxford, 1984), chaps. 1–2; and, most recently, Stephen Buckle, *Natural Law and the Theory of Property: Grotius to Hume* (Oxford, 1991).

revolutionaries had "opposed the natural rights of the people to all the nonsense of the civilians on the conventions set up against them,"[9] also rejected a merely historical, "negative" interpretation of common property. Instead he insisted that communal property rights still obtained. He thus promoted a contemporary right to property that a strictly stadial theory—insofar as it historicized rights claims, acknowledging only those original rights that had been unsecured by subsequent contracts—necessarily rejected, at least in this form. Natural law texts usually conceded the recurrent validity of original common property rights in one crucial respect. For some, at least, argued that the needy, if facing starvation, could invoke the right of charity from the rich and could demand that grain be sold to them at the normal market price, and even (a few added) rightfully steal in cases of dire necessity. But Paine's conception of the application of original rights to the modern world was wider than this, and it only succeeded because of a theologically based workmanship model. Man had not made the earth, and "though he had a natural right to *occupy* it, he had no right to *locate as his property* in perpetuity any part of it; neither did the Creator of the earth open a land-office, from whence the first title-deeds should issue."[1] Since cultivation began, however, landed monopolies had dispossessed at least half the population of their portion of the soil. If they were compensated by receiving £15 at age twenty-one (or about half a year's wage for an agricultural laborer) and £10 annually from age fifty onward, a "revolution in the state of civilization" analogous to a republican revolution in government would result.[2]

To strengthen this argument still further, *Agrarian Justice* also urged two further claims on behalf of the dispossessed. The first of these, Paine's "principle of civilization," invoked a tacit original contract in asserting that "no person ought to be in a worse condition when born under what is called a state of civilization, than he would have been had he been born in a state of nature." If necessary, provision had consequently to be made "by subtracting from property a portion equal in value to the natural inheritance it has absorbed."[3] Second, Paine suggested that while land was given by God to all, personal property was "the *effect of society*," without which no one could acquire more than their own hands could produce. Consequently the rich owed "on every principle of justice, of gratitude, and of civilization, a part of that accumulation back again to society from whence the whole came." Like the principle of civilization, this secular argument aimed to bolster theologically based rights. But it also

9. *Speeches of M. Mirabeau the Elder* (Dublin, 1792), p. 18.
1. Paine, *Complete Writings* (n. 1, p. 274), 1:611.
2. Ibid., pp. 612–13, 621.
3. Ibid., pp. 613–20.

permitted all property, not only land, to be taxed or otherwise appropriated for the common good. The funds, or government bonds, by which the national debt was serviced, for example—which Paine wished to tax—here faced a burden of social responsibility that divine intention seemingly had not assigned them, Genesis having shortsightedly referred only to landed property, not financial speculation. Wealth derived from manufacturing was similarly liable. A claim of justice for wage labor was thus presented here that could not be deduced from divine intention, which referred only to the landless, and that was difficult to deduce (because of the vagueness of the precept) from the principle of civilization. This concern with wage labor represented a dramatic development in Paine's theory of justice and clearly proceeded from the belief that "the accumulation of personal property is, in many instances, the effect of paying too little for the labor that produced it; the consequence of which is that the working hand perishes in old age, and the employer abounds in affluence."[4]

Paine thus developed three arguments for redistributing property in *Agrarian Justice*. He agreed that land ownership arose with cultivation and had existed neither "in the first state of man, that of hunters, nor in the second state, that of shepherds," where property was only in flocks and herds. But he urged a broader interpretation of the consequences of God's bequest of property to all than most natural jurists conceded. A contemporary right was extended—not merely to the needy but to all without land—of a portion of any improvements on land in perpetuity, not only subsistence goods during famine. This variation on natural law claims for soft or imperfect rights to charity substituted a general right to subsistence for the specific right of the necessitous, or, if we like, transmuted an imperfect right to charity for the starving few into a perfect right to assistance of the dispossessed laboring classes in general.[5] Paine's two further arguments, one based on a principle of civilization, the other on a general duty owed by the wealthy to society, gave his claims a much greater scope than his deductions from divine intention allowed, though without being centrally focused on the claim (often associated with Locke) of the laborer to a proportion of his or her produce because of the labor invested therein.

After Paine fled to France in late 1792 to avoid imprisonment for sedition, the leading republican writer in Britain was John Thelwall, an interesting and relatively sophisticated writer whose views have been unduly neglected by historians of this period. Born in Covent Garden in 1764, apprenticed as a silk-mercer and tailor, and later a

---

4. Ibid., p. 442.
5. Ibid., p. 611. See, e.g., Hugo Grotius, 2:188–89, for the origins of this view.

student of divinity, medicine, and law, Thelwall became a lecturer, journalist, and political pamphleteer. Tried for treason in 1794 and acquitted after six months' imprisonment, he remained one of the leaders of the London Corresponding Society, the main reform organization in Britain during the 1790s.[6] Among his various poetical, literary, and political writings, Thelwall's *The Rights of Nature against the Usurpations of Establishments* (1796) in particular restated the problem of the rights of the majority to subsistence and property. Like Paine (though at least initially the two were likely unaware of each other's tracts),[7] Thelwall argued that republican demands for greater social equality could be reconciled with Britain's increasing opulence by a more just distribution of wealth to the laboring classes. But while Thelwall became one of the leading procommercial democratic republicans writing in the 1790s, he retained important Stoic and antiluxury arguments in his views, notably in the three volumes of his poetry and essays published as *The Peripatetic* in 1793.[8] In his London lectures of 1795–96, too, Thelwall still emphasized the need for more abstemious, stoical, and republican manners, urging his listeners to

> labour to abolish luxury . . . Let us in our own houses, at our own tables, by our exhortations to our friends, by our admonitions to our enemies, persuade mankind to discard those tinsel ornaments and ridiculous superfluities which enfeeble our minds, and entail voluptuous diseases on the affluent, while diseases of a still more calamitous description overwhelm the oppressed orders of society, from the scarcity resulting from this extravagance. Thus let us administer to the relief of those who, having the same powers of enjoyment with ourselves, have

6. A recent perceptive evaluation of his intellectual achievements is given in Iain Hampsher-Monk, "John Thelwall and the Eighteenth-Century Radical Response to Political Economy," *Historical Journal* 34 (1991): 1–20. Also useful is Geoffrey Gallop, "Ideology and the English Jacobins: The Case of John Thelwall," *Enlightenment and Dissent* 5 (1986): 3–20. See generally my edition of *John Thelwall: Political Writings* (University Park, Pa., in press).

7. *Agrarian Justice* was written in the winter of 1795–96 and published in early 1796 in Paris. A London edition appeared in 1797. One copy of Thelwall's political lectures (in the Cambridge University Library), published as *The Tribune* in 1795–96 (3 vols. [London]) is inscribed to "Citizen Thomas Paine, with the respect and sincere admiration of the author," though there is no way of knowing whether or when Paine, who remained in Paris until 1802, received it.

8. In *The Peripatetic*, Thelwall gave considerable emphasis to pastoral, agrarian, and anticommercial themes. He regretted the passing of a time when lands were rented out in small portions, and master and laborer "were near enough to a level of sympathy in each other's misfortunes" that "the reciprocity of kindness might rationally be expected," which was ended by the concentration of landed wealth (*The Peripatetic, or, Sketches of the Heart, of Nature and Society*, 3 vols. [London, 1793], 1:145). In a poem entitled "To Luxury," written in 1794, Thelwall castigated the "noxious weeds" of luxury that threatened liberty, which could subsist only on "virtuous poverty." In "To Simplicity of Manners," too, he praised "those ancient Manners—simple and severe," cultivated by Sparta in particular (reprinted in John Thelwall, *The Poetical Recreations of the Champion* [London, 1822], pp. 169–70).

a right to, at least, an equal participation of all the necessaries of life, which are the product of their labour.[9]

The notion of "an equal participation of all the necessaries of life, which are the product of their labour" would, as we will see, become particularly important in Thelwall's *Rights of Nature*. In his lectures, however, Thelwall also emphasized his acceptance of commerce and pleaded for an end of scarcity through establishing universal freedom of trade in surplus produce. Throughout this period, moreover, Thelwall's views of luxury appear to have undergone further alteration. Against a scheme (strongly reminiscent of his friend William Godwin's position in the first edition of his *Enquiry Concerning Political Justice* [1793]) for reducing human labor to half an hour daily by abolishing luxuries and producing only necessities, Thelwall now stressed that buildings, books, paintings, and the like were good things, provided they did not grind down the poor.[1] Thus, without neglecting the effects of luxury on manners, Thelwall saw its chief threat as lying less in a tendency to engender moral and political corruption than to exacerbate social inequality (a conclusion, we will see, that Godwin reached at about the same time). Thelwall still reprinted one of his own earlier poems from *The Peripatetic* that termed commerce a "doubtful" and "partial good" because it often engendered war and its luxuries resulted in monopoly. But it seems that his chief concern now was more with the monopolistic effects of commerce than the moral consequences of luxury.[2]

This shift in Thelwall's views toward a more procommercial stance certainly resulted in part from reading the *Wealth of Nations* at this time, which led him, more than most other radicals in this period, to take up the categories of political economy and especially the all-important language of "productive and unproductive labor."[3] Examining in several lectures in 1795 the causes of the dearness and scarcity of provisions in this near-famine year, Thelwall agreed with Smith that "real wealth" lay only in "the quantum of real necessaries and comforts," and he praised "the fair, the just, and rational system of commerce" that exported a surplus only after meeting home demand. "My idea of the first and genuine principles of just government, with respect to agriculture," he asserted, was "to produce the largest quantity of the necessaries of life, and to promote the most equal distribution of those articles." Agriculture ought not to aim at

9. Thelwall, *The Tribune*, 1:13.
1. William Godwin, *Enquiry Concerning Political Justice*, 2 vols. (London, 1793), 2:823.
2. Thelwall, *The Tribune*, 2:8.
3. See my "The Reaction to Political Radicalism and the Popularization of Political Economy in Early Nineteenth Century Britain: The Case of 'Productive and Unproductive Labour,'" in *Expository Science: Forms and Functions of Popularization*, ed. Terry Shin and Richard Whitley (Dordrecht, 1985), pp. 119–36.

"commerce" or to fall prey to "monied speculators" but should satisfy "the comfort and accommodation of the people." Praising the ideal of "imperceptible gradations of rank, where step rises above step by slow degrees . . . till the whole society [is] connected together by inseparable interests" as superior even to any "golden age of absolute equality," Thelwall argued that this was attainable only where competition made monopoly impossible. Speculation, "the over eager pursuit of opulence among one class of the people," had eroded the moral effects of a "fair and equitable process of exchange."[4]

Embracing unlimited "fair" commerce entailed a new look at luxury and its relation to virtue. Referring to a plan by an African colonization projector, C. B. Wadstrom, which proposed distributing produce only according to real rather than "artificial" wants, Thelwall noted that this raised "the important dilemma of simplicity or luxury." But he then crucially argued at length that luxury introduced through commerce did not inevitably corrupt a nation. Athenian republicanism, for example, had sprung from a "generous and magnanimous virtue" that a commercial nation might also possess, and that was thus derived less from abstemious poverty than from limiting the dependency of its citizens. Such independence, he stressed, resulted only when individuals reaped "the profits of their individual exertions," and where true freedom of trade lowered prices to the point where only "a living profit" was attainable. But commercial freedom in a republic still required civil and political liberty, which in turn rested on "a simplicity of manners, a fortitude of character, and a pure and generous system of morality." At present these attributes, Thelwall confessed, were more often found in noncommercial countries like Switzerland. Where they flourished in earlier republics, like ancient Greece, this had occurred only because commerce had increased the independence of all by being "made to produce equal advantage to every citizen of the community": "Every man participated not only in the labour, but in the profit . . . when the rich merchant, the great landed proprietor, and higher classes of society, are enabled to enjoy more luxuries, and live in great pomp, the tendency of the laws and institutions of society ought to be such, that the labourer also will have his proportion of the advantage, eat with more comfort, sleep in a better cabin, and be enabled to give his offspring a better education, and a better knowledge of their rights and duties."[5] The crucial question for Thelwall, therefore, was how to replicate such conditions in a modern commercial society.

4. Thelwall, *The Tribune*, 2:38, 46, 59, 66–67, 150, and 3:38–39.
5. Ibid., 3:43, 46, 248. For a possible source of this view of the Greeks, see William Jones, *The Spirit of Athens* (London, 1777), pp. 191–92. The notion that the best commerce was that which furnished the greatest employment to all and nourished the health and strength of the inhabitants, as well as being "most certain," was also shared by writers

Contrary to some interpretations, the *Rights of Nature* thus considerably refined Thelwall's new vision of egalitarian commercial republicanism.[6] His central premise was now that every man and woman had "a sacred and inviolable claim, growing out of the fundamental maxim, upon which alone all property is supported, to some comforts and enjoyments, in addition to the necessaries of life, and to some 'tolerable leisure for such discussion, and some means of such information,' as may lead to an understanding of their *rights*; without which they can never understand their *duties*." This was clearly an appeal for the right of the poor and laboring classes to greater independence. Society had the duty "not merely to *protect*, but to *improve* [my emphasis] the physical, the moral, and intellectual enjoyments . . . of the whole population of the state. It ought to expand the faculties, encrease the sympathies, harmonize the passions, and promote the general welfare."[7] This principle was defended in *The Rights of Nature* in four ways. First, Thelwall proposed that all had "naturally an equal claim to the elements of nature," of which light, air, and water in particular remained in common. ("Naturally" here meant taking each individual as an "abstraction," devoid of social and political ties, with natural rights being determined by wants, faculties, and means.) This implied that each person also possessed "*a right to exercise his faculties upon those powers and elements, so as to render them subservient to his wants, and conducive to his enjoyments*." This right, however, applied to all, and those who monopolized the means of support violated the rights of others. For all social rights implied a reciprocal duty to secure similar rights for others.[8] Thus, Thelwall's first rights claim was that, since this natural inheritance had been shared by all in the state of nature, society must compensate for its subsequent loss.[9] As we have seen, this paralleled exactly Paine's similar claim in *Agrarian Justice*. It also echoed, albeit in a more secular form, the familiar natural law description of the

---

like Capel Lofft (*Elements of Universal Law* [London, 1779], pp. 120–21). But Lofft also opposed luxury and insisted that "luxury in a *commonwealth* is either extinct the instant it springs up, or the *commonwealth*" (p. 106).

6. Thelwall's biographer, Charles Cestre, assumed he "chiefly aimed at reducing the excessive consumption of luxuries by the few, in order to increase the share of necessaries for the many," and saw commerce as at best only a doubtful good. This was true for the early 1790s but must be considerably qualified after 1794–95 (*John Thelwall* [London, 1906], pp. 59, 61).

7. John Thelwall, *The Rights of Nature* (London, 1796), pt. 1:16; pt. 2:46. It ought, in short, actively to promote the ends of "society," as Pufendorf had used the term, and as Paine had concluded at the end of *Rights of Man* (n. 3, pp. 265–66), pt. 2, or to follow the obligation to improve both body and soul, as Hutcheson phrased it, or the "talents," as Sharp had insisted (Francis Hutcheson, *A System of Moral Philosophy*, 2 vols. [London, 1755], 2:111–12; Granville Sharp, *A Tract on the Law of Nature* [London, 1777], p. 23).

8. Thelwall, *The Rights of Nature*, pt. 2:39–42. Natural law writers agreed that the chief obligation of property was not hindering the rights of others to enjoy their own. On this obligation, see, e.g., Thomas Rutherforth, *Institutes of Natural Law*, 2 vols. (London, 1754), 1:138–39.

9. Thelwall, *The Rights of Nature*, pt. 2:27, 38–39.

Creation and of God's intention that the earth should always support all its inhabitants. But this was also the most theologically oriented of Thelwall's claims, for his other arguments focused solely on social consent and a reconstruction of the "rights of labourers."

Thelwall's conclusion regarding natural inheritance was reached by reviewing the progress of society through the savage, pastoral, and agricultural stages. He agreed that, in the pastoral state, herds alone had been owned, with land being appropriated only after the widespread introduction of agriculture. Thereafter, if property was the "fruit of useful industry," "the means of being usefully industrious" remained "the common right of all." This clearly implied a right to labor and to receive a reasonable reward therefrom, and was the second pillar supporting Thelwall's claims.[1] But while agriculture brought many benefits, land became appropriated by "moral and political expediency," not merely occupancy or labor. This ended the relatively equal distribution of property that had long prevailed.[2] The invention of primogeniture and governmental protection of privilege and wealth helped divide society into proprietor and laborer, with the few monopolizing the advantages secured by the labor of all. Thelwall conceded that returning to an equality of landed property was impossible. The question, therefore, was what rights laborers in the existing system had. And these, he argued, rested on "the triple basis of *nature*, of *implied contract*, and *the principles of civil association*."[3]

The natural rights of laborers rested on the fact that as "men" (women do not enter into the discussion), they were heirs to "the common bounties of nature." At birth, however, each found "his inheritance is alienated, and his common right appropriated," though when individuals worked on the common elements of nature they retained the right to the "advantages" of their industry. Nonetheless, everywhere else, where inequality had generated sharp distinctions between proprietor and laborer, society was still "responsible . . . for an equivalent for that which society has taken away." For instead of being grounded in natural right, the permanent possession of land was merely expedient, being based especially on the tendency of private ownership to increase production. Such expediency did not, however, invalidate a prior right that the laborer possessed, Thelwall argued (on the basis of an unexplored principle of reciprocity), to receive as much in return as he or she had given to society, as well as to employ his or her faculties beneficially. Any unjust agreement

1. Ibid., pp. 54–55. Thelwall may here have followed Blackstone's account of the evolution of property (*Commentaries on the Laws of England* [1765–69] [Washington, D.C., 1902], 2:1–9).
2. Thelwall, *The Rights of Nature*, pt. 2:62.
3. Ibid., pp. 77–86.

"extorted by the power of an oppressor" for inadequate wages was thus morally and politically void, the genuine basis of property here being not expediency but labor alone.[4] There were echoes of Locke in particular in this account.[5] But Thelwall's path was no longer well trodden, touching a familiar series of stages on the road to a moderate plea for social justice without upsetting the existing distribution of property. As he well knew, his departure now was sharp, abrupt, and dramatic. His course was set for a generalized account of wage labor that went well beyond the theories of any of his predecessors.

So far, we have seen, Thelwall argued for a redistribution of property first to compensate for the loss of natural inheritance and second in recognition of the reciprocal nature of social labor. Thelwall's third and most striking argument for redistribution rested on the notion of an "implied compact" that had been entered into tacitly by all upon leaving the state of nature, but that was now, he insisted, relevant to any agreement between laborer and employer.[6] This compact, as we have seen, was the only means by which Thelwall presumed that commerce and republicanism were compatible, because it allowed the laborer a right to the produce of his or her employer *proportionate* to the profit of the employer. Consequently the position of the laborer had to improve with the growing opulence of a commercial society. This contract was "implied in the very distinction of labourer and employer . . . by the reason of the thing, and the rules of moral justice," specifically because capital could not be productive without labor, and vice versa. Civil association, Thelwall insisted, had been constituted for the general good. Mankind had left the state of nature for "the comforts and abundance of all" rather than particular advantage, and cultivation also required common labor. When the wealthy few tyrannized over the many, this was "not a compact of civil association, but a wicked and lawless anarchy," analogous to the presocial state, which altered "the very nature" of the tenure of the property holder by substituting usurpation and

4. Ibid., pp. 54–79. This extended the natural law view that contracts that tended to ruin the community were no longer binding (e.g., Grotius [n. 8, p. 276], 2:125; Francis Hutcheson, *A Short Introduction to Moral Philosophy*, 2d ed. [Glasgow, 1753], p. 168). Thelwall reflected of his law studies that he had suffered under a "surfeit . . . of the glossing and barbarous jargon of the law." Here he mentioned Grotius and Pufendorf and quoted frequently from Blackstone, though disgustedly dismissing "Sir W. Blackstone, and the fraternity of Lincoln's Inn" for their slavish devotion to ancient custom (Thelwall, *The Rights of Nature*, pt. 2:24, pt. 3:110).

5. See James Tully, *A Discourse on Property: John Locke and His Adversaries* (Cambridge, 1980). It might be added that some have found a general right to subsistence, prior to any act of labor, in Locke as well (see Richard Ashcraft, *Locke's "Two Treatises of Government"* [London, 1987], p. 88).

6. On the background to the concept of "implied contract," see Peter Birks and Grant MacLeod, "The Implied Contract Theory of Quasi-Contract: Civilian Opinion Current in the Century before Blackstone," *Oxford Journal of Legal Studies* 6 (1986): 46–85.

plunder for legitimate possession.[7] To Thelwall, however, civilization implied that the laborer had the right not merely to a subsistence but also to the education of his family and their improvement and participation in "all the sweets of polished society." The rights of society were thus not fixed in Thelwall's view but were, in a sense, now indexed to the inflation of needs. Consequently, "natural" entitlements also increased and now encompassed the produce of commerce and manufacturing as well as agriculture."[8]

We see here how important a claim to recall the original intention of the founders of civil society was. To Grotius, for example, the defense of rights of necessity was based upon the supposition that this was what the founders of private property would have given (and which hypothetical intention obviated the need for more detailed discussions of the original contract itself). For Pufendorf, a "tacit compact" permitted the introduction of private property, while for Locke this contract recognized the original mixing of labor with raw materials that founded property.[9] But as Istvan Hont in particular has emphasized, the more the "negative community" theorists stressed a gradual and historical emergence of private property, the less likely was any reliance upon a contract; Hutcheson, for example, simply denied the need to assume such a compact.[1] For Thelwall, however, an "implied contract" supported the fourth great pillar of his argument, a proportionate right of labor to the profits of capital, and required a much more contemporary role for the original contract than earlier writers assumed. This was a stark and forceful restatement of contract theory that embraced economic relations much more clearly than it did the general rules of civil association.

Thelwall's first two arguments clearly paralleled the two principles of "progress" and "social duty" that Paine offered in *Agrarian Justice*. Both agreed that compensation for the loss of a natural inheritance justified greater equality of property. What was particularly distinctive to the *Rights of Nature*, however, and what most clearly signaled its acceptance of commercial progress, was the view

---

7. This argument may have been indebted to Paine (see *Rights of Man* [n. 3, pp. 265–66], p. 171).

8. Thelwall, *The Rights of Nature* (n. 7, p. 282), pt. 2:80–82, 45, 76. For Blackstone on implied contracts, see 3:159–67.

9. Grotius, 1:238–93; Samuel Pufendorf, *The Whole Duty of Man According to the Law of Nature*, 5th ed. (London, 1735), pp. 135–36; Hutcheson, *A System of Moral Philosophy* (n. 52 above), 1:330; John Locke, *Two Treatises of Government*, ed. Peter Laslett (Cambridge, 1970), p. 317. Rutherforth (n. 6, p. 282) follows the doctrine of tacit consent by occupation (1:48, 81), emphasizing that this would have been seen as "for the convenience of all," while rejecting Locke's theory that labor contributed to property (p. 56).

1. See Istvan Hont, "From Pufendorf to Adam Smith: Sociability, Commercial Society and the Four Stages Theory," in *The Languages of Political Theory in Early-Modern Europe*, ed. Anthony Pagden (Cambridge, 1987), p. 270. On Grotius and the introduction of a contract in the transition from common property, see Richard Tuck, *Natural Rights Theories* (Cambridge, 1979), p. 77.

that the laborer could claim a proportion of the employer's *profits* because society rested on common labor. Here Paine, while agreeing that "personal property is the effect of society," proposed that a fixed sum be paid to all at certain points in their lives as restitution for their loss of land. This was a static, welfare-oriented approach to poverty and subsistence. Appropriately, given his greater stress on the labor basis of property, Thelwall, through the rule of proportionate advantage, instead considered the problem of how to cope with wages generally and how to raise the standard of living of the working classes as society became progressively richer. This certainly helped to give him a greater emphasis on manufacturing (upon which he planned at one point to lecture) than Paine offered. Otherwise these are remarkably similar viewpoints that represented a major turning away from previous republican treatments of the limitation of landed property by an agrarian law. Instead, both Paine and Thelwall embraced, if only tentatively, a new radical approach to commercial and manufacturing wealth that allowed Thelwall, in particular, to insist in a dramatic assertion (given his nagging Stoic impulses) that he "would extend civilization: I would increase refinement" while meeting the demands of social justice.[2]

Given its centrality to this new emphasis, Thelwall's rule of proportionate advantage merits closer examination here. Broadly, this argument had two aims. First, in keeping with his dictum that society should not merely protect but also improve the welfare of all, Thelwall's juristic strategy can be described as in a sense socializing existing accounts of property rights by construing all property relationships as occurring not between master and servant but between consenting equals, like brothers in a family, albeit possessing less than equal property[3] Social obligation here assumed priority over rights assigned by the system of ranks, which for Thelwall led to an economic exploitation that he explicitly termed "anti-social" in its effects. From a natural law viewpoint, this strategy invoked familiar emphases on the interdependence of all ranks and the primordial duty of the wealthy to support and recognize the claims of the poor, albeit from a much more radical perspective that laid far more stress on the intent of the founders of society to retain a sense of its communal basis. In addition, Thelwall's new emphasis was a radical *republican* interpretation of jurisprudential discussions of contract that extended "politics" into "society" by adapting ideas of the original political contract to the existing system of labor relations. This strategy required a theory of original political equality, a conception

2. Thelwall, *The Rights of Nature*, pt. 3:83–84.
3. Grotius, e.g., distinguishes between societies of equals, such as brothers, or unequals, such as masters and servants (*De Jure Belli et Pacis*, ed. William Whewell, 3 vols. [Cambridge, 1853], 1:4).

of the continuing relevance of a particular account of how society had been formed, and a Lockean and Smithian stress on the value of labor in production.

Thelwall's argument relied equally on a more narrowly legalistic reinterpretation of existing contractual relations, a move for which his own brief legal training provided some preparation. His claim that all property was social in nature, and specifically that all cultivation rested on social labor, was only a reworking of the early eighteenth-century natural law doctrine that the chief advantage of society lay, as Hutcheson put it, in the division of labor and the increasing expertise and production it permitted. And this of course was also one basis of Smith's commercial sociability.[4] But Thelwall applied the idea of sociability rather differently in *The Rights of Nature*. By emphasizing the equal contributions of capital and labor, he clearly did not conceive of the relationship of master and servant (the basis of most existing discussions of wage relations) merely in terms of a contractual compromise of interests—for this meant, as Burke, for example, had argued, that no further conflict of interests existed between employer and employee once wages had been agreed.[5] Instead, Thelwall took up the law of partnership and its discussion of the pursuit of common gain, and he assumed these to be that part of the "implied contract" that justified proportionate advantage in distributing profit.[6] Wage labor, therefore, was no longer to be conceived as normally defined by the market, that is, by the usefulness of the labor and the number of laborers, as Grotius's British disciples like Thomas Rutherforth had contended. The latter interpretation permitted the payment of mere subsistence wages, indeed less if charity supplemented wages, as it commonly did (and it offered little if any reward at all for those unable to work, by the time Malthus took up the theory). Instead, wage labor embodied not merely a "contract for mutual benefit" (to use Rutherforth's phrasing), as the hiring of labor had been construed previously, but a full partnership governed by the rules of "comparative share" or proportionate gain. This for Thelwall was the only form of contractual relationship fully compatible with the general obligation to mutual advantage of the social compact (which Rutherforth, for example,

---

4. Hutcheson, *A System of Moral Philosophy*, 1:288. For Smith, see Knud Haakonssen, *The Science of a Legislator: The Natural Jurisprudence of David Hume and Adam Smith* (Cambridge, 1981).
5. Edmund Burke, "Thoughts and Details on Scarcity" (1795), in his *Works* (London, 1887), 5:139.
6. This also involved the restitution of what Thelwall clearly understood to be natural equity, whose protection Grotius (n. 3, p. 286) and others had also understood as one of the goals of the original establishment of private property (1:237). The best contemporary account of partnership was William Watson, *A Treatise of the Law of Partnership* (1794). On partnerships between labor and capital, see pp. 135–37.

admitted should not be violated in such contracts).[7] This, for Thelwall, was the meaning of the assertion that the implied contract rested on the principles of civil association generally, the state of nature having been left only for common, not particular, advantage.[8] And this was clearly the only definition of employment compatible with an egalitarian, democratic, and procommercial form of republicanism, in Thelwall's view.

The key problem here was, of course, the question of what right anyone had to use the "property" of others (which for Thelwall crucially included labor) for their own profit. In the best known natural law writer in eighteenth-century Britain, Pufendorf, for example, we find both a plea for a "just equality" in contractual relationships, and, more specifically, the injunction that in partnerships "when any Labour is bestow'd in the *Improvement* of any Commodity, which is put in by another, he is suppos'd to have such a Share in the Thing it Self, as is proportionable to the *Improvement* it has received." But Pufendorf admitted that many types of "accessional advantages" existed, even where human industry added to the value of a commodity, which belonged to the owner of the property, not the laborer. And this of course was the usual understanding of wage labor.[9] But partners, natural law writers concurred, were entitled to a return from any enterprise proportionate to their contribution, whether this be in labor or capital.[1]

What Thelwall evidently did was to envision every employment contract in these terms, and thus he extended the rule of proportionate advantage to all. Both Locke and Smith had demonstrated the importance of labor to production. But while Thelwall agreed that the genuine basis of property was labor and that the agricultural laborer was the true cultivator, he put forward no claim for "the whole produce of labour" (the position that, in Anton Menger's well-known but overly teleological book, commenced the nineteenth-century debate over the rights of labor). His concern instead was solely with reciprocal, proportionate rights or an equivalency based upon the constitution of society for the benefit of all. Landed property was founded not only in labour but also in a moral and political expediency intended by the first contractors of society and in a natural right to property granted by God.[2] Nonetheless, the crucial question here was not which rights had existed in the state of nature, where labor might or might not have given a right to property, but

7. Rutherforth, 1:231, 214, 276, and 2:255.
8. Thelwall, *The Rights of Nature*, pt. 3:80.
9. Pufendorf, *The Whole Duty of Man* (n. 9, p. 285), pp. 162–63, 169, 140–41.
1. A position followed by, e.g., William Paley, "Principles of Moral and Political Philosophy," in *The Works of William Paley* (London, 1831), p. 37.
2. Thelwall, *The Rights of Nature* (n. 7, p. 282), pt. 2:76.

which ones were retained in later social stages. For Thelwall, these centered both on labor and "the means of being usefully industrious," which was the common right of all, as well as proportionate and equivalency rights based on the implicit contract and the constitution of society as a collective enterprise.[3] Thelwall did not, therefore, merely echo jurisprudential discussions of the poor's claim to subsistence. Virtually every natural law writer had conceded that the poor had the right to be supported through their labor.[4] But while writers like Ogilvie acknowledged a right to the improvements of landed property, the right to a proportionate return for all property, in any form of labor relationship, was generated only as a consequence of partnership—for example, where one individual lent money to another to use for profit and was thereby entitled to a share of the profit. Such claims were clearly impossible in a relation of servitude.[5] Consequently Thelwall did not attempt to revive a "moral economy" of just prices and fair wages either, since wages were to be proportionate to profit, not to the cost of living. Instead he proposed a new vision of economic justice centering on the contractual relations between worker and employer.[6]

※　※　※

3. This solved the Lockean problem of the right to the produce of others' labor outside of the common materials of nature. For Locke, the mixing of labor with common property created private property in the natural state. But "my servant's turfs" belonged to me in later social stages, even if he or she had cut and stacked them, presumably even if they were cut on common land. For Thelwall, no servant ought ever to labor at such a disadvantage. See Locke (n. 9, p. 285), pp. 306–7. Blackstone (n. 1, p. 283) merely acknowledged that in return for work a servant was entitled to wages (1:428).

4. For Hutcheson (n. 7, p. 282), e.g., "the indigent must be supported by the compensations they get" for their labour (*A System of Moral Philosophy*, 2:1). Grotius (n. 3, p. 286) had insisted that the poor had the right to purchase necessities at a fair price (1:252). Pufendorf (n. 9, p. 285) reiterated cases where extreme necessity superseded existing rights (*The Whole Duty of Man*, pp. 87–88). Richard Cumberland agreed that no right of dominion permitted the removal of necessities from the innocent (*A Treatise of the Law of Nature* [London, 1727], p. 68). Paley also recognized the imperfect right of the poor to relief by the rich on the basis of original divine intention ("Principles of Moral and Political Philosophy," pp. 20, 50). For Paley's view, see generally Horne, chap. 4.

5. Ogilvie, p. 12. For treatments of partnership, see, e.g., Hutcheson, *A System of Moral Philosophy*, 2:71; Pufendorf, *The Whole Duty of Man*, pp. 168–69.

6. But unlike the later Owenite socialist view, for which it clearly laid the foundations by concentrating on the contractual relationship between laborer and employer, Thelwall's theory did not enjoin the exact exchange of equal amounts of labor in contracts in order for justice to be fulfilled. In Grotian terms, Thelwall demanded beneficial contracts, with a limited degree of equality, and Owenism, commutative contracts that guaranteed complete equality (see Grotius, 2:65). On the relations between early British socialism and natural jurisprudence, and the ideal of partnership and "cooperation" as a new form of sociability, see my *Citizens and Saints: Politics and Anti-Politics in Early British Socialism* (Cambridge, 1989), pp. 23–62.

Selected Bibliography

Allison, Robert. *The Crescent Obscured: The United States and the Muslim World, 1776–1815*. Chicago: University of Chicago Press, 1995.

Anderson, Fred, and Cayton, Andrew. *The Dominion of War: Empire and Liberty in North America, 1500–2000*. New York: Penguin Books, 2005.

Appleby, Joyce. "Commercial Farming and the 'Agrarian Myth' in the Early Republic." *The Journal of American History* 68 (March 1982): 833–49.

Bailyn, Bernard. *The Ideological Origins of the American Revolution*. Cambridge: Belknap Press of Harvard University, 1967.

Banning, Lance. *The Jeffersonian Persuasion: Evolution of a Party Ideology*. London: Cornell University Press, 1978.

Bender, Thomas. *A Nation Among Nations: America's Place in World History*. New York: Hill and Wang, 2006.

Berlin, Ira. *Many Thousands Gone: The First Two Centuries of Slavery in North America*. Cambridge: Belknap Press of Harvard University, 1998.

Bouton, Terry. *Taming Democracy: The Founders, "The People," and the Troubled Ending of the American Revolution*. New York: Oxford University Press, 2006.

Cornell, Saul. *A Well-Regulated Militia: The Founding Fathers and the Origins of Gun Control in America*. New York: Oxford University Press, 2006.

Cotlar, Seth. "Radical Conceptions of Property Rights and Economic Equality in the Early Republic: The Trans-Atlantic Dimension," *Explorations in Early American Culture* 4 (2000): 191–219.

Egerton, Douglas R. *Death or Liberty: African Americans and Revolutionary America*. New York: Oxford University Press, 2009.

Einhorn, Robin, *American Slavery, American Taxation*. Chicago: University of Chicago Press, 2005.

Elkins, Stanley, and McKitrick, Eric. *The Age of Federalism: The Early American Republic, 1788–1840*. New York: Oxford University Press, 1995.

Ellis, Joseph J. *Founding Brothers: The Revolutionary Generation*. New York: Vintage Press, 2001.

Eustace, Nicole. *Passion Is the Gale: Emotion, Power, and the Coming of the American Revolution*. Chapel Hill: University of North Carolina Press, 2008.

Fischer, David Hackett. *Paul Revere's Ride*. New York: Oxford University Press, 1995.

———. *Washington's Crossing*. New York: Oxford University Press, 2004.

Fitzsimons, David. "Tom Paine's New World Order: Idealistic Internationalism in the Ideology of Early American Foreign Relations," *Diplomatic History* 19 (fall 1995): 569–82.

Foner, Eric. *The Story of American Freedom*. Norton, 1999.

———. *Tom Paine and Revolutionary America*. New York: Oxford University Press, 1976.

Freeman, Joanne B. *Affairs of Honor: National Politics in the New Republic*. New Haven, Conn.: Yale University Press, 2002.

Frey, Sylvia. *Water from the Rock: Black Resistance in a Revolutionary Age*. Princeton N.J.: Princeton University Press, 1991.

Fruchtman, Jack Jr. *The Political Philosophy of Thomas Paine*. Baltimore: Johns Hopkins University Press, 2009

————. *Thomas Paine and the Religion of Nature*. Baltimore: Johns Hopkins University Press, 1993.

————. *Thomas Paine: Apostle of Freedom*. New York: Basic Books, 1996

Gimbel, Richard. *A Biographical Check List of "Common Sense," with an Account of Its Publication*. New Haven, Conn.: Yale University Press, 1956.

Hendrickson, David C. *Peace Pact: The Lost World of the American Founding*. Lawrence: University of Kansas Press, 2003.

————. *Union, Nation, or Empire: The American Debate over International Relations, 1789–1941*. Lawrence: University of Kansas Press, 2009

Hofstadter, Richard. *The American Political Tradition and the Men Who Made It*. New York: Vintage Books, 1948.

Holton, Woody. "Did Democracy Cause the Recession That led to the Constitution?" *Journal of American History* 92 (September 2005): 442–69.

Jordan, Winthrop. *White over Black: American Attitudes Towards the Negro, 1550–1812*. Chapel Hill: University of North Carolina Press, 1968.

Kagan, Robert. *Dangerous Nation: America's Foreign Policy from Its Earliest Days to the Dawn of the Twentieth Century*. New York: Vintage Books, 2006.

Kaye, Harvey. *Thomas Paine and the Promise of America*. New York: Hill and Wang, 2006.

Keane, John. *Tom Paine: A Political Biography*. Boston: Little, Brown, 1995.

Keyssar, Alexander. *The Right to Vote: The Contested History of Democracy in the United States*. New York: Basic Books, 2000.

Kohn, Richard. *Eagle and Sword: The Federalists and the Creation of the Military Establishment in America, 1783–1802*. London: Free Press, 1975.

Kolchin, Peter. *American Slavery, 1619–1877*. New York: Hill and Wang, 1993.

Kramnick, Isaac. *Republicanism and Bourgeois Radicalism: Political Ideology in Late Eighteenth-Century England and America*. Ithaca, N.Y.: Cornell University Press, 1990.

Kukla, Jon. *A Wilderness so Immense: The Louisiana Purchase and the Destiny of America*. New York: Anchor Books, 2003.

Lambert, Frank. *The Barbary Wars: American Independence in the Atlantic World*. New York: Hill and Wang, 2007.

Larkin, Edward. *Thomas Paine and the Literature of Revolution*. New York: Cambridge University Press, 2005.

Leill, Scott. *Forty-Six Pages: Thomas Paine, "Common Sense," and the Turning Point to American Independence*. Philadelphia: University of Pennsylvania Press, 2003.

Loughram, Trish. "Disseminating *Common Sense*: Thomas Paine and the Problem of the Early National Bestseller," *American Literature* 78 (March 2006): 1–28.

Maier, Pauline. *American Scripture: Making the Declaration of Independence*. New York: Vintage Books, 1997.

Mann, Bruce. *Republic of Debtors: Bankruptcy in the Age of American Independence*. Cambridge: Harvard University Press, 2002.

McDonald, Forrest. *The Presidency of Thomas Jefferson*. Lawrence: University of Kansas Press, 1976.

McWilliams, Wilson Carey. "Civil Religion in the Age of Reason: Thomas Paine on Liberalism, Redemption, and Revolution," *Social Research* 54 (Autumn, 1987), 447–90.

Middlekauff, Robert. *The Glorious Cause: The American Revolution, 1763–1789*. New York: Oxford University Press, 1982.

Murrin, John M. "The Jeffersonian Triumph and American Exceptionalism." *Journal of the Early Republic* 20 (Spring 2000): 1–25.

Nash, Gary B. *The Unknown American Revolution: The Unruly Birth of Democracy and the Struggle to Create America*. New York: Penguin Books, 2005

Nash, Gary B., with Soderlund, Jean R. *Freedom by Degrees: Emancipation in Pennsylvania and Its Aftermath*. New York: Oxford University Press, 1991.

Onuf, Nicholas and Onuf, Peter. *Federal Union, Modern World: The Law of Nations in an Age of Revolution, 1776–1814*. New York: Madison House Publishers, 1994.

Opal, J. M. *Beyond the Farm: National Ambitions in Rural New England*. Philadelphia: University of Pennsylvania Press, 2008

———. "*Common Sense* and Imperial Atrocity: How Tom Paine Saw South Asia in North America," *Common-Place* 8 (July 2009), www.common-place.org.

———. "The Labors of Liberality: Christian Benevolence and National Prejudice in the American Founding," *Journal of American History* 94 (March 2008): 1082–107

Peskin, Lawrence A. *Captives and Countrymen: Barbary Slavery and the American Public, 1785–1816*. Baltimore: Johns Hopkins University Press, 2009.

Peterson, Merrill D. *Thomas Jefferson and the New Nation: A Biography*. New York: Oxford University Press, 1970.

Philp, Mark. *Paine*. New York: Oxford University Press, 1989.

Porter, Roy. *English Society in the Eighteenth Century*. Rev. ed. New York: Penguin Books, 1991.

Radcliffe, Evan. "Revolutionary Writing, Moral Philosophy, and Universal Benevolence in the Eighteenth Century," *Journal of the History of Ideas* 54 (April 1993): 221–40.

Robbins, Caroline. "The Lifelong Education of Thomas Paine (1737–1809): Some Reflections Upon His Acquaintance among Books," *Proceedings of the American Philosophical Society* 127 (June 1983): 135–142.

Schama, Simon. *Citizens: A Chronicle of the French Revolution*. New York: Vintage Books, 1989.

Shankman, Andrew. *Crucible of American Democracy: The Struggle to Fuse Egalitarianism and Capitalism in Jeffersonian Pennsylvania*. Lawrence: University of Kansas Press, 2004.

Sharp, James Roger. *American Politics in the Early Republic: The New Nation in Crisis*. New Haven, Conn.: Yale University Press, 1993.

Silver, Peter. *Our Savage Neighbors: How Indian War Transformed Early America*. New York: Norton, 2008.

Smith, Frank. "New Light on Thomas Paine's First Year in America, 1775," *American Literature*, 1 (January 1930): 347–71.

Smith-Rosenberg, Carroll. *This Violent Empire: The Birth of an American National Identity*. Chapel Hill: University of North Carolina Press, 2010.

Stansell, Christine. *The Feminist Promise: 1792 to the Present*. New York: Modern Library, 2010.

Taylor, Alan. *The Divided Ground: Indians, Settlers, and the Northern Borderland of the American Revolution*. New York: Vintage Books, 2007

———. *Liberty Men and Great Proprietors: The Revolutionary Settlement on the Maine Frontier, 1760–1820*. Chapel Hill: University of North Carolina Press, 1990.

Waldstreicher, David. *In the Midst of Perpetual Fetes: The Making of American Nationalism, 1776–1820*. Chapel Hill: University of North Carolina Press, 1997

———. *Runaway America: Benjamin Franklin, Slavery, and the American Revolution*. New York: Hill and Wang, 2004.

Walker, Thomas C. "The Forgotten Prophet: Tom Paine's Cosmopolitanism and International Relations," *International Studies Quarterly* 44 (2000), 51–72.

Wilentz, Sean. *The Rise of American Democracy: Jefferson to Lincoln*. New York: Norton, 2005.

Williamson, Audrey. *Thomas Paine: His Life, Work, and Times*. London: George Allen and Unwin, 1973.

Wood, Gordon S. *The Creation of the American Republic, 1776–1787*. Chapel Hill: University of North Carolina Press, 1969.

———. *Empire of Liberty: A History of the Early Republic, 1789–1815*. New York: Oxford University Press, 2009

Zagarrie, Rosemary. *Revolutionary Backlash: Women and Politics in the Early American Republic*. Philadelphia: University of Pennsylvania Press, 2007.

Index

NOTE: Entries referencing footnotes are indicated with an *n* following the page number.